THE SOVIET ASSET

THE SOVIET ASSET
Military Power in the Competition over Europe

Edited by
UWE NERLICH

Volume I
of
Soviet Power and Western
Negotiating Policies

BALLINGER PUBLISHING COMPANY
Cambridge, Massachusetts
A Subsidiary of Harper & Row, Publishers, Inc.

UA
770
S6675
1983
v. 1

International Standard Book Number: 0-88410-905-4 (v. 1)

Library of Congress Catalog Card Number: 82-22694

Printed in the United States of America

Library of Congress Cataloging in Publication Data

Main entry under title:

Soviet power and Western negotiating policies.

  Included index.
  Contents: v. 1. The Soviet asset, military power in the competition
over Europe.
  1. Soviet Union—Military policy—Addresses, essays, lectures.
  2. Soviet Union—Armed Forces—Addresses, essays, lectures.
  3. Soviet Union—Foreign relations—1945- —Addresses, essays, lectures.
  4. World Politics—1945- —Addresses, essays, lectures. I. Nerlich, Uwe.
UA770.S6675 1983   355'.033047   82-22694
ISBN 0-88410-905-4 (v. 1)

CONTENTS

Map and List of Figures   ix

List of Tables   xi

Preface   xiii

Editor's Introduction   1

PART I   THE SHIFTING BALANCE: THE WAY IT WAS

Chapter 1
To Lose an Arms Race: The Competition in
Conventional Forces Deployed in Central
Europe 1965–1980
—Phillip A. Karber   31

Chapter 2
How the Soviet Union Came to Gain Escalation
Dominance: Trends and Asymmetries in the
Theater Nuclear Balance
—James J. Martin   89

v

*PART II   POLITICAL PURPOSE IN THE PURSUIT
OF THE ARMS COMPETITION*

Chapter 3
Military Power in International Politics:
Soviet Doctrine on Its Centrality and
Instrumentality
— Robert Legvold   123

Chapter 4
The Soviet Conception of Europe and Arms
Negotiations
— John van Oudenaren   161

Chapter 5
The Threat Perceived? Leverage of Soviet
Military Power in Western Europe
— Lothar Ruehl   195

Chapter 6
The Battle of Unengaged Military Strategies
— Phillip A. Karber   207

*PART III   SOVIET MILITARY POWER: THE CONTEXT
OF RESTRAINT*

Chapter 7
Sustaining the Burden of Soviet Defense:
Retrospect and Prospect
— Abraham S. Becker   233

Chapter 8
Reconstructing the Soviet Perspective
on U.S. Global Policy
— Harry Gelman   277

Chapter 9
Prospects and Requirements for the Containment
of Matured Soviet Military Power
— *Fritz Ermarth* 307

Chapter 10
Alliance Strategy in the 1980s and the Political
Approach to Soviet Power
— *Uwe Nerlich* 331

List of Abbreviations 343

Index 347

About the Editor 361

About the Contributors 363

MAP AND LIST OF FIGURES

Map

Central European Force Deployment 1980   33

Figures

1-1   Center Region Balance Trends: Ground Force
       Manpower/Divisions   36

1-2   Center Region Balance Trends: Main Battle
       Tanks/Armored Personnel Vehicles   43

1-3   Center Region Balance Trends: Antitank
       Guns/Antitank Guided Missile Launchers   51

1-4   Center Region Balance Trends: Artillery/Multiple
       Rocked Launchers   55

1-5   Center Region Balance Trends: Combat Aircraft/
       Armored Attack Helicopters   60

1-6   Center Region Balance Trends: Air Defense Guns/
       Surface to Air Missile Launchers   71

2-1   Trends in NATO and Warsaw Pact TNFs   95

7-1   Comparative Growth of U.S., Soviet, and Chinese
       Military Outlays, 1968-1978   236

LIST OF TABLES

1-1   Distribution of Increase in Conventional Armament
      (Combined NATO and Warsaw Pact Expansion in
      Central Europe: 1965–1980)   41

1-2   Comparative Force Levels: Warsaw Pact versus NATO   81

1-3   Increase in Conventional Armament Deployed in
      Central Europe between 1965 and 1980   86

2-1   Trends in NATO and Warsaw Pact TNFs   94

2-2   NATO and Warsaw Pact Modernization Programs
      for Offensive TNFs   97

2A-1 Trends in NATO Offensive TNFs   110

2A-2 NATO Mid-Range Land-Based Dual-Capable Aircraft
      In Europe   112

2A-3 U. S. Offensive Nuclear Warheads in Europe   113

2A-4 Trends in Warsaw Pact Offensive TNFs   114

2A-5 FROG and SS–21 Launchers   116

2A-6 SCUD/SS–X–23 Launchers   116

2A-7 GOLF and HOTEL Ballistic Missile Submarines with
      Theater Missions (Worldwide Deployments, 1980)   116

2A–8   GOLF and HOTEL Ballistic Missile Submarines
       with Theater Missions (Worldwide Deployments, 1975)   116

6–1   Expansion of Forward Deployed and Mobilization
       Conventional Weapons, 1965–80   214

PREFACE

This book is the first of two volumes presenting studies on Soviet military power and Western negotiating behavior. (Volume 2 is titled *The Western Panacea: Constraining Soviet Power through Negotiations.*) Libraries abound with work on both the Soviet military posture and the diplomacy and policies of ongoing arms control negotiations. Work in both fields characteristically reflects the very polarizations that prevail in the bodies politic at large. What is ominously lacking is work on the political instrumentalities of Soviet military power as well as on how negotiation—the process and the outcomes—actually affect arms competitions. Work on what arms control has achieved or failed to achieve in terms of constraining Soviet power is virtually nonexistent even though this question pertains to the very rationale for arms negotiations with the Soviet Union.

The state of the academic art tends to suggest something more profoundly important: While arms negotiations with the Soviet Union have increasingly become a crucial context for a nonalarming, yet most effective buildup of Soviet military power as well as for the display of some of its most essential political instrumentalities, because of the ways in which it shaped Western security policies, Western negotiating policies have been increasingly indifferent toward such developments. In fact, the more Western negotiating policies tend to be determined by domestic considerations, the more they seem to run out of serious negotiating options while at the same

time increasingly constraining *Western* military efforts, which were
already undertaken in a piecemeal manner. In other words, among
the most important yet least explored aspects of both Soviet military power and Western negotiating policy are the patterns by which
Soviet political objectives in the pursuit of global power interact with
Western political constraints in a sustained competition as those patterns affect both sides' grand strategy options. Arms negotiations
have become the level at which these interactive patterns are most
observable. The absence of a body of research on these aspects thus
reflects the very distortions that flow from political approaches that
have prevailed in the West for more than twenty years.

It is only in the most recent endeavors that the interrelations
between Soviet power and Western negotiating behavior have begun
to be a focus of analytical interest. There may be a growing body of
research at last. These volumes are meant as a forum for such work,
both American and West European.

Along with the companion volume, this one originated from a
comprehensive project carried out for several years under the sponsorship of the Stiftung Wissenschaft und Politik (SWP) in Ebenhausen in the Federal Republic of Germany, the largest West European
research institute in the field of foreign and security affairs. In the
project some thirty key analysts from the United States and Western
Europe participated as principal authors. Contributions were reviewed during several project workshops. Somewhat different versions of the texts have been published in German as well.

The project was guided by three principal observations: First, the
political role of Soviet military power and the Soviet approach to
arms control has to be seen in terms of *how the Soviets hope to
shape the process of political change* in Europe and elsewhere (with
change in Europe on top of the Soviet agenda). Second, *Western
defense and negotiating policies tend to play directly into Soviet
hands* (and mostly for structural reasons). Third, while the Soviet
Union is likely to remain a cautious risk-taker, as a result of the
lingering process of political change through arms buildup and arms
negotiations the role of *Soviet military power may in fact become
decisive.* Expansion of Soviet political control becomes conceivable
precisely because the Soviet Union increasingly succeeds in denying
Western responses and negating Western strategy where military
power matters most: in regional contexts.

Soviet military power thus has to be seen primarily in terms of its
roles in a sustained process of political change in Europe and else-

where, which tends to deprive the United States progressively of its protective options vis-à-vis third countries and thus much of its influence on a global scale. This process could result in profoundly changed political structures in relations between the United States and Western Europe and between the West and the Soviet Union.

In this perspective the volumes are intended as systematic efforts to induce a redirection of Western thinking on military security. At the very least they should help further recognition of the limitations of prevailing approaches. It is hoped that they will stimulate research in a number of new directions.

It seemed important to start with longitudinal analyses of military change over the recent decades. In order to manage the vast amounts of data, changes have been primarily studied in Central Europe during the period from 1965 to 1980. The area is the principal area of confrontation, the only one where superpower forces face each other directly across a common border; the period is most crucial for the behavior of the two sides in the military competition.

The comprehensive project represented by these books was made possible only through the committed participation of many. The wealth of perspectives generated by the personal responsibility of each of the authors gains in value precisely because these different perspectives are presented in a systematic framework developed by all.

Several of the authors on both sides of the Atlantic wrote their contributions prior to assuming governmental responsibility or as holders of public office. These contributions do not represent the views of the institutions involved; rather, they document the authors' independence of judgment based on their commitment to the cause. The long gestation period of the project inevitably contributed to the problem that not all contributions were written at the same time; in some instances it proved impossible to bring the material up to date. We must thank the authors for their patience in this regard.

In addition to the chapters in this colume, contributions to the project have been made by Manfred Bertele, Seweryn Bialer, Falk Bomsdorf, the late Donald G. Brennan, Hedley Bull, Richard Burt, Lawrence Freedman, Colin Gray, Jean–Marie Guéhenno, Pierre Hassner, Robert Hermann, Johan Holst, Cecil Hudson, Fred Iklé, Stephen Lukasik, Andrew Marshall, Robin Ranger, Hans Rattinger, Trutz Rendtorff, Henry Rowen, Lothar Ruehl, Peter Stratmann, and Philip Windsor. Many of those contributions are included in the second volume. Invaluable advise has come from Christoph Bertram, Josef Joffe,

Klaus Ritter, Friedrich Ruth, Thomas Schelling, Enid Schoettle, Helmut Sonnenfeldt, Albert Wohlstetter, and David Yost. Falk Bomsdorf, Hanns Maull, and Grant Whitney have facilitated the utilization of workshop deliberations as congenious rapporteurs; Denis Mercer and Cornelia Schweigler turned the teutonic language of several chapters into English.

The organizational and editorial burdens of the project rested above all with the SWP institute, my colleagues. Klaus Ritter, the institute's director, displayed the patient understanding required for such an effort. Falk Bomsdorf has ably assumed wide organizational and editorial responsibilities. Albrecht Zunker's skills time and again helped avoiding obstacles. Gisela Helms, Christa Hille, and Kurt Jacob have gone over most pages several times, while Gerda Exner helped turn earlier workshops into smooth operations. Petra Pfadisch, Elisabeth Quaet–Faslem, and last, but not least, my daughter Carolin provided essential help that resulted in a deliverable manuscript

While the Stiftung Wissenschaft und Politik proved to be a most suitable operational base for this project, various other institutions have also been instrumental in the process, in particular the Foreign and the Defense Ministery in Bonn, the BDM Corporation in McLean, Virginia, the Naval Postgraduate School in Monterey, California, and the European–American Institute for Security Research in Los Angeles.

Without substantive financial support from the Stiftung Volkswagenwerk in Hannover the project would have exceeded the SWP institute's resources.

At a stage where energies tend to decline, work with Ballinger Publishing Company turned out to be encouragingly smooth, in particular with Carol Franco, Senior Editor, and Steven Cramer, Associate Editor.

Uwe Nerlich
1983

EDITOR'S INTRODUCTION

For three decades enduring political structures in Europe have guaranteed an unprecedented period of peace. It is not the kind of peace that European humanism described as a political and cultural responsibility. Europe at the height of its power showed itself to be incapable of such peace with disastrous consequences. Rather, the political structures securing today's peace in Europe are derived from the vision and political acumen of a generation that sought to ensure that the catastrophe of the Second World War would never be repeated. Unavoidably, however, both the consequences of decades of self-destructiveness in Europe and the forces released in the disaster of the Second World War are also manifested in these structures.

After no other European war was a restoration of previous conditions as unthinkable as after World War II. Yet past European experiences did repeat themselves in this new situation. Securing its hold over Alsace-Lorraine after 1871 required Germany to maintain large military forces, which necessitated a further rearmament of France, which in turn required other European nations like Austria, Italy, and Russia to seek to maintain a military balance. Similarly, the policy of Stalin and his successors of controlling political developments in Eastern Europe and the Eastern part of Germany through a large Soviet military presence forced the West to heed the requirements of military balance, which to a large extent determined the further course of events.

1

As a result the two superpowers that emerged after the Second World War have faced each other in Europe ever since. Peace in Europe is maintained in the context of a military confrontation unprecedented in peacetime. Furthermore, in this confrontation the West seeks to check superior Soviet conventional forces on the European continent through nuclear deterrence, while the Soviet Union has discovered the potential offensive advantages of nuclear weapons. In extreme crises nuclear deterrence is to prevail through a degree of irrationality that Moscow assumes to exist in the West—a situation that in the long run cannot serve as a solid foundation for the West's image of itself.

Under these conditions a repetition of solely European catastrophes seems inconceivable, since the traditional powers of Europe are deprived of the causes for conflicts as well as of the means for carrying them out. But Europe's impotence also implies that in the end the conduct of the two superpowers will decide the fate of Europe. Western Europe can influence its own fate only to the extent that it avoids extreme situations that would accentuate the power potential of the two superpowers. Thus West European policy is for the most part limited to an exercise of influence. With such a policy Western Europe has repeatedly sought to establish a *modus vivendi* with the Soviet Union without opening itself to Soviet influence, just as it time and again had to maintain the United States' engagement on its soil without allowing the resulting military confrontation to become the decisive structural element of European policy.

Thus the peace prevailing for more than three decades also has placed Europe in a consistently precarious position. In addition the perennial interplay of national self-interest in Western Europe has prevented the establishment of a political community that might have served as a model in world politics. This failure at political integration showed that the forces that led Europe down the path of self-destruction are not limited to the level of military-political rivalry.

The dimensions of this failure to build a political community in Western Europe can be estimated by the fact that during the last decades Western Europe has realized unprecedented levels of prosperity, tolerance, and mobility. A politically integrated Western Europe would thus have represented a community without comparison. For this there will probably be no second chance. But if Western

Europe's lack of strategic leverage coincided with a peak in the political and social development of most Western European states, this should not only be attributed to the features of the present system of European security. It is also important to remember that this realization of general prosperity, of tolerance, and of mobility occurred in the course of decades of competition with the Soviet Union as a different system and above all as the result of the United States' liberal policies encompassing large economic areas. Indeed, the policy of peace as pursued by the West in the past was so successful because the political structures supporting this peace remained relatively unaffected by alternative political trends.

Peace in Europe, it follows, could be jeopardized not only by developments that might alter the strategic situation in Europe. If this peace appears increasingly endangered in the early 1980s, it is because the strategic relationship with the Soviet Union *and* political conditions in the West are changing at the same time. In an effort spanning roughly twenty years, the Soviet Union has succeeded in rendering the Western deterrence strategy, the so-called strategy of flexible response, so ineffective that only a systematic and costly effort by the Western alliance to regain a range of response options can promise to limit decisively over the long run Soviet use of military power. At the same time — and here the Soviet leadership's well-honed sense for developments in the West may be evident — criticism in the West, and particularly in Western Europe, of the prevailing methods of security policy has grown to such an extent that the continued existence of the European security system in its present form has become questionable. The internal prerequisites for maintaining this system of European security are thus no longer reliably present at the very moment when the demands made on the system have significantly increased.

Western criticism of current methods of security policy is dominated by a feeling that has moved the great political philosophers since the nineteenth century, the unsettling realization that the capability for political action in the face of growing demands seems ever more limited. "Throughout Europe," wrote Lorenz von Stein some 130 years ago, "there is the feeling that this situation cannot continue, will not continue. Mighty, dreadful movements are preparing themselves; no one dares say where they will lead."[1] Such warnings have since proved true more than once. During the past three decades, however, a sense of acute crisis regarding the existing security system has been the twin of actual well-being.

Until now the Western public has not been made aware of sound political concepts for a basic change. Change will not come naturally but, rather, will depend on the leadership and political vision of Western governments. Solutions will have to be sought under difficult domestic conditions and in the face of the political weight of Soviet military power, which favors the current Western trend toward ever greater accommodation.

Any change in domestic preconditions that has already taken place has resulted largely from factors having nothing directly to do with changes in the West's strategic relationship with the Soviet Union. Two new developments in particular could increasingly shape the further course of events. One is the political *change of generation*, which provides access to the political process to a young generation that experienced neither the Second World War nor the formative years of the existing system of European security. This generation became acquainted with the rules and realities of the present security system at a time of ever more ambivalent policies, ever greater demands on the system, and simultaneous waning of faith in its effectiveness. At the same time more than previous generations, this one has avoided becoming politically absorbed into the system, as demonstrated by the various ways in which it has organized itself and developed the means of passing on its own traditions.[2] Parts of this generation have remained outside the established political systems of Western countries, and for many young people the methods and structures of the existing security order have become symbols of that which they emphatically reject. Nevertheless the established parties, considering the small majorities prevalent throughout Western Europe, must view this young generation as potential voters whose endorsement can determine their own access to power. Every attempt in the West to build a new consensus for the maintenance of military security as a prerequisite for political development must face this new challenge.

The other new situation is a result of the new means of communication. Traditionally journalism served the function of reporting and interpreting. But now the success of political action is often determined by its mere presence in the media, particularly television. The modern mass media thus have caused a change in political behavior akin to the effects of the invention of the printing press. The way political action is presented defines the conditions for political success and thus has ever more influence over initiative, orientation, and resolve in political behavior. This change to *communication* as action creates the danger that political behavior, to the extent that it must seek media attention can also be manipulated since those in control of the new media, themselves without responsibility, can vary considerably the criteria for success. This form of political behavior, by which success is measured in terms of "the greatest possible emotional impact on the greatest possible number," is not uniformly present in all Western countries.[3] It is most apparent where, given the growing domestic political immobilism, political actors seek to gain space for *visible* political action. Foreign and security policy is a preferred arena for symbolic activities, despite the fact that its very complexity is particularly ill-served by those simplifications essential for establishing a "tele-presence."

These two new developments, serving to change the quality of Western politics, demonstrate, especially in their interaction, how domestic changes are impeding the formation of a new security consensus. Moreover these changes have become part of the political landscape of Western countries even though they bear almost no relation to any changes in the military threats presented by the Soviet Union.

However one views the effects of this new situation, two consequences must be emphasized. First, it is even less possible than in previous decades to pursue a policy that, based on a systematic analysis of the growing Soviet military power, aims to establish stable conditions for further political development in Europe. Western policy toward the Soviet Union was never guided by long-range goals and clearly defined priorities. Western governments' existing tendencies toward "constructive ambiguity," as Kissinger called it, are thus only strengthened under today's conditions. These features of Western security policy are evident in domestic political controversies, between the partners of the Western alliance, and in all of their relations with the Soviet Union.

Second, given the usually rather diffuse policies of Western governments, limited for the most part to the management of complicated situations, under conditions prevailing now small minorities have more opportunity to express their viewpoints, at times with dramatic effects. This is accomplished through the media, which spreads the

views. The dimensions of the political controversy over the goals of
security policy are becoming so distorted that governments are concentrating on merely maintaining a security system when actually
the system is in urgent need of reformulation. It is in the nature of
the multiplier effect that the ideas of fringe groups seeking security
mainly as the result of a unilateral exercise of self-restraint have become recognized as alternative concepts. With this orientation, it is
possible to arrive at simple and seemingly plausible formulas for consensus which define important political questions, set goals and tactics and interpret Soviet policy and its manifestations.

The political effects of such unilateralism are evident in the way in
which the political predisposition to self-restraint, long implicit in
Western security policy, is being reinforced. For years Western policymakers have reacted more strongly to internal demands for unilateral restraint than to the evident need for measures to limit the
growing military capabilities of the Soviet Union.

The dimensions of the current debate about the future security
policy of the West—which is taking place in terms of war and peace—
is circumscribed by the alternatives of either maintaining the present
security system or dismantling it unilaterally. The possibility of improving the present system through a more effective strategy of military deterrence is increasingly remote from serious debate, as is the
possibility of placing greater emphasis on *mutual* restraint in the relations between the Soviet Union and the West.

The forms the policy of maintaining the present security system
takes in the West alternate with characteristic regularity among the
individual partners. For example, the attempt on the part of the Reagan administration to reestablish a military balance in critically important areas that it considers threatened is just as much aimed at
this goal of preservation as is the attempt on the part of the social-
liberal coalition in Bonn to maintain the political priority of arms
control over defense in those or other critical areas. In the 1970s
the situation was exactly reversed. The government of the Federal
Republic of Germany then saw a need to express its concern over
certain aspects of the American SALT position (the question of the
so-called forward-based system [FBS]) or complained about insufficient defense efforts of the United States (as in December 1978 regarding a 3 percent increase of defense expenditures). The American
administration in turn urged politically sensitive arms control ele-

ments on the Federal Republic, e.g. the so-called Option III in the Vienna negotiations on mutual and balanced force reductions in 1975 (MBFR), or subordinated German military requirements to its own arms control goals, demanding in summer 1977 limitations on long-range cruise missiles intended for NATO. Pursuing such contradictory courses at different times, the United States and the Federal Republic each find occasion to claim that the other country's actions are not conducive to the maintenance of an effective alliance. From one perspective the alliance's ability to function effectively seems threatened; from the other its basis of legitimacy. Every attempt at maintaining the previous security system must therefore be based on a stretched and thus fragile consensus.

In reviewing the developments within the Western alliance one could argue that on the American side characteristic oscillations and periodic switches between defense and arms control priorities seem to be the rule.[4] The Federal Republic considers itself particularly affected by such oscillations and generally attempts to stabilize that American trend to which it has just adapted with difficulty. It does so by meeting the American challenge, the change in priorities usually resulting from primarily domestic processes, with nervous persistence. The ups and downs of U.S. policy originate within U.S. politics itself; the oscillations are usually strongest within the general public, somewhat more subdued in Congress, and weakest within the administration. In 1982, however, this process of oscillations was for the first time affected by political repercussions emanating from Western Europe, particularly the Federal Republic, as the foreseeable dampening of Reagan's policy of placing a high priority on defense was prematurely given an added impetus.

Each time that its policies run counter to those of the United States, West Germany's European partners in the alliance fear that it is drifting away from the United States and the alliance. Such fears were expressed during the 1960s on the question of nuclear codetermination. Such fears are now expressed whenever German counterpressure is exerted in the direction of maintaining the priority of arms control. As soon as the Federal Republic appears to be following a course similar to that of its West European partners, such as France's Eastern policy during the sixties or the so-called peace movement in the Netherlands in the late seventies and early eighties, the allies begin to reverse their behavior. Trends in their own policies, which are in fact reinforced by German behavior, are dampened in the hope of leading the Federal Republic back to the middle of the road, a policy pursued not the least in order to enhance their own political maneuverability. Such behavior can be observed most clearly in the case of France. As a result the respective countercyclical policies initiated in the United States and West Germany intersect only briefly. At the very moment when the policy of the Federal Republic is once again aimed at establishing new common ground with the United States, the latter is already starting its next policy switch.

Given the dynamics within the Western alliance, which in each phase interfere decisively with the alliance's capacity to develop political initiatives supported by a broad consensus, the Soviet Union naturally favors all trends toward arms control and opposes those toward defense. In light of strong dynamics of their own, widespread Western assumptions about Soviet influence often seem exaggerated; usually it can only support already existing trends or weaken unfavorable developments. From the Soviet point of view developments in the United States and West Germany enjoy absolute priority. Given the frequently countercyclical character of these developments, Soviet diplomacy thus often needs to operate with a high degree of flexibility.[5]

These dynamic processes emphasize in characteristic ways the primacy of domestic politics in all countries of the alliance. The fact that in such a situation the Atlantic alliance has continued to function at all may be considered a stroke of historical luck, but in the end it was probably due to this dynamic and the typical behavior of the individual countries in assigning political priority to either defense or arms control that the alliance was repeatedly able to converge on a middle course. Since the midsixties, however, the activities of all alliance members have increasingly been directed at arms control and away from defense.

The price paid for alliance cohesion is a limited ability to undertake far-reaching initiatives and to review systematically relations wih the Soviet Union.[6] The policy of *management* of relations with the Soviet Union, with its many variations, has revealed the sensitive internal limits on Western ability to counter Soviet policy strategically. But it made possible over a long period of time a security consensus in the West whose importance ultimately lay in relations with the Soviet Union.[7] It was not just an accident that developments in relations with the Soviet Union (the Vietnam War, détente, and the growing military power of the Soviet Union) triggered reactions in the West that could not be completely absorbed by the political system of the alliance that has progressively weakened the security consensus in the West.

Thus a strategic approach vis-à-vis the Soviet Union was hampered ever more. At the same time resistance to the prevailing security system increased a resistance that took the form of an actionism necessarily limited to achieving changes in relations with the Soviet Union through changes in Western policies. The present security consensus has long excluded a goal-oriented, strategic approach toward the Soviet Union. On the other hand it could be called into question only by a unilateralism that seeks to gain freedom of maneuver by unilaterally giving up certain elements of the prevailing security system or even by attempting actively to eliminate or obstruct them.

This unilaterlism, which found only one form of expression in the so-called peace movement, is manifested most explicitly as protest or open rejection, without actually being able to threaten the Western security consensus. The more latent forms of unilateralism are politically of much greater consequence, as is apparent in their influence on the setting of the political agenda, on the way certain proposals are publicly advanced, and on the manner in which certain interpretations — particularly regarding Soviet policy — are offered.

Those intent on influencing the political agenda tend to describe certain measures or questions, which from a systematic point of view are of only limited importance, as if they were destabilizing threats to the whole security system (a system they themselves are actually trying to eliminate) or as if they even involved questions of war and peace. Controversies about the so-called neutron weapons or about the deployment of long-range theater nuclear forces (LRTNF) in some West European countries are striking examples of agenda-building, insofar as the likelihood of a large conflict is made to appear dependent on whether the West refrains from taking certain measures to reestablish a military equilibrium.[8] Suggestions advanced for a unilateral renunciation of certain options (first use of nuclear weapons) or programs (modernization in certain areas like LRTNF), for unilaterally effective agreements (a freeze on nuclear weapons, which would codify a Soviet advantage), or for the unilateral reduction or withdrawal of certain weapons systems sufficiently illustrate additional techniques for effective agenda-building.

Agenda-building through criticism and proposals is reinforced by the positive estimates of the consequences of such unilateral actions vis-à-vis the Soviet Union and the minimization of their attendant dangers. They form an unusual contrast to the allegedly peace-threatening effects resulting, in this viewpoint, from Western countermeasures. This technique of interpreting Soviet behavior began first throughout the United States and more recently spread to Western Europe. It applies primarily to the presentation of the military balance, to analyses of Soviet behavior (as in Afghanistan) and to interpretations of the Soviet arms buildup, for example its intercontinental first-strike capability (SS–18 and –19) and continental first-strike capability (SS–20).[9]

The more often and the more exclusively alliance policy is determined by the debate about preserving or unilaterally limiting the existing security system, the more alliance policy shifts away from the requirements of military effectiveness and the more the postwar security consensus erodes. Yet until now no other kinds of measures have been proposed, much less initiated, that might keep the political influence and military power of the Soviet Union out of the life and relationships of Western and particularly West European industrialized nations.

In this way unilateralism is about to become the secret pacesetter of alliance policy, without itself having to attain any kind of declared goals. In addition, the more it advances, the more hopeless the West's situation becomes. Increasingly, unlimited Soviet military capability could only be contained by giving Western defense efforts top priority, yet unilateralism is becoming an essential component of the foundation upon which alliance legitimacy rests.

Such a tendency would find its expression in a policy of meeting unilateral actionism almost to the limits of formal alliance membership. Proponents of this policy seek to establish mutual security in the sense of a "security partnership" with the Soviet Union, while avoiding any definition of what they actually expect from such a partnership in the face of the realities of Soviet power. Indeed, the proponents of this policy strive to create the impression that such a partnership is already a matter of fact.[10]

A security partnership with the Soviet Union has always been a matter of hope, at least since the earliest manifestations of certain common interests, such as were defined during the 1955 Geneva summit conference (today often considered the peak of the Cold War). Yet since the beginning of the 1960s it has become more than clear, occasional political rhetoric to the contrary notwithstanding, that the Soviet Union is in principle not yet prepared to recognize

Western security interests. The Soviets rely instead on their own strength, the further enhancement of which is to help them in achieving the goals of their *Westpolitik.*

In view of the constantly shifting priorities in the course of the continuing debate about maintaining or unilaterally limiting the existing security system, a policy of mere management will become ever less adequate for securing the effectiveness of the alliance. So far there are no foreseeable developments within the West that might enable the West, better than has been the case, to design a strategic approach towards the Soviet Union; that is, to develop with sufficient unity and the political stamina necessary for the gradual realization of long-term goals the political, economic, social, and military elements for a coherent policy vis-à-vis the Soviet Union. At least the realization is gradually taking hold, however, that despite a lack of domestic preconditions a strategic approach toward the Soviet Union has become necessary if only to provide for the continued existence of the alliance.

First, the possibility of dangerous developments is becoming more real, where Soviet military power might prove decisive. Thus a further weakening from within the Soviet empire or the increasingly unstable situation in the Persian Gulf region (which, directly and indirectly, is of vital importance to all Western industrialized countries) could lead to a potentially uncontrollable expansion of the Soviets' use of military power. Such contingencies are much more likely than planned aggression, yet their results would be similarly disastrous. This incidentally provides the methodologically important insight that the danger to peace can be determined only on the basis of a strategic analysis of political interest and not on the basis of abstract comparisons of military power or, much less, of imaginary consequences of partial Western measures designed to redress existing or developing military imbalances.

Second, faced with such potential conflict situations and the most likely Soviet military-political responses, the need for a global orientation of Western strategy clearly emerges. In the framework of such a global strategy selective military reactions could be adequate, if they were suitably prepared. The effectiveness of Western deterrence strategy will have to prove itself against the background of an increasingly broad specrum of disquieting conflict possibilities; but it will also depend more and more on whether the West can, through selective responses, deny the Soviet leadership the means and operations to become sufficiently certain about the outcome of a conflict. This strategic approach is very different from a Western war-fighting capability, yet it implies more than the kind of deterrence position that can presumably guarantee Soviet restraint only through the threat of a nuclear catastrophe.

Third, one lesson from the negotiations conducted with the Soviet Union in the 1970s is increasingly clear: Military security cannot generally be strengthened through an institutionalized process of arms control negotiations aimed for the most part at mere arms limitations while at the same time subordinating Western military preparations in critical areas of defense to the course of these negotiations. Instead, major reductions—disarmament—must be the goal thereby enabling the West to base the negotiations on assessments of concrete threats and to accept discontinuities in the negotiating process, discontinuities that in turn protect the West from feeling permanently pressured.

Fourth, in view of the growing internal difficulties that any Soviet leadership must face, the West has been rediscovering a possibility with which the Soviet Union has always reckoned (as evidenced by the Soviet attempts to shut itself off): namely, the possibility of Western political influence on events within the Soviet empire. The West is deeply divided over the usefulness, the goals, and the methods of exercising such influence. However, these disagreements are founded increasingly on the realization shared by most that the stability of Soviet rule, relying as it does on military strength, is not inaccessible to Western political influence. The possibility for a long-term design of East–West relations is based on this realization.

Although the West cannot forgo nuclear deterrence, the predominant categories of Western deterrence policy have for the most part blinded Western policymakers to four elements on which any future Western security policy should focus: real strategic threats, the necessity for selective military capabilities, disarmament as a political goal, and influencing development within the Soviet empire. By linking these four elements in various ways, options could be developed that would help the West regain the political initiative, and this in such a way that the structure of relations with the Soviet Union would once again become a matter of political decisionmaking and diplomatic negotiations. If sound policies could be designed, it seems reasonable to expect that a new security consensus could be built, whereas a mere continuation of the policy of management will contribute to the disintegration of the present consensus within the foreseeable future.

What then is the nature of the present debate in the West, in which all sides so emphatically claim to be speaking for peace? The peculiarly smooth transition in recent years from a situation in which Europe was thought to be an island of peace to one where fear has become the determinant of political action suggests the shallowness of prevailing attitudes.[11] In fact, current political developments in the West could well prove decisive for war and peace, but in the debate of the early 1980s practically no consideration has been given to categories of war and peace, nor have any attempts been made to define possible political causes of renewed and inevitably catastrophic military conflict in Europe. It seems rather ironic that a movement has developed in several Western countries that protests passionately against war without having the slightest idea under which political-strategic circumstance war could occur in a Europe that has enjoyed nearly forty years of peace. It is also strange that in these countries a type of study has grown that calls itself peace research yet that has never shown any interest in analyzing the conditions for the very peace that will soon enter its fifth decade.[12]

This may not be surprising if one recalls that the most comprehensive research effort on the causes of war was started "in the hopeful atmosphere of Locarno (1926) and completed in the midst of a general war" (1941).[13] Ironically, 1941 was also exactly the time when the United States and the Soviet Union had begun work on those weapons that were to change completely the problem of war but that also helped create a situation that has kept war out of Europe since 1945.[14] In addition, consider the historian's complaint that in the twentieth century, during a period of unprecedented risks of war, no new ideas have been conceived for the creation of international order—yet this lack of thought is not even considered a problem.[15]

The present debate, conducted in the name of peace and war, is thus actually concerned with keeping or gaining political power in the countries involved. As a consequence of this debate the political influence of Soviet military power may be expanded, the domestic preconditions of the present security system in the West may be further weakened, and thus the possibilities for political action vis-à-vis the Soviet Union may be reduced. To this extent the debate does in fact involve questions of war and peace. Yet no answers to the question of what are the real threats to European peace and what will be the future role of military power in the political development of Europe can be drawn from this debate. Rather, the strange situation is developing in which the realization of the prerequisites for a peaceful political order in Europe will be hindered by a movement that believes itself particularly committed to peace.

Given today's controversies, political reason may once again feel discouraged. Historical experiences, situations that overwhelmingly demand pragmatic responses and domestic political calculations which have politicized the security policy agenda do indeed leave little room for reasoned and responsible policies. But political reason would abandon itself and, with it, the possibility of maintaining peaceful political developments in Europe if it did not continually rethink, develop, and/or discard the guiding political principles concerning the maintainance of peace. In this sense the necessity for increased knowledge is grounded in the very purpose of political action.

Beyond these controversies it will become necessary for the West to identify those additional measures or even far-reaching changes necessary for peaceful evolution in Europe. Four basic questions must be addressed: Which conditions have preserved peace in Europe during the last decades? What changes contribute to a reduction in self-restraint in the use of military power in non-European regions, resulting in a greater number of conflicts characterized by the use of modern arms technology and the desire for military solutions? Which political-strategic conditions could make a military conflict in Europe more conceivable in the foreseeable future than in past decades? In other words, with what serious threats to peace in Europe must a responsible Western security policy be prepared to deal? Finally, to what extent can the political structures of the peace that Europe has enjoyed for decades change—either through changes in basic strategic relations, political developments, or political methods used to limit military power, to the point that the political situation in Europe shifts decisively, and without actual military conflict, to the benefit of one side only? In other words, when dealing with the value of military power in Europe, we are dealing not with the avoidance of war, but, rather, with the future design for peace. Does not the continued growth of Soviet military strength, as well as the Soviets' way of negotiating over security issues, serve their *political* purposes in a protracted process of political change in which the West stands to lose its staying power?

A Western peace policy worthy of the name must address all four questions. The questions are independent to the extent that each requires a specific answer and the answers to all four could easily come into conflict. There is presently no Western government whose policy is adequately geared to any of these questions. On the other hand there is reason to assume that Soviet policy emphasizes precisely the questions most ignored in the West, namely the potential for conflict outside of Europe and the political effects of military power in a protracted process. A Western peace policy must first be able to define the conditions for peace in Europe today in such a way that their preservation or restoration, should this be practical, would not run counter to this policy but, rather, be one of its potential goals. This also means that the analysis of the preconditions of the current peace must be consistent with the depiction of future threats.

The criticism of nuclear deterrence prevailing in a number of Western countries alleges that the present peace can be attributed not to nuclear deterrence but to political restraint. In the future, it is argued, the threat to peace will come from the nuclear buildup, while political restraint, for unexplained reasons, will cease to exist. Conversely, proponents of Western deterrence policy attribute the fact that peace prevails primarily to the existence of nuclear weapons; more recently, some agreements concerning a symbolic limitation of nuclear weapons are cited as a second, occasionally even as the more important, explanation. From such a perspective it is easy to lose sight of the political structures without which an effective nuclear deterrence cannot be maintained. In fact, it seems inappropriate to attribute peace in Europe *solely* to the effectiveness of nuclear deterrence. Nuclear deterrence can only be and remain effective within the context of political structures stable in the face of isolated changes and potentially unstable only as a result of fundamental political shifts that would affect all the elements of European politics.

A Western peace policy must take account of political changes that have led to a rediscovery of classical warfare in regions Western liberal thought has long assumed would remain peaceful if only they were left to their own political evolution and kept out of the East–West conflict. In fact care must be taken to keep East–West relations immune from conflicts in non-European areas. Indeed, the Soviets must not be presented with opportunities to intervene in such conflicts and must be given sufficient reasons for exercising restraint. Iraq's attack on Iran, South Africa's attack on Angola, Argentina's attack on the Falkland Islands, or Israel's attack on the Palestinians in Lebanon certainly created situations involving Soviet interests and in part even Soviet obligations.

A conclusion can be drawn from such developments that third parties in non-European regions are now more likely to solve political conflict through military means than in the days of bipolarity. Yet in spite of some unsettling cases, the stability of East–West relations in the face of such incidents in non-European regions has *so far* not been upset. Given the vital importance of certain non-European crisis areas for the viability of Western industrial societies, however, it is also foreseeable that the greatest threats to what remains of East–West stability are to be found in the possibility that conflicts, particularly in the Near and Middle East, could spread. The dimensions of these threats are clearly determined by the state of the direct political-strategic relationship between the Soviet Union and the West.

The dynamics of all serious East–West crises have demonstrated that within the given military structures in Europe, neither side at any point has been willing to risk war, even if this could not be predicted with certainty in the course of some of these crises. If, as is the concern of many, the probability of a military conflict in Europe seems to be growing at the present time, this could be the result of either a change in the structures responsible for maintaining peace or a change in the way in which past decades are now viewed. Both can be mutually reinforcing. Third, therefore, a peace policy must now even more specifically address the question whether war in Europe is in fact a political possibility or to what extent such contentions can be related to political-strategic considerations or else tend to ignore real threats to Western security.

The debate about this question suffers from characteristic conceptual deficits. As a rule the definition of threat is formulated to satisfy certain political purposes, which usually creates a tendency to neglect troubling elements. Occasionally, however, it also overemphasizes certain threatening aspects. At the same time threat analyses for the most part ignore the goals of the other side, which realistically should determine the suitability of one's own means. This tendency leads on the one hand to a generalization of threats that would need to be considerably narrowed if political goals were taken into account. On the other hand it often implies that situations in which use of military force could actually give one side decisive political advantages are not adequately diagnosed.

A further difficulty arises from the fact that the Atlantic alliance represents a politically complicated coalition for the common defense which, in the face of the warfare capabilities systematically pursued by the other side, depends on the deterrent effect of potentially irrational reactions. Such a coalition furthermore is incapable of formulating reasonable goals in case of war and, confronted with the sensitive political task of defining its mutual commitments, almost unavoidably defines the threat it must face on the basis of administrative and legalistic structures. A coalition such as the Atlantic alliance can orient itself only on a bureaucratically defined and administered threat, which carries the danger of misinterpreting or ignoring actual threats.[16]

A realistic analysis of future threats to Europe must be based on three facts. For one, the range of military response options open to the Western alliance is narrowing, while the potential threats derive increasingly from developments that are rarely or barely taken into consideration. This applies particularly to the possible effects of extra-European conflicts. Furthermore on the Soviet side a combination of internal weakness and actually usable military power makes the prediction of Soviet behavior even more difficult, especially in view of the growing vulnerabilities of the West in sensitive non-European areas, such as the Gulf region, and the waning reaction capabilities of the West. Finally it becomes obvious in retrospect that the doubts expressed in the West about the effectiveness of the strategy pursued by the alliance are directly related to constant attempts on the part of the Soviet Union to negate through its own efforts the strategy of the Western alliance, to deny the Western alliance the ways and means for effective countermeasures.[17]

Fourth, this bears direct consequences for the question about the role of military power in the long-term political development of Europe. For more than two decades Western expectations have been grounded in the belief that it was possible to achieve a stability in military relations that required similar behavior patterns from the Soviet Union. A situation in which one side, however encouraged by the behavior of the other side, attempted to deny the other side the response options upon which its strategy is based, yet at the same time has acquired military maneuverability of its own, is incompatible with expectations of military stability. Indeed, it necessitates a reconsideration of the course of the military competition over the past decades. Moreover, there can be little doubt that all political actors are guided in questions of European security by calculations about the outcome of conceivable military conflicts. If one side fears that all or most *virtual* wars would in the end redound to the benefit of the other side,[18] this is bound to influence its peacetime behavior and ultimately its political will to maintain prevailing political structures. This is particularly true for Western Europe's relationship with the United States.

In a basic sense, this fourth question includes the other three and requires additional attention to the course of the East–West military competition during the last decades and to the accompanying political efforts to regulate it. From this perspective the question of how to design peace in Europe must be at the center of the political debate. The stability of peace-keeping structures will be decided primarily from this perspective, and change would result primarily from changes in the political role of military power in the course of the political development of Europe.

In the West and particularly in Western Europe, military power is being viewed increasingly in the nonpolitical terms that characterized American foreign policy in earlier years. The political instrumentality of such power has been largely forgotten. To make matters worse, the use of military power is denied as a rational option and at the same time taken into consideration as a catastrophic possibility. The idea of political order in Europe no longer seems to include a regulated military competition as a potential goal. Since this competition nevertheless is proceeding—albeit with different levels of intensity on both sides—the idea of a political order has disappeared completely from the European agenda. It has been replaced by a redefinition of the nature of antagonism in Europe, and political behavior has been adjusted accordingly. This might still meet the Western desire for normality if it were shared equally on both sides. In fact, however, the Soviet Union at no time has expressed its political recognition of Western security interests. Instead, it has subjected its political-economic system to the limits of what it could bear in order to achieve a systematic buildup of its military power—this under conditions where different approaches might have furthered internal reform opportunities and thus the acceptance of Soviet rule. The fact that the Soviet leadership has been willing to accept such costs can find its explanation only in Soviet political objectives and a political understanding of military power, which is utterly different from the understanding shared in the West.

The idea of a balance of military power—where both sides accept military stability through a mutual neutralization of strategic attack options and hence a progressive political uselessness of military power—must indeed have appeared strange to the Soviet Union as a superpower not yet fully consolidated. The maintenance of its political system depends on both political protection from and competition with the West, and military power is needed to achieve both objectives. The political necessities for military power and presence are all too readily apparent throughout Eastern Europe. In competing with the West the Soviet Union is either relegated to the level of mere military power, or it is forced to discover an alternative to systemic competition, which would change the nature of Soviet politics. As long as the Soviet Union continues to regard its relations with the West in terms of systemic conflict, it will be left without any other means of carrying out the competition.

The fact that, from the Soviet perspective, military power can be a suitable instrument—which justifies the political and military costs incurred in its buildup—is the result of Soviet interpretations of *Western* policies and politics; actual developments during the last decades have tended to confirm such interpretations. The political culture of Western countries is ill suited for protracted conflict, and even less so when such conflict requires a long and costly arms competition even in peacetime. The structures of American–West European cooperation, on the other hand, were formed primarily in terms of providing for a common defense. (That at least is the public's understanding that to a large degree corresponds with reality.) Were they to become dissolved, the relationship between the United States and Western Europe would change radically, far beyond that based on military necessities. In addition, it was clear—not least because of the division of Europe and, most importantly, of Germany—that the question of how to structure relations with the Soviet Union would remain a central one for political decisionmaking processes in the West; that is, one that would pit political forces within each country and all of the countries against each other. The constant conflicts resulting from such political disagreements were bound not only to eliminate considerably the chances for designing a durable Western political strategy vis-à-vis the Soviet Union, but also to offer the Soviet Union time and again possibilities for counterinfluence.

Given these conditions, the concept of arms control—which is of Western origin—opened up for the Soviet Union perspectives of certain developments in East–West relations where the mere continuity of negotiations seemed to become a primary need of Western politics. It followed that the continuing buildup of Soviet military power would take place in a mutually accepted context of negotiations that subjected the Soviet Union to no limitations whatsoever while forcing the West increasingly into a posture of self-denial; as a final result, political conditions would be created—symbolized by actual agreements—that seemed to make the protection of Western Europe by the United States ever more difficult militarily and ever less necessary politically. The constantly shifting balance of military power was bound to narrow the range of negotiating options for the West. At the same time, it forced the West more firmly onto the road of negotiating about its military security.

In this sense the Soviet military buildup, to a considerable degree, served the purposes of a long-term political double strategy towards the West. The Soviet Union, precisely because it was successful on the political level, widened the opportunities for using its military power with impunity, either to intervene directly or to prevent outside intervention where favorable political changes were taking place. In addition,the constantly changing "correlation of forces" favored the otherwise potentially hopeless expectation of systemic stabilization within the Soviet sphere of influence. The mere fact of negotiations, which finds the West in the role of a *demandeur* urging continuity with ever fewer bargaining options, is of extreme importance for the Soviet Union, because negotiations serve two political functions. First, they lend legitimacy to the Soviet Union both within its borders and outside (i.e., the Soviet military presence in Eastern Europe through MBFR). Second, they symbolize a certain kind of progress in the competition with the West that is made possible by the military buildup of the Soviet Union and finds its expression in categories of negotiations that imply their recognition by the West.

The long-term political strategy of the Soviet Union, where the buildup of military power and a willingness to enter into negotiations are designed mutually to reinforce each other in pursuing the goal of gradual political changes in Europe, aims to dissolve the structures of American–West European cooperation and thus the commitment to share all risks. Were this strategy to succeed, it would mean not only the end of those conditions that for decades now have guaranteed peace in Europe. Rather, the logic of such a development would also imply that the increase in Soviet power available for conflict situations inside and outside of Europe would enter ever more forcefully into the political consciousness of Western European countries, to the point where the danger of war in Europe might become real. Unless basic relations within the Atlantic alliance experience a decisive change for the better, such a course of events would accelerate developments favorable to the Soviet Union. The actual use of Soviet military power in the pursuit of political objectives would then become less necessary. It would be limited in its role to that of protecting favorable political changes in Europe or other critical regions such as the Near and Middle East (or even, in the longer run, the Caribbean) against intervention from the United States.

To that extent the degree of the actual military threat to the West can serve as one indicator for the effectiveness of the most important instrument available to the Soviet Union in its long-term pursuit of Westpolitik. But the point of view prevailing in the West is generally limited to a perception and estimation of Soviet military power in any *given* situation; this is true as much for alarmists as for appeasers. Hence, the ironic developments since the early sixties: The idea of a steady and increasingly irreversible process of political and military change in Europe was expressed in the declaratory objectives of the Soviets' political strategy and is being realized through the constant buildup of Soviet military power and through their specific approach to negotiations. By now, however, it is primarily the West and above all Western Europe who are insisting on the continuity of this political process, although they are neither prepared to engage in the military competition nor ready to seek structural changes as a result of negotiations. The West is not even capable of understanding the dynamics of the process itself or the structural changes taking place in its course; neither is it willing to make those changes the yardstick by which to measure the new requirements of a Western security policy. In that sense, too, Western security policy is limited merely to managing a process or, in rare instances, to short-lived demands for discontinuity.

Under these circumstances the slowness of political change in Europe may come as a surprise. In marked contrast to Eastern Europe, the West could always take recourse to a seemingly endless array of fall-back positions and was thus able constantly to adjust to new—though usually worse—situations. This has given rise to a political mentality that the German poet Hölderlin once described in the following way: "Wherever there is danger, help will become available." Still, the process of political change in the West is proceeding in one direction only, even if at different speeds and with occasional, though slight, course corrections. From a medium-range perspective this is likely the most promising development as far as the Soviet Union is concerned. For the first time a situation has now become conceivable in which the United States and Western Europe will react to each other so that the continued existence of cooperative structures in the military economic, and political fields will become questionable. Foreseeably, disagreements over how to deal with the Soviet Union will assume increasing importance; recent developments have shown that Western Europe will tend to seek to reestablish alliance consensus precisely on that level where mere continuity in relations with the Soviet Union can most easily be achieved—arms control negotiations.

For the Soviet Union this development—reinforced by increasingly frequent European–American disagreements in other areas—must now seem the most promising. Two factors need mention in this context, however. First, the Soviet Union, while it obviously succeeded in setting such a development in motion, must still rely primarily on the dynamic that Western policies tend to develop. If the nature and course of political change in Europe during the past years is taken into account, and if Soviet military power and the effects of prevailing Western approaches to negotiating with the Soviet Union can be reflected more appropriately in Western political thinking, then this course of action could be slowed down or even reversed. Second, this would be especially true if Western policies were geared to the fact that political change in Europe and in East–West relations cannot disregard developments in Eastern Europe and in the Soviet Union, which in turn contribute to overall changes. Of course such internal changes in East European countries are much less subject to Western influence than are comparable changes in the West to Soviet interventions. In addition, they are much more circumscribed by the political effects of military power than in the West. Still, it is incumbent upon the West to develop appropriate long-term political objectives that might be realized in the general process of political change in Europe.

Needless to say, the pursuit of such political objectives for a future state of affairs in continental Europe would require appropriate military preparations in order to preclude potential Soviet efforts at forestalling such changes. The most important goal of a Western deterrence policy must be to secure the possibility for political change in Europe without Soviet power playing such an overwhelming role as in past decades. This includes the goal of preventing all wars, but the political objectives must go beyond that. Under prevailing conditions, negotiations with the Soviet Union are exclusively geared to political and domestic crisis management, tend to strengthen the political effects of military power, reduce the military capabilities of the West, and further the political goals of the Soviet Union. Hence, they should *not* be given political priority over defense policies. Both approaches—deterrence and negotiations—should be pursued with one goal in mind: to design long-term sustainable policies for the creation of political structures in Europe. This would presuppose a development whereby common political responsibilities gain preponderance over the mere management of military competition, which so far has been conducted by one side as a variant of political competition and understood by the other side as a necessary means of avoiding conflict.

Such a reorientation of Western security policy would open up many new possibilities for establishing alliance consensus. It would free the West from those very basic goal conflicts that are no longer limited to nuclear deterrence and for that very reason serve to discredit it. It would make feasible a policy in which *moralism* would no longer be confined to positions that do not show a *political* way out of a given situation and rarely go beyond the principle of mere negation. Finally, it would lay the groundwork for a policy in which *realism* is no longer limited to positions that—in the extreme consequence of political action to which it is committed—put the very foundations of the political community in question or leave it open to the danger of destruction.

This perspective informed the research project undertaken by the Stiftung Wissenschaft und Politik, presented in this and its companion volume, *The Western Panacea*. This volume focuses on the *only*

ingredient of Soviet power that induces political change in the West—
military power. In Part I, Phillip Karber and James Martin describe
what advantages the Soviet Union actually gained during a sustained
effort vis-à-vis the Western alliance for both the conventional and the
theater nuclear balance. This has never been done before in those
terms, since force comparisons are usually provided on an annual
basis—that is, in static terms—or else in extremely aggregated ways
by simply showing changes over time in most general measures like
expenditure or aggregates of nuclear weapons. Several explanations
are offered for how and why the Soviet Union pursued the arms
competition. In Part II, Robert Legvold considers the political instrumentality of Soviet military power in terms of Soviet doctrine, John
van Oudenaren examines the Soviet conception of Europe, Lothar
Ruehl shows how that conception tends to shape Western perceptions, and Phillip Karber deals with the Soviets' systematic effort to
negate Western deterrence strategy as a viable policy. Part III puts
Soviet military power in a political context. Abraham Becker reviews
Soviet military activity with regard to Soviet objectives and economic constraints. Then Harry Gelman reconstructs the Soviet
leadership's perception of what challenges U.S. global policy poses
to the Soviet Union and what opportunities may arise to broaden
the scope of Soviet displays of power. On this basis, Fritz Ermarth
assesses the needs and chances for containing Soviet power under
currently emerging circumstances. And finally Uwe Nerlich considers the political need for linking a strategy for military containment
to a broader long-term political approach toward Soviet power.

The second volume looks at arms negotiations, the one field where
the political influence of Soviet military power may be most obvious,
but which nevertheless happens to be the dominant context for the
West to assess and manage military power. This volume states at the
outset that in recent decades there has been a reversal of roles, turning the West into the *demandeur* in a process that it feels necessary
to continue, despite the synergism of Soviet arms and negotiating
policies, as well as the fact that the West is increasingly running out
of meaningful negotiating options.

Two broad conclusions follow from these volumes. First, neither
confrontational policies nor the détente policies of the 1970s are
adequate to cope with Soviet military power and Soviet negotiating
policy. While the former rightly recognizes the importance of Soviet
military power but tends to ignore the political context within which

it primarily matters—the sustained effort toward political change—the latter encourages engagement in a long-term process without coping with military power as either a threat or an instrument to control this process. Second, arms negotiation policies ought to be designed to meet strategic requirements—that is, deterrence strategy should determine the scope for what is negotiable—yet deterrence strategy ought to be seen within the framework of a broadly gauged policy toward the Soviet Union. The pursuit of that policy, oriented toward political structures of Soviet–Western relations should be the very essence of the West's engagement in a long-term process of competition and conflict management.

NOTES

1. Lorenz von Stein, *Geschichte der sozialen Bewegung in Frankreich von 1879 bis auf unsere Tage*, 3 vols. (Munich: 1921, reprint of 1850 ed.), vol. 3, p. 208.
2. Cf. Steven Szabo, ed., *The Successor Generations: International Perspectives of Postwar Europeans* (London: Butterworth, 1982).
3. The quote is from Ted Koppel, a news moderator for the American Broadcasting Company. In an important speech William P. Clark, security adviser to President Reagan, summarized the reevaluation of American strategy toward the Soviet Union the following way: "a successful strategy [*must*] have diplomatic, political, economic, and *informational* components built on a foundation of military strength" (speech on May 21, 1982, at Georgetown University, in *Wireless Bulletin from Washington* 97, (May 24, 1982): 3; emphasis added.) On television in the United States as a medium for politics see Theodore H. White, *America in Search of Itself: The Making of the President 1956–1980* (New York: Harper & Row, 1982), esp. ch. 6; see also William L. Rivers, *The Other Government: Power and the Washington Media* (New York: Universe Books, 1982).
4. See also the observations of Henry Kissinger in *Kissinger: The White House Years* (Boston: Little, Brown, 1979), p. 195.
5. As far as Germany and the United States are concerned, predominantly cooperative trends in their relations with the Soviet Union in the sense of an active diplomacy coincided only between 1971 and 1973. This immediately heightened the maneuverability of both and made possible a real negotiating strategy vis-à-vis the Soviet Union.
6. It was primarily this viscosity of the alliance that made Charles de Gaulle appear such a dramatic exception.

7. A precise characterization of this policy of "management," focusing on the United States, is to be found in John van Oudenaren, "U.S. Leadership Perceptions of the Soviet Problem since 1945," R-2843-NA, The Rand Corporation, Santa Monica, Calif., March 1982, pp. 43ff. According to this analysis, the management approach is based on the assumption that the causes of conflict in relations with the Soviet Union are structurally and geopolitically determined and therefore not to be eliminated through "solutions." Accordingly, instead of setting long-range goals, the "managers" place their confidence in the effects of a process of long and, if possible, uninterrupted duration.

8. Examples become more numerous during the last years, primarily on the European side, above all in the Federal Republic of Germany, whereas previously they were to be found mainly on the American side. The process of agenda-building is one of the most important and least studied phases of the political process; for a survey of the state of research in this field see Barbara J. Nelson, "Setting the Public Agenda: The Case of Child Abuse," in Judith V. May and Aaron B. Wildavsky, eds., *The Policy Cycle* (Beverly Hills, Calif., 1978), pp. 18-23. Aaron Wildavsky has aptly characterized one further dimension of such agenda-building: "The ways in which the dominant problems of the time are handled may set the style for dealing with other areas of policy. . . . The characteristic mode through which major policies are attacked thus becomes an independent variable which may be given explanatory power in accounting for ways of problem solving." (In Wildavsky, *The Revolt against the Masses* [New York: Basic Books, 1971], p. 174.)

9. Cf. the critical statements by Albert Wohlstetter, "Optimal Ways to Confuse Ourselves," in *Foreign Policy* 20 (Fall 1975): 170-198; and K.-Peter Stratmann, "Das 'eurostrategische" Kräfteverhältnis. Zweifelhafte Bewertungen als Folge der Anwendung unterschiedlicher Kriterien," in *Europa-Archiv* 36, no. 13 (July 1981): 387-98.

10. The concept of shared security includes the old idea of a mutual interest in survival, which at the end of the 1950s informed the concept of arms control. This concept does not, in principle, answer the question of what performance and behavior one should expect from the Soviet Union in the interest of partnership. Furthermore, the concept is advanced at a time when it is becoming clear that common interest in survival from the Soviet perspective could and can be safeguarded by a policy contrary to the interest of the West.

11. The political nature of this change becomes obvious from the fact that although a break came with the Soviet aggression in Afghanistan, with the hostage-taking in Teheran (in which the Soviet Union did play an opportunistic and hostile role), with the realization of an unchecked Soviet arms buildup, and with the repression of the Polish reform movement, the

manipulated fear in the West appeared directed more at the reactions of the United States than at Soviet behavior. In this instance the peculiar dynamics of earlier events, such as the Cuban missile crisis and Soviet intervention in Czechoslovakia or in the Vietnam War, repeated itself, which released a political need in the West — above all in the United States — for rapprochement with the Soviet Union. New under the current situation is the fact that Western reactions are not based on expectations of a new détente but rather on the fear of a dangerous crisis in relations with the Soviet Union, a crisis that many fear might be triggered as a result of *Western reactions.* Consequently the current situation is marked by more than the usual attempts at détente in order to repair relations.

12.   This kind of research was, in regard to this perspective, guided only by efforts to interpret the peace of the past decades as an "organized peacelessness," which eliminated the question pertaining to the preconditions for the prevailing peace, or to depict Soviet Western policy (including its arms buildup) as merely reactive, thus assigning the blame for all tensions to the West.

13.   Quincy Wright in the introduction to his monumental two-volume work, *A Study of War* (Chicago: University of Chicago Press, 1942), vol. 1, p. viii).

14.   On the origin of the nuclear arms race on the part of the United States and the Soviet Union see Nerlich, *The Precarious Peace: European Security in Its Fourth Decade* (forthcoming).

15.   F.H. Hinsley, *Power and the Pursuit of Peace: Theory and Practice in the History of Relations between States* (Cambridge, England: 1963), p. 3.

16.   This practice of a bureaucratized threat is in some Western countries politically opposed by groups that believe in the concept of reactive causes of war; they assume, in other words, that the way in which the West intends to react to aggression makes war itself more likely. The debate over the so-called theater nuclear force-modernization has provided many examples for this kind of attitude.

17.   See Chapters 1 and 6 by Phillip Karber and Chapter 2 by James J. Martin in this volume.

THE SHIFTING BALANCE
The Way it Was

1

TO LOSE AN ARMS RACE
The Competition in Conventional Forces Deployed in Central Europe 1965–1980

Phillip A. Karber

For some years almost every major defense program before the North Atlantic Treaty Organization (NATO) has been scrutinized, indeed criticized, as a stimulant to the interbloc competition frequently described as an arms race. The Western alliance has actively pursued an arms control agreement, and its member governments have actively sold their respective electorates on the prospect of a European arms accord between NATO and the Warsaw Treaty Organization (the Warsaw Pact) that if successfully negotiated would relieve some of the burden of defense expenditure and reduce the risks of war. Yet to date no agreement has been reached. Negotiations on mutual and balanced force reductions (MBFR) are stalled; SALT II was relegated to an indefinite purgatory, and the new theater nuclear force (TNF) discussions are giving every evidence of continuing the "dialogue" where *process* is given precedence over *progress*. While this mating dance drones on unconsummated, the armament competition in and around Central Europe continues unabated.

Editor's note: This chapter and Chapter 6 represent parts of a comprehensive study on the European arms competition between 1948 and 1980. (A draft version of the full study was presented at a workshop in Ebenhausen in summer 1980. Publication of the full study that will include extensive documentation is considered for a later state). See also Karber's discussion of arms control implications in Uwe Nerlich, ed., *The Western Panacea: Constraining Soviet Power through Negotiation* (Cambridge, Mass.: Ballinger Publishing Company, 1983).

In Central Europe the armies of NATO and the Warsaw Pact have increased their combined inventory of major weapons by 50 percent since 1965, adding over 31,000 major combattant systems (see Map). Another aspect compels interest in this arms race, moreover. Today Central Europe has the heaviest concentration on earth of conventional and nuclear weapons deployed in operational units. It is the only region where the forces of the two superpowers stand face to face across a common border. It is the only area where both parties to a potential conflict not only possess nuclear weapons but have integrated their anticipated use as an explicit element of their military strategy and gone go considerable effort to link in doctrine the fortunes of the conventional military balance to a strategic exchange between the superpowers.

The term "arms race" is widely used, and to the extent that it offers a generally understood, succinct description of a complex phenomenon, it is a useful term. But like all metaphors, it can be abused. Indeed its use to describe a strategic competition between East and West is not without critics or problems. Usage of the "race" analogy is relatively modern, dating from the first years of this century. As critics have pointed out, the word connotes not only a competition but one with an identifiable starting position, prescribed parameters for competition, and an end state or finish line. It has been suggested that unless these properties can be demonstrated in an arms competition the term *arms race* is not only of no value but is dangerous in that it inaccurately purports to describe a relationship that may not exist.

The Central European arms competition does fit the race analogy. It has a starting date before which the currently opposing forces were not only not in a competitive posture but actually cooperated in the defeat of a common opponent. In retrospect the competition has been conducted within identifiable parameters. One of these is the geography of the region. Central Europe is naturally defined in north and south by the obstacles of the Baltic Sea and the Bavarian Alps. Longitudinally, it is defined by the geographic infinity of oriental Russia and the cultural continuity of the Gallic Occident. Militarily, the competition has remained remarkably symmetrical in form and function if not intensity and hue. This is not to say that Central Europe has not experienced a spillover of its arms competition to other domains nor been free of exogenous contamination. Nevertheless, the competition remains a struggle for the heart of Europe.

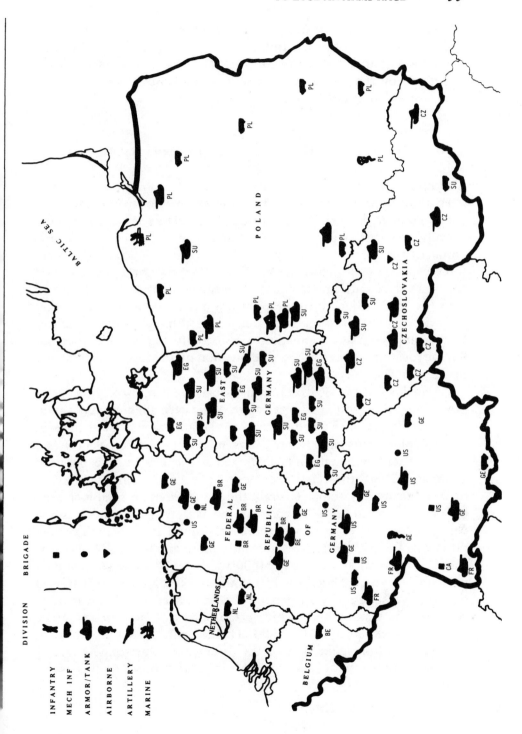

Whoever controls the land between the Rhine and the Vistula exercises influence out of proportion to the size of the population or economic potential of the immediate area. The Central Europe of today, as defined by the MBFR guidelines, is no less central to the future of civilization than it was in the Thirty Years War.

THE CONVENTIONAL FORCE COMPETITION

Although there are numerous ways to assess the conventional combat strength of opposing military forces, the quantity of troops and number of combat units that constitute the respective forces have traditionally been the two indices most frequently employed. Despite the popularity of these two measures, their utility in portraying overall force capabilities is highly suspect since they do not address a third and at least equally important factor—the weapon systems deployed with the force. Unmanned weapons are relatively harmless and combat without organization is anarchy, yet although factors such as force manpower and combatant units modify the balance, they are but surrogate measures of the sine qua non of an arms race: the competition in weaponry.

An analysis of the Central European balance based solely on aggregate changes in divisional units deployed by each alliance would indicate that little had changed since 1965. Despite a series of changes in force deployments and fluctuations in the number of NATO and Warsaw Pact divisional units deployed in Central Europe between 1965 and 1980, the relative balance between the alliances has remained remarkably stable. Overall, the NATO division total increased by one (from 26 to 27), whereas the Warsaw Pact total was unchanged (at 57). In contrast, the total ground force manpower deployed in the region has grown steadily more disparate as NATO personnel were reduced by nearly 50,000 after 1965, while Warsaw Pact personnel were expanded by 150,000. As a result, the small NATO quantitative superiority in personnel that existed in 1965 was overcome by the Warsaw Pact, which established a 20 percent advantage over NATO in personnel by 1980. The comparative stability of divisional establishments in view of the divergence in personnel requires further examination to address the nature and causes of this asymmetry.

A number of problems are entailed in focusing on divisional units as a measure of combat capability: Both the size and combat capabilities of units called divisions differ substantially; increases in combat capability can occur within the division rather than by adding additional units; and the combat capabilities of units at echelons other than the division are omitted entirely. The variance in unit structures must be assessed for their impact on combat capabilities, the process of force reorganization over time must be closely examined, and all force elements, regardless of echelon, must be included in a comprehensive balance assessment. The impact of differences in unit structure can also be seen in the manpower area. While the Warsaw Pact had more than twice the number of NATO divisions in 1965, NATO personnel totals were slightly greater since NATO divisions were considerably larger than their Warsaw Pact counterparts and existed with a much heavier supporting structure than Warsaw Pact units.

The disparity between the trends in manpower and divisional units in Central Europe from 1965 to 1980 can be explained through a comparative examination of the relative effort devoted by each alliance to force improvement, which is reflected in the various force deployment and reorganization schemes that took place during this period. In retrospect the approaches taken by NATO and the Warsaw Pact were diametrically opposed and resulted in a shift in the balance of conventional force capabilities in favor of the Warsaw Pact. Although various attempts were made to enhance NATO conventional combat capabilities in Europe, they were negated by both cutbacks in deployed forces and postponement of modernization initiatives due to economic constraints throughout the alliance. Although these economic considerations shaped NATO force development over the years, the Warsaw Pact embarked on extensive force development and modernization that has already yielded substantial results and shows no signs of abating. The impact of these trends is not readily apparent in a comparison of manpower and division totals because in both alliances the changes either occurred within the existing unit structures or involved combat forces subordinate to echelons other than the division—corps, army, and front.

Between 1965 and 1970 NATO personnel were reduced by nearly 36,000 as actual force levels were reduced in nearly all NATO armies (see Figure 1–1). Although the reductions were relatively small on an

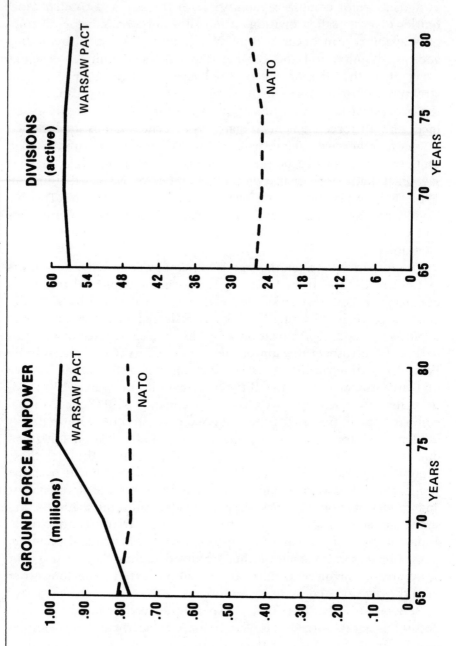

Figure 1-1.   Center Region Balance Trends: Ground Force Manpower/Divisions.

individual basis, they would cumulatively have been of even greater magnitude without the continuing buildup and deployment of West German forces that took place to offset most of the decreases in the other national forces. During this period NATO's hopes of increasing force capabilities were not fulfilled, and NATO combat capability declined relative to the Warsaw Pact.

The United States withdrew one of its five divisions in the theater in addition to one of its three armored cavalry regiments in 1968 to meet resource constraints during the Vietnam conflict. Of the division withdrawn, only a single mechanized brigade remained stationed in the forward area under the "reforger" concept: Thus unit served as the forward element of a U.S.-based mechanized division that was to be rapidly transported to Europe in case of crisis to reinforce peacetime in-place forces. Clearly a compromise, this move affected the readiness of U.S. forces for a conflict and also set the stage for other cost-cutting adjustments. A number of force reorganizations in other armies either reduced or at best maintained the force capabilities that existed prior to the reorganization. The British reorganized the three divisions in the British Army on the Rhine (BAOR), resulting in a reduction of combat brigades form seven to six. The Belgians disbanded an active brigade within each of their two divisions in the Federal Republic of Germany, reducing in-place force capabilities by one-third. The Canadians cut the strength of their forces in the theater by one-half and the remaining elements of the mechanized brigade group were redeployed form the Northern Army Group (NORTHAG) to the Central Army Group (CENTAG), more than doubling their deployment distance from the inter-German border. In spite of these changes there was some improvement in the force posture. The French reorganized their two divisions in West Germany (one armored, one infantry), resulting in two mechanized divisions that were more suitably structured to modern mechanized combat and had materially greater combat strength than the previous formations.

The NATO force reductions occurred at a time when Warsaw Pact capabilities were changing dramatically. Following the massive invasion to suppress the Dubcek regime in Czechoslovakia in 1968, the Soviets created the Central Group of Forces and stationed five additional divisions in that country on a permanent basis. The net result of the invasion increased the Warsaw Pact division total by only one, however, as four low-category-readiness Czech motorized rifle divisions and an infantry regiment were abolished nearly simultaneously. Although not reflected in division totals, the deployment of five category I Soviet divisions in place of the low-readiness and marginally capable Czech units represented a substantial improvement in overall Warsaw Pact force capabilities and readiness for combat in Europe. In addition, the Poles reorganized one mechanized division to form a sea-landing division capable of amphibious operations in the Baltic area. Little in the way of reorganization occurred in either Soviet or East European units during this time, but an attempt was made to resolve associated readiness problems with a continuous fleshing out of existing unit personnel and equipment requirements. As a result, Warsaw Pact capabilities were steadily improving across the board within the existing force posture while NATO capabilities stagnated in an environment dominated by budgetary rather than military considerations.

The expansion of Warsaw Pact force capabilities, particularly Soviet, within existing units that had been seen in earlier years was vigorously pursued between 1970 and 1975. Armor, antiarmor, artillery, and air defense assets were increased on a large scale throughout the forces, although personnel increases during those years were modest at 50,000 and not a single division was added to the Warsaw Pact force structure. Rather, by increasing force capabilities within the divisions and in army and front support regiments and brigades, this expansion was largely concealed from Western perceptions and analyses of their force posture.

The period between 1970 and 1975 was decidedly more stable within NATO. Although personnel levels did decline slightly again, previous force levels were largely maintained or incrementally increased over time. The United States deployed an armored brigade within the Seventh Corps to serve as another forward element of a U.S. reinforcing division under Reforger. West Germany created two new tank regiments to serve as corps-level reserve units for two of the three corps. Notwithstanding these initiatives, NATO lost ground relative to the Warsaw Pact force expansion program through 1975.

After 1975 a new round of force reorganizations began in both alliances. NATO led this cycle with changes in virtually every army deployed in Central Europe. The United States deployed another mechanized brigade to the forward area and also restationed one brigade from the Seventh Corps to Garlstedt in NORTHAG with the establishment of U.S. Third Corps as a reserve element in that army group. The West Germans reorganized a number of their divisions, adding three brigades fully mechanizing motorized units, and establishing several new Panzer units as well. Late 1970s British and French army reorganizations affected all units in the two corps and resulted in the establishment of one new division organization by each country. Since these efforts were again driven more by economic than military considerations, however, the new divisions were roughly equal to other NATO brigades in combat strength and the impact of the reorganizations is more accurately assessed as a reduction from 12 brigades to 7 brigade equivalents. To make matters worse, the Belgians redeployed their mechanized division in West Germany back to Belgium, further reducing combat readiness in the theater.

At the same time the focus of Soviet and Warsaw Pact modernization efforts was again on improving force capabilities within the existing force structure. The most significant of these efforts was the Soviet modernization of an entire motorized rifle regiment in every division in Europe to create an independent combined arms force with combat capabilities equivalent to a NATO brigade. Each of these new style regiments was given 90 BMP infantry combat vehicles and a full battalion of artillery in addition to expanded and more sophisticated armor, antiarmor, and air defense assets. These changes greatly increased Soviet offensive capabilities by lowering the level of combined arms integration and providing these units much greater freedom for independent maneuver. Similar trends have been seen in the East European armies and will be of particular significance for NATO if widely adopted within the Warsaw Pact.

Although the Soviet and Warsaw Pact force levels were decidedly more static between 1975 and 1979 than in previous years, this was only the quiet before the storm. In 1980 a Soviet tank division was withdrawn from the Group of Soviet Forces in Germany (GSFG). This move was the first Soviet force reduction since the 1958 reorganization, but, rather than signaling a reduction in force capabilities, it represented the beginning of a new and massive restructuring of all tank regiments in the forward area, which is leading to increases in weapon assets and force capabilities.

Thus in contrast to NATO personnel reductions and reorganization schemes that did little to enhance combat capabilities, Warsaw Pact forces were steadily expanded through three mechanisms: the establishment of Soviet Central Group of Forces; the expansion of unit structures, particularly Soviet, already deployed in Europe; and the introduction of additional combat units at army and front levels of subordination. These actions increased 1965 Warsaw Pact personnel totals by 20 percent as they brought 150,000 new personnel into forward area units. Moreover these organizational developments were intended to expand unit combat capabilities in a meaningful way and resulted in Warsaw Pact weapon inventories being expanded to a much greater extent than the personnel figures would suggest. Hence a comparison of the weaponry of the two alliances is needed in order to assess the balance of forces.

The competition in conventional weaponry can be broken down into five general categories of armament: armored vehicles (tanks and armored personnel carriers [APCs]); antiarmor systems (antitank guns and antitank guided missiles [ATGMs]); artillery fire support (conventional artillery and multiple rocket launchers [MRLs]); aerial weapons (tactical aircraft and attack helicopters); and air defense systems (air defense guns and surface-to-air missiles [SAMs]). The total number of systems for each alliance in each category has been traced between 1965 and 1980. Included in the count were systems in active operational combat units located within Central Europe that were manned at 50 percent or greater of wartime strength. Thus weapons systems held by reserve units, in prepositioned stocks, territorial defense units, and reinforcing forces have been excluded. Although the weapons categories do include systems of widely varying capabilities, the long-term trends in total systems not only show an upward competitive spiral but also quite clearly illustrate the major conventional areas of emphasis in the arms race to date.

Considering all five armament categories within the central region, there has been a significant increase in the number of both NATO and Warsaw Pact systems deployed. These aggregate trends also show considerable disparity in the relative effort devoted to force developments in the two blocs. Since 1965 the Warsaw Pact expansion has accounted for more than 80 percent of the increased armament levels in Central Europe, while NATO's share is less than 20 percent. In 1965 the Warsaw Pact with 57 divisions had a 50 percent advantage in total weapons, and in 1980 with 57 divisions it has expanded its lead over NATO to 100 percent. Over the same period the Warsaw Pact has added 4.4 weapons for every 1 added by NATO.

Even important from the perspective of a long-term competitive race, there is an asymmetrical momentum to the quantitative race.

NATO's rate of growth for the 1970s has declined from that of the mid-1960s, whereas for the Warsaw Pact the rate of growth over the same period has accelerated. Had the rate of acquisition for both alliances stayed the same for the following decade as it was between 1965 and 1970, NATO today would have 10 percent more weapons systems in its inventory and the Warsaw Pact 10 percent less. There is not a single weapons category where the Eastern bloc is not numerically superior; qualitatively there is not a single area where NATO's technological advantage has not declined faster than the numerical imbalance has grown. Also interesting is the relative emphasis placed by the alliances across the five weapon categories (see Table 1-1). Armored vehicle systems dominate the increases on both sides and account for half of all systems deployed since the mid-1960s. The growth in armored assets was brought about in the mechanization that began in both alliances in the 1950s and has been the most significant aspect of the conventional arms competition for the entire period. The deployment of tanks and armored personnel carriers (APCs) for supporting infantry has totally reshaped modern maneuver warfare, and the continuing imbalance in tanks, the dominant armored system, has had a great impact in determining the nature of the competition in the other armament areas as well. Indeed this cross-category fertilization of the action–reaction cycle not only

Table 1-1. Distribution of Increase in Conventional Armament (*Combined NATO and Warsaw Pact Expansion in Central Europe: 1965-1980*).

Functional Balance	Weapon Category	Proportion of Total Armament Increase, %
Armor	Tanks; APC/IFV	50
Antiarmor	Antitank guns; antitank guided missile launchers	29
Artillery	Tube artillery; multiple rocket launchers	14
Aerial	Combat aircraft; armed attack helicopters	3
Air defense	Air defense guns; SAM launchers	4

drives the quantitative expansion but directs the qualitative acceleration of weapons technology as well.

In terms of ground warfare, tanks required APC/IFV so that associated infantry could keep up with the pace of battle; the continued growth of armor stimulated the expansion of antiarmor systems; the need to suppress the latter has driven the demand for artillery fire support. Even the aerial and air defense balances were affected by the emphasis on armor. The aerial balance was altered with the introduction of a new category of armament, the ATGM attack helicopter. In addition virtually all new SAMs and air defense guns introduced since 1965 have been specifically designed for the mechanized battlefield and thus to provide armor freedom of maneuver from air attack.

Armor Balance

The Warsaw Pact's 2-to-1 advantage in tanks over NATO in the central region in the mid-1960s was not viewed with alarm because of a number of compensatory factors. Western tanks had a significant technological advantage. The two blocs were virtually equal in number of armored personnel carriers. And given that NATO forces were defensively oriented, their quantitative and qualitative lead in antitank weapons appeared to offset their numerical inferiority in tanks.

Since 1965 the Warsaw Pact inventory of main battletanks deployed in operational units in Central Europe has grown from 12,000 to more than 16,000 (see Figure 1–2). This 35 percent expansion contrasts dramatically to the addition of fewer than 500 tanks to NATO in active units in the central region and was accomplished in several stages. First, after the 1968 intervention in Czechoslovakia the five Soviet divisions that remained replaced four Czech reserve divisions that had not had a full unit complement of tanks, which were of World War II vintage. Second, as the Soviets began modernizing their tank divisions with the T–62 rather than withdrawing the replaced T–54 and T–55s on one for one, these older systems were transferred to the motorized rifle divisions to increase their tank strength by 30 percent, via the addition of an independent tank battalion and the equivalent increase of an added tank company to each of the divisions's three motorized rifle regiments. In the third stage the Soviets reinforced their army and front-level independent tank

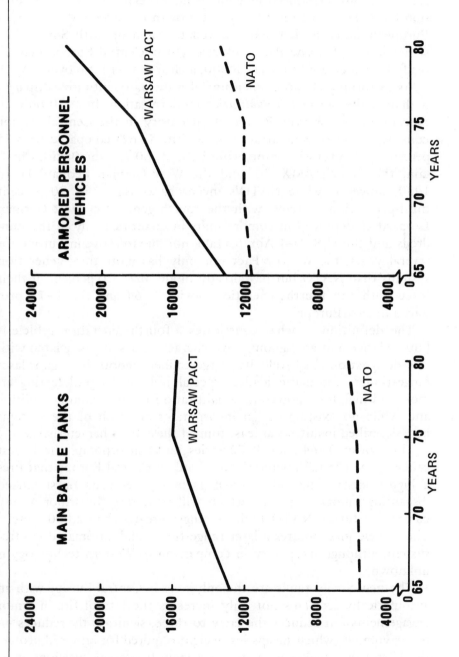

Figure 1-2. Center Region Balance Trends: Main Battle Tanks/Armored Personnel Vehicles.

regiments and introduced new independent regiments above the division level. The most recent stage of growth has occurred in the East European units as they have moved to catch up with Soviet divisional norms. Warsaw Pact tank strength in Central Europe may already have increased to over 18,000, a clear 3-to-1 ratio over NATO.

As disturbing as the momentum of growing quantitative disparity is that of the Soviet-led *qualitative* modernization. In 1970 only 20 percent of the Warsaw Pact tank inventory in the Central Region consisted of third-generation vehicles (the T-62) compared with 75 percent of NATO's inventory (the U.S. M-60 A1, the British Chieftain, the French AMX-30, and the West German Leopard I). In 1980, however, while NATO's inventory consisted of 90 percent third-generation systems, with the fourth-generation West German Leopard II deployed in combat units in quantities only in the hundreds and the U.S. M-1 Abrams tank not due to arrive in Europe for several years, the Warsaw Pact not only has more third-generation systems than NATO but has already modernized 20 percent of their force with the fourth-generation Soviet T-64 and the T-72 produced in East Europe.

The definition of what constitutes a fourth-generation vehicle is both relative and ambiguous. Five characteristics are associated with this designation—high-velocity, large-caliber smooth-bore gun; laser range-finder; automatic loader; special hollow-charge-defeating armor; and high horsepower-to-weight ratio for cross-country agility—and while no existing design incorporates all, each of the systems here described manifests at least four of these five characteristics.

The Soviet T-64 and T-72 series tanks incorporate the largest caliber gun (125 millimeters) of any tank in Central Europe that fires a high-velocity long-rod APFSDS (armor-penetrating fin-stabilized discarding sabot) projectile, which will penetrate the armor of any current or future NATO tank at ranges greater than 2,000 meters. The vehicle incorporates a laser range-finder and automated control system, although its quality in comparison to Western technology is unknown.

The new Soviet tanks are the only ones in Central Europe with an automatic loader. This not only increases the rate of fire in armor engagements but reduces the crew to three, significantly reduces interior volume (which means less weight required for armored protection), and thus makes it unique as a main battletank weighing in at

40 tons, one-quarter lighter than its nearest Western fourth-generation competitor.

The T-64 and T-72 have a 70 degree obliquity on the hull glacis plate, conical turrets, low silhouettes, and retractable fender skirts, making them more difficult targets than any NATO third-generation tank. And if this survivability is complemented by some form of special armor (which they are widely believed to have, although it is rated inferior to Western types), it would bring their survivability close to Western fourth-generation systems. This series of Soviet vehicles also possesses a new engine and return roller suspension system, although the horsepower-to-weight ratio and acceleration or agility are not considered the equivalent of Western fourth-generation counterparts.

The Warsaw Pact tank production of T-64 and T-72 tanks until the mid-1980s by the Soviet Union, Czechoslovakia, and Poland is estimated to be more than 22,000 units, at least double the tank production by all of NATO's 15 nations. Nor has the Eastern bloc been content to leave its earlier systems technologically stagnant. There have been persistent reports of the retrofitting of laser range-finders and the introduction of new and more effective ammunition for their earlier T-54, T-55, and T-62 tanks. Thus the West can no longer be content to assume that its qualitative superiority will make up for quantitative inferiority. Indeed it is the NATO alliance that lags in the date of introduction of fourth-generation tanks and their rate of production. NATO faces a severe problem of technological catch-up.

The most significant armored vehicle developments in NATO are the West Germany's new Leopard II and America's M-1 Abrams tank. The technology they incorporate will have a radical impact on the Western approach to tank warfare. Most significant is their utilization of special armor (Chobham type), with the result that, on the aspects most frequently penetrated (turret, glacis plate, and frontal hull), they will have at least 200 percent of current protection against HEAT warheads (hollow charges) and nearly 50 percent more than current protection against high-velocity armor-piercing rounds. These new tanks will be relatively immune to the increasing proliferation of antitank rockets and missiles. This will allow Western armor to operate much more actively on the modern battlefield, not nearly as inhibited by its vulnerability as would otherwise be the case; to hold defensive positions longer, and to exploit the attacker's flank vulnerabilities through counterattack far more often than would be possible today. With the new German high-velocity 120-mm gun, the Leopard II and XM-1 can penetrate any known armor array; and coupled with new laser range-finders, ballistic computers, and stabilization, their accuracy of fire falls well within the definition of precision guidance. The M-1 has a better hit probability on the move than its predecessor the M-60 has while stationary, over the same range. The new horsepower-to-weight ratio, coupled with advanced suspension, not only double the cross-country speed but also provide an acceleration rate that can be employed to reduce the tanks' vulnerability to opposing gunlaying. With its integral thermal sight the Abrams tank can drive and engage targets at night and under conditions of reduced visibility—a tactical combat capability that current vehicles do not even approach.

Thus the new U.S. and West German main battletanks will help redress the armor balance when they are fielded, but it must be remembered that Soviet forces have more of their new T-64 and T-72 tanks in Central Europe today than NATO will have M-1 and Leopard II tanks in 1985. There are indications, however, that the Soviets are developing yet another tank, the T-80, which will mount advanced armor and which could be in serial production by the mid-1980s.

In the midsixties NATO and the Warsaw Pact were at near parity in the number of deployed APCs and the quality of the Western system (the U.S. M-13, British FV-432, German HS-30, French AMX-13 VTT and Dutch YP-408) was equivalent to that of the Warsaw Pact system (the BTR-50, BTR-60, and OT-64). For NATO this was actually an advantage because quantitative parity meant that it had a much higher ratio of APCs to troop units carried, which permitted assigning one APC per infantry squad whereas Warsaw Pact infantry had to double up and permitted the use of armored carriers for command and control, ammunition resupply, and specialized functions whereas the Eastern bloc had to depend on soft-skinned vehicles.

But two factors have significantly altered the APC balance in Central Europe. First, Warsaw Pact forces increased their quantity of APCs so that by the early 1970s every infantry squad had its own armored carrier and the supporting arms had been equipped with armored vehicles based on APC design variants to achieve equivalent unit mechanization saturation with NATO.

The second major factor was the Soviet introduction in 1967 of the first infantry fighting vehicle (BMP) and still one of the best and its large-scale rapid deployment since the early 1970s. What made the BMP unique (in contrast to traditional APCs) was its incorporation of a dual antiarmor combat capability in addition to superior cross-country mobility, the ability to be amphibious without preparation, full CBR collective protection and side-firing ports so that the mounted infantry could use its small arms under complete protective cover. The antiarmor fire power consists of a turret-mounted 73 mm automatic-loaded low-pressure gun firing a rocket-assisted HEAT round capable of penetrating a third-generation main battle-tank at 1,000 meters. In addition the BMP has a turret-mounted antitank guided missile with 3,000-meter range that could be loaded and operated under armored protection. With every third BMP carrying an onboard SA–7 air defense missile (which has been observed being fired from the infantry compartment while the vehicle is in movement), the BMP became the first truly combined arms vehicle. By 1980 the BMP has been widely introduced in each of the Soviet and East European armies in the Central Region and the Warsaw Pact superiority over NATO in infantry fighting vehicles today is at least 3 to 1.

The first NATO counterpart to the BMP was the West German Marder, still the West's best overall design of the deployed IFVs. The Marder, deployed only in the West German army and armed with a 20 mm cannon and retrofitted with the Milan ATGM represents 80 percent of NATO's current IFV inventory in the central region. Its counterparts, the French AMX–10 and Dutch AIFV, also mount a rapid-fire cannon—but due to size constraints have not mounted an ATGM on the squad carrier but include instead a longer range ATGM (HOT for the French and TOW for the Dutch) on a separate variant. Today U.S., British, Belgian, and Canadian infantry are still carried into battle in armored taxis which, reflecting a design concept two decades old, mount no antiarmor capability, no infantry support cannon, and no provision for the troops to fire their small arms under protective cover.

The new U.S. M–2 IFV, which should be introduced into Central Europe around 1983, will be the first NATO counterpart matching the BMP's long-range ATGM capability with its own dual-pod TOW mount. The M-2 IFV turret also includes a 25 mm Bushmaster chain gun, which unlike its smaller caliber Western counterparts will be able to penetrate the Soviet BMP well beyond 500 meters. In fact, the TOW Bushmaster turret, combined with a thermal imaging sight, offers a significant fire-power improvement and, had the M-2 been deployed in Central Europe in the mid-1970s when it was originally scheduled, it would have given NATO a significant edge over the Warsaw Pact. When it finally appears, however, it will no longer be a valued luxury, but an overdue necessity.

Unfortunately the M-2 has a number of limitations that, while insufficient to cancel its acquisition, nonetheless dampen enthusiasm for its late arrival. The system has an excellent horsepower-to-weight ratio and cross-country agility and the rationale for this significant upgrading of automotive and suspension performance was the perceived necessity for an IFV that could operate in close conjunction with the M-1 main battletank. This logic unravels, however, given the radical difference in survivability between the two systems, since the IFV does not incorporate the armor protection available on third-generation tanks. While the M-2 has improved ballistic protection over the M-113 against small arms, it is extremely vulnerable to all Warsaw Pact infantry and vehicle-fired HEAT warheads, ranging from the RPG-7 rocket and BMP gun to the new longer range ATGMs.

This asymmetry in survivability between tanks and the mechanized infantry fighting vehicles creates a severe imbalance in the conduct of either active defense or counterattack, both of which are dependent upon mounted supporting infantry. Thus the mechanized infantry vehicles, which can be penetrated by even the smallest ATGM or gun HEAT warhead, will suffer vastly disproportionate attrition. When hit IFVs are much more prone to catastrophic destruction, and the casualties for vehicles will be three times higher than a tank. As one Israeli infantry commander observed from the 1973 Middle East War: "In the first engagement we had trouble getting the troops to dismount from the protective womb of the APCs, but after witnessing the flaming destruction of entire squads in vehicles hit by antitank fire, we had trouble getting the troops back in."

The U.S. M-2 shares this vulnerability to HEAT warheads with all currently designed IFVs, including the BMP, and its boxlike configuration and high silhouette make it proportionately more visible and thus more vulnerable. In contrast to BMPs, the infantry firing ports do not give equivalent flank protection and the troops do not have opportunity to look out an open hatch during movement. While the system is rated as amphibious, unlike the BMP it cannot enter the water directly but requires the time-consuming erection of a vulnerable flotation screen.

Infantry fighting vehicles not only greatly increase the offensive power of combined arms formations but are also of enormous utility to the defense. Armed with rapid-fire automatic cannon, they provide accompanying suppressive fire for tanks in fluid battle, reduce the target overload by weeding out the opposing APCs, and give infantry a strong base fire for dismounted maneuver. Armed with ATGMs they not only increase the quantity of antiarmor systems and complement the high rate of fire provided by tank guns with the longer range fires of the missile, but allow infantry to operate more independently, thus freeing additional numbers of tanks for critical sectors. They permit the defending infantry to avoid being pinned down in static positions, reducing their vulnerability on the highly mobile battlefield, and, when combined with active defense tactics, make it feasible not only to stop offensive breakthroughs but to destroy them. Given NATO's large number of infantry units, there is no single other weapon investment that could provide as high a return in countering a Warsaw Pact offensive as a new generation of heavy armor infantry fighting vehicles with special armor—yet none is under active development. It will be 1990 before any is likely to appear in the NATO force structure.

Antiarmor Balance

Since the mid-1960s, the assumption has been widespread and oft-repeated in the West that NATO's inferiority in tanks was compensated for by its lead in antitank weapons. This was specious reasoning at best, because NATO's technological advantage in ATGMs and antitank guns was only marginal. Moreover, the quantities of both kinds of systems were only a fraction of NATO's already outgunned tank strength. While in the mid-1960s NATO possessed more ATGMs than the Warsaw Pact, the available number of these weapons, no more than 1,000, was trivial compared to the size of the Warsaw Pact armored forces that NATO faced. Over the intervening decade NATO tripled the number of these systems and introduced highly accurate second-generation guidance technology that greatly improves their accuracy.

Nevertheless, in 1980 the Warsaw Pact had twice as many ATGMs in Central Europe as did NATO although it is NATO that is on the defensive. It has long been thought that the quality of NATO's ATGM technology was years ahead of the Soviets. The Soviets have introduced at least three new ATGM systems, however, all with range and guidance capability equal to NATO's best. One of these systems incorporates terminal guidance, a technology that will not be available on attack helicopters in NATO until the mid-1980s. Of the Warsaw Pact's 7,000 ATGM launchers, over 80 percent are now mounted on armored vehicles, providing not only enhanced mobility but also increased survivability, since the launcher can be loaded and fired under protective armor cover. By contrast, less than 50 percent of NATO's ATGMs are mounted on armored vehicles, only one-third can be loaded and fired under armored protective cover. It is also interesting to note that half of NATO's inventory of ATGMs in the central region are deployed with U.S. forces, covering only 25 percent of the front. And, while NATO has substituted ATGMs for its older antitank guns, the Warsaw Pact has increased its inventories of both (see Figure 1-3).

The introduction of new ATGM systems, and the impact they had early in the 1973 Middle East War, have led some observers to conclude that these weapons signal the demise of the tank on the modern battlefield. The ATGM does offer substantial advantages to the defense but *not* as a replacement of the tank. Instead the value of ATGMs is to give infantry effective antiarmor capability of their own so that NATO's tanks, rather than being scattered along the front, can be massed to counter Warsaw Pact breakthrough attempts and to exploit weaknesses on the attacking units' flanks.

But the ATGM has substantial limitations. Although ATGMs possess longer range than tank guns, the terrain features of Western Europe make it difficult to exploit fully the ATGM's range superiority. ATGMs have one-fifth the rate of fire of tanks, which means that in close engagements if the attacker is willing to accept attrition a static infantry defense will be breached. Because of the size and weight of the missile, only several rounds are usually available for each launcher; the new American TOW ITV and West German JPZ–HOT have one-sixth the ammunition load of a tank, while the British

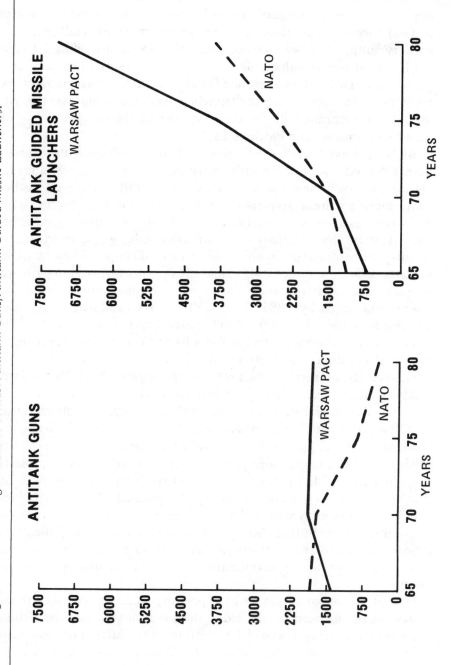

Figure 1-3. Center Region Balance Trends: Antitank Guns/Antitank Guided Missile Launchers.

Swingfire has one-tenth and uses first-generation guidance technology. Dismounted launchers cannot be fired from enclosed positions or field fortifications; thus they expose the crews to small arms and artillery suppressive fire. Second-generation forward-looking infrared (FLIR) guidance is vulnerable to inexpensive countermeasures, and its use through battlefield smoke requires a thermal imaging sight six times more expensive than the launcher. And, most important, existing ATGM warheads will not penetrate the Chobham-type armor of fourth-generation main battletanks.

As NATO has lost its qualitative lead and the Warsaw Pact forces have achieved quantitative superiority in antitank weapons, a growing asymmetry in how those systems are tactically employed has become more apparent and acute. For the Warsaw Pact forces, with their emphasis on the mounting of ATGMs on armored vehicles, these systems have acquired an offensive role: giving mechanized infantry formations an organic assault capability; providing tanks in the attack with a direct long-range means of overmatching fire to suppress static defenses and impede the active mobility of defending armor (since even by 1985 all of NATO's APCs and half of its tanks will not have special armor); allowing even larger tank concentrations in breakthrough areas by giving the adjacent economy of force units enhanced capability; and effectively doubling the shock effect and flank security of formations that have penetrated NATO's forward defenses. While expanding their inventory of ATGMs, the Warsaw Pact has also modernized their antitank guns, replacing short-range recoilless guns and truck-towed cannons with high-velocity guns (100 mm T–12A) limbered by a tracked armored vehicle (M–1970) or large-caliber smooth-bore guns (115 mm) mounted on a new self-propelled chassis. In contrast, for NATO the quantitative growth of the ATGM has been accompanied by a combined 55 percent reduction in antitank guns with a defensive orientation and been achieved primarily by distributing short-range dismounted systems (Milan and Dragon) to the infantry, in essence utilizing existing formations and force structures as an economical means of expanding antitank assets.

One of the major problems of depending on defensive antitank infantry on the modern battlefield is that, contrary to popular belief, the need for infantry is expanding with the introduction of new technology, rather than being reduced. Mechanized, the infantry is expected to accompany tanks in both active defense and counterattack, to provide suppression of the opposing antitank weapons; it is expected to be the major medium through which NATO's antiarmor capability will be enhanced; it is expected to be the primary means by which indirect fire is directed onto the battlefield; all in addition to its traditional missions of assaulting and defending forested terrain, built-up areas, emplaced minefields, etc. But at the very time infantry's role is expanding, the strength of NATO infantry units is not only not keeping pace but declining in numbers and quality of troop training.

The most severe imbalance that antitank infantry will face on the future battlefield, characterized by its high intensity of fire and rapid maneuver, is in survivability. Recent field exercises show that dismounted infantry firing portable ATGMs (the Milan and Dragon together account for the majority of NATO's ATGM inventory), will, in the face of a typical Warsaw Pact artillery suppression, suffer 90 percent crew casualties when firing from unprepared positions. When firing from trenches without overhead cover, casualties are reduced to 30 percent, but it takes an average of 18 hours to prepare these positions; and while the construction of bunkers will reduce casualties further, this will require even longer for field preparation. Given the current absence of any prepared positions across the breadth of the Central European frontier and the already severe problem of getting units into battle positions—because of the problems of readiness compounded by the need to displace units on an active defense so that they are not overrun in static positions—survivability will continue to be a serious problem. If the Warsaw Pact believes that large quantities of vehicle-mounted and armor-protected ATGMs have a growing utility to the offensive doctrine, can NATO afford so few for its defense? If the Western forces had a clear superiority in artillery assets or at least were not numerically inferior, that question might be avoided, but given the growing imbalance in suppressive capability NATO's quantitative and qualitative antiarmor imbalance becomes increasingly decisive.

Artillery Balance

Although NATO has long been outnumbered in artillery assets, thoughout the 1960s its forces more than compensated for this numerical deficiency by a clear qualitative superiority: the majority of

NATO systems were self-propelled, while those of the Warsaw Pact were towed. NATO's inventory consisted of 30 percent large-caliber 175-mm or 203-mm guns and cannons, while the Warsaw Pact fielded none above the medium 152 mm. The West had lowered the level of combined arms integration to provide each maneuver brigade with an artillery battalion for direct support, while Warsaw Pact artillery was centralized at division and army level with inadequate assets to support all the Pact maneuver units. NATO forces had sophisticated fire control to permit coordinating decentralized firing units, while the rudimentary Soviet technology left no option but centralization (see Figure 1–4).

NATO's technological modernization of its artillery assets has been focused less on the development of new delivery systems than on increasing munitions lethality, target acquisition, and fire control for the weapons that it already has fielded. It is interesting to note that, whereas in the past NATO has had the vast majority of its artillery self-propelled and the Warsaw Pact forces depended upon towed artillery, Western armies have recently begun reexamining the value of towed systems. At the same time the former have begun to deploy self-propelled artillery. Although self-propelled artillery provides greater tactical mobility and system survivability, the latest designs in towed artillery have advantages in operational mobility, rapid long-distance travel by truck or carriage by helicopter, and are much cheaper to procure and maintain. Thus currently entering service is the joint British–German FH–70 and the U.S. M–198 towed artillery pieces, although none of the latter is scheduled for Europe before the mid-1980s and the total procurement of the former will be less than 10 percent of NATO's total inventory. Various Western armies have new self-propelled designs intended to replicate the automatic loaders of the newly deployed Soviet self-propelled systems. But the French GCT SP 155 mm system, which has completed development, will only be produced in very limited numbers, and the joint British–German SP–80 and U.S. ESPAWs 155 mm will not be available for field deployment for another decade.

Far more significant were the developments, primarily in the United States, making artillery munitions far more lethal, thereby significantly increasing the effectiveness of each tube. With the increasing concern for the ability of Western defenses to hold against large and high-speed armored assaults, traditional artillery has been perceived as progressively less effective as the thickness and resis-

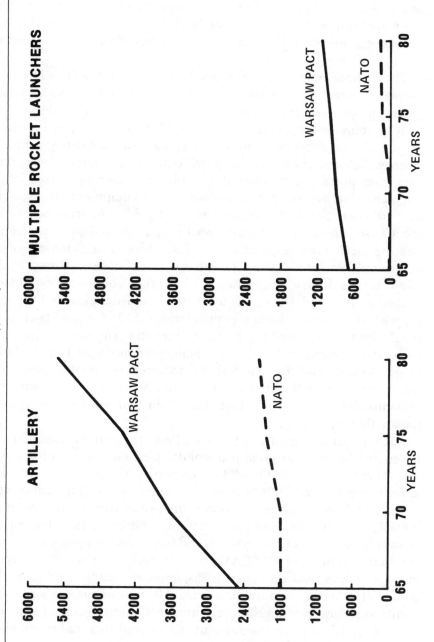

Figure 1–4. Center Region Balance Trends: Artillery/Multiple Rocket Launchers.

tance of armor has increased. The U.S. army has developed three new types of ammunition for its self-propelled 155 mm artillery, the most predominant weapon among NATO forces, which could vastly increase the utility of indirect artillery fire power on the armor-intensive battlefield.

These three new types of artillery rounds are the DPICM (dual-purpose improved conventional munitions), CLGP (cannon-launched guided projectile), and FASCAM (family of scatterable mines). The DPICM round incorporates a cluster of 75 bomblets, each a small, shaped charge designed to penetrate top armor on fighting vehicles, destroy lighter unarmored material (trucks, air defense weapons, command posts, logistics vehicles) while producing optimized lethal fragmentation against personnel and fragile equipment. The second new round is the first artillery precision-guided munitions (PGM): the CLGP, an antitank HEAT warhead, is guided by a projectile steering mechanism responding to a laser designator mounted on air or ground platforms. The CLGP has a range of approximately 20 kilometers, although designation at that range could only be accomplished by flying platforms; its most frequent use is expected to be in support of maneuver units equipped with GLLD (ground laser locator designator) for artillery forward observers. The same device will be used to designate for the new helicopter-mounted Hellfire long-range ATGM, and for tactical air-delivered scatterable mines, in which the base shell dispenses nine antitank mines, each of which is influence-fused and has a high probability of penetration against tank belly armor.

Each of these munitions gives artillery an antitank capability it never had before, but none is a wonder weapon, for each has not a few operational limitations. For example, to be really effective against area targets, DPICM must be salvoed in very high concentrations. CLGP, with its slow response time (half the rate of fire of an ATGM, and at least one-sixth that of a tank), does not compare favorably with direct fire systems and is dependent upon continuous communications. For FASCAM to be effective, it must also be fired in large volleys, and the mines it dispenses are readily visible on the ground, facilitating removal or bypass. All three of these systems will significantly increase logistics requirements, and the cost of this new technology is far from insignificant: Compared to a traditional high-explosive artillery round, DPICM is two to three times more expensive, CLGP at least ten times, and FASCAM twenty times.

The effectiveness of the new antiarmor artillery munitions is critically dependent upon the target acquisition and fire control capability of the systems that fire them. This is even more the case with the U.S. army's recently developed concept of deep engagement, whereby the target servicing load on the direct fire antiarmor system is relieved by breaking up the momentum and reducing the closure rate of Warsaw Pact second-echelon forces. However, the abandoning of the American TACFIRE computerized fire direction system and the cancellation of their SOTAS target acquisition system seriously undermine the potential utility of artillery in helping to offset the armor–antiarmor imbalance.

The rebuilding of Warsaw Pact artillery began in earnest in the late 1960s and through succeeding stages of growth that combined quantitative expansion with qualitative modernization to maximum effect. First came the return of army and front-level artillery brigades that had originally been withdrawn with the introduction of tactical surface-to-surface missiles. Second, with the introduction of the new D–30 122 mm gun-howitzer (still one of the finest designed towed artillery pieces in any army) and the new BM–21 multiple rocket launcher (which significantly increased range, accuracy, and a number of rounds over its predecessors), Soviet division-level assets in both categories were increased by 50 percent. However, it was in the third stage throughout the 1970s that the most significant increase in performance was achieved. This involved the lowering of the level of artillery subordination from the division to the maneuver regiment level by the addition of first a battery and then a full battalion of new self-propelled artillery, yet retaining the concentration of assets at the higher echelons. In the mid-1970s this expansion was limited to Soviet motorized rifle regiments, but by the end of the decade was being implemented in Soviet tank regiments with the East European armies starting to follow suit. This not only mirrors NATO's concept of a direct support artillery battalion for each brigade (regiment) but goes beyond it since the Warsaw Pact has four maneuver regiments per division, whereas the strongest of NATO's divisions has only three brigades. As a result of this growth Warsaw Pact fire support effectiveness has more than tripled in the last fifteen years. With 5,000 pieces of artillery compared to NATO's 2,400, and with 1,200 multiple rocket launchers compared with NATO's 170, the sheer weight of numbers gives the Warsaw Pact forces in Central Europe a substantial superiority in conventional fire support.

This imbalance, however, is not limited to the Warsaw Pact's quantitative growth in artillery assets (which may grow even further as East European armies follow Soviet unit expansion), but encompasses qualitative improvement as well. During the last several years, Soviet forces have been equipped with nearly 1,000 of their two new self-propelled and armored artillery weapons (SP 122 mm and SP 152 mm). Unlike NATO systems, both are designed to be fired "buttoned-up," with full CBR protection, and they incorporate an automatic loading system mechanism that can more than triple their rate of fire under surge conditions. Most of the remaining towed artillery has been modernized, producing longer ranges and higher rates of fire. Like NATO, the Soviets have developed rocket-assisted projectiles (RAP) which can add 30–50 percent to the ranges of their existing artillery pieces. Recognizing NATO's increased dependence on centralized fire control systems for decentralized fire units, the Soviets are placing increased emphasis upon counterbattery suppression and neutralization. This may be achieved by combining the advantage of longer range guns with an extensive electronic warfare signal direction-finding capability, recently augmented by advanced technology computerized fire direction, laser target acquisition, and counterbattery radar systems mounted on armored vehicles that are being deployed with the new self-propelled artillery. Although the initial modernization was Soviet led and focused on the introduction of medium self-propelled systems, East European armies are now acquiring these systems (with the Czechs producing their own uniquely designed wheeled version of the SP 152 mm) and the Soviets are introducing self-propelled versions of their long-range 130 mm guns that outrange any artillery deployed by NATO and have not only matched the West's largest caliber weapon (203 mm) but surpassed it with the fielding of a self-propelled ultraheavy howitzer or mortar.

Since the late 1960s the Warsaw Pact inventory of multiple rocket launchers (MRLs) has been increased by 40 percent and the early models mounting only 8–16 tubes per launcher have been replaced with a new 40-round system. The combined impact results in a fivefold increase in MRL salvo capability. This is impressive in that a single salvo of a BM–21 MRL battalion (18 systems) has the same fire power as 720 rounds of conventional tube artillery. In addition, the Czech RM-70 system has an automatic reload capability that permits it to fire two of these salvos in very rapid succession, providing a massive fire power for the suppression mission. In contrast to the opponent's preference for the MRL, NATO has only deployed one system, the West German LARS, in Central Europe, and then only in small numbers. Although the U.S. army has designed a new long-range general support rocket system (GSRS) capable of dispensing fragmenting bomblets and large numbers of mines, the Soviets have already deployed in East Germany a 240 mm self-propelled large system very similar in range accuracy and ammunition effectiveness to that which will be available to NATO no earlier than the mid-1980s.

Aerial Balance

Of all the categories of conventional weaponry, the respective aerial postures of the two alliances are the most difficult to analyze. The cause of difficulty is the very feature that makes tactical aircraft attractive as a weapons system—the inherent flexibility of the platform for performing a broad range of different missions: interception, fighter escort, close air support, battlefield interdiction, deep strike, reconnaissance, air defense suppression, electronic warfare, and nuclear delivery. A complicating factor is that the performance of the platform is heavily dependent on the ordnance available and the quality of the pilot training, both of which can and do vary widely within and between the respective alliance air forces. Last, whereas the focus on the Central European region (see Figure 1–5) is a useful guideline for measuring ground systems (reflecting immediately available forces), for tactical aircraft this boundary distinction is far more arbitrary since tactical air assets can be introduced via rebasing almost overnight and combat aircraft deployed in adjacent areas can and will flow combat missions over the central front.

Given these limitations, several other aspects of the Central European competitive air balance are noteworthy. Tactical aircraft have been more sensitive than any other conventional weapon to technological obsolescence; a relatively small advance in component design (propulsion, fire control, or avionics) can drastically change the relative standing of a platform. It is thus the one balance area in which technological improvements are given such close scrutiny by the participants and where an innovation on one side can trigger a response from the other side even before the activating system has been oper-

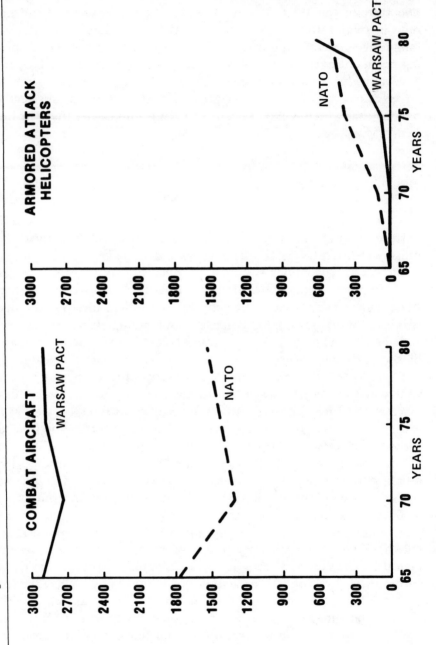

Figure 1-5.   Center Region Balance Trends: Combat Aircraft/Armored Attack Helicopters.

ationally deployed. Despite the reaction to every action on the technological level, the overall fleet structure and mission orientation of the respective alliance air forces have tended to be more internally derived than competitively driven. Given the intensity of qualitative competition, the quantitative levels, although unequal, have remained fairly stable and it is no small irony that the aerial balance, consisting of the most flexible conventional and sophisticated weaponry, has not had as much impact on other balance areas as they have had on the mission orientation and technological design of the tactical air forces. Thus since the mid-1960s NATO has increasingly depended upon tactical aircraft and introduced a new category of aerial armament—the ATGM-armed attack helicopter (AAH)—to offset its growing inferiority in ground-based antiarmor capability.

Although the Eastern bloc had maintained since the end of World War II a quantitative margin that never fell below a 1,000 aircraft advantage, nevertheless by the mid-1960s the technological advantage of Western platforms qualitatively offset the numerical disparity. Thus in 1965 half of the Warsaw Pact air fleet was still composed of first-generation jet aircraft (Mig 15 and Mig 17 fighters) and their second-generation systems (Mig 19 interceptors, SU-7 ground attack, Yak-28 strike or reconnaissance, and early model Mig 21 fighters) were technologically inferior to Western platforms. In 1965 over 90 percent of NATO's fleet consisted of second-generation systems, the F-100 Super Sabre, RF-101 Voodoo, F-102 Delta Dagger, F-104 Starfighter, F-105 Thunderchief, Javelin, Canberra, Lightning, Buccaneer, Mirage III, and G-91). While this variety of systems represented no small standardization problem for the West, the diversity of capability and breadth of mission potential was of little comfort for the East. Between comparable systems NATO aircraft generally had a much more versatile multimission capability and were superior in avionics, range payloads, loiter time, and air-to-air munitions. Oriented toward deep-strike interdiction and nuclear strike missions, they had a high prospect of success. Western pilots were better trained, had twice the flying time of their Warsaw Pact counterparts per person, and operated with flexible tactics that stressed individual initiative in contrast to the overcontrolled and rigid intercept procedures of the other side.

The growing recognition of this qualitative asymmetry again offered NATO the hope that its technological advantage would compensate not only for numerical air advantage of the Eastern bloc but also for the conventional ground force disparity. The belief was enhanced by the introduction of third-generation aircraft, particularly the U.S. F–4 Phantom, a multipurpose fighter whose performance was unequaled in any combatant role: air superiority, conventional ground attack, nuclear strike, electronic countermeasures (ECM), and armed reconnaissance. Nevertheless, no sooner did Western optimism become widespread than the material basis upon which it was assumed began to erode. First, NATO's adoption of "flexible response" placed a much heavier burden on tactical air than the previous strategy in that large conventional requirements were added without a concomitant reduction in nuclear strike demands or an increase in assets. In fact combat experience showed that even under conventional conditions the sheer quantitative demands for aircraft were growing. Thus the 1967 Middle East war illustrated the high loss rates produced by vulnerable air bases; Vietnam demonstrated that strike aircraft over the opponent's territory needed a substantial number of air-to-air escorts and ECM/air defense suppression platforms when encountering a Soviet-designed SAM/interceptor integrated defense; and the 1973 Middle East war taught a bitter lesson in terms of the attrition rates to be expected when using aircraft over a battlefield saturated with modern, mobile, and advanced guidance air defense guns and missiles.

Second, the total inventory of Western aircraft deployed in the Central Region actually declined—with the Americans redeploying aircraft back to the United States (necessitated by air base overcrowding due to the loss of French facilities and the increasing demands of Southeast Asia) coupled with noticeable reduction in the numerical size of European squadrons as newer, higher performance systems were introduced. Third, while NATO continued to modernize, the rate of introduction of third-generation systems was significantly slower (half that experienced with second-generation systems) and many of the new planes were not camparable to the F–4 Phantom in that they were designed for a single mission (Mirage V, Harrier, and Jaguar: ground attack) or were third-generation systems in date of production only (F–5 and Alpha Jet). In fact even though the British and German fleets acquired the Phantom, their urgent requirements for a high-performance interceptor resulted in it being relegated to an air-to-air role rather than conventional ground attack or nuclear strike.

By far the biggest strain posed to NATO's overcommitment of its finite and dwindling aerial assets was the phased but intensive modernization program of Soviet frontal aviation deployed in Central Europe and the new options this gave to the Warsaw Pact. First, in 1970 came modified versions of the two most popular second-generation systems, which, while representing incremental improvements, boosted performance into the class of third-generation aircraft. Thus the Mig–21 J/K/L/N Fishbed, with a new engine giving almost 50 percent more thrust and much improved avionics, not only replaced the earlier model Mig 21s in the traditional interceptor role but added a counterair, battlefield interdiction and strike capability as well. Likewise, the SU–17/20 Fitter C was a variable-geometry replacement of its second-generation namesake (SU–7 Fitter A) in which the combination of a higher performance engine and swing wing configuration improved range, runway performance and nearly doubled the ordnance payload.

Between 1971 and 1975 the Soviets introduced two versions of the new Flogger series. While both have a similar variable-geometry air frame, are rated with a nuclear delivery capability, and can be used in a multimission role, nevertheless, each has been outfitted with mission-specific high-technology components. The Mig–23 Flogger B is designed as an air superiority fighter with such advanced features as laser gunsight, advanced intercept radar, and new high-performance air-to-air missiles capable of "all aspect" (head-on) engagement. The Mig–27 Flogger D, designed for ground support and interdiction strike missions and engineered to employ air-to-ground laser/TV precision-guided munitions, more than doubled the range and the ordnance payload of the aircraft it replaced.

Warsaw Pact aircraft modernization since 1975 has involved the introduction of third-generation aircraft into the East European air forces (with several squadrons of Mig–23 in GDR and Czech units, several squadrons of SU–17 and SU–20 in Czech and Polish units, but over 450 late-model Mig–21 J/K/L/N deployed in all three fleets) and the Soviet forward deployment of aircraft with unique characteristics for frontal aviation. In this latter category is the stationing of the Mig–25 high-altitude reconnaissance aircraft in the Soviet tactical air army deployed in Poland, a system that can fly over Europe with impunity and could also mount a stand-off air-to-surface nuclear missile. Also in this category is the SU–24 (or SU–19) Fencer, a variable-geometry deep-strike interdiction aircraft that falls in the performance category of a medium bomber (for example in a nuclear delivery high–low penetration it has 85 percent of the combat range of a U.S. F–111 E or F and is equal to the French Mirage IV A). Like the Mig 25, only several squadrons of Fencer are typically located forward, although larger numbers have been quickly restaged to East Germany for air exercises, and from current bases in the Western USSR the SU–24 is capable of covering all NATO targets in Central Europe, thus presenting a potent offensive threat of conventional air base preemption or theater nuclear delivery.

Thus within the space of less than a decade, the Warsaw Pact air potential vis-à-vis NATO changed radically. From a force preoccupied with air defense (depending on Soviet-based medium bombers and MR/IRBMs to carry the weight of theater nuclear strikes) to one which, led by Soviet frontal aviation, is now clearly oriented to offensively influencing the course of a conventional campaign. From a force that was clearly technologically inferior in 1965 it was changed to one that in 1980 had more third-generation systems deployed in Central Europe than NATO had aircraft. The introduction of high-technology aircraft has been associated with the implementation of a new theater "air offensive" strategy in which, during the initial period of conventional operations, frontal aviation fighters and ECM aircraft cut corridors through the NATO air defense belt and escort medium bombers to strike NATO's critical rear area installations. Attacks against NATO's most important air bases, nuclear storage sites, and key command and communication facilities would not only degrade its conduct of a conventional campaign but also offer the prospect of anesthetizing the West's central nervous system for release of nuclear options. Amid this confusion fighter bombers would return to disrupt the mobilization and forward deployment of NATO's ground formations, interdict its lines of communication (LOCs), and severely inhibit tactical mobility over the battlefield. Thus, over the last decade, the prospective locale of a battle for air supremacy has moved several hundred kilometers West and it is NATO's ground units rather than those of the Warsaw Pact that will receive disproportionate losses from air attack.

With the introduction of the new multimission aircraft, the Eastern bloc has also closed the gap in pilot training and, while the West had a substantial lead in aerial munitions technology, the costs, developmental problems, and limited Western production have combined to give the Soviets time to achieve an advantage in the quality, variety, and quantity of deployed air-delivered munitions technology, both in air-to-ground precision-guided munitions (PGM) and in air-to-air intercept missiles (AIM). The defensive potential of PGMs has been widely anticipated in the West. However, the introduction of these systems into the Warsaw Pact forces now suggest that early expectations were overoptimistic. Evidently the PGM revolution will do more to increase the offensive power of Warsaw Pact frontal aviation than it will for NATO's defensive utilization of tactical air for several reasons. First, the number of PGMs carried into combat tends to be restricted by operational limitations; given that Warsaw Pact combat aircraft outnumber NATO's by 2 to 1 in the central region, this suggests that qualitative platform differences will be equalized. Second, stand-off PGMs will automatically increase the range of Warsaw Pact fighters, putting NATO rear targets well within their reach. Third, there is a major asymmetry in the target orientation of the two fleets. NATO tactical aircraft (trying to offset the ground imbalance) will be attempting to destroy tens of thousands of mobile dispersed and semihard targets (35,000 tanks and APCs, and 6,000 artillery systems) extensively protected by the densest low-altitude air defense system in the world (3,500 air defense guns and 1,500 SAMs), subject to the vagaries of inclement weather and the difficulties of target acquisition and identification. On the other hand Warsaw Pact tactical aircraft are likely to utilize PGMs against NATO's rear targets, which are fixed, generally soft, and relatively few in number.

Reflecting the Eastern bloc exploitation of their newly acquired offensive platform capability a varied assortment of air-to-surface ordnance has been developed including laser-guided bombs, cluster munitions, electrooptical and laser-guided tactical air-to-surface missiles, large-caliber unguided rockets, fuel-air explosives, and an airfield attack/runway cratering warhead. Likewise, an entire new generation of air-to-air missiles is being fielded, the most significant being the "all-aspect" missile, which permits long-range head-on engagements. Western operational tests of this type of system have shown that, when both sides have equal technology, the employment of the all-aspect missile exacerbates, rather than compensates, quantitative disparities. This new technology is likely to produce a radical change in aerial engagement, with this "defensive" system facilitating deep offensive strikes in which flights of Eastern bloc escorting fighters sweep corridors for low penetrating bombers while high-altitude air superiority fighters prevent the intervention of NATO's defensive interceptors. Thus the new two-seat Soviet Mig–25 E "Super" Foxbat incorporating look-down/shoot-down radar and new all-aspect missiles may make an early and noticeable entrance into the Central European air balance. With the Warsaw Pact having closed the third-generation platform gap in the late 1970s, NATO again led in the introduction of a new generation of tactical combat aircraft with the U.S.-developed F–15 Eagle, F–16, and A–10 Thunderbolt.

The latest Western aircraft can still outperform their nearest Soviet competitors, however, In 1980 the F–15 was still the world's best air-to-air combat aircraft, with excellent radar and a high-energy and high-maneuverability platform. The F–16 likewise is an excellent dogfight machine and has the added advantage of a well-rounded multimission capability, including ground attack and nuclear delivery. The A–10, with its armor-piercing gun, high-ordnance load and long loiter time, was specifically designed for survivable close air support over the battlefield. Unfortunately the high cost of the F–15 and the lack of sufficient sheltered "bed-down" space for the A–10 have greatly constricted the numbers deployed in Central Europe. None of the European allies are planning to purchase either of these systems because they cannot afford to expend limited resources on single-mission aircraft. A number of NATO countries are purchasing the F–16 but are trying to maximize its utility in the area in which they feel weakest: Thus NATO's primary orientation, including the purchase of ordnance and the training of pilots, will be the air defense role. Given the Soviet fielding of a force to sustain offensive combat in all-weather conditions, the lack of any of those three systems of an all-environment (nighttime, low-altitude, below weather) ground attack capability is particularly noticeable. In what has to be one of the stranger examples of intentional technological self-denial, the current F–15 was purposely designed to exclude ground attack and nuclear delivery capability while both the A–10 and F–16 lack the avionics for all-environment missions.

NATO's first fourth-generation multimission aircraft will be the European-designed, multirole combat aircraft (MRCA) Tornado, a two-seat variable-geometry platform that falls between the U.S. tactical F–111 E/F and the Soviet Flogger system. Closer to the former in cost and the latter in capability, the Tornado will be deployed in two versions (air superiority interceptor and deep interdiction/

nuclear strike) replacing Vulcan medium bombers, Buccaneer light bombers, and F-4 interceptors in the British Air Force and the aging F-104 in the West German Luftwaffe. Even if the Tornado is deployed on schedule and in the programed quantities (increasingly dubious assumptions), nevertheless NATO's rate of introduction of all fourth-generation systems will be half that achieved with the fielding of third-generation planes and one-quarter the deployment rate of second-generation aircraft. Meanwhile, the Soviets have been observed conducting final flight testing a number of new fourth-generation systems to be deployed in the early 1980s. These include late-model improvements to the Fencer and Flogger entering accelerated production; a Mig-29 Ram-K air superiority fighter, the equivalent of the U.S. Naval F-14; a Sukhoi Ram-L fighter, virtually an F-16 with advanced radar "all-aspect" missiles and mounting a 30 mm gun; a Ram-J ground attack machine, resembling the A-10; and a possible frontal aviation version of the vertical short take-off and landing (VSTOL) Yak-36, a Soviet version of the British Harrier. The prospect of NATO offsetting its quantitative imbalance in the air with clear qualitative superiority (not to mention compensating for the growing ground imbalance) does not seem to be in the cards.

Given NATO's quantitative inferiority in fixed-wing tactical aircraft, its late 1960s, early 1970s advantage in the number of deployed helicopters in Central Europe, and its qualitative lead in their armament were viewed as an important area of technological leadership. The United States introduced the first military application of a helicopter into Europe in 1952 and by 1968 the U.S. Seventh Army was the first to experiment with the mounting of armament on a rotary-wing platform. However, it was the French in the mid-1960s who made the initial breakthrough in combining the mobility of the helicopter with the accuracy and lethality of the long-range ATGM. Over the 1970s the number of helicopters available to both NATO and Warsaw Pact forces deployed in Central Europe has grown until there are as many rotary-wing aircraft as fixed-wing. While the vast majority of helicopters are not armed combatants but used for battlefield command, observation, resupply, medical evacuation, and general support functions, nevertheless both NATO and the Warsaw Pact have been adding substantial numbers of armed attack helicopters (AAH) to their respective inventories by introducing new systems and retrofitting ATGM weapons on older platforms.

By 1980 the numerical balance of ATGM-equipped attack helicopters was at parity, and although the total quantity deployed remain relatively trivial compared to the inventories of other combat
systems in Central Europe several noticeable trends are beginning to
emerge. First, despite joining this competition late the Eastern bloc
has not only caught up but is introducing these systems at almost
twice the rate of the West. Second, given current deployment patterns, the Warsaw Pact will have at least a 50 percent advantage (and
possibly double) in the number of attack helicopters fielded by
1982. Third is a trend toward unique battle helicopters specifically
designed for the attack mission and armed with technologically
sophisticated third-generation ATGM ordnance.

There has been much optimism in the West about the defensive
value of AAH mounting ATGMs as a means of offsetting Warsaw
Pact armor superiority. The armed helicopter provides a surge capability for the defense and can fill many of the roles of a mobile reserve by being able to move from one threatened sector to another
far faster than ground forces. On the other hand the Warsaw Pact
seems to be placing heavy emphasis on the offensive role of the AAH
in order to exploit gaps in NATO's defensive line, to disrupt the mobility required by forward defense, and provide ready suppressive fire
and real-time intelligence for its own maneuver forces. They have deployed several hundred Mi–24 Hind D gunships armed with a long-
range third-generation fire and target terminal (infrared) homing
ATGM, and have outfitted hundreds of the older MI–8 helicopters
with air-to-surface ATGMs. Even though the success of the armed
helicopter over the Central European battlefield will depend on the
effectiveness and density of the opposing air defenses, the potential
of the new systems incorporating advanced technology is likely
to influence the modern battlefield out of all proportion to their
number.

The current generation of NATO's armed helicopters (the American TOW Cobra, British Lynx, French Gazelle, and the German
PAH-1) are severely restricted in the effectiveness of their armament
(first-generation guidance ATGMs, range-limited second-generation
ATGMs, and very slow rate of target engagement) and their operational capability in degraded conditions (lack of avionics and sight
for all-weather and night operations). The next generation of AAH,
currently under development, will be required to fly and fight under
nighttime and adverse weather conditions at low altitudes with

greater stand-off range capability (the French/FRG PAH–2, and U.S. AH–64). By far the most radical innovations were to be incorporated on the U.S. Hellfire system, a third-generation guided ATGM with an 8,000-meter range and a combination of three different guidance modes—laser designation, RF/IR signature homing, and launch-and-leave fire-and-forget thermal contrast. With coded laser guidance the ATGMs can be rapid-fired (multiple missiles against the same target or the same helicopter rapidly engaging multiple targets) and remotely designated (from the ground or another helicopter). Signature homing is critical to suppressing ground-based air defense guns and missiles by targeting their radar emissions. The capability of a missile to home in on thermal contrast permits the helicopter to fire (then either take evasive action or engage another target) without having to track the missile for the entire duration of its flight.

However, the American cancellation of the last two versions of the Hellfire (for reasons of economy rather than effectiveness) leaves the Soviet Hind D unmatched in third-generation fire-and-forget homing technology, which not only has very promising tactical target servicing applications under surge conditions but is also critical to platform survivability over a battlefield saturated with modern air defenses. As attack helicopters acquire a growing prominence over the land battle there is the increasing prospect of aerial engagement between helicopters; thus it is interesting that the Soviets are now adding as collateral armament for the Mi–24 infrared-seeking air-to-air missiles.

The current balance in AAH numbers thus belies a competitive asymmetry that does not favor the West. The Warsaw Pact has a five-year lead in the fielding of multimission battle helicopters and third-generation ATGM armament. Perhaps most significant for the survivability and effectiveness of the helicopters is the difference between the two blocs in the quantitative density and qualitative capability of modern battlefield air defense (self-propelled low-altitude SAMs and radar-directed guns) provided to the respective maneuver forces.

Air Defense Balance

As a category of weaponry, air defense systems have shared several common developmental characteristics with antitank systems. Neither stands alone as a balance area but rather has its importance defined by the class of weaponry to which its capabilities are juxta-posed. The technological trends in both areas are similar: Originally guns were replaced with missiles, but within the last decade the for-mer have made a comeback, a combination of guns and missiles being viewed by both blocs as the best posture. Although the employment of antitank and antiair weaponry is inherently defensive at the tacti-cal level, when these systems are integrated into a broader combined arms force structure they can produce a synergistic result with in-herently offensive capability. In both areas the Eastern bloc had early quantitative leads in guns that were heavily cut back in the 1960s, at which time NATO led in the introduction of missiles, only for the Warsaw Pact to achieve quantitative superiority and qualita-tive parity by the mid-1970s (see Figure 1-6).

The introduction of air-delivered nuclear warheads into Central Europe in the late 1950s tolled the deathknell of the World War II vintage large-caliber fixed-installation air defense artillery. The op-posing air threat was no longer large formations of bombers but indi-vidual flights of strike aircraft whose probability of delivering their ordnance was virtually independent of the numbers of guns de-ployed. Only the SAM, with its much greater range, altitude, and probability of hit, offered any prospect of defense against aerial nuclear attack.

Thus both sides divested their inventories of air defense artillery (ADA), but NATO, having far fewer systems to lose, emphasized the development and deployment of SAMs and maintained only minimal levels of optically directed medium-caliber (20–40 mm) air defense guns in the maneuver force (primarily the dual-barrel U.S. M–42) and limited rear-area terminal defenses (Bofors 2–60/70). The War-saw Pact, with a far greater ADA investment reduced its inventory by a much larger percentage than NATO but also retained many more systems fielded. These reductions took place in two stages; in the early 1960s large-caliber ststems were withdrawn on a massive scale and in the late 1960s towed and non–radar-directed systems were replaced at less than one-for-one with far more effective guns and low-altitude SAMs mounted on armored vehicles. The Warsaw Pact has consistently placed a much heavier emphasis than NATO on re-taining small- and medium-caliber guns in large quantities within their maneuver divisions and focused their effort at technological improvement.

Figure 1-6.   Center Region Balance Trends: Air Defense Guns/Surface to Air Missile Launchers.

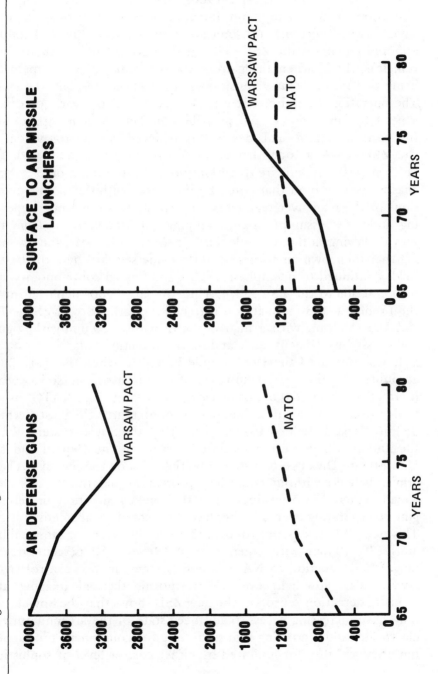

In the late 1950s and early 1960s, the Soviets focused their modernization on the 57 mm gun, introduced in two versions—the divisional radar–directed S–60 gun (mounted on a towed trailer) and for armored regiments the ZSU–57/2 dual gun (mounted on an armored vehicle), which, when firing from a fixed position, was capable of being tied into a radar-acquisition gun-direction fire-control system. The operational requirement was clear; the Soviets clearly perceived a need for an armored, self-propelled air defense gun with a radar fire control system. This design was achieved in the deployment of the ZSU–23/4, a four-barreled rapid-fire 23 mm system with full radar acquisition and fire direction mounted on an armored tracked chassis, as a weapon that could be integrated with the mobile operations of the maneuver regiments. Meanwhile Western armies, operating under the assumption of a minimal air attack threat from the East, believing in the technological superiority of SAMs, and presuming that their own air forces would provide security over the battlefield, continued to deemphasize ADA and fielded contemporary systems inferior to the ZSU–23/4. Thus the late 1960s deployment of the French dual 30 mm at best matched the earlier Soviet ZSU–57/2 and U.S. Vulcan, with a high cyclic firing rate 20 mm gatling gun, had grossly insufficient range and no fire-direction radar.

It was not until the 1973 Middle East War, when the ZSU–23/4 accounted for the highest numbers of aircraft attrition (so large that it effectively inhibited opposing close-air support) that NATO rushed to design an equivalent technological counterpart—the West German 35 mm Gepard, fielded twelve years after the Soviet system. While the Dutch will procure a modified version of the Gepard and the U.S. 40 mm Divad system should be fielded soon the rest of NATO's armies will do without equivalent protection and the Soviets have already entered into production of their next generation air defense gun incorporating even a higher level of technological sophistication. This new ZSU is superior to its predecessor in mounting large-caliber guns (30–40 mm with equal rate of fire and 50 percent greater range) and superior to NATO's new systems in fire control (with laser, radar, low-light-level electrooptical, thermal imaging and acoustic detection sensors). The new ZSU shows that the Soviets not only have increasing access to advanced state-of-the-art miniaturized electronics and a growing industrial base for component production but they are also not inhibited by either cost or level of sophistication from rapidly incorporating this technology into new weapons systems.

In no area of weaponry has the coming of age of Soviet technology been more manifest than in the competitive development of SAMs. The appearance of SAMs in both alliances in the late 1950s, designed initially for medium- and high-altitude intercept, also greatly extended range, accuracy, and responsiveness over the best large-caliber air defense guns. NATO took an early lead with the deployment of a comprehensive air defense early warning radar network (NADGE), and by the early 1960s this system was reinforced in Central Europe with the dual-echelon deployment of a high-altitude, long-range Nike-Hercules belt covering the western two-thirds of Germany from Bremen to Stuttgart and complemented by a forward belt of the medium-altitude Hawk, which extended forward protection from the Baltic to Bavaria. These systems represented NATO's ultimate success at weapons standardization with only the British holding out to deploy their nationally produced Bloodhound and Thunderbird for the United Kingdom sectors. The Nike-Hercules was unique in that it was located in permanent sites and equipped with a dual-capable warhead. The Warsaw Pact soon also fielded an area defense SAM network, based on the high-altitude SA-2 and medium SA-3, although in deployment it differed from NATO in that by dispersing launch positions, it covered a much larger area with three successive concave (from the inter-German border to Warsaw) belts of integrated defenses. Under this umbrella the self-propelled SA-4 was introduced at front and army level to provide mobile, quickly displaced medium-altitude coverage for ground maneuver formations. While NATO's trailer-mounted Hawks could be moved, they were not operationally mobile, and a U.S. developed self-propelled version was never deployed.

The next stage of SAM development came to fruition in the late 1960s and early 1970s with the introduction of low-altitude short-range IR-seeking missile deployed at the level of maneuver units. These were the U.S. Chapparal, the British Rapier, and the Soviet SA-9. Both alliances received these systems in the same period, but their deployment favored the Eastern bloc: Unlike its Western counterparts, the SA-9 was designed with a data link to interface with the acquisition radar of the ZSU-23/4 (with which it is deployed as a regiment system); the British Rapier was not mounted on an armored vehicle; and of NATO's armies only the U.S. and British forces were equipped with a low-altitude battlefield SAM, whereas the SA-9 has been distributed throughout the Warsaw Pact.

The Eastern bloc clearly won the third phase of missile air defense competition with the SA-6 and SA-8 systems demonstrating Soviet interest in overlapping low- to medium-altitude coverage with multiple guidance modes. The SA-6, which demonstrated its effectiveness in the 1973 Middle East War, is deployed at both division and army level and has been introduced into all three of the East European armies. The increasing proliferation of the SA-6, combined with the introduction of the SA-8 (also deployed at division level) are responsible for the late 1970s growth in Warsaw Pact SAM inventories, which with current momentum will continue to expand well into the 1980s.

The only visible Western response in the late 1970s was the completion of the incremental improvement program for existing Hawk batteries, a move necessitated by the systems increasing vulnerability to ECM. NATO's recent and infamous example of weapons standardization, the Roland (a counterpart to the SA-8 but to be limited to corps deployment) reached operational status in 1980 as the first French and German units were fielded. Because of massive acceleration in cost, the U.S. canceled its purchase of Roland and West Germany significantly cut its programmed acquisition.

The U.S. Patriot, in development for nearly twenty years, is scheduled to replace a portion of the obsolete Nike-Hercules by the mid-1980s (although fewer than half of these batteries are currently planned for Patriot modernization). Meanwhile, the Soviets are entering production of no fewer than four new SAMs: the SA-10, a replacement for the large number of SA-2/SA-3 in the Soviet Union, which could also be introduced into Central Europe; the SA-11, yet another battlefield system (with altitude and range between the SA-6 and SA-8 but with highly sophisticated three-dimensional radar); the SA-12, an apparent replacement for the medium-altitude SA-4 with a phased-array radar system for multiple target handling (thus, similar in range acquisition to the Patriot); and the SA-13, a tracked vehicle replacement for the SA-9, which, unlike its predecessor, mounts an acquisition/ranging radar and passive RF detectors. The introduction of only the SA-12, combined with what is already deployed, would be sufficient to maintain Eastern bloc SAM qualitative superiority through the decade of the 1980s and given NATO's current plans, there is no danger of the Warsaw Pact losing its quantitative advantage.

The real impact of the imbalance in NATO/Warsaw Pact air defenses is not limited to the asymmetry in their respective protection but, rather, is represented in the offensive potential opened up for Eastern bloc tactical air and ground forces. Where NATO armies are under increasing threat from Warsaw Pact aerial interdiction and close-air support, the Soviet Army, more than any other in the world, has become self-reliant in defending the air space over the battlefield and its second-echelon units. This consists of a series of overlapping missile envelopes, each of which are then protected by an integrated system of point defenses, while the armored vehicle-mounted guns and low-altitude SAMs provide mobile air defense coverage for the maneuver regiments. In addition, the Warsaw Pact ground forces have a 2-to-1 advantage over NATO in man-portable missiles (SA-7 versus Redeye) for close-in protection. Where NATO tactical air forces are increasingly preoccupied with defending their own air space, the Soviet tactical air armies can concentrate on exploiting the offensive capability provided by their recent modernization since their rear-area infrastructure is protected by hardened air bases (underground facilities for command and control, hangarettes and revetments for aircraft) and redundant airfields and dispersal strips, covered by a well-integrated air defense network composed of a large interceptor fleet and dense SAM coverage. NATO's aircraft sheltering program has not kept pace with Warsaw Pact's in quantity or quality. Unlike the latter, Western hangarettes do not permit aircraft to rearm or refuel while sheltered; cannot handle more than one aircraft; do not utilize earth covering and camouflage for reduction of target signature (particularly important vis-à-vis PGMs); and were not designed for even minimal nuclear blast or chemical protection. Western airfields have but a fraction of Eastern bloc terminal active defenses and are grossly behind in the deployment of rapid runway repair assets.

NATO's tactical air interceptors are limited not only in quantity but in effectiveness. They depend on a small and highly vulnerable set of fixed-site early warning radars (located close to the inter-German border) without which they cannot be vectored to incoming bombers but are encumbered by an archaic command and control system and are reduced to visual identification of targets because in the absence of a functioning IFF (identification of friend or foe) capability they are as likely to fire on other NATO aircraft as on the enemy. The procurement of the AWACS (Airborne Warning and Control System) aircraft in Central Europe ameliorates some of these problems, but the fielding of Soviet Mig–29 class long-range air-superiority fighter with advanced radar and "all-aspect missiles" will mean that NATO interceptors must add AWACS to their defensive missions. Warsaw Pact introduction of their IL–76 version of AWACS and sophisticated ECM platforms will give them an air offensive battle management system and defense degradation capability NATO is not currently prepared to handle.

Thus it is the combination of Eastern bloc air defense and aircraft modernization that has compounded NATO's tactical air problem. The range of missions NATO's tactical air forces are expected to fulfill has increased, while the modernization needed has not kept pace. Today they are expected to defend their own air bases against a potent Soviet preemptive capability, compensate for an obsolescent ground-based air defense network, provide on-call close air support to help NATO's outnumbered ground forces defeat Soviet armor, and interdict Soviet second-echelon reinforcement while all the time holding back systems for nuclear delivery. There are just not enough modern aircraft to go around. The growing aerial/air defense imbalance has compounded NATO's inferiority in armored, antiarmor and fire-support capability so that the prospect of a successful Western conventional defense is increasingly bleak.

IN SEARCH OF ACTION AND REACTION

The trends surveyed in the first section illustrate that an asymmetrical expansion of conventional armament has occurred in Central Europe. Given the disproportionate effort between the two blocs, this raises the question why. One of the traditional explanations of arms race theorists is that of action and reaction, a competitive cycle in which force development by one side stimulates a reaction by the other, which in turn pushes the initiator to further heights of armament. This hypothesis has been advanced by some to suggest that the Soviet-led Warsaw Pact, rather than initiating a new round in the conventional arms competition, has merely been defensively *reacting* (usually in quantity of force) to U.S.-led NATO actions (particularly in quality of force). There are several different ways of examining this hypothesis:

1. Technical development. Which side has led in advanced weapon design and new systems introduction?
2. Force structure. Has the size of one side's forces driven the other or has there been apparent copying of combined arms unit organization?
3. Alliance leadership. Even though NATO as an aggregate has not kept pace with the Warsaw Pact, has the United States served as a stimulant?

Despite clear evidence of Western *qualitative* initiatives in the areas of technology and force structure, which the Eastern military establishments have found it prudent to emulate, nevertheless evidence also very clearly shows that the Soviet Union has been the responsible agent for the *quantitative* arms race in Central Europe, which time and again induced the West to look for ways to compensate for quantitative inferiority through qualitative quick fixes.

Technological Development

Since the end of the Second World War, Western leadership in advanced weapons technology has been a significant factor in the Central European military balance. It was real but it was also necessary. Numerically inferior in conventional weaponry, NATO has repeatedly sought qualitative advantages. This was particularly true in traditional conventional weaponry—tanks, APCs, antitank guns, artillery, MRLs, jet aircraft, and air defense guns. But in three areas NATO was the first to develop and field a new type of armament: SAMs in the late 1950s; ATGMs in the early 1960s; and AAHs mounting ATGM in the late 1960s. These new categories had several points in common. In all three the ordnance involved was a form of guided missile. These systems were developed by Western aerospace industries, generally more technologically advanced than their Eastern counterparts, particularly in propulsion and miniaturized guidance electronics. Each of these weapon categories was focused on a defensive mission—antiarmor or antiair—and against a category of armament where the other side had a significant numerical superiority, either tanks or aircraft.

A pattern is also discernible in the Eastern bloc reaction. Within three to five years of the introduction of the first NATO system in a new armament category the Soviet Union had deployed a technological counterpart with its forces in Central Europe. And in each case it has taken less time between the Warsaw Pact's first fielding of one of these technologies, initial operational capability (IOC), and the date when their quantity of these new systems caught up to level of the West (SAMs 1960 IOC/1970 crossover; ATGM 1963 IOC/1972 crossover; AAH 1973 IOC/1979 crossover). At about the time of numerical crossover, the Eastern bloc has also introduced in each of these three armament categories an entire new generation of advanced systems at least the technological equal of anything in the West (SA-6 SA, 1973; AT-5 ATGM, 1976; Mi-24 AAH, 1977). The combination of numerical expansion at the point of crossover with the proliferation of new generation technology has produced in each case an acceleration of qualitative growth while the Western forces are reaching a point of quantitative saturation. By the end of 1981 the Warsaw Pact had a 2-to-1 superiority in SAMs, ATGMs, and AAS, the number of the latter deployed in Central Europe having doubled since the end of 1980.

Perhaps the most telling point is that in each of the cases where the Warsaw Pact forces have achieved quantitative crossover and qualitative parity, the tactical concept for employing these *defensive* systems has been converted into an *offensive* role. Thus where the majority of NATO SAMs are in permanent or semifixed sites, the majority of WTO SAMs are mounted on armored vehicles, designed for rapid movement, and integrated into the maneuver doctrine of combined arms formations. Where the majority of NATO ATGMs are short-range troop-carried systems, the majority of Warsaw Pact ATGMs are longer range, mounted on armored vehicles designed to provide overwatching fire support for tanks in the offensive and to secure the flanks of a breakthrough against counterattack. Whereas NATO plans to use its AAHs as a target-servicing supplement to weak or overloaded sectors of its front, the Warsaw Pact plans to use its AAH for surprise vertical envelopment, forestalling the deployment of Western reserves, and conducting raiding operations deep in NATO territory. The Warsaw Pact has not only caught up but today fields a force of SAMs, ATGMs, and AAH systems that surpass NATO's deployed counterparts in quantity and quality.

The examples involving new postwar armament categories demonstrate a dramatic pattern of action–overreaction and the intent of the Eastern bloc to couple technological parity with quantitative superiority is evident in a multitude of areas. In the mid-1970s the West had under development an assortment of radically new components and munitions that, when deployed, were believed not only to improve greatly the combat capabilities of traditional weaponry (tanks, artillery, and tactical aircraft) but also to provide at least a decade lead over the Eastern bloc. These included special composite armor and laser range-finders for tanks; rocket-assisted projectiles, antiarmor submunitions, counterbattery radar, millimeter-wave target acquisition, and computerized fire control for artillery; all-aspect air-to-air missiles, electrooptical "smart" bombs, fuel air explosives, hard-target munitions, high-energy and high-maneuverability engines, and map-of-the-earth avionics for tactical aircraft. By the end of 1980 every one of these technologies had been deployed with Soviet forces in Central Europe—no later and indeed in some cases earlier than the arrival of this capability in Western units and always in greater quantity. The complexity of design, sophistication of subcomponents, and skill required in manufacture suggests that the majority of these developments were not reactive at all but, rather, already being pursued simultaneously with those in the West. Thus it was an asymmetry in intelligence, not high technology, that gave NATO a misleading self-confidence.

This plagiarism is the sincerest form of flattery to an author. Reactive system design is the equivalent to a technologist. And in the early 1970s the Soviets were not shy about borrowing Western vehicular design concepts, self-propelled artillery and multipurpose fighter bombers being the clear examples of abandoning an entrenched design philosophy (towed artillery and single-mission aircraft) in favor of a demonstrated successful approach by the other side. But in the late 1970s the tables had turned, for it was NATO that was clearly reacting, using Eastern bloc systems and components as design prototypes—high-velocity, smooth-bore guns and automatic loaders for antitank weapons; combined gun and ATGM armament for infantry fighting vehicles; radar-directed, high-rate-of-fire self-propelled air defense guns; shock effect and salvo capability of MRLs. In fact in late 1980 the Soviets were discovered to be pursuing a new technological area of conventional armament, the armored vehicle-mounted laser, for use in antipersonnel, armor/antiarmor suppression, and air defense roles. If the Soviets are able to maintain current developmental momentum, the Eastern bloc will have a tactical battlefield laser weapon fielded at least five years in advance of NATO.

Evidence is growing that the Warsaw Pact has finally caught up to the West's leadership in advanced conventional technology. Where the East has made an extraordinary effort, NATO's response has been laconic, with canceled or redirected development programs, procurement delays, prolonged and inefficient production runs, failure to achieve a rational division of labor (let alone standardization), and ever-escalating costs. All of these result in more expensive systems, which means fewer systems and creates a demand for even greater performance, which means higher acquisition risk and therefore retarded arrival and exponential expense. If Western qualitative superiority is needed to offset its quantitative inferiority, as has been the traditional assumption, then quite clearly the Soviet-led Warsaw Pact has won the technological race for the early 1980s. If that was their objective (and the level of resource commitment over the last decade required to achieve it suggests a very conscious decision), then this reaction was driven less by the fear of Western technological stimuli than it was by the hope of NATO developmental inaction.

Force Structure

Since the beginning of the Central European arms race competition in the late 1940s the Eastern bloc has maintained numerical superiority in conventional weapons. Since the late 1960s it has conducted a successful but nonetheless costly campaign to achieve technological leadership in the quality of deployed armament. This raises the question why if the Eastern bloc already possessed numerical superiority and were exhibiting a high rate of technological modernization, they found it necessary to expand even further the size of armament inventories. Various Western Sovietologists believe that the buildup was driven by a set of prescribed "equipment norms" calibrated to the inventory levels of the opposing NATO armies.

There is a relatively strong association between Warsaw Pact introduction of advanced technological systems and change in their overall assets (see Table 1–2). For example, the reduction in air defense

Table 1-2. Comparative Force Levels: Warsaw Pact versus NATO.[a]

	Force Ratio 1965	Ratio of Weapons Added, 1965–1980	Force Ratio 1980
Tanks	2.3: 1	4.5: 1	2.7: 1
APC/IFV	1.1: 1	3.0: 1	1.7: 1
Antitank guns	.8: 1	—[b]	2.6: 1
ATGM	.6: 1	2.4: 1	1.9: 1
Artillery	1.2: 1	8.2: 1	2.6: 1
MRL	No NATO	3.0: 1	7.1: 1
Tac air	1.6: 1	—[b]	1.9: 1
AAH	None	1.2: 1	1.2: 1
Air defense guns	4.8: 1	—[c]	2.7: 1
SAM	.6: 1	6.0: 1	1.5: 1
Total	1.5: 1	4.4: 1	2.0: 1

a. Ratios calculated to nearest tenth.
b. Net reduction by NATO.
c. Net reduction by Warsaw Pact.

guns (the only armament category to register a declining ratio) is related directly to the expansion and modernizations of SAMs and the introduction of a far more sophisticated self-propelled gun design, which replaced the older systems at an exchange of less than one for one although the overall capability vastly increased. In artillery the introduction of the new self-propelled guns was added on top of an expanding inventory of 1960s-designed towed systems. In the category of main battletanks over 8,000 third- and fourth-generation systems were introduced between 1965 and 1980, but only half that number of older systems were withdrawn. In tactical aircraft the numerical impact of modernization had a different effect between the initial early-1970s introduction phase (in which the overall force inventory declined) and the subsequent phase of the late 1970s, when the introduction of new platforms was associated with an overall rise in inventory level. Within individual categories, technology therefore clearly had an impact on quantity, but this relationship was not consistent across the various categories of armament and appears to be independent of any actions taken by the West.

Although aggregate force levels demonstrated little evidence of an arms race action–reaction phenomena, at the level of combatant units a strong case can nevertheless be made that much of the Eastern bloc armament expansion was a function of mirror-imaging of the organizational structure of NATO rivals. The trend throughout the early 1970s, in which the Soviet units took the lead within the Warsaw Pact, was to bring the inventories of these subunits up to level comparable with those of the West. Thus the Soviets followed the NATO pattern of making an APC or IFV available to each infantry squad; artillery batteries were increased by 50 percent so that they were numerically equivalent to those of NATO (18 tubes per battalion); and many tank battalions were increased by as much as one-third in assets. It is interesting to note that while the Soviets were increasing the size of their tank battalions, several of the leading NATO allies were experimenting or in fact implementing a reduction in the size of theirs, following a realization that the more compact "Soviet-style" formations had significant advantages in unit integrity, tactical flexibility, and crew performance.

By far the clearest example of force structure mirror-imaging has been the Warsaw Pact adoption of NATO's concept of combined arms integration below the organizational level of the division. In the early 1960s Western armies selected the brigade as the lowest level of maneuver unit incorporating combined arms assets—tanks, mechanized infantry, and artillery fire support. The rationale for this was compelling. It permitted greater dispersion on a battlefield where nuclear weapons might be employed. It allowed the brigades to be tailored for anticipated missions (infantry-heavy units for defense and armored heavy units for counterattack). Yet because they were semi-independent in artillery and logistics support, they could be employed with a high degree of tactical flexibility. Within NATO the structure of these brigades varied considerably (most European armies having a fixed number of battalions, whereas the United States emphasized a more flexible task force approach), but the average division had three of these brigades. In contrast the divisions of the Warsaw Pact consisted of four maneuver regiments, which, unlike the brigade structure of NATO, had a significantly smaller degree of combined arms integration. Thus, for example, Soviet tank regiments contained no infantry or artillery and for these regiments to operate successfully over the course of a campaign required preplanned allocation of divisional artillery assets and colocation or cross-attachment with other types of regiments. It was this asymmetry in the level of combined arms integration that led many Western assessments to conclude that although the Warsaw Pact had twice as many divisions as NATO in the central region, this numerical advantage was more than compensated by the fact that these divisions were weaker than their Western counterparts in the total amount of conventional armament and disadvantaged in the flexibility of tactical employment.

Over the course of the 1970s this organizational asymmetry between NATO and the Warsaw Pact changed radically. In 1965 every NATO division was stronger in active manpower and armament than the best Eastern bloc counterpart and in the next fifteen years only two Western armies expanded their divisional assets (with an average unit growth of 25 percent for the Federal Republic of Germany and 30 percent for the United States). In 1980 only the divisions of these two NATO members were comparable in conventional weaponry to those of the Warsaw Pact, all of which have increased armament inventories (with the average Polish division up by 10 percent; Czechoslovak up by 20 percent; East German up by 40 percent; Soviet tank divisions up by 64 percent and Soviet motorized rifle divisions up by 91 percent). The driving factor in the growth of divisional armament has been the Soviet adoption of NATO's concept to combined arms brigades for each of the four regiments in every division. Thus the current Soviet tank regiment today consists of not only three battalions of main battletanks but a full battalion of infantry-mounted IFVs and a battalion of self-propelled artillery. The motorized rifle regiments (over half of which are now equipped with infantry fighting vehicles) have had their inventory of tanks expanded by 30 percent and also been assigned a full battalion of artillery. In keeping with NATO's concept of semi-independent brigades, each of these regiments has had its logistics, transport, engineering, air defense, and command assets expanded to the point where they are at least the equal of Western brigades in fire power, sustainability, and capacity for autonomous operations. In terms of an action–reaction phenomena it is this mirror-imaging of the regimental formations that has driven much of the quantitative expansion of the Eastern bloc. The numerical impact, however, is magnified and the conventional imbalance exacerbated by three additional anomalies: First, the Warsaw Pact not only has twice as many divisions but each has a third more regiments than Western units have brigades. Second, in the process of lowering the level of combined arms integration, the Eastern bloc retained the centralized assets (particularly artillery, air defense, and logistics) that previously existed at the divisional, army, and front level. Third, while only Soviet units have fully adopted the brigade concept at regimental level, as East European armies continued to follow their example, the quantity of arms in Eastern bloc units will expand proportionately.

It is with no little irony that, as the Warsaw Pact has, over the last decade, moved in the direction of NATO's force structure design of the mid-1960s, many Western armies have moved in the opposite direction. Today's Belgian division has only two brigades (having dropped one in the late-1960s reorganization); the British and French armies in Germany have abolished the brigade level altogether, their new divisions less than half the strength of a comparable Soviet division in conventional weaponry. Moreover, where the Eastern bloc has significantly increased the readiness and sustainability of its divisions, NATO has suffered in these areas. The British army of the Rhine would require large-scale precombat reinforcement and augmentation of a level that would have been unacceptable in the mid-1960s; two of the remaining four Belgian brigades have been redeployed home from their former forward positions in Germany; five of the six Dutch brigades have subordinant tank, infantry, and artillery battalions in reserve mobilization (RIM) status. Since the mid-1970s the U.S. Army has reintroduced two brigades (one in 1975 and one in 1976—the equivalent of three having been withdrawn in 1968) and the West German army has increased its force structure from 33 to 36 brigades, but in the case of the former this came at the expense of sustainability (the manpower having been drawn from in-theater logistics units) and in the case of the latter at the expense of readiness (one battalion in each German armored or mechanized brigade being manned by either trainees or reservists). In summary the Eastern bloc mirror-imaging of Western force structure has focused on force expansion but ignored resource constraint.

Alliance Leadership

Both NATO and the Warsaw Pact represent military alliances between sovereign states; yet both the United States and the Soviet Union have a unique status, *primus inter pares.* Within their respective blocs this is a function of history, both having emerged from the Second World War significantly stronger than other European countries or combination of countries. Their status is also a product of their massive inventories of nuclear weapons unmatched by any combination of European states. It is a result of both superpowers arbitrating their respective alliance decisionmaking and the deference accorded their leadership by the other members. Had it not been for the political confrontation between East and West over Central Europe, it is not axiomatic that the United States and the Soviet Union would have been natural rivals. As events developed both assumed the mantle of alliance leadership, however, and competition between the two took on a dynamic of its own.

With each superpower being the champion of its alliance, one explanation of the expansion of conventional armament within Central Europe is that the two superpowers were primarily competing against each other and merely dragging their respective alliances along with them. Given the precedence in which the Eastern bloc evolved from a superpower–client relationship and the intermittent role of the United States within NATO in sounding the alarm with respect to countering the growth of Soviet military power, this hypothesis is intuitively attractive. Empirical data suggesting that the Soviet Union has since the mid-1960s attempted to match U.S. technological leadership makes it tempting to assume that the Warsaw Pact's quantitative expansion has likewise been a reaction to U.S. stimuli.

In disaggregating the trend data for conventional force expansion in terms of superpower contribution, there is dramatic proof that *the Soviet Union has been the responsible agent for the quantitative arms race* (see Table 1–3). In contrast, not only has the United States, as NATO's champion, not kept up with the Soviet conventional force expansion, but there is virtually no evidence that American numerical increases in weaponry have served as a plausible rationale for the rate, scope, or magnitude of Soviet growth (see Table 1–3). Since 1965 over 30,000 conventional weapons have been added to the forces of the two alliances deployed in Central Europe; the Soviet Union represents 46 percent (14,000 systems) of this expansion, whereas the United States has accounted for less than 7 percent. In main battletanks the Soviets have added 18 systems for every one of the United States; in APC/IFV the ratio is 16 to 1; in ATGM 2.4 to 1; in conventional tube artillery 30 to 1; in MRLs the Soviets have expanded their inventory by 75 percent and the United States has not deployed any; in tactical aircraft the Soviets have added 5 planes to every 1 of the United States; and in SAMs the ratio of additional

Table 1-3. Increase in Conventional Armament Deployed in Central Europe between 1965 and 1980.

	Combined Increase of Systems by both Alliances: 1965–1980	Distribution of Combined Increase, %			
	Percentage Increase	Non-U.S. NATO	U.S.	Non-Soviet Warsaw Pact	Soviet
Main battle tanks	25	12	4	14	72
APC/IFV	43	14	2	53	31
Antitank guns	12 (reduction)	NATO reduction of 55%*		WTO increase by 40%*	
ATGM	500	15	19	27	39
Artillery	84	9	2	37	52
MRLs	96	25	0	30	45
Tactical air	5 (reduction)	NATO reduction of 14%* — U.S. increase by 6%*		WTO total no change — Soviet increase by 8%*	
Attack helicopters	(none in 1965)	14	32	9	45
Air defense guns	4 (reduction)	NATO increase by 50%*		WTO reduction of 18%*	
SAM	84	6	9	21	64
Total	47 / 30,210 systems	12 (19%)	7	35 (81%)	46

*Percentage change over 1965 assets, not combined increase.

systems added has been 7.5 to 1. In only two categories was there an asymmetrical quantitative trend: in air defense guns where the Soviets reduced their inventory by 29 percent while the United States introduced systems in categories where it had none deployed in 1965 and in antitank guns where the United States replaced all of its systems with ATGMs while the Soviets expanded theirs by 50 percent.

If a single culprit is to be identified, a nation whose forces in Central Europe have accounted for the largest expansion of conventional weaponry, it is clearly the Soviet Union. In the ten armament categories, the Soviets numerically outdistanced the U.S. in all but one, unilaterally surpassed NATO (the United States combined with its European allies) in all but two, and increased at a faster rate than its own Warsaw Pact allies in eight. On the other hand the United States led NATO's quantitative expansion in only three categories (ATGM, AAH, and SAM), all of which, interestingly, are areas where the United States also had a technological advantage due to its superior aerospace industrial base.

One of the most frequent bromides charged by Americans vis-à-vis their European allies is that the United States has been burdened with a disproportionate share of NATO's defense effort. In terms of NATO's conventional forces in Central Europe, this claim is at best marginal. The United States, with 24 percent of the ground force manpower and responsibility for defending one-quarter of the front, represents 28 percent of the alliance's conventional armaments. As the recognized technological leader of the West the United States is behind the Soviets, the East Europeans, and its own allies in fielding a fourth-generation tank (U.S. M–1 versus West German Leopard II and Soviet T–64 and T–72); an infantry fighting vehicle (U.S. IFV versus West German Marder, French AMX–10P, Dutch AIFV, and Soviet BMP); an automatic loading self-propelled artillery piece (U.S. ESPAWS versus French GCT–155, Soviet SP–122 and 152, and Czech SP–152); a multiple rocket launcher (U.S. MLRs versus West German LARS and Soviet 122 mm BM–21 and 240 mm GSRS); a radar-directed self-propelled air defense gun (U.S. Divad versus West German Gepard and Soviet ZSU–23/4); and an advanced-guidance vehicle-mounted battlefield SAM (U.S. canceled Roland versus British Rapier, West German Roland and Soviet SA–6, SA–8, SA–11, and SA–13).

In terms of the United States being NATO's champion vis-à-vis the rival superpower, a Western David to the Eastern Goliath, it is neither evident in technological leadership nor quantitative expansion. Since 1965 the Soviets have expanded their conventional weapons deployed in the central region on a ratio of seven weapons added to each system increase by the United States. For the American forces to have matched just the Soviet increase over the same period, the United States would have had to deploy three times their 1965 total inventory of armament in Central Europe. In 1980 Soviet forces alone have more conventional armament deployed in Central Europe than all of the opposing armies of NATO.

2 HOW THE SOVIET UNION CAME TO GAIN ESCALATION DOMINANCE
Trends and Asymmetries in the Theater Nuclear Balance

James J. Martin

Since the late 1960s the USSR has made a sustained effort to improve the theater nuclear force (TNF) posture of the Warsaw Pact while at the same time making major improvements in conventional, chemical, and strategic forces. NATO on the other hand has made only sporadic efforts to improve its TNF posture. Soviet operational concepts and military forces have been remarkably adaptive to shifts in NATO doctrine and forces, seeking particularly to negate Western nuclear options. A fundamental problem for NATO is the Soviet doctrine of and capabilities for preemptive theaterwide nuclear strikes in Europe.

The Warsaw Pact is now far better prepared than NATO to fight a combined conventional-chemical-nuclear war in Europe, the kind of war they see as most likely if war does break out between NATO and the Warsaw Pact. This advantage results from asymmetries in military doctrine, TNF survivability, resiliency in command, control, and communications (C^3), and general-purpose force capabilities to operate in a nuclear-chemical environment.

As a consequence, political-military initiatives are increasingly passing to the Soviet Union—negotiation of arms control agreements from a position of strength, deterrence of a wider range of NATO actions, the ability to drive crisis outcomes in directions favoring the Soviet Union, and the capability to dominate the escalation process. The Soviets increasingly are able to dominate the escalation process, in the sense of forcing upon NATO difficult choices about escalation, choices made more difficult by Soviet military advantages at each level of escalation. NATO has the military potential to restore the TNF balance. The problems that have led to the current imbalance are, however, basically political in nature and therefore require NATO political as well as military action.

NATO AND WARSAW PACT APPROACHES TO NUCLEAR WAR

Both NATO and the Warsaw Pact attach great importance to nuclear weapons in their strategies. The roles for nuclear weapons and the relation of these weapons to other force elements are markedly different for each side, however. For NATO the strategic and political aspects of TNF traditionally have transcended their tactical importance. Theater nuclear forces are held by NATO to contribute primarily to deterrence of war in Europe; this contribution is seen as consisting largely of the threat they pose of escalation to intercontinental nuclear war. They are not to be tactical substitutes for a strong conventional force posture; nor are they to be the primary nuclear defense of Europe. Rather, TNFs are viewed as an important symbol of the U.S. commitment to Europe's defense and of the linkage of U.S. strategic forces to NATO.

NATO leaders are nevertheless concerned about at least one of the growing asymmetries between NATO and the Warsaw Pact: long-range TNF capabilities. Through the High Level Group and the Special Consultative Group, NATO is carrying out a program of TNF modernization and arms control negotiations to deal with this problem. At the military-technical level NATO has increased emphasis on TNF capabilities and plans to help stop the Warsaw Pact's combined arms offensive. Despite progress in planning, major improvements in NATO's TNF capabilities are largely future prospects, not present realities. Of even greater significance, movement at the military-technical level toward improving the military aspects of NATO's TNF posture has not been matched at political levels in all NATO countries, and there is potent domestic opposition in many countries to NATO nuclear forces.

The Soviet Union tries to foster a public image as a reluctant and defensive nuclear power. In this image the Soviet Union is portrayed by itself as besieged by Western imperialism, nuclear war as a horrible

prospect that would devastate the world and Soviet readiness to reduce its nuclear armaments as stymied by an alleged arms buildup by
the West. In practice the Soviet view of theater nuclear forces has far
greater military content than NATO's.[1] The Soviets believe that nuclear weapons have great military importance and that decisive military advantages can be gained by the side that uses them first. Even
if a NATO–Warsaw Pact war were to begin conventionally, the Soviets believe, NATO would be forced to use nuclear weapons, the Warsaw Pact must make every effort to preempt NATO's nuclear use,
and the Warsaw Pact must be prepared to win a nuclear war with
NATO, in the sense of occupying Western Europe and recovery rapidly from the war.[2]

Thus theater nuclear forces are an integral part of Warsaw Pact
military strategy, force posture, and training. A key element of this
strategy is preemption of NATO nuclear use with large-scale, theaterwide nuclear and chemical strikes. The targeting of these strikes supports the high-speed combined arms offensive of the Warsaw Pact,
whose general-purpose forces are equipped and trained to exploit
rapidly the damage and disruption caused by these strikes.

The United States and NATO are seeking to stabilize and reduce
military imbalances through arms control negotiations. To the Soviets, however, arms control is a means to undercut U.S. and NATO
responses to Warsaw Pact military programs. The Soviet Union is
adept, moreover, at propaganda campaigns aimed at exacerbating
domestic opposition to NATO nuclear force modernization. They
did this with evident effectiveness when NATO was considering
deployment of enhanced-radiation/reduced-blast nuclear weapons
in 1977–78. They are now engaged in a similar campaign to undercut the fragile European consensus on modernizing long-range
TNFs, combining disinformation about Soviet TNFs and doctrine
with threats of further TNF deployments and promises of force reductions that would have little impact on Warsaw Pact military
capabilities.[3]

NATO AND WARSAW PACT THEATER
NUCLEAR FORCES

A shortcoming of past efforts to assess the theater nuclear balance
resulted from lack of comprehensive publicly available data showing
trends and asymmetries in theater nuclear forces over time. While

The Military Balance series of the International Institute for Strategic Studies (IISS) provides the elements for such a data base, it does not assemble TNF data for a span of years in a single volume and it has gaps in the data. In recent years the IISS has published an assessment of the theater nuclear force balance in the annual volumes of that series, but this assessment does not treat trends over time in the data and excludes short-range TNF systems.[4] Collins provides TNF data over time but not in sufficient detail for a thorough assessment.[5] Metzger and Doty performed a TNF balance assessment as background for analyzing TNF arms control approaches but did not include trends from the past and excluded all systems with ranges less than 400 nm.[6] Treverton, in a recent Adelphi paper, includes all TNF systems but provides no historical trend data, only future projections.[7] Some recent articles analyze historical TNF trends but focus only on long-range TNFs and in some cases only on trends in Soviet forces.[8] None of these sources treats the important matter of reloads for TNF systems, recently confirmed for Soviet systems by the Department of Defense (DoD) publication, *Soviet Military Power*, and implied for NATO TNF systems by that department's annual report for fiscal year 1981.[9]

The appendix to this chapter seeks to overcome these problems by developing a detailed data base on the number of NATO and Warsaw offensive TNF delivery vehicles and nuclear warheads in four snapshot years—1970, 1975, 1980, and 1985 (projected). "Offensive" TNFs are defined as those with the primary mission of attacking fixed or mobile targets ashore in the European theater, and include short-range, mid-range, and long-range TNFs. Excluded from the data are defensive TNF systems (surface-to-air missiles (SAMs) with nuclear warheads; atomic demolition munitions) and TNF systems for fleet air defense, antisubmarine warfare and antiship warfare.

Of course many uncertainties exist about these data, but the nature of the uncertainties is different for NATO and Warsaw Pact TNFs. For both sides publicly available data on the number of TNF delivery vehicles are probably reasonably accurate, at least for purposes of establishing trends in the mix for each side and in the relative force levels. Less data are publicly available on the number of TNF nuclear warheads for each side, so the appendix makes inferences about warhead levels and mix from delivery system data. Since the DoD has announced that the United States deployed about 7,000 nuclear warheads in Europe up to 1980, then withdrew 1,000 warheads, reasonable assumptions can be made about the number of defensive TNF warheads included in these numbers and derive the approximate size of the total NATO stockpile of offensive TNF warheads.[10] No approximation of the size of the total Warsaw Pact TNF stockpile is possible. The appendix resolves uncertainties about that stockpile conservatively, probably underestimating its size. Thus the total number of Warsaw Pact TNF warheads shown in Table 2–1 and Figure 2–1 should be interpreted as a lower bound on the actual size of the stockpile.

Table 2–1 summarizes the TNF data of the appendix according to the categories currently in use by the DoD and the NATO High Level Group: short-range systems (0–159 km), mid-range systems (150–1500 km), and long-range systems (1,500 km and greater).

The totals from Table 2–1 are graphed in Figure 2–1, where the contribution of French TNF systems is shown separately. The overall trends are clear. The Warsaw Pact has been ahead of NATO in TNF delivery vehicles since the 1960s and is adding delivery vehicles at a significant rate, projected to have more than twice the number of offensive TNF delivery vehicles as NATO by the mid-1980s. The number of NATO's TNF delivery vehicles increased only slightly in the 1970s; no significant increase is projected by the mid-1980s.

The Warsaw Pact started the decade of the 1970s with fewer TNF warheads than NATO but has steadily increased its stockpile, reaching parity with NATO around 1980, or perhaps earlier (keeping in mind the conservative nature of the estimate of the number of its nuclear warheads). The rate of deployment of Warsaw Pact TNF warheads is actually increasing in the 1980s, as the Soviet Union deploys SS–20 launchers with MIRVs and reloads, and Backfire bombers with greater payload (at comparable ranges) than the older Badger and Blinder medium bombers. By the mid-1980s, the Warsaw Pact is projected to lead NATO in offensive TNF warheads by about 1.5 to 1. The NATO stockpile, in fact, is declining since 1975, as the obsolete but warhead-intensive short-range Honest John system is phased down.

Table 2–1 shows that more than half of the NATO stockpile of TNF warheads has been associated with short-range systems such as nuclear artillery, Honest John, and Lance. This fraction is projected to decline in the 1980s, as Honest John continues to be phased down and the number of NATO long-range TNF warheads is increased. Nuclear warheads for mid-range systems, almost all tactical aircraft,

Table 2-1. Trends in NATO and Warsaw Pact TNFs.

	Delivery Vehicles				Nuclear Warheads			
	1970	1975	1980	1985	1970	1975	1980	1985
NATO TNFs								
Short-range	920	968	911	856	3,600	3,828	3,150	2,492
Mid-range	1,332	1,263	1,228	1,185	2,114	1,872	1,795	1,730
Long-range	194	347	461	569	194	432	991	1,283
Totals	2,446	2,578	2,600	2,610	5,908	6,132	5,936	5,505
Warsaw Pact TNFs								
Short-range	455	662	991	1,291	910	1,324	1,682	2,582
Mid-range	1,734	3,024	3,391	3,672	1,095	1,743	2,332	2,619
Long-range	1,144	1,000	900	710–860	2,288	2,042	2,120	2,660–2,960
Totals	3,333	4,686	5,282	5,673–5,823	4,293	5,109	6,134	7,861–8,161

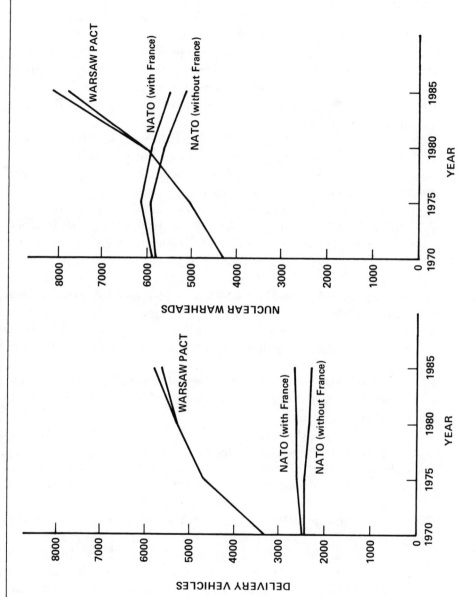

Figure 2-1. Trends in NATO and Warsaw Pact TNFs.

constitute about 30 percent of the NATO stockpile during the period under examination. Warheads for long-range systems have been increasing during this period. In 1970 NATO long-range systems consisted of a small number of submarine-launched ballistic missiles (SLBMs) and British and French medium bombers. U.S. F-111s and Poseidon SLBMs, and French intermediate-range ballistic missiles (IRBMs) and SLBMs were added during the 1970s; the buildup of long-range systems is projected to continue during the 1980s with deployment of Pershing II, ground-launched cruise missile (GLCM), and an additional French SSBN.

The Warsaw Pact started the 1970s with a substantial lead over NATO in long-range TNF delivery vehicles and warheads. Despite some reduction in the number of long-range delivery vehicles during the 1970s, the number of warheads has declined only slightly and is projected to increase substantially in the 1980s as a result of the SS-20 and Backfire modernization. The Warsaw Pact has maintained a lead over NATO in mid-range TNF delivery vehicles, deploying a mix of tactical surface-to-surface missiles (SSMs), tactical aircraft, and SLBMs. The number of Warsaw Pact mid-range TNF warheads exceeds that of NATO in the mid-1970s and is projected to continue to increase in the 1980s. The Warsaw Pact was substantially behind NATO in short-range TNF delivery vehicles and warheads in 1970 but has been building up here, as well. The Pact achieved the lead over NATO in short-range TNF delivery systems during the late 1970s and is still deploying nuclear-capable artillery units. By the mid-1980s, the Warsaw Pact is projected to lead NATO in short-range nuclear warheads.

Table 2-2 shows the strong momentum of the Pact's modernization program for TNFs as compared with NATO's. In every category the Warsaw Pact has new systems currently being deployed. Almost all of NATO's TNF modernization programs are in development.

Current Warsaw Pact TNF modernization programs are impressive. The SS-20 mobile MIRVed IRBM, which provides significant improvements in survivability, range, accuracy, and number of warheads compared with the fixed-base SS-4 and SS-5 MR/IRBMs, is a major element of this modernization effort. The SS-20s will by the mid-1980s provide over 1,500 nuclear warheads, a substantial and survivable theater reserve for coercion or restrike of targets. Other Warsaw Pact TNF modernization programs are equally impressive, providing theater nuclear forces with greater range, accuracy, and

Table 2-2. NATO and Warsaw Pact Modernization Program for Offensive TNFs.

	Systems Currently Being Deployed	Systems under Development
NATO	F-16	New 8-in. artillery round Tornado Pershing II GLCM SLCM UK Trident (Polaris replacement)
Warsaw Pact	Nuclear artillery SS-21 (Frog replacement) SS-22 (Scaleboard replacement) Improved tactical aircraft Backfire SS-20	SS-X-23 (Scud replacement)

Sources: DoD, *Annual Report, Fiscal Year 1982* and *Soviet Military Power*.

operational flexibility. These programs include a number of new TNF systems now being deployed: nuclear artillery; the SS-21 replacement for the Frog rocket (proceeding slowly); the SS-22 replacement for the Scaleboard SSM; high-performance nuclear-capable attack aircraft in frontal aviation (Fencer) with greatly improved range-payload capabilities as compared with older nuclear-capable tactical aircraft; and the Backfire medium bomber.

NATO is currently deploying the nuclear-capable F-16 tactical aircraft. All other NATO TNF modernization programs are in various phases of research and development. These include a new nuclear artillery projectile for the 8-in. howitzer that will have longer range than the current W33 round; the nuclear-capable Tornado aircraft; the Pershing II SSM; and cruise missiles for ground and sea launch (GLCM and SLCM). Deployment of Pershing II and GLCM depends upon maintaining a fragile European consensus in the face of vocal domestic opposition and a continuing Soviet propaganda campaign against NATO TNF modernization. The United States is examining options for deployment of land-attack sea-launched cruise missiles with nuclear warheads. Britain plans to modernize its Polaris SLBM force in the 1990s with the U.S. Trident I missile.

The Warsaw Pact gains a number of important benefits from its modernized theater nuclear forces. The general trends are toward more theater nuclear delivery vehicles and warheads, longer range while maintaining or increasing payload, greater accuracy, and a balanced mix of short-range, mid-range, and long-range TNF systems. These trends contribute to improved survivability through more rearward deployment and greater mobility, improved operational availability of TNF systems when required by operational commanders, and dual TNF coverage of all important military targets in NATO Europe. This last point is significant. With increased numbers of short-range and mid-range TNF systems (currently about 4,000 nuclear warheads) and improved military characteristics as these systems are modernized, Warsaw Pact tactical commanders are gaining an extensive capability with TNF systems intrinsic to their units to target throughout the depth of NATO Europe. These systems are not covered by SALT or long-range TNF arms control negotiations. This tactical TNF capability is backed up by over 2,000 long-range TNF warheads on systems based in the Soviet Union that provide a theater reserve and a hedge against excessive attrition of tactical theater nuclear forces or C^3 failures between Moscow and Warsaw Pact tactical commanders.

Other qualitative aspects of the TNF balance are also important. For example, regarding TNF survivability under enemy attack, both sides have vulnerabilities, but NATO's appear to be worse. About one-third of each side's TNF warheads are associated with aircraft that operate from fixed bases, vulnerable to nuclear and chemical attacks, and to a lesser extent vulnerable to conventional air attacks, depending on such factors as the state of the counterair battle and the effectiveness of each side's air defenses. But certain asymmetries favor the Warsaw Pact. They have more dispersal bases for tactical aircraft than NATO and heavier air defenses. Moreover, their medium bombers are based in the Soviet Union, where they are more survivable than systems in Eastern or Western Europe during certain phases of conflict. This is an example of a more general TNF basing asymmetry that favors the Warsaw Pact. All Warsaw Pact long-range TNF systems are based in the Soviet Union and have sufficient range to attack all targets in NATO Europe from these bases. Thus, Warsaw Pact's long-range TNFs are able to hold NATO targets at risk from bases that are in sanctuary during conventional conflict, since NATO currently has virtually no conventional attack capability against Soviet territory. Soviet long-range TNFs may also be in sanctuary during limited nuclear conflict if NATO leaders choose not to attack Soviet territory. NATO long-range TNFs on the other hand are all based in Western Europe or on submarines at sea, where they are exposed to a full range of threats (unconventional, conventional, chemical, and nuclear) during all phases of conflict.

Another TNF basing asymmetry that enhances the survivability of Warsaw Pact theater nuclear forces deployed with the ground forces relates to the dispersal of these mobile units from their peacetime kassernes and nuclear weapons storage sites (nuclear artillery and SSM systems). Both sides are vulnerable to attacks on TNFs in their peacetime basing locations and during the TNF dispersal process. Since a war in Europe would be initiated by the Warsaw Pact, WP theater nuclear forces presumably will be fully dispersed and ready for operations at the start of the war. Depending on the degree of surprise achieved by the Warsaw Pact, NATO mobile TNFs may not be fully dispersed at the opening of the war and could be subjected to effective attacks by enemy tactical aircraft and unconventional warfare forces during the dispersal process.[11]

Another important qualitative aspect of the TNF balance relates to the capabilities of each side's general-purpose forces. Warsaw Pact combined arms forces are equipped and trained for operations in a nuclear-chemical environment. Little effort has been devoted to equipping and training NATO general-purpose forces for military operations in such conditions. By every measure the Warsaw Pact is ahead of NATO in offensive and defensive chemical warfare capabilities. Although it is difficult to assess the potential military effectiveness efforts to enable forces to operate in a nuclear-chemical environment, it is clear the Pact is devoting more effort than NATO to this problem. This must provide them with some advantage in the kind of war they see as most probable in Europe, a combined conventional-chemical-nuclear war.[12]

NATO AND WARSAW PACT THEATER
NUCLEAR OPERATIONAL CONCEPTS

NATO concepts of military operations have undergone considerable change since the inception of the alliance, in part because of Soviet efforts to negate NATO nuclear options. In the 1950s NATO's military concept rested on massive nuclear retaliation in the event of any form of Communist aggression. This concept exploited U.S. strategic nuclear superiority over the Soviet Union and sought to extend that superiority by building up TNFs in Europe. In the 1960s as the Soviet Union deployed a secure second-strike capability against the United States and counters to NATO's TNF, U.S. and NATO military concepts moved away from massive retaliation toward mutual assured destruction (MAD) and limiting damage in intercontinental war and toward flexible responses in Europe. NATO's military committee document 14/3 eventually formalized the flexible response concept in 1967 but did not resolve a fundamental difference within the alliance about what it meant. The Americans emphasized conventional forces as the primary deterrent to Warsaw Pact nonnuclear attacks, while the Europeans emphasized deterrence of such attacks by threats of early first use of nuclear weapons and escalation. NATO military concepts of the 1970s placed more emphasis on military options for engaging in conflict if deterrence failed—the use of conventional weapons technology and limited nuclear options to enhance flexible responses. In the early 1980s NATO concepts show inconclusive signs of moving toward more emphasis on deterring Warsaw Pact first use of nuclear weapons and on doctrine for combined conventional-nuclear operations.

The NATO nations, in their political deliberations, their force acquisition planning, and even to a considerable extent their military operational planning, act as if there are sharp dichotomies among conventional, theater nuclear, and strategic nuclear war. NATO has not made as thorough preparations as has the Warsaw Pact at the interfaces of the various types of conflict. In fact Warsaw Pact military doctrine, strategy, forces, training, and operational planning treat conventional, theater nuclear, and strategic nuclear much more as a continuum in the context of general war with the West. As a consequence the Warsaw Pact appears to make more thorough and extensive preparations than NATO for fighting a combined conventional-chemical-nuclear war in Europe.

The Soviets see a high probability that a war between NATO and the Warsaw Pact will ultimately involve the use of nuclear weapons. They apparently remain skeptical of the possibility for controlling escalation. Their quantitative and qualitative force improvements and operational concepts for employing these forces reflect a concerted effort to negate NATO's military (especially nuclear) options and to dominate the escalation process. While their TNFs and C^3 appear to have the capabilities for a range of flexible response options, the Warsaw Pact's strategy for war in Europe still appears to be focused on large-scale, preemptive, theaterwide nuclear attacks in support of the combined arms offensive.[13] This emphasis on nuclear preemption is a major means by which the Warsaw Pact seeks to counter NATO's nuclear options, but other aspects of Warsaw Pact strategy, forces, and operational planning have been directed as well at negating three key elements of NATO's strategy—unconditional reliance on U.S. strategic forces, NATO TNF threats to targets in East Europe and the USSR, and TNF operations against the Warsaw Pact combined arms ground offensive.[14]

In an effort to negate the reliance of U.S. allies on U.S. strategic forces, the Soviets have made a sustained effort over several decades to acquire and maintain offensive and defensive capabilities to destroy or neutralize U.S. strategic forces. These means include a variety of nuclear and nonnuclear capabilities for strikes on U.S. ICBMs, bomber bases, naval bases, aircraft carriers (which the Soviets continue to regard as a strategic threat to their homeland), and C^3 installations; for antisubmarine warfare (ASW) campaigns against ballistic missile submarines (SSBNs); for air defense, ballistic missile defense, and civil defense; and for secure second-strike nuclear responses against political and military targets in the United States. Even though they have achieved considerable capabilities to negate U.S. strategic forces, the Soviets are continuing to seek counters to U.S. strategic force improvements and to effect further shifts in the correlation of forces.

Many years of conditioning by a MAD approach to strategic force planning makes it easy to overlook the fundamental connection between a secure Soviet strategic attack capability and Warsaw Pact prospects for successful military operations in Europe. Soviet deployment of a secure intercontinental retaliatory capability against the United States successfully negated NATO's strategy of massive retaliation for theater aggression. Soviet movement in the late 1960s away from a doctrine of early escalation of war in Europe to intercontinental nuclear warfare[15] no doubt reflected their increasing confidence in deterring U.S. first use of strategic forces in response to theater aggression, as well as the growing Warsaw Pact nonnuclear force capabilities. Improvements during the 1970s in the size, survivability, hard target destruction potential, and preemption capabilities of Soviet intercontinental forces further undercut the viability of U.S. strategic forces for deterrence of Soviet aggression in Europe. Further, the Soviet capability for secure retaliation against the United States creates substantial doubt in both the United States and Europe about U.S. willingness to employ strategic forces for defense of Western Europe or for any other purpose except to respond to attacks on the U.S. homeland. Even if the United States is willing to carry out such operations, the Soviet capability to hold major elements of U.S. strategic forces and other military targets in the United States at risk complicates the military viability of using strategic forces to support theater operations.

Consequently the contribution of U.S. strategic forces to deterrence of Soviet attacks in Europe now consists to a considerable extent of nonspecific threats of uncontrolled escalation to general nuclear war, with widespread devastation and massive uncertainties about postwar political, economic, and social conditions that, it is presumed, the Soviets as well as the West desire overwhelmingly to avoid. In light of continued Soviet efforts to achieve a large measure of strategic superiority and to deny effective theater nuclear options to NATO, this may not be an adequate deterrent to Warsaw Pact aggression.

The Soviet Union and Warsaw Pact have similarly been engaged in sustained efforts to negate NATO's TNF threats to targets in East Europe and the USSR. Since the 1950s NATO has had TNFs that threatened East European and Soviet territory—medium bombers, tactical aircraft, Pershing missiles, SLBMs, and IRBMs. By virtue of being based in Europe, in many instances being manned by Europeans, and, in the case of British and French nuclear forces, being under European national release authorities, these theater nuclear strike forces provide NATO with options for attacking Soviet and East European territory that might be employed earlier and more credibly than U.S. strategic forces.

It is for precisely these reasons that the Soviets have been making systematic efforts since the 1950s to deny effective long-range and mid-range TNF options to NATO. In the 1950s, partly because of technology limitations and partly for strategic reasons, the bulk of Warsaw Pact nuclear forces were medium bombers and IRBMs that threatened large, theaterwide nuclear responses against Europe to counter NATO's TNF strike options. The threat perceived by Europeans was—and is—widespread devastation from Soviet nuclear responses to NATO TNF strikes. Actually the Warsaw Pact has maintained a number of military means for the more specific purposes of destroying or neutralizing NATO long-range and mid-range theater nuclear forces in order to improve their prospects for successful combined arms operations in Europe, while also reaping deterrent and propaganda benefits from the generalized image of widespread nuclear devastation.

Warsaw Pact theater targeting and attack goals have remained constant since the 1950s. They include use of all available military resources (nuclear, conventional, chemical, unconventional) to destroy NATO theater nuclear delivery systems, nuclear weapons and C^3, and use of weapons of mass destruction to hold at risk or destroy political-military controls and industrial war-making potential in West Europe. Priority Warsaw Pact targets include NATO theater nuclear strike forces—airbases, Pershing launchers, aircraft carriers, French IRBMs, and U.S., UK, and French SSBNs. Not only are these targets accorded high priority in Warsaw Pact nuclear employment planning, but high priority during all phases of conflict is given to destruction of NATO theater nuclear forces by nonnuclear means—covert agents, long-range reconnaissance patrols, conventional air operations against airbases and Pershing, conventional naval operations against aircraft carriers, ASW versus SSBNs, and attrition of NATO's dual-capable aircraft by Warsaw Pact air defenses.

The Warsaw Pact's successful and systematic effort over the decades to improve its nuclear and nonnuclear counters to NATO's theater nuclear strike forces continues. It is directed toward increased numbers of nuclear and nonnuclear delivery systems and warheads for theater targeting; systems with greater range and payload capability to facilitate more survivable rearward basing; faster response times to enhance preemption; improved accuracy for greater hard-target destructive capability; and improved air defenses to protect Warsaw Pact TNFs and inflict attrition on NATO dual-capable aircraft. These threats to NATO's theater nuclear strike forces are complemented by the Warsaw Pact's coercive threats of theaterwide nuclear responses to NATO TNF strikes. The effects are to undercut substantially NATO's first use of theater nuclear strike forces, to create substantial doubts about the survivability and retaliatory viability of all NATO's current long-range and mid-range TNFs except SLBMs, and to raise questions about the military viability of Pershing II and GLCM—questions that have not been sufficiently examined because of the continued strong first-use orientation of NATO's nuclear strategy.

A third major element of NATO's nuclear strategy is nuclear attacks on Warsaw Pact ground forces and their air and logistics support, using short-range TNFs against targets in the battle area and mid-range theater nuclear forces against deeper tactical targets in Eastern Europe. As is the case with Warsaw Pact efforts to negate other elements of NATO nuclear strategy, Warsaw Pact objectives have remained the same since the 1950s; the Warsaw Pact has been steadily improving its military capabilities to support these objectives.

Warsaw Pact targeting and attack goals in support of the combined arms offensive have been to use all available military resources to destroy NATO TNF delivery vehicles, nuclear warheads, and C^3, and to use weapons of mass destruction (if necessary) to destroy or neutralize NATO military forces or bases that threaten significant opposition to the combined-arms ground offensive. These targets include NATO tactical airbases, groupings of NATO ground forces, tactical C^3, and ports and airfields through which NATO could move reinforcements.

Nuclear operations are an integral part of WP strategy and doctrine for combined arms ground operations in Europe. This aspect of WP military strategy includes the following:

- Preemption with massive, theaterwide nuclear attacks to destroy or neutralize threats to the combined arms offensive.

- High-speed exploitation of Warsaw Pact nuclear strikes by combined-arms ground forces to destroy, neutralize, or envelop NATO ground forces, seize territory and recovery resources, and win the war.

- A doctrine of echeloned ground force operations to reduce NATO's nuclear targeting opportunities against Warsaw Pact combined-arms forces and to preclude damage to nearby Warsaw Pact units if one is successfully attacked by NATO nuclear forces. Echeloned operations seek to gain the benefits of a nuclear dispersed posture by physical separation and frequent movement of major ground force units while maintaining the shock and momentum of ground operations by directing the movement of successive echelons against NATO weak points.

Tactical C^3 redundancy and mobility that, combined with a skip-echelon operating doctrine, seeks to provide command and control resiliency in a nuclear environment.[16]

Since the late 1960s, the Soviets have also recognized the possibility that they may effectively deter or delay NATO's decision to initiate use of nuclear weapons against Warsaw Pact combined-arms forces. Accordingly doctrine, training, and equipping of Warsaw Pact general-purpose forces have provided capabilities for extended non-nuclear operations in Europe, as well as for an early transition to combined conventional-chemical-nuclear conflict.

In support of the foregoing goals the Soviets have made a sustained effort to improve their capabilities to negate NATO TNF operations against Warsaw Pact combined arms forces. As in other areas these Soviet efforts continue unabated. They include upgrading of the firepower and maneuver capabilities of ground-force artillery, tanks, antitank systems, armored personnel carriers, air defenses, and (more recently) helicopters; major improvements in the range, payload, avionics, and performance characteristics of frontal aviation aircraft; deployment of nuclear artillery; and the initial deployment of a new generation of tactical nuclear missiles to replace the Frog, Scud, and Scaleboard systems.[17]

IMPLICATIONS FOR NATO

The foregoing analysis leads to the conclusion that the Warsaw Pact is in a far better position than NATO to fight a combined conventional-chemical-nuclear war in Europe. The Warsaw Pact has advantages for such a war in forces, doctrine, C^3, operational plans and training. This capability combined with the doctrine and capabilities for nuclear preemption and Soviet and Warsaw Pact advantages in conventional and strategic forces all lead to increased Soviet dominance of the escalation process. This exacerbates the ever-present West European concern about U.S. decoupling of its strategic forces from the defense of Europe, which in turn contributes to the erosion of the allies' confidence in the United States. As a result of this chain of events, political-military initiatives increasingly are passing to the Soviet Union—negotiation of arms control agreements from a position of strength, deterrence of a wide range of NATO actions, and the capability to drive crisis outcomes in directions preferred by the Soviets. It is these consequences that make the theater nuclear balance important in its own right, not just a footnote to the strategic balance.

The great asymmetry between NATO and the Warsaw Pact concerning purposes for nuclear weapons and doctrine and strategy for their use, coupled with the growing Soviet and Warsaw Pact capabilities to negate NATO's nuclear options, raise serious questions about the efficacy of NATO's deterrent threats of early first use of nuclear weapons and escalation to intercontinental nuclear war. A fundamental problem now facing NATO is how to deter Warsaw Pact first use of nuclear weapons in a European conflict, as well as how to strengthen deterrence of Warsaw Pact nonnuclear aggression. Resolution of this problem requires tailoring forces, operational concepts, war plans, C^3, logistics and training in specific ways to counter Warsaw Pact operational concepts and exploit Warsaw Pact weaknesses. Some would dismiss this as nuclear war-fighting and, therefore, destabilizing. It is more accurate to characterize this approach as enhancing deterrence of Warsaw Pact aggression in a world already made less stable by Warsaw Pact political and military trends, through means for which the Soviets and other Warsaw Pact nations have shown evident respect in the past.

Some lines along which to proceed are as follows:

- Shift NATO's strategic concept for nuclear weapons employment away from a fixation on early first use of nuclear weapons to emphasis on a survivable conventional-nuclear military capability to counter the Warsaw Pact combined-arms offensive.

- Make a variety of operational, force posture, and C^3 improvements designed to thwart the Soviet doctrine of nuclear preemption.

- Make improvements in U.S. and NATO capabilities for general war with the Soviet Union, to counter Soviet escalation dominance at this level of conflict. These improvements should, for example, enhance the endurance and survivability (under both conventional and nuclear attack) of strategic and theater nuclear forces, and give more attention to general-purpose ground, air, and naval operations in general war.

- Improve U.S. and NATO forces, doctrine, employment plans, C^3, and logistics in ways designed to deny the Warsaw Pact quick victory in a war in Europe. There may be substantial leverage on the Soviets in this regard. It is not clear that the Soviet Union would be willing to take the risks of a long war, because of the questionable reliability of their Warsaw Pact allies, problems in the Soviet economy, and problems with the non-Russian nationalities.

NATO should take advantage of a number of Warsaw Pact strategic and military weaknesses in redirecting its operational concepts. There is no single critical weakness that, if properly exploited, could seriously undercut the opponent's military strategy, but exploitation of the following in a coherent NATO strategy for war could have telling synergistic effect in enhancing deterrence:

- The probable difficulties of the Warsaw Pact in adapting the combined-arms offensive to unexpected changes during the course of war.

- Soviet preoccupation with control over operational timelines and with concluding military operations rapidly and decisively.

- The political reliability of the non-Soviet Warsaw Pact nations. One recent study suggests that the Soviet strategy of short mobilization time, short-warning attack, and "lightning war" may in part be motivated by the Soviet Union's desire to limit opportunities for its allies to opt out of the conflict.[18]

- The extensive dependence of many elements of Warsaw Pact military power on fixed bases in the Soviet Union and East Europe (medium bombers, Soviet naval aviation, C^3, sustaining logistics for land and sea operations).

- The apparent continued Soviet preference for highly favorable force correlations before committing to military operations. This means that even the start of additional NATO efforts to improve the theater nuclear balance can have considerable deterrent effect, provided these efforts are sustained.

The United States and NATO can and must restore the theater nuclear balance in Europe. Military actions in the area of doctrine, force posture, C^3, and employment planning to accomplish this restoration are feasible for the NATO nations; some are in progress. But there are political prerequisites: agreement within the U.S. government on the importance and nature of a sustained TNF improvement program, sustained political leadership within the NATO nations to implement such a program, and, perhaps most urgently needed at this time, a return to quiet diplomacy within NATO on TNF planning.

APPENDIX A

Open sources of information on NATO and Warsaw Pact TNFs are individually fragmentary and often inconsistent with one another. When these sources are evaluated for accuracy according to the extent to which their authors are likely to have had access to official data and are cross-checked by means of some simple consistency rules, however, they collectively can provide a reasonably accurate picture of trends in the level and mix of theater nuclear forces. Details of estimated trends and the rules and assumptions used in deriving them are set forth here; sources used are listed at the end of the appendix. These sources fall into four categories, ranked in order of their authority:

1. Department of Defense documents available to the public (e.g., annual DoD reports; the recently published document, *Soviet Military Power* (Data source 2 f)).

2. Books and articles by former DoD officials who are likely to have had access to accurate data (Collins (1); Kennedy (6); Moore (8)).

3. *The Military Balance* series published annually by the International Institute for Strategic Studies (4). This series is useful for efficient access to historical data since it is compiled from public documents of the DoD and defense ministries of allied nations.

4. Books and articles by other researchers (Joshua and Hahn (5); Metzger and Doty (7); Treverton (9)).

During the last several years, a number of publications have developed data bases comparing NATO and Warsaw Pact TNFs (e.g., 2d; 4a: 126–129; 6; 7; 9). None of these is totally adequate. Most are incomplete, focusing on a subset of the TNF balance, such as long-range TNFs. None contain trend data prior to the late 1970s, although such data are important for understanding changes that have been taking place over time in the TNF balance. A particularly serious omission in previously published TNF data bases is the lack of data on reload warheads. Recent DoD publications (especially 2c and 2f) allow more accurate treatment of TNF reloads for both NATO and the Warsaw Pact.

The data presented in Tables 2A–1 through 2A–8 below seek to remedy these deficiencies.[19] NATO and Warsaw Pact offensive TNF delivery vehicles and warheads are estimated in four years—1970, 1975, 1980, and 1985 (projected). The TNF systems shown are those with the primary mission of attacking fixed or mobile targets ashore in the European theater. These systems include nuclear artillerty, surface-to-surface missiles deployed with the ground forces, land-based aircraft, carrier-based aircraft, medium-range and intermediate-range ballistic missiles, submarine-launched ballistic missiles, and ground-launched cruise missiles. They are grouped into the categories currently in use within the DoD and the NATO High Level Group: short-range systems (0–150 km), mid-range systems (150–1500 km), and long-range systems (1,500 km and greater), although there are some minor variations from this categorization in order to keep systems with common missions within the same range category. Excluded from the data shown below are atomic demolition munitions (ADMs), nuclear-capable SAMs, and fleet antiair, antisubmarine, and antiship TNF systems.

Many delivery vehicles carry more than one nuclear warhead. A "delivery vehicle" is defined as a TNF launch platform in ways that have become commonly accepted for nuclear force data bases. Delivery vehicles include artillery tubes, mobile SSM launchers, aircraft, SLBM launch tubes, IR/MRBM launch pads, silos or mobile launchers, and GLCM launchers. "Nuclear warheads," as defined in the data below, are the independently targetable warheads carried by these delivery vehicles and reload warheads for these vehicles. Thus the counts of NATO and Warsaw Pact offensive theater nuclear warheads estimate the nuclear stockpile that each side has earmarked primarily for use against targets ashore in the European theater.

The data below show the total number of delivery vehicles and warheads estimated to be available for operations in Europe. In recent years, the IISS has estimated "arriving" TNF warheads to

Table 2A–1.   Trends in NATO Offensive TNFs.

System	Range/Combat Radius (km)	Delivery Vehicles				Nuclear Warheads			
		1970	1975	1980	1985	1970	1975	1980	1985
Short-Range Systems (0–150 km)									
Nuclear artillery (8–in. 155 mm)	14/29	700	700	700	700	1,400	1,400	1,400	1,400
Lance	110	0	36	90	90	0	216	810	810
Honest John	40	200	200	91	24	2,000	2,000	910	240
Sergeant	140	20	20	0	0	200	200	0	0
French Systems Pluton	120	0	12	30	42	0	12	30	42
Subtotal (short-range systems)		920	968	911	856	3,600	3,828	3,150	2,492
Mid-Range Systems (150–1,500 km)									
Pershing IA	740	180	180	180	72	270	270	270	108
Land-based dual-capable aircraft (F–104, F–4, Buccaneer, Jaguar, F–16, Tornado)	Various	1,052	967	882	947	1,708	1,450	1,323	1,420
Carrier-based dual-capable aircraft (A–6, A–7, Buccaneer S2)	Various	100	86	72	72	136	122	108	108
French dual-capable aircraft									
Land-based (Mirage IIIE, Jaguar)	Various	0	30	70	70	0	30	70	70
Carrier-based (Super Etendard)	Various	0	0	24	24	0	0	24	24
Subtotal (mid-range systems)		1,332	1,263	1,228	1,185	2,114	1,872	1,795	1,730

Long-Range Systems (1,500 km and Greater)

Vulcan medium bomber	> 2,000	70	56	56	0	70	56	56	0
F-111 dual-capable aircraft	1,800	0	85	170	170	0	170	340	340
Pershing II	1,600	0	0	0	108	0	0	0	108
GLCM	2,500	0	0	0	40	0	0	0	160
SLBM	4,600	88	104	104	104	88	104	464	464
French Systems									
Mirage IV medium bomber	1,600	36	36	33	33	36	36	33	33
IRBM	3,000	0	18	18	18	0	18	18	18
SLBM	3,000	0	48	80	96	0	48	80	160
Subtotal (long-range systems)		194	347	461	569	194	432	991	1,283
Grand Total		2,446	2,578	2,600	2,610	5,908	6,132	5,936	5,505
U.S. Offensive Nuclear Warheads in Europe[a]						5,503	5,631	4,918	4,451

a. Does not include nuclear warheads based at sea.

Table 2A-2. NATO Mid-Range Land-Based Dual-Capable Aircraft in Europe.

	1980	1985
U.S. F–4	250	250
UK Buccaneer	50	0
UK Jaguar	40	40
Allied F–104	367	102
Allied F–4	175	175
Allied Tornado	0	230
Allied F–16	0	150
	882	947

make its assessment of the TNF balance, using utilization and service-ability factors, and survivability, reliability, and penetration indices (4a: 126–29). Although this method reflects asymmetries in pre-launch survivability and defenses, it is highly arbitrary unless carried out through complex and scenario-dependent war gaming calculations. It is preferable to present inventory data and to discuss (in the assessment of the main article) trends and asymmetries in survivability and penetration, as well as other important qualitative factors not included in the IISS analysis.

NATO theater nuclear forces are composed of delivery vehicles operated in the European theater by various NATO nations, U.S. nuclear warheads for these delivery vehicles (held in U.S. custody until their use is authorized (2b: 68)), and the delivery vehicles and nuclear warheads of Britain and France. The NATO TNF data shown in Table 2A–1 aggregate U.S., British and other NATO TNF delivery vehicles and the associated warheads except for those of France, since these forces are all part of the integrated military structure in Allied Command Europe (ACE). Inasmuch as French forces are not part of ACE, French TNF systems are shown separately. Table 2A–2 summarizes the detailed contents of NATO dual capable aircraft for 1980 and 1985 that underlie the data in Table 2A–1. Table 2A–3 presents the data on warheads contained in Table 2A–1.

Table 2A–3.   U.S. Offensive Nuclear Warheads in Europe.[a]

System	1970	1975	1980	1985
Nuclear artillery	1,400	1,400	1,400	1,400
Lance	0	216	810	810
Honest John	2,000	2,000	910	240
Sergeant	200	200	0	0
Pershing IA	270	270	270	108
Land-based dual-capable aircraft[b]	1,633	1,375	1,188	1,285
F–111 dual-capable aircraft	0	170	340	340
Pershing II	0	0	0	108
GLCM	0	0	0	160
	5,503	5,631	4,918	4,451

a. Does not include nuclear war heads based at sea.

b. Data from Table 2A–1 less 135 UK nuclear bombs in 1980 and 1985, and less 75 UK nuclear bombs in 1970 and 1975. This accounts for nuclear weapons assumed in Table 2A–1 to be associated with the UK Buccaneer and Jaguar; the Jaguar was first deployed in 1974 and Table 2A–1 assumes nuclear-capable Jaguars came into the force after 1975.

The TNF of the Warsaw Pact consist of delivery vehicles in the Western Part of the Soviet Union, Eastern Europe, and the sea environs, operated by the Soviet Union and other Warsaw Pact nations (2d: 64), and Soviet nuclear warheads for these delivery vehicles (held in Soviet custody in peacetime (2b: 69)). The TNF data shown in Table 2A–4 aggregate Soviet and non-Soviet delivery vehicles and nuclear warheads, since these forces are all part of an integrated military structure. Table 2A–4 assumes one reload (two warheads) per FROG or SS–21 launcher, SCUD or SS–X–23 launcher, and Scaleboard or SS–22 launchers.

Table 2A-4. Trends in Warsaw Pact Offensive TNFs.

System	Range/Combat Radius (km)	Delivery Vehicles				Nuclear Warheads			
		1970	1975	1980	1985	1970	1975	1980	1985
Short-Range Systems (0–150 km)									
Nuclear artillery (203 mm, 240 mm)	29	0	0	300	600	0	0	300	1,200
FROG/SS-21	70/120	455	662	691	691	910	1,324	1,382	1,382
Subtotal (short-range systems)		455	662	991	1,291	910	1,324	1,682	2,582
Mid-Range Systems (150–1,500 km)									
SCUD/SS-X-23	300/350	263	384	539	539	526	768	1,078	1,078
Scaleboard/SS-22	900/1,000	43	85	85	85	86	170	170	170
Land-based dual-capable aircraft (Fitter, Flogger, Fencer, others)	Various	1,350	2,500	2,725	3,000	405	750	1,042	1,275
SLBMs*	1,400	78	55	42	48	78	55	42	96
Subtotal (mid-range systems)		1,734	3,024	3,391	3,672	1,095	1,743	2,332	2,619

Long-Range Systems (1,500 km and Greater)

Medium bombers (Badger, Blinder, Backfire)	2,900–5,500	544	500	390	400	1,088	1,042	860	1,000
SS–4/SS–5 MR/IRBM	2,000/4,100	600	500	450	50–200	1,200	1,000	900	100–400
SS–20 IRBM	5,000	0	0	60	260	0	0	360	1,560
Subtotal (long-range systems)		1,144	1,000	900	710–860	2,288	2,042	2,120	2,660–2,960
Grand Total		3,333	4,686	5,282	5,673–5,823	4,293	5,109	6,134	7,861–8,161

*Includes some SS–N–6 SLBMs (2,400–3000 km).

Table 2A–5. FROG and SS–21 Launchers.

	1970	1975	1980	1985
Soviet Systems (Collins)	355	462	483	483
NSWP Systems (*Military Balance*)	100	200	208	208
	455	662	691	691

Table 2A–6. SCUD/SS–X–23 Launchers.

	1970	1975	1980	1985
Soviet Systems (Collins)	213	284	376	376
NSWP System (*Military Balance*)	50	100	163	163
	263	384	539	539

Table 2A–7. GOLF and HOTEL Ballistic Missile Submarines with Theater Missions (*Worldwide Deployments, 1980*).

Class	Missile/Range (km)	Number of Submarines	Tubes per Submarine	Total SLBM Tubes
H–II	SS–N–5/1400	7	3	21
G–II	SS–N–5/1400	13	3	39
G–IV	SS–N–6/2400–3000	1	5	5
				65

Table 2A–8. GOLF and HOTEL Ballistic Missile Submarines with Theater Missions (*Worldwide Deployments, 1975*).

Class	Missile/Range (km)	Number of Submarines	Tubes per Submarine	Total SLBM Tubes
H	SS–N–5/1400	8	3	24
G–I	SS–N–4/560	9	3	27
G–II	SS–N–5/1400	11	3	33
				84

Data Sources

1. John M. Collins, *U.S.-Soviet Military Balance, Concepts and Capabilities: 1960-1980* (New York: McGraw-Hill, 1980).
2a. Department of Defense, *Annual Defense Department Report, FY 1978*, Washington, D.C., January 17, 1977.
 b. ____ , *Annual Report, Fiscal Year 1979*, Washington, D.C., February 2, 1978.
 c. ____ , *Annual Report, Fiscal Year 1981*, Washington, D.C., January 29, 1980.
 d. ____ , *Annual Report, Fiscal Year 1982*, Washington, D.C., January 19, 1981.
 e. ____ , *The Theater Nuclear Force Posture in Europe*, a report by the Secretary of Defense to Congress, Washington, D.C. (April 1975), reprinted in *Nuclear Strategy and National Security: Points of View*, edited by Robert J. Pranger and Roger P. Labrie, (Washington, D.C.: American Enterprise Institute for Public Policy Research, 1977), pp. 167–88.
 f. ____ , *Soviet Military Power* (Washington, D.C.: Government Printing Office, 1981).
3. Justin Galen, "The Changing Missions and Structure of the French Air Force in the 1980s: The Views of the Senior Planner," *Armed Forces Journal International* (November 1979): 18, 20, 66.
4a. The International Institute for Strategic Studies, *The Military Balance, 1981-1982* (London: September 1981).
 b. ____ , *The Military Balance, 1980-1981* (London: September 1980).
 c. ____ , *The Military Balance, 1975-1976* (London: September 1975).
 d. ____ , *The Military Balance, 1970-1971* (London: September 1970).
5. Wynfred Joshua and Walter F. Hahn, *Nuclear Politics: America, France, and Britain*, The Washington Papers, vol. 1, no. 9, The Center for Strategic and International Studies, Georgetown University (Beverly Hills, Calif.: Sage, 1973).
6. Robert Kennedy, "Soviet Theater Nuclear Forces," *Air Force Magazine* (March 1981): 78–83.
7. Robert Metzger and Paul Doty, "Arms Control Enters the Gray Area," *International Security* 3, no. 3 (Winter 1978-79): 17–52.
8. Robert A. Moore, "Theatre Nuclear Forces: Thinking the Unthinkable," *International Defense Review* 14, no. 4 (1981): 401–408.
9. Gregory Treverton, *Nuclear Weapons in Europe*, Adelphi Paper no. 168, The International Institute for Strategic Studies, London, Summer 1981.

NOTES

1. For more detailed discussion of nuclear weapons in Soviet doctrine and strategy, see, for example, J.J. Martin, "Nuclear Weapons in NATO's Deterrent Strategy," *Orbis* 22, no. 4 (Winter 1979): 875–95; Benjamin S. Lambeth, "Selective Nuclear Operations and Soviet Strategy," in *Beyond Nuclear Deterrence: New Aims, New Arms*, edited by Johan J. Holst and Uwe Nerlich (New York: Crane, Russak, 1977), pp. 79–104; and Fritz W. Ermarth, "Contrasts in American and Soviet Strategic Thought," *International Security* 3, no. 2 (Fall 1978): 138–55.

2. "Preemption" is a technical term in Soviet military strategy that implies the Soviets expect to have advance indication of NATO preparations to employ nuclear weapons and will make every effort to preempt that employment by launching their own nuclear attacks first.

3. For further discussion of Soviet uses of arms control and propaganda to counter Western military responses, see Helmut Sonnenfeldt and William G. Hyland, *Soviet Perspectives on Security*, Adelphi Paper 150, The International Institute for Strategic Studies, London, Spring 1979: 21–23. See also Hyland's "Soviet Theatre Forces and Arms Control Policy," *Survival* 23, no. 5 (September–October 1981): 194–99.

4. See, for example, *The Military Balance, 1981–1982*, The International Institute for Strategic Studies, London, September 1981, pp. 126–29.

5. John M. Collins, *U.S.-Soviet Military Balance, Concepts and Capabilities: 1960–1980* (New York: McGraw-Hill, 1980).

6. Robert Metzger and Paul Doty, "Arms Control Enters the Gray Area," *International Security* 3, no. 3 (Winter 1978–79): 17–52.

7. Gregory Treverton, *Nuclear Weapons in Europe*, Adelphi Paper 168, The International Institute for Strategic Studies, London, Summer 1981.

8. Raymond L. Garthoff, "Brezhnev's Opening: The TNF Tangle," *Foreign Policy* 41 (Winter 1980–81): 82–94; Lawrence Freedman, "The Dilemma of Theatre Nuclear Arms Control," *Survival* 23, no. 1 (January–February 1981): 2–10; Hyland, "Soviet Theater Forces."

9. U.S. Department of Defense, *Soviet Military Power* (Washington, D.C.: Government Printing Office, September 1981) and *Annual Report, Fiscal Year 1981*, Washington, D.C., January 29, 1980, p. 146.

10. For the number of U.S. nuclear warheads in Europe, see DoD annual reports, *Fiscal Year 1981*, pp. 91, 95, and *Fiscal Year 1982*, p. 125.

11. One analyst estimates it will take 48–72 hours to disperse NATO's TNFs to their wartime posture; see Justin Galen, "Can NATO Meet Its Toughest Test? Strategic and Theater Nuclear Forces for the 1980s," *Armed Forces Journal International* (November 1979): 50. For discussion of Soviet unconventional warfare forces, see DoD, *Soviet Military Power*, pp. 38–39.

12. See DoD *Annual Report, Fiscal Year 1981*, p. 92. For discussion of Warsaw Pact chemical warfare capabilities, see DoD, *Soviet Military Power*, pp. 37–38.

13. Soviet nuclear doctrine is discussed in a number of publicly available Soviet documents. For a summary and analysis of these sources, see Lambeth, "Selective Nuclear Operations and Soviet Strategy."

14. See Uwe Nerlich, "Theatre Nuclear Forces in Europe: Is NATO Running Out of Options?," in *NATO: The Next Thirty Years*, edited by Kenneth A. Myers, (Boulder, Colo.: Westview Press, 1980), pp. 63–93, for a political and strategic analysis of these Soviet moves toward "nuclear counter-deterrence."

15. Lambeth, "Selective Nuclear Operations and Soviet Strategy," pp. 83–86.

16. For more detailed discussion see *The Theater Nuclear Force Posture in Europe*, a report submitted to Congress in April 1975, by Secretary of Defense James R. Schlesinger. Most of this report is reprinted in *Nuclear Strategy and National Security: Points of View*, edited by Robert J. Pranger and Roger P. Labrie, (Washington, D.C.: American Enterprise Institute for Public Policy Research, 1977), pp. 167–68. See also J.J. Martin, "Nuclear Weapons in NATO's Deterrent Strategy."

17. See DoD, *Soviet Military Power*, pp. 27–35.

18. A Ross Johnson, Robert W. Dean, and Alexander Alexiev, *East European Military Establishments: The Warsaw Pact Northern Tier*, Rand Report R-2417/1-AF/FF, Santa Monica, Calif., December 1980.

19. For a fuller presentation and discussion of this data base see James Martin's chapter in Uwe Nerlich ed., *Sowjetische Macht und westliche Verhandlungspolitik im Wandel militärischer Kräfteverhältnisse* (Baden-Baden: Nomos-Verlag, 1982), pp. 159–83.

POLITICAL PURPOSE IN THE PURSUIT OF THE ARMS COMPETITION

3 MILITARY POWER IN INTERNATIONAL POLITICS
Soviet Doctrine on Its Centrality and Instrumentality

Robert Legvold

The more Soviet military power grows, the more important are Soviet views on the role of military power in international politics. Not that outsiders can lay bare the Soviet mind or even agree on a single plausible image of what it might be. Nor, could they, would this be the last word on the nature of the Soviet military challenge. For the challenge embraces many elements, including specific Soviet military capabilities, the way these are used, and the way others fear they may be used. Soviet thoughts about semiabstractions like the functioning of force in contemporary international politics are but a fragment of the larger issue.

Historical experience, prevailing military doctrine, politics at home, and the momentum of a massive military establishment, too, shape the Soviet arsenal. Insecurity, ambition, and opportunity contribute to its exploitation. As for the apprehensions of others, a problem no less real than the Soviet Union's precise capabilities and intentions, these owe far more to fluctuating national psychologies, stirred by the whole range of a nation's problems, than to any profound acquaintance with Soviet thinking about military power.

This said, it makes no sense to assess the threat posed by the size and quality of Soviet forces with no thought to Soviet perspectives on their political role. A part of reality is the Soviet view of it. In this case, how Soviet leaders judge the political utility of arms, the foreign policy function of strategic doctrine, and the link between the prevailing military balance and political opportunities abroad gives more precise meaning to the arms they have. So does their notion of how Western leaders do the same. As Stanley Hoffmann wrote some years ago, "The student of politics who looks only at patterns of behavior but leaves out the meanings that actors give to their own and to each other's conduct turns into a specialist of shadows."[1]

This, then, is to be a look at the way the Soviet leaders integrate the process of arming and the resort to arms into their daily dealings with the outside world—or, more precisely, at the way they apparently think about the integration.[2] The real issues here are rather simple: How key is military power to the conduct of Soviet foreign policy, and how systematically is it integrated into policy? The first concern reflects widely held notions about the very nature of the Soviet Union, which according to conventional wisdom, relies on military power above all nations. Scarcely anyone discusses the challenge of growing Soviet military strength without making the point, sometimes attributing this trait to time-encrusted Russian tradition but more often these days to the peculiar dependency of a country poor in the other elements of power. Military power, however, can be central to the Soviet outlook for different, less simplistic reasons.

If military power is central to the Soviet view of international politics for whatever reason, we on the outside have a stake in exploring the purposefulness and coherence with which the Soviet leaders exploit it. Does the USSR, said to be so reliant on the military instrument, have some reasonably well-integrated concept for proceeding? The question is not whether a grand design or master plan for Soviet foreign policy exists, but whether that country has a clear notion of where and how military power is to be put to political use. The question touches everything from the portent of the Soviet Union's new readiness to meddle with force in Third World crises (the traces of a new political-military doctrine?) to the meaning of Soviet military efforts in Europe (are these directed at denying NATO all options, including wholly defensive ones, expressly to intimidate the West Europeans, forcing from them clearly conceived political concessions?).

This may seem an odd way to simplify the analysis. Western writers tend to deal more abstractly with the political role of military power, preoccupied as they are with the revolutionary implications of nuclear weapons. Most of their intellectual energy has been applied to rethinking the function of military force since these weapons have transformed war, its quintessence. One part of the enterprise has focused on trends altering the utility of force[3] ; the other on criteria for utilizing force or more precisely for bargaining with arms in the shadow of nuclear war.[4] Both make military power an abstraction, an object shaped by changes in its social and political context and governed by principles of mathematical, communications, or game theory.

Nothing is inherently wrong in this. Arguing about the utility (and the "usability") of force or deriving "principles" for what Thomas Schelling calls the "diplomacy of violence" (juxtaposing it to military strategy defined as "the art or science of military victory") are perfectly valid pursuits, though with certain costs.[5] The tendency of the debate over the utility of force seems to be an irrepressible facet of the way Americans understand and argue over the nature of the contemporary international political order.[6] And the older intellectual fascination with the "art of coercion short of war and on the brink" underpins the whole of U.S. deterrence theory.[7] One preoccupation plays a key part in explaining the world to us: "When states dare not resort to war, yet dare not renounce the resort to war, international politics is bound to depend heavily upon the threat or prospect of war."[8] The other profoundly influences the way we cope with this world: "The power to hurt is bargaining power. To exploit it is diplomacy—vicious diplomacy, but diplomacy."[9]

These preoccupations also set the terms within which Western leaders and analysts think about military power, constricting as well as skewing perspectives. By stressing the question of utility—force as an instrument of policy—they obscure military power's other realms. For apart from the conscious uses of military power, the military balance among states exercises an independent, indirect political effect, the apprehensions of many suggest. Thus, for example, a link is commonly thought to exist between shifts in the central balance and a growing Soviet willingness to intervene in distant conflicts.

Given the intellectual priorities of most Western analysts, this part of the analysis remains vague and impressionistic, however. Even the subtlest among them settle for the loosest formulas. How to explain the supposed eagerness of West Europeans to trade with the Soviet Union on terms favorable to the Soviets, the likelihood that the West will make the concessions in arms control talks, the reluctance of some West European governments to join in NATO exercises thought provocative to the Soviet Union, or the tendency in Scandinavia and elsewhere to apply a double standard in East–West relations? Such "deference," says one of the ablest students of military affairs, "is inexplicable except in terms of [the Soviet Union's] immense military power."[10] Perhaps. But the point is far from self-evident, and the failure to go beyond casual inference contrasts with the elaborate (though abstract) interest of most Western analysts in the formal, calculated actual or threatened applications of force.

The bias or preoccupation of Western analysis has a second consequence for the U.S. approach to the Soviet Union and military power. In the midsixties, Robert Osgood and Robert Tucker published a book in which they argued that military strategy had now become a far broader concept, embracing "not only the waging of war but all the uses of force as an instrument of policy short of war."[11] "In fact," they contended, military strategy "is itself a major instrument of policy in peacetime." "Thus strategic pronouncements can have the impact of major diplomatic statements, and the strategic 'dialogue' with one's allies can be as politically significant as the communication of strategic intentions to one's adversaries."

Construing so broadly the proper sphere of strategic thought made good sense, but in fact the American policymaker and the majority of specialists did not go in this direction. Instead, both the policymaker and the academic strategist continued to devote themselves to the intricacies of deterrence theory, with its emphasis on the complex but narrow problem of nuclear bargaining. Strategy, understood (to follow Michael Howard) as a fundamental amalgam of operational skill, logistical underpinning, social (and political) cohesion, and technological adequacy intended to meet the test of actual warfare, fell by the wayside.[12] Most Western analysts lost interest in the mundane side of war and the ramified dimensions involved in preparing for it—lost interest in struggling with the hopelessly uncertain social and political requirements of war in the nuclear age.

The Soviets did not. Lately a growing number of Western commentators have begun lamenting the damage done to a sound defense by the circumscribed preoccupations of nuclear-fixated deterrence, or, to use the strategist's phrase, by "extended deterrence."[13] No one, however, has yet begun untangling the particular effect of these preoccupations on Western perceptions of those like the Soviets who deal differently with these issues.[14]

In short, any effort to understand the political significance of Soviet military power is twice burdened: once by the automatic but unexamined political effect attributed to the sheer existence of this power and once by the twist given to Western perspectives by the West's own peculiar concepts of (nuclear) deterrence. The first failing poses a subtle obstacle to dispassionate analysis, making it harder to bring an open mind to the question of how in reality the Soviets conceive the political returns to military power. The second leads Western analysts to infer Soviet intentions from Western notions of nuclear war, to judge Soviet defense preparation by the principles implicit in Western notions of "crisis stability," "intrawar deterrence," and "escalation dominance."

To shake free of these handicaps, one needs categories forcing the analysis beyond conventional, and rather empty, frames of reference. Two seem to me useful. The first reckons that military power has no single political significance for the Soviet Union, nor for any nation, but, rather, possesses significance at several levels. Like any great nuclear power and some that are nonnuclear and not so great, the Soviet Union confronts, cares about, appraises, and exploits military power on different levels. The waging of war is one—now transformed when waged among nuclear states into something very special. Another is the use of force short of war, including the threat to wage war, now separated from the actual waging of war by practicality. (Using force is still practical; waging nuclear war is not.) In between, the ever-changing military balance constitutes a third dimension. At each level the utility of military power, its political meaning, and the criteria by which these are judged vary. Only by looking at each level can the Soviet political stake be sensibly discussed. And only by looking at all three levels can the first of my two basic questions be answered: How is military power central to Soviet foreign policy (not, how central is military power to Soviet foreign policy)?

The second basic question is also a second basic category pushing the analysis beyond the usual: that is, the question of how systematically military power is integrated into Soviet foreign policy or, to put the same point differently, how thoroughly the Soviet leaders plot the political tasks they assign their military power. The ultimate question is whether they have what might be called a "strategy of use" or strategy for exploiting military power to achieve political ends. The prior questions, however, are (1) what links exist among Soviet military capabilities, military strategy, and, to borrow Uwe Nerlich's category, political rationale, particularly in Europe, and (2) what links Soviet policymakers establish among the different military balances, again, including the one in Europe.

THE THREE LEVELS OF UTILITY

The Instrumentality of War

Force, Laurence Martin has commented, is the instrument that "trumps all others."[15] So highly prized is it by Soviet leaders, according to the dominant image in the West, that they scarcely recoil even before the horror of nuclear war. No one suggests that the Soviet leaders want a nuclear war or would launch one out of coldly calculated ambition, and few doubt that they grasp the awful implications of having one. But, to the consternation of a great many, they treat wars, including nuclear wars, as "winnable." They continue to perfect "war-fighting" capabilities and concepts. And they continue to repeat Clausewitz's dictum that "war is the continuation of politics by other means." Thus, while the Soviet leaders may not regard nuclear war any more cavalierly than Western leaders, in the view of many they are less paralyzed by the notion of its madness or unthinkability and less reluctant to go about their business, making sure that in whatever comes, nuclear war included, their country shall prevail.

The Soviet leadership, in fact, does not believe in the political utility of war any more than Western leaders. Rather, they say, should war occur, it will be the result of "imperialism's"—always imperialism's—struggle against socialism, and the contest between the two will continue even in conditions of war. Says one Soviet specialist, director of the foreign relations department of the Institute of the United States of America and Canada, "When the instrument of war can no longer be rationally controlled or when the aggressor is destroyed in the struggle for 'victory,' then war loses its character as a practical instrument of policy."[16] Many people have made the point, including Soviet military commentators. Some, such as the late N.A. Talensky, a military man of admittedly "advanced" views, have long condemned the "dangerous illusion" that thermonuclear war "can still serve as an instrument of politics, that it is possible to achieve political aims by using nuclear weapons and still survive."[17]

The military, no less than the intellectuals in the international affairs institutes, censure Western specialists for "deliberately lumping together the theoretical proposition characterizing the essence of war and the proposition concerning the expediency or otherwise of war as a means of achieving political objectives."[18] Soviet spokesmen of all kinds have made it quite plain that they do not regard war as a legitimate recourse of policy save for wars of "national liberation" fought against colonial masters or wars of national defense. One may believe their claim or not, but their words cannot be used to prove the case against them.

Not even the benevolent connection between war and revolution survives in contemporary analyses. Historically it has been good Marxist–Leninist teaching to represent war as the catalyst for revolution, but the teaching has changed. Wars that once the proletariat turned against their instigators "to speed up revolution and social progress" now exact too heavy a price "for the world to pay for the destruction of capitalism, already doomed by history."[19] Indeed, according to Georgy Arbatov, if revolutionaries start wars, like their class enemies, they will only succeed in turning "the indignation of the masses against themselves."[20]

War, therefore, is not what distinguishes the Soviets' approach to military power from that of the West. For them as for us, the political significance of military power resides elsewhere.

The Instrumentality of Military Trends

There is more to military power than its use. Long before the first tank surges across somebody else's border, the might of nations weighs on world politics. But how? Leaders and publicists on both sides have always worried about military trends and the psychological hazards of seeming to have fallen off the pace. They assume a direct connection between the state of the military balance and the aggressiveness of the other side's foreign policy. They take for granted that military power casts a political shadow.

Western leaders and writers, however, worry about the impact of military trends viscerally, vaguely, desultorily. The Soviets, while far from knowing how to map the precise effects of a changing balance, have a clearer and more self-confident approach to the problem. They start with the assumption that the growth of Soviet military power works a substantial and salutary effect on the shape of world affairs. Because many in the West make no such axiomatic assumption about their own countries' military power, the contrast at this level is elemental. Détente, the "national liberation revolution," the muffling of German "revanchism," and the defeat of a postwar U.S. policy predicated on "positions of strength" are all said to be the blessings of Soviet military efforts.[21] Never in their analyses are the disintegration of détente, the increasing contrariness of Western governments, and the passing of the so-called "Vietnam syndrome" of the United States also its products.

Soviet observers clearly believe that military power has some larger political impact, that it influences the orientation of governments and, thus, the basic direction of events. Whatever the Soviet faith in the good coming from military power, Soviet observers make no effort to explain the process by which it functions, however. The Soviet faith in military power is neither absolute nor narrowly based, moreover. On the contrary, Soviet analysis denies the military factor an independent and preeminent importance, inserting it instead into a broader theory of international politics dominated by what Soviet writers call the "correlation of forces."

The correlation of forces is a sweeping concept, incorporating virtually all critical trends in international politics—from the economic performance of the socialist countries to the strength of the European Left, from the clash of interests among capitalist nations to the momentum of the "national liberation struggle."[22] It stands as a balance sheet of the forces shaping an age. For Westerners brought up on "balance of power" theory, it should be underscored that the Soviet formula is not a theory of equilibrium and has little to say about the circumstances that preserve a given international order. But then neither is it simply a way of tallying comparative gross national products, fates of technology growth, let alone the balance among armies, strategic rocket forces, and the like. Rather, it is about the direction of events, history's scorecard, a device for commenting on the underlying pattern of change, and, as such, it assumes a particular movement to international politics. Least of all is it a surrogate phrase for the military balance. When Soviet speakers boast of a favorable shift in the correlation of forces, they are not, as many Western commentators apparently think, specifically talking about shifts in the military balance.[23]

Here, however, the concept is introduced not for what it reveals of the Soviet grasp of international politics, but for what it tells us of the place assigned military power. The place is subordinate. In the Soviet scheme of things, military power plays a partial and indirect role. Change, such as the West's turn toward détente in the early 1970s, arises out of the overall transformation of the international environment, not merely from shifts in the military balance. Change, in turn, shapes the correlation of forces. Détente, for example, by constraining "imperialist aggressiveness," improved the correlation of forces. In this interplay between détente and the shifting correlation of forces, the growing military strength of the socialist countries, while significant, was still only a component.

Three elements are essential to a balanced reconstruction of the Soviet approach to military power. First, Soviet analysts are inclined to stress the limits placed on the West's military options by diverse changes in the international environment, that is, by the shifting "correlation of forces" in its broadest sense. This leaves the interaction between Soviet and Western military power real but indirect and indeterminate.

Soviet analysts also stress the importance of dealing with military power in context, never judging the significance of military trends in isolation. In what remains the most thorough Soviet analysis of the political role of military power, Vasilii Kulish emphasizes that the effectiveness of military power is "determined not only by the forces themselves" but "depends upon the specific international-political situation."[24] Important as the military balance between adversaries may be, he says, it is "moderated" by the political setting and the role of third parties. The military balance is not something that Soviet analysts think can be determined by simply inventorying each side's "capabilities." "In the nuclear age," Kulish says, "it has become increasingly difficult to define or determine military superiority or to evaluate the balance of military force."[25] So many other elements enter the picture, including, to take his examples, a great confusion of third parties and alliances of widely varying economic and military potential, "the complicated interlacing" of national interests, the political constraints imposed on the use of force, and the strength of "revolutionary and national liberation movements."

Soviet analysts, too, are beginning to acknowledge the declining utility of military force in international politics. They, too, discuss the irony of nuclear weapons, an arm too powerful to be used for anything other than avoiding its use, the limits placed on the resort to force by the lurking fear of nuclear war, and the growing array of problems for which the military solution is no solution at all.

Military power has always been, they say, the "supreme ruler of interstate relations."[26] Among the many factors constituting the correlation of forces, it has long been regarded as decisive.[27] But over the last several years Soviet writers have begun conceding military power less preeminence. To make their point they often borrow from Western authors: "Even representatives of bourgeois science and diplomacy are beginning to reckon with . . . the increasing obsolescence of military solutions to international problems."[28] The technique is disingenuous, but it does allow them to quote those who contend "that the next decade will be par excellence an era emphasizing and depending upon diplomacy and diplomatic skills," and to attack those "bourgeois theorists" who maintain that force "is the decisive factor in international relations."[29] Today, they stress, these bourgeois theorists confess " 'the paradox of force,' admitting that it is no longer possible to achieve the desired political results by using force."[30]

Over the years Soviet speakers have made it a basic premise of analysis that the United States with its allies seeks a military balance that can be put to work, that is, a balance salvaging the largest possible role for military power as an instrument of policy. The Americans they say instinctively insist on dealing with the Soviet Union from a "position of strength," meaning from a position of military superiority. "The United States throughout the cold war," to repeat a point made a thousand times over, "has pursued a strategic concept based on the maintenance of military superiority over the USSR. There have been some interludes of negotiation and advocacy of reduced tension, but always in the context of the United States bargaining from positions of superior military strength."[31]

What constitutes a "position of strength"—how it is measured and used—receives little elaboration, but the implication is clear that American leaders believe discrepancies in the military balance are politically useful and, therefore, are constantly trying to accentuate them.[32] The more interesting aspect of the argument comes at the next step.

In striving to achieve a military advantage and to turn it to practical advantage, the United States is said to pursue a formal strategy. Strategy in this case—what Westerners call strategic doctrine—they represent as a determined effort to accentuate the political effect of a military posture. Rather than an abstraction designed to cope with the risk of nuclear war, in Soviet analysis Western deterrence theory becomes a political concept, preoccupied with the foreign policy utility of nuclear weapons. Such doctrines as "massive retaliation," "flexible response," and "selective options," are not merely defense concepts, say Soviet commentators; they are "instruments" of foreign policy. They are inventions expressly intended to increase the political resonance of Western military power and the flexibility with which it can be used.

Soviet intellectuals and leaders, like their Western counterparts, indulge a casual certainty that some nations live according to a larger strategic design built around great stores of military power and a determination to perfect its political exploitation. (In this case, of course, they mean the United States, its principal NATO allies, and maybe China.) They arrive at this conclusion by a different route, however, imparting different meanings to much of the language and many of the ideas used on both sides.

For example, they read the intellectual patrons of deterrence theory and the annual posture statements and think they are encountering not a defense doctrine but a foreign policy strategy, not a scheme for coping with nuclear war but a device for harnessing nuclear weapons to political objectives. In one of their more striking departures, they suggest that the "foreign policy role of military force" is shifting "from the sphere of war and military action to the sphere of deterrence."[33] With force less usable among great powers, naturally more attention turns to the exploitation of force short of war, but Soviet analysts seem to be saying something more. They seem to be saying that U.S. policymakers are not only struggling with the problem of structuring a military threat to avert war or cut war short should one occur but with the possibility of using the shadow of war to serve workaday foreign policy—to control events, others' behavior, and the course of change.

Because the grand policy of the United States has always been viewed as offensive, strategic doctrine takes on an ambitious, assertive character. And containment, in Soviet eyes, was never merely an attempt to prevent Soviet aggression or to check the spread of Soviet influence beyond Eastern Europe. It and its more ambiguous sequels, they say, have always been more concerned with larger twin objectives: To weaken and, if possible, undo Soviet power within its own sphere and to dictate the pace and character of change elsewhere. Any defense posture in the service of these objectives inevitably assumes a highly political character.[34] For good reason, therefore, in another striking contrast with Western usage, Soviet writers rarely refer to the ideas of "massive retaliation," "flexible response," "limited nuclear options," or the Carter administration's Presidential

Directive 59 as "strategic doctrine." They call them instead "military-political doctrine."

These conceptual qua semantic discrepancies, however, only scratch the surface. Traced further, they lead back to a dense and massive tangle of assumptions about the place of military power in American history, of geopolitics in American conceptions, and of strategic designs in American policy. In article after article, book after book, Soviet writers take up these themes, spinning them out, embroidering them, interweaving them.[35]

One of the more remarkable examples is a book by Henry Trofimenko that tracks U.S. theories of deterrence, geopolitical analysis, and balance-of-power politics back to Alexander Hamilton and his contemporaries.[36] From his elaborate account, the United States emerges as (1) historically prone to deal with weaker adversaries from a "position of strength"; (2) long persuaded of a "manifest destiny" and of a right to bring its way of life to others, a conviction affecting its notions of "just war," "enlightened self-interest," and so on; (3) attached to the nineteenth-century concept of the balance of power and increasingly determined to become its arbiter; and (4) since the turn of the century, smitten with the ideas of Mahan and Mackinder, a fascination, Trofimenko maintains, that persists today. Says he, the whole postwar policy of containment derives from "traditional geopolitical postulates."[37] Trofimenko, one of the Soviet Union's most accomplished students of U.S. strategic doctrine, then goes on to the arcana of postwar deterrence theory, but he starts his analysis with this basic set of propositions.

Soviet leaders may not follow Trofimenko's argument in all its intricacy, but they accept, indeed insist on, essentially the same view of the United States in a cruder form, and that has at least three practical consequences. First, the tendency to put the United States at the center of Soviet concerns and then to portray it as a military challenge drives the Soviet leadership to stress the military side of its own policy. Soviet images in this case add to the general militarization of choice. Conservatives in the Soviet Union argue that the imperialists only understand military power, that only a militarily strong Soviet Union can hope to promote détente or safely undertake arms control negotiations. When relations sour, the argument for facing the United States and other potential adversaries with increased military power accentuates the natural tendency to rationalize Soviet efforts by others' efforts. But in neither case, due to the role the United States plays in Soviet images, are the advocates of increased military power obliged or inclined to defend it as the path to Soviet aggrandizement or hegemony.

Second, because they take seriously the political significance of military trends, Soviet observers worry about who is seen as up and who as down in the military competition. Appearances have been important to the Soviet leaders. Someone like Nikita Khrushchev made them the essence of his approach to nuclear diplomacy, counting on blustery talk about Soviet missiles and the apparent momentum of the Soviet nuclear program to cow the West Europeans.[38] His successors have done less simple-minded rocket-rattling, almost in proportion to the growth and refinement of Soviet nuclear capability, but they are not above vague allusions to the awful risks run by neighbors who would let the Americans put a new generation of ground-launched cruise missiles on their soil. They also reduce U.S. crisis initiatives to the same level: "Since the end of the Second World War," writes Vadim Kortunov, "the United States has issued at least twelve standby orders to its armed forces in order to pressure the Soviet Union and other socialist states."[39] Perhaps Kortunov is only peddling propaganda when he writes that "imperialism has on more than one occasion used its nuclear missile potential in an attempt to intimidate the socialist countries." But the spirit of his comment conforms to an old Soviet habit of playing rhetorically to popular fears in a moment of crisis, divorcing nuclear diplomacy from closely calculated assessments of the balance. Such simplistic, heavy-handed, and semireflexive incantations of nuclear threat, it should be underscored, are nearly the opposite of a truly systematic and discriminating use of nuclear weapons to achieve political ends.

Military trends and Soviet notions about the United States also coalesce in the elusive but politically potent issue of military superiority. Precisely what military superiority means, how it is to be identified, and of what proportions of naval, conventional, and nuclear power it consists are no more thoroughly discussed by Soviet analysts than by Western analysts. But Soviet writers are clear that military superiority has long been a central goal of the United States. For their own part the Soviet leaders have decided that it is better politics to disclaim an interest in military superiority, or what the Soviet military as late as 1976 called with obvious sympathy "military-technical superiority."[40]

Because the nuclear balance overshadows other dimensions of military power, the issue of military superiority is often reduced to strategic nuclear superiority, a notion Soviet analysts tend to portray as an ability to deliver a "disarming first strike." The consequence of Soviet concern over strategic nuclear trends is a critical ambivalence. For Soviet analysts are at once confident that neither side can again forge ahead of the other: Trofimenko says, "We in the Soviet Union are well aware that if we attempted to outstrip the United States in strategic arms, it would not bring any positive results because of the inevitable U.S. countermeasures (and this is true for either country)."[41] At the same time, they admit marginal advances by one side over the other are possible, and these, they warn, may beguile incautious leaders into acting as though they had a real advantage. Thus, in effect, they divide trends at the strategic nuclear level by objective and subjective criteria, trusting the first, worrying about the second.

Finally, there is a third context in which Soviet analysts judge the political significance of military trends: the instrumentality of force itself. Here, too, when Soviet commentators link the state of the military balance to the active use of force, they have the option of starting with American conceptions. "Our strategic arsenal must be made adequate to prevent the Soviet Union or any other country from using, or threatening to use, nuclear weapons in world politics," one expert American group has written. "If that is accomplished, U.S. conventional forces can again become the effective bulwark of our diplomacy."[42] For the Soviets, as a consequence, the question of how the central balances relate to the exploitation of force has several sides, not merely that stressed by Western analysts since the Soviet–Cuban intervention in Angola. This scarcely means that the Soviet approach to the use of force is purely reactive or defensive, but it does mean that analyses focusing on unilateral Soviet ambitions will miss an important dimension of the problem.

The Instrumentality of Force

Nuclear weapons have not ended the use of force. Nowhere has military power been a more regular and palpable part of foreign policy than at the level of local wars. Strategic theory and a great deal of defense analysis may have little to say about the daily mundane uses of force, but by any measure it is this dimension that gives military power its steadiest, most immediate political significance.[43] To understand the Soviet response to military power at this level, the analyst needs to track two loosely connected issues: the place occupied by the United States in Soviet perspectives, and the place that force occupies in Soviet foreign policy quite apart from the Americans.

Over the years, Western analysts have paid too little attention to the extraordinary centrality the Soviet Union assigns the United States in its approach to the outside world.[44] They have paid even less attention to the effect this bias has on the character of Soviet foreign policy. And they have paid virtually no attention to the central role Soviet observers attach to military power in the foreign policy of the country central to Soviet concerns. Yet no notion more dominates the Soviet analysis of American foreign policy, none figures more prominently in their assessment of international politics and the role of force. U.S. policy, they say, is the creature of military power, and the application of force its most trusted recourse.[45]

This preoccupation brings us back to the question of military superiority, particularly its strategic nuclear dimension. Soviet analysts appear to be of two minds: Some have long charged the United States with seeking an ability to deliver a disarming first strike. The means may have been inadequate, the doctrines incomplete, and the declarations of U.S. leaders otherwise, but a first-strike capability, they insist, has been the inherent logic of U.S. efforts.[46] Others have been less quick to reduce the issue so starkly. That the United States seeks some form of strategic advantage they do not challenge. But whether the U.S. objective is as crude and unrealistic as a capacity to deliver a disarming first strike is another matter. Trofimenko, for example, considers recent adjustments in U.S. programs and ideas, and suggests that, though an effort to "break through the constraints of mutual deterrence, [they] may have a more modest interpretation than the desire to return to unilateral deterrence of the Soviet Union," a euphemism presumably for the massive U.S. advantages of the 1950s and 1960s.

> They may, for instance, be interpreted as a way to favor the United States (without violating the letter of the arms limitation treaties) with certain partial advantages that would not guarantee the success of the first strike but would still allow for greater flexibility in the use of strategic offensive arms, thus making it possible to impose on the other side the 'rules of exchange' (in case of conflict), unilaterally beneficial for the United States.[47]

The reason the United States plays around with the idea of "partial advantage" within the strategic nuclear competition, Trofimenko says, and he is echoed by other Soviet commentators, is to make good the use of force at lower levels. By striving to make U.S. deterrence of the Soviet Union "more efficient" than Soviet deterrence of the United States, he says, the American leadership hopes to give itself "the opportunity to increase political pressure" and to "open up the prospect of using military force with impunity at the lower rungs of the escalation ladder."[48] Doctrine, arms, and alliances are still all designed to provide the United States with a maximum of usable force in the pursuit of its daily policy concerns.

For all the stress on American efforts to preserve a role for the use of force, however, Soviet writers rarely analyze these efforts in any detail. The exception is a book by Vitaly Zhurkin, the Deputy Director of the Institute of the United States and Canada, dealing with what he calls U.S. "crisis policy" or "crisis diplomacy."[49] The phrase includes everything from gunboat diplomacy to the movement of forces in the Berlin crises of the late fifties and early sixties, from the American intervention in Guatemala in 1955 to its part in the Vietnam War.

To deal with the larger issue of strategic doctrine and the U.S. approach to the use of force, Zhurkin divides the last thirty-five years into four periods: In Era I, from 1945 to 1952, according to Zhurkin, the United States did not have an elaborate strategy "for the use of military force at different levels and in different situations," concentrating instead on the preparations for a decisive war against the Soviet Union. Era II, from 1953 to 1960, was marked by the first integral American doctrine designed not only for war but for the "calculated use of American military might as a policy instrument in peacetime."[50] The doctrine of massive retaliation, Zhurkin maintains, represented an attempt to make the threat of nuclear war an all-purpose instrument of foreign policy, providing not only for the West's basic security, but serving as well to dictate the outcome of local crises and conflicts. Against a nonnuclear adversary it might have made sense, he comments; against a nuclear power like the Soviet Union it did not, and eventually it was abandoned.

Era III is from 1961 to 1968. It represents, Zhurkin argues, a watershed in the development of U.S. foreign and defense policy, out of which emerged the doctrine of flexible response. He treats this concept as both a more elaborate attempt to integrate force into U.S. policy and as a reflection of the narrowing opportunities for its use. On the one hand the United States was enlarging its military options and doing a better job of matching resources to the opportunities.[51] On the other hand the shifting "correlation of forces" was compelling the United States to resort to more indirect strategies, stressing limited and local war. And flexible response, for all its sophistication, says Zhurkin, was a reflection of this trend.[52]

Era IV, from 1969 to roughly 1974, the years of détente, Zhurkin characterizes as a period of increasing realism in U.S. foreign policy. Largely as a result of Vietnam, he argues, Americans were learning the limits of interventionism. A growing portion of the U.S. political and intellectual elite was coming to recognize that even at the lower end of the spectrum, American military power could accomplish only so much. Zhurkin is not saying that everyone had grown so wise. Rather, he is arguing that American leaders and many influential voices around them were gradually coming to see just how "selective" and "discriminating" the use of force must be.

Does Era IV still endure? Does the challenge of coming up with a strategic posture guaranteeing a role for force grow even more discouraging? Despite the wreckage of U.S.–Soviet détente and the gloomy things the Soviets have begun to think about the prospects of U.S.–Soviet relations, the Soviets have not yet pronounced themselves. The stirrings, however, suggest that when they do, the result will be a sharp shift back to a conservative image of evolving American attitudes. Soviet commentators talk of a U.S. return to a "position of strength" policy, of a renewed preoccupation with the military competition, and of a restored will to intervene with military power.[53] This time, Mikhail Milshtein writes, they are going beyond earlier emphases, talking about the use of tactical nuclear weapons in third-area conflicts, treating the Middle East and Persian Gulf as a new strategic theater, and so on.

This is one side of the story. The other is the Soviet Union's own independent appreciation of military force as a policy instrument. Khrushchev gives us an arresting example in recalling the Korean War. Brezhnev has provided another by sending his armies into Afghanistan.

Khrushchev, in his memoirs, candidly admits that the North Koreans started the 1950 war because they "wanted to prod South Korea with the point of the bayonet."[54] He makes no effort to explain the attack as a justified response to imperialist designs, and he says nothing about the Soviet Union's sacred duty to defend a fellow socialist state from the South's aggression. The North Koreans, with Soviet approval and help, were simply making revolution, at the "point of the bayonet." By invading, he confesses, Kim Il-sung expected "to touch off an internal explosion in South Korea" out of which "the power of the people would prevail." The North Koreans "wanted to give a helping hand to their brethren who were under the heel of Syngman Rhee," and, as far as Khrushchev was concerned, this was and remained long after a legitimate use of force, deserving Soviet material aid and even direct logistical and command support.[55]

In Afghanistan, for all the clamor over a U.S.–Chinese–Pakistani-sponsored insurgency, the Soviet leadership knows the problem is a failed "revolution" that could only be saved by a massive military intervention.[56] When the situation grew sufficiently desperate, having the ability to act, the Soviet Union acted. Neither Afghanistan's place outside the socialist camp nor oft repeated words about not exporting revolution had much to do with the decision. And it would be stretching an argument to the extreme to think that theories about the U.S. "crisis diplomacy" had any more to do with it. Simply, the Soviets were presented with a severe problem, and, for a variety of reasons beyond the concern of this essay, picked force, lots of it, as the way out.

In Korea, Afghanistan, perhaps the 1977 Ogaden War, and Vietnam's conquest of socialist Kampuchea, the Soviet leadership used force or sanctioned its use when neither the specific threat of U.S. intervention or "imperialist theories" on the role of force could have been much on its mind. Where does this leave us? Does not the Soviet Union's periodic readiness to use force for its own reasons make Soviet perspectives on Western practices distinctly incidental?

Though the Korean, Afghan, and other cases are obviously important, until now they have also been the exception rather than the rule. Most often when the Soviets have resorted to force outside their own camp, whether as in the Arab–Israeli wars of the 1960s and 1970s or in the Angolan civil war of 1975–76, the role they see military power playing in Western policy has been a natural element in their definition of the problem. Their perception of the role of force in Western policy shaped the outlook within which relevant Soviet capabilities and strategies take form.

The point is not that the role of force in Western policy renders Soviet military policy defensive or purely reactive. In a competitive world checkmating, let alone outbidding, the other side's use of force can scarcely be considered defensive. The point is that the Soviet notion of the role force plays in Western policy affects the role they assign their own, influencing the way priorities are set, stakes assessed, utility defined, and strategies devised. Soviet policy, as a consequence, is not the free-floating, independent product of Soviet ambition so often implied in Western analysis.

THE INTEGRATION OF SOVIET MILITARY POWER INTO SOVIET FOREIGN POLICY

Focusing on Soviet conceptions of the military role in international politics tells us little about the way military power is integrated into Soviet foreign policy. The role Soviet analysts assign military power in Western foreign policy sheds light on the value, functions, and limitations attached to its role in Soviet foreign policy. But it does not reveal the degree of care, preconception, or thoroughness with which it is made a part of policy. The question of how *systematically* the Soviet Union incorporates military power into policy requires separate analysis.

Three areas shed light on this dimension: the Soviet approach to the use of force in regions of instability, the Soviet political exploitation of military power in Europe, and Soviet security policy in the strategic theaters surrounding the Soviet Union. The core of the analysis centers on the relationship in each instance among Soviet military capabilities, military strategy, and political rationale. The key question, again, is whether the Soviets have a "strategy of use" or a strategy for exploiting military power to achieve political ends.

The Soviet Use of Force in Regional Instability

For more than a decade the Soviet Union steadily expanded its ability to use force far from home and then, to the alarm of most, actually began using it. Even before the invasion of Afghanistan Western analysts were asking "whether the Angolan, Ethiopian, and other African adventures" were the "harbingers of a major shift in Soviet strategy, tending toward larger military operations as a major tool of high policy," or were "merely a spin-off from a rising tide of Soviet military power designed and acquired for the more central purposes of national security."[57] After Afghanistan many answered that indeed Soviet power and opportunism had congealed into a more assertive and coherent strategy in the Third World, arguing that the Soviet leadership meant to promote radical change wherever it had likely clients, underwriting these changes with its military power. Afghanistan, some said, signaled the extension of the Brezhnev doctrine to countries that yesterday had been nonaligned or even friendly to the West, under the flimsiest pretext of protecting "revolutionary" change.

The answer has been too quick in coming: It is far from clear that this Soviet leadership has a more coherent notion of what it is doing in the Third World, including those critical and unstable areas near the Soviet Union. It is even less clear that it has thought through the use of force at this level and begun developing a strategy for its incorporation into daily policy. Some years ago Kulish stressed how "difficult, dangerous, and responsible" the task of defining "the actual functions of military force in specific situations" had become.[58] He added how equally difficult the task had become of determining the "limits and probable consequences of its use." So difficult, indeed, he argued, that while in the past these problems could be "resolved by political and military leaders based upon their experience," this was no longer adequate. "The new conditions" (in the early 1970s), he wrote, "require new scientific methods."[59] New methods since have not produced even a modest sharpening of policy, however.

Soviet intellectuals and publicists have simply not wrestled with these problems. And not because these are the order of issues that never get discussed in the Soviet Union: Kulish and his coauthors had rather boldly opened the matter. By Soviet standards they were frank in the forces they advocated and the uses to which they would have them put. They, for example, wrote of the possibility that the Soviet Union "may require mobile, well-trained, and well-equipped armed forces" if it is to "prevent local wars" and to provide "military support" to "nations fighting for their freedom and independence against the forces of internal reaction and imperialist intervention."[60] Moreover, they went on to say, while "in some situations the very knowledge of a Soviet military presence in an area in which a conflict situation is developing may serve to restrain the imperialists and local reaction," in other cases "the actual situation may require the Soviet Union to carry out measures aimed at restraining the aggressive acts of imperialism."

Never has the discourse in the Soviet Union recovered even this level of specificity. The closest that anyone has come is Admiral Sergei Gorshkov, but his shadowy references to the "peacetime role" of the Soviet navy and to the task of protecting "state interests" and defending the "national liberation struggle" contain no hint of a modestly coherent behind-the-scenes discussion of how these things are to be accomplished.[61] Most of the time Soviet commentary is at the level of bromides on the role of "socialism's military might" in assisting "revolutionary liberation movements" and in "hindering the export of imperialist counterrevolution," something that General Aleksei Yepishev, the head of the Soviet military's political arm, calls "one of the most important manifestations of the external function of the armed forces of a socialist state."[62]

Granted the Soviet leaders hardly need a carefully polished strategy before putting their country's military power to work. Nonetheless it makes a difference whether they became embroiled in Angola because the opportunity arose or because they thought the time had come to make more use of military force to shape outcomes in such settings and were busy developing a notion of when, where, and how force is to be employed. It makes a difference too whether the Soviets invaded Afghanistan because of peculiar circumstances or because they now have in place a new standard assuring Third World clients of salvation, provided if necessary by invading Soviet military forces.

It makes a difference, in short, whether the Soviet leaders are not only methodically building force-projection capabilities, but also developing a (military) strategy for their use and, beyond that, a political rationale ordering priorities. The first they are doing, but not methodically. (The gaps and unevenness in Soviet capabilities have been often noted.[63]) The second they are doing at a narrow operational level, according to the requirements dictated by their interventions in Angola and Ethiopia. (A larger, more integral, and general-purpose strategy such as that required by the U.S. commitment to a Rapid Deployment Force has not been undertaken.) The third, the development of a political rationale, may be forming piecemeal around an amorphous mix of instincts, opportunism, and existing involvements. (But the result does not add up to a self-conscious and well-integrated sense of priorities; nothing on the scale of, say, the Eisenhower doctrine, or Kennedy's counterinsurgency planning, or even the emerging U.S. tendency to deal with a critical region like the Persian Gulf as a new strategic theater.) Because advances in each of these three areas remains fragmentary and inchoate, the integration among the three is still scarcely underway. Thus, while it is important to recognize the striking departures represented by the Soviet–Cuban intervention in Angola and the Soviet invasion of Afghanistan, it is also important not to confuse the unprecedented use of force with the systematic use of force.

As a result the challenge to Western policy is not so much a headstrong Soviet leadership possessed of perfectly balanced capabilities and a well-heeled doctrine but one with deeply ingrained notions about Western doctrine, increased capabilities, and a predilection for controlling or constricting the use of U.S. military power. When Soviet naval spokesmen write about the use of force at lower levels of tension, they inevitably focus on the West's ability to move freely along the sealanes, treating these as "important tools of colonial politics and aggression."[64] When other military spokesmen discuss the Soviet Union's increasingly far-flung military resources, they invariably do so in the context of the United States' vast foreign military infrastructure. And when the Soviet political leadership identifies the successes of its "fraternal assistance" to warring local clients, it usually involves the thwarting of Western power.

In the years ahead the greater risk is not of a supremely ambitious Soviet Union resorting with impunity to force, interested only in capitalizing on the moment to secure political gain in this or that troubled quarter. It is that both countries, increasingly well-endowed with the necessary capabilities, will set about *using* force to control the other's *use* of force. This may not unfold in every instance. There will be cases where the Soviet Union assumes the situation gives it a semifree hand, as in some situations it will be prepared to concede the same to the United States. But the great majority of cases are likely to be somewhere in between.

The Politics of Soviet Military Power in Europe

In the case of the Soviet Union's military policy in Europe, the severed link is between military capabilities and military strategy on the one hand and political rationale on the other. Soviet military capa-

bilities and strategy, a strategy designed for war, are closely inter-
woven, but they are not then carefully integrated into a larger political strategy. Not that the Soviet leaders anticipate no political effect
from their massive military power in Central Europe. (That they do
as a matter of faith has already been discussed.) And not that were
they to manage an overwhelming military advantage, they would not
use it to force specific political concessions from the West Europeans. (Khrushchev tried in the Berlin crises of 1958 and 1961 even
without a crushing superiority.) Rather, the argument is that the Soviet military effort in Europe is not systematically integrated into the
Soviet Union's working foreign policy. By and large the Soviet Union
does not consciously make military choices expecting thereby to
influence West European policy at the Madrid Conference, a decision
to admit Greece or Portugal to the Common Market, or even the
West European position on the Arab–Israeli conflict.

Testing how systematically the Soviet leaders integrate military
power into their European policy, of course, is not easy. So many
criteria can be applied, so few conclusions verified. Still, in a fundamental sense, the issue comes down to one essential question: Do the
Soviet leaders purposely press forward with military programs, determined to eliminate all NATO counteroptions, even, or perhaps
particularly, those that are clearly defensive? Is it a concerted Soviet
objective, in other words, to leave Western Europe defenseless, a
Western Europe that would then, and while it was happening, be
easier prey to Soviet political desires?

Those who see a clear and methodical political intent behind Soviet military preparation would presumably say yes. My answer is no.
I have no doubt that Soviet military planners are bent on denying
NATO and the United States defense options, particularly escalatory
options, that might by any stretch of the imagination turn the outcome of war against the Soviet Union. And I assume that the Soviet
political leadership wants to have behind it military power guaranteeing that in any European political crisis the West's *military* options
are not superior to its own. But neither aim necessarily means that
the Soviet leaders have set out systematically to undermine all of
NATO's defense options, knowing that at a certain point they will
undermine critical political options as well.

In effect I am drawing a distinction among Soviet ambitions vis-à-
vis Western defense options in peace, war, and crises. It is admittedly
a fine one. Who knows all the reasons the Soviet Union wants to be

able to deny NATO a tactical nuclear option? Who can say precisely why the Soviet Union has deployed the SS–20, a weapon that menaces a whole range of Western defense options?[65] So many Soviet military measures admit of more than one interpretation. So many fit with a strategy directed at undermining NATO defense options in all three settings.

It seems reasonable to assume the most immediate explanation for the *systematic* growth of Soviet military power is the best one, or at least an adequate one. The most immediate explanation is that this growth is in response to the requirements of war and the Soviet Union's preferred strategy for fighting it. Provided the West then focuses its own attention on a balanced defense in the event of war, it is prudent to hypothesize that the Soviet Union has the military machine it has because it is principally the work of military men, and military men worry, plan, and build for one major event: war.[66]

If the four or five major phases in the development of Soviet military power in postwar Europe are examined, their single central feature has been the desire to maintain a preferred *military* strategy, one constantly (and quite legitimately) threatened by planned Western responses. From 1947 to 1954, for the most part the end of the Stalin era, the Soviet Union went about building a leaner, pared down, but consolidated and forward defense in Eastern Europe. By then Soviet defenses were already concentrated around armor, a massive number of combat units, and "shock-power," that is, fire power enhanced by maneuver. Above all, Stalin's notion of "active defense" assumed a rapid counteroffensive, transferring the battle to the other side's homeland.

When after 1954 the West, despairing of coping with the Soviet conventional threat in kind, embraced theater nuclear weapons, the Soviet command moved rapidly to counter. Even before Zhukov's ouster in 1957, the Soviet ground forces were set on their modern course: "active defense" and the counteroffensive gave way to a clearcut commitment to the swift forward offensive, a Soviet version of a blitzkrieg strategy. The modernization of the infantry, the integration of tank forces into the motorized infantry, the creation of more compact tank divisions, and the incorporation of tactical missiles—all steps designed to increase the mobility of Soviet forces—were the Soviet response to a nuclear-armed enemy. From this point forward, Soviet military efforts in Europe were to be heavily influenced by the "nuclear imperative"; that is, by the need to smash though the forward defenses of the enemy, "close quickly" on his nuclear installations, and overwhelm his rear areas before he could collect himself.

Khrushchev confused the issue in 1960–1964 with his emphasis on strategic nuclear war, leading him to downgrade the importance of conventional and tactical nuclear war in Europe. But even during this peculiar interlude, so objectionable to much of the Soviet military command, the process of enhancing the shock power and mobility in the Soviet Union's reduced ground forces continued.

With Khrushchev's departure, indeed even before, the Soviet Union began the fourth phase in the development of its military power in Europe. In the decade from 1965 to 1975, the Soviet Union gradually built the comprehensive "combined arms" capability about which its military command had doubtless dreamed since the late 1950s. On the ground this meant still greater shock power and mobility derived from the growth and modernization of Soviet armor, the development of self-propelled artillery and improved organic antiair capability, and the introduction of armored APC fighting vehicles and a substantial increase (40 percent) in the motorized rifle divisions' tank strength. When these were combined with the improvement in Soviet reinforcement capabilities, particularly by air, the incipient development of an air force with deep-interdiction capabilities, and an increased ability to cut NATO's transatlantic reinforcement, the Soviet Union had moved much closer to a genuine conventional war option, or to what Thomas Wolfe once called a "dual war-fighting capability."[67]

To be sure, the Soviet military does mean to parry NATO's military options in the course of a war, starting from the low end of the spectrum. If war comes, the Soviet Union is determined to shift the nuclear onus to the West (based on an ability to wage and win conventional war), to close off NATO's nuclear option (based on an ability to suppress low-level NATO nuclear responses as well as large-scale strategic nuclear responses from within the theater), and to decouple NATO's active defense from U.S. strategic nuclear forces (based on strategic "parity" between U.S. and Soviet forces).

But again it makes a difference whether we interpret this as primarily the inspiration of a military strategy or of a political strategy. By reading too much into Soviet efforts, we panic and choose self-defeating "quick fixes." NATO's historic nuclear solution, for example, may not only have undercut a more balanced defense but may well have accentuated the Soviet challenge by intensifying all the elements of the Soviet "combined arms" approach charged with throttling our theater nuclear weapons. More recently the storm over the Soviet SS–20 has preempted a more measured but comprehensive approach to the broader theater nuclear problem and in the process precipitated remedies that are sure to compound Western Europe's security problem in the 1990s.

The Soviet Approach to Security and the Rimland

Were all these arguments conceded—were it agreed that the Soviet Union does not have a refined political strategy for the use of force and is not more proficient than the West in integrating military power into its foreign policy—are not its natural instincts an adequate substitute? Many would say so. The Soviet leaders by nature seek to be what Fritz Ermarth calls a "regional security manager" in all the critical theaters ringing the Soviet Union. Like a lodestar the Soviet desire to clear these regions of alien military alliances, competitive security structures, and major outside powers, they assert, guides the Soviet approach to military power as surely as any carefully crafted design.

Despite its basic validity the image offers little guidance for interpreting working policy. As an insight into Soviet preferences and into the direction the Soviet leaders would take events if only they could, it tells us a great deal. The Soviets have an unusually strong urge to be unoppressed by the security arrangements of others and to be accepted by all in the area as a benevolent guarantor of peace and safety. But this image is basically a portrait of Soviet objectives, maximum objectives at that, and explains nothing of how the Soviets mean to get there.

There are three practical implications of all this hair-splitting. First, where one stands with respect to fine lines determines one's approach to the Soviet military threat. Those who ignore or dismiss them will tend constantly either to overestimate or to underestimate the Soviet challenge. They will convince themselves that worrying about surviving throw-weight exchange ratios does address a politically significant element of this challenge; or they will conclude that no sensible Soviet leader believes nuclear weapons matter politically provided a loose balance of terror prevails. For those who care about fine lines, on the other hand, the military balance is likely to be a many-sided affair, created by both camps' weaknesses as well as strengths, measured in physical capabilities but determined by the intangibles of will, alliance cohesion, and threat. Those who think refined distinctions are important tend to focus on tangible defense weaknesses, such as a dwindling ability to counter the Soviet use of force in Third World conflicts or a hollowing conventional defense in Europe. They usually stress less aspects of the strategic nuclear competition whose meaning derives from intricate and abstract notions of how a nuclear exchange would be effected. And when they set about solving a particular defense problem, say the hazards of a deteriorating Eurostrategic balance, they are more inclined to look beyond the immediate solution to its longer term consequences. Ground-launched cruise missiles, for example, may appear an appropriate answer to the Soviet SS–20 as the world is today; whether they are if having them ends any chance of dissuading the Soviet Union from going forward with its own cruise missile program may be another matter, particularly if the Soviet military finds an alternative mission for its cruise missiles presenting the Western alliance with a whole new challenge (for example, were the Soviet Union to develop strategic conventional cruise missiles as a substitute for the deep-interdiction air force it has never had). In short, those who attach importance to nuances in the Soviet understanding of military power are likely also to recognize both the complexity and the ambiguity of the Soviet military challenge.

Second, the fine line is important in shaping one's approach to superpower rivalry in areas of conflict. Those who see few nuances or complications in the Soviet use of force, only an increasing boldness, are not likely to harbor much hope for anything other than a response in kind. Those who think the evolving Soviet strategy in conflict areas is more incomplete, tentative, and circumscribed are more likely to envisage reaching mutually acceptable limitations on each superpower's use of force. There ought to be no illusion that the Soviets can be talked into greater restraint, but, if they are still feeling their way when it comes to military involvement abroad, a balanced Western strategy combining firmness (meaning military strength) with dialogue has a chance of affecting the way the Soviet Union intrudes in local conflicts.

Third, one's view of the Soviet approach to military power decisively influences one's attitude toward arms control. If one disbelieves in the mixed character of Soviet military efforts, in the impact of Western, particularly U.S., military policy on Soviet thinking, and in the Soviet capacity to show restraint, arms control becomes a marginal proposition, with deservedly dim prospects. If one sees the sources and nature of the Soviet military effort as more complex and the Soviet capacity to adjust to Western concerns as greater, then arms control becomes more sensible and important. Only those who are willing to entertain the idea of something other than a one-dimensional Soviet approach to military power are likely to notice the changes taking place in basic Soviet attitudes. In truth, the Soviets have come a long way toward embracing notions of "strategic parity," mutual deterrence (and, ironically, in some circles even the notion of mutual assured destruction), and crisis stability. They do not always define these concepts as Westerners do, but the impression of those who debunk the possibilities of arms control because Soviet concepts are fundamentally at odds with Western ones cannot be sustained if one will but look at what is happening to Soviet perspectives.

Similarly, there is an obvious connection between what one thinks the Soviets are up to by increasing their military power in Europe and the expectations one has for arms control. Anyone who believes the Soviet Union is driven to add to its military power by political ambition must doubt the utility of arms control in Europe. Those who think the Soviet Union is at least as much influenced by a more direct set of military considerations are more likely to trust in the basis for arms control if only the process can be wisely structured.

In all this there are two utterly crucial objectives: the first, to persuade Soviet leaders, who have long felt secure only in the confidence that their armies can prevail in war, that their security is better built on knowing only that the other side cannot prevail in war. The second is to persuade them, but not them alone, that the more sensible objective is not to ensure that the gravest risks in any crisis are transferred to the other side, but that they cannot be transferred to your side. For some, these objectives will appear a pipe dream. For others who care about the nuances in the Soviet approach to the political significance of military power they will appear reasonable, even urgent.

NOTES

1. Stanley Hoffmann, "Perception, Reality, and the Franco-American Conflict," *Journal of International Affairs* 21 (1967): 57.

2. Divining Soviet perspectives is a difficult, elusive, and contentious process. Few people, with good reason, are willing to make the effort. Instead, the tendency is to infer Soviet attitudes or even Soviet intentions from Soviet behavior; then to check these impressions against the Soviet literature. The last involves scanning Soviet sources for fragments bearing on the theme under exploration, forming these into patterns responding to hypotheses judged appropriate by Western analysts.

   Although this may be a useful research stage, the study of Soviet foreign policy must be pushed beyond. If we are to be accurate in assessing Soviet views, we will have to build from the ground up: getting to know individuals, not merely by reading them but by speaking with them, deriving images of how different segments of the foreign and military policy elite think from specific knowledge of the way particular individuals within it think, and reconstructing prevailing Soviet perspectives from a complex pattern of specific views, rather than imputing to Soviet leaders and elites frameworks of thought that are largely a residual category of our notions about the nature of the Soviet system or the essence of Soviet foreign policy.

3. I have in mind essays such as the following:

   Robert J. Art, "To What Ends Military Power?" *International Security* (Spring 1980): 3-35;

   Laurence Martin, "The Role of Military Force in the Nuclear Age," in *Strategic Thought in the Nuclear Age* edited by Laurence Martin (Baltimore: The Johns Hopkins University Press, 1979), pp. 1-29;

   and older classics such as

   Klaus Knorr, *On the Uses of Military Power in the Nuclear Age* (Princeton, N.J.: Princeton University Press, 1966);

   Stanley Hoffmann, *The State of War* (New York: Praeger, 1965);

   Robert E. Osgood and Robert W. Tucker, *Force, Order, and Justice* (Baltimore: The Johns Hopkins University Press, 1967);

   and Bernard Brodie, *War and Politics* (New York: Macmillan, 1973).

4. The best illustrations are

   Thomas C. Schelling, *Arms and Influence* (New Haven, Conn.: Yale University Press, 1966);

   Glenn H. Snyder, *Deterrence and Defense* (Princeton, N.J.: Princeton University Press, 1961);

   Herman Kahn, *On Escalation: Metaphors and Scenarios* (New York: Praeger, 1965);

Oran Young, *The Politics of Force* (Princeton, N.J.: Princeton University Press, 1968);

Robert Jervis, "Deterrence Theory Revisited," *World Politics* (January 1979), pp. 289-324.

5. Schelling, *Arms and Influence*, p. vi.

6. Still, the quarrel is a bit of a phony, and has been for most of the last twenty years. In fact an essential consensus exists on the following proposition: Force is of diminishing utility (because the range of problems for which it offers no solution is growing) but far from useless (because the problems which it does address remain important); it is of diminishing "usability" (because of the increasing costs associated with the application of force) but far from unused (because the costs do not in all cases outweigh anticipated gains nor are they in all cases well-calculated). Though the degree of change in all four categories is a real and crucial source of disagreement, one ought not to overlook this underlying consensus.

7. The phrase is Osgood and Tucker's in *Force, Order, and Justice*, p. 26.

8. Ibid.

9. Schelling, *Arms and Influence*, p. 2.

10. Martin, "The Role of Military Force in the Nuclear Age," p. 12.

11. Osgood and Tucker, *Force, Order, and Justice*, p. 26.

12. Michael Howard, "The Forgotten Dimensions of Strategy," *Foreign Affairs* (Summer 1979): 975-86.

13. In addition to Michael Howard, who has long argued the point, see Jan M. Lodal, "Deterrence and Nuclear Strategy," *Daedalus* (Fall 1980), especially pp. 157-60; and Richard R. Burt, "Washington and the Atlantic Alliance: The Hidden Crisis," in *National Security in the 1980s: From Weakness to Strength* edited by W. Scott Thompson (San Francisco: Institute for Contemporary Studies, 1980), especially pp. 119-21.

14. I am mindful that several Western authors have wrestled with the ethnocentric aspects of U.S. deterrence theory. See the interesting though idiosyncratic book of Ken Booth, *Strategy and Ethnocentrism* (New York: Holmes and Meier, 1979), especially pp. 63-93; for indirect commentary, the important early essay of Bruce Russett, "The Calculus of Deterrence," *Journal of Conflict Resolution* (June 1963): 97-109; and the excellent study by Alexander George and Richard Smoke, *Deterrence in American Foreign Policy* (New York: Columbia University Press, 1974), especially pp. 58-87.

But here I am not concerned with the fact that the United States and the Soviet Union, or for that matter France and China, deal differently with the threat of nuclear war; rather, that the way the United States has chosen to deal with the threat of nuclear war affects its interpretation of the Soviet Union's choice. It is a matter of our assuming that, were we doing as the Soviets, we would be doing it for certain reasons, which in fact may not be theirs.

15. Laurence Martin, "Force in Modern Societies: Its Place in International Politics," *Adelphi Papers* 102 (Winter 1973): 14.

16. G. A. Trofimenko, *SShA: Politika, voina, ideologiya* (Moscow: Mysl, 1976), p. 293. One commentator has even found support for the Soviet position in Clausewitz's work, which given Lenin's admiration for *On War*, a fact this author notes, serves as something of a substitute for Lenin's own writings. He has located a quote in the Clausewitz book contending that as politics grow more "grandiose and powerful," so does war, until, at some point, "war attains its absolute form." He uses this to argue that, "In other words, [Clausewitz] anticipated that war might exceed its political bounds, begin to act according to its own laws, and, when this happens, cease to be a means of rational policy, turning into an end in itself." (Vadim Kortunov, "Za vysokii uroven effektivnosti ideologicheskoi raboty," *Kommunist* 10 (July 1980): 96–97.)

17. General-Major N. A. Talensky, "The Late War: Some Reflections," *International Affairs* 5 (May 1965), p. 15.

18. Rear Admiral V. Shelyag, *Krasnaya Zvezda*, February 7, 1974, p. 2. Marxist–Leninists, other significant military spokesmen have said, "do not confuse" the problem of war's essence with the "problem of war as a means of policy." (A. S. Milovidov and V. G. Kozlov, *The Philosophical Heritage of V. I. Lenin and Problems of Contemporary War* (Moscow: Voennoe Izdatelstvo, 1972), p. 50.)

19. Tomashevsky, *Leninskie idei.*

20. G. A. Arbatov, *Ideologicheskaya borba v sovremennykh mezhdunarodnykh otnosheniyakh* (Moscow: Politizdat, 1970), p. 72.

21. See V. M. Kulish, "Détente, International Relations, and Military Might," *Co-existence* 14, no. 2 (1977), p. 182. And on the influence of Soviet military power on West Germany's policy toward the USSR, see V. I. Popov, *A Study of Soviet Foreign Policy*, quoted by David D. Finley, *Some Aspects of Conventional Military Capability in Soviet Foreign Relations*, ACIS Working Paper no. 20, University of California at Los Angeles, February 1980, pp. 39–40.

22. Soviet writers also use the term *correlation of forces* in more specific ways. Georgy Shakhnazarov refers to the correlation of forces in "some sectors" or quarters, by which he presumably means geographical regions, suggesting that "short-run prognoses" or comparisons are possible in this instance. (See G. Shakhnazarov, "K probleme sootnosheniya sil v mire," *Kommunist* 3 [February 1974] : 86.)

At times in the past, military men have talked about a "correlation of forces of nuclear weapons," a term referring to the factors determining the strategic nuclear balance before and after a nuclear exchange. For a sample, see the items from declassified issues of *Voennaya Mysl* in *Strategic Review* (Fall 1979): 90-95.

23. As a practical tool for understanding international politics, however, the concept of the correlation of forces is almost worthless—at least in its present rudimentary form. The Soviets themselves confess the near impossibility of calculating something as elusive as "the level and nature of the political and economic development of the two social systems, the military potential of different countries, the influence on the masses of various views and ideas, the role and influence of social movements, the prestige and appeal of state policies," and a great many more equally difficult comparisons. (A Vakhrameyev, "Détente and the World Balance of Forces," *International Affairs* 1 [January 1979]: 81.) "Many of the factors" comprising the "general correlation of forces in the world," Georgy Shakhnazarov writes, "are exceedingly difficult to calculate. Some of them fluctuate and are capable of unpredictability." In private, Soviet academics admit that the process of giving the concept content and turning it into something analytically useful has scarcely begun.

24. V.M. Kulish, ed., *Voennaya sila i mezhdunarodnye otnosheniya* (Moscow: Mezhdunarodnye otnosheniya, 1972), p. 37.

25. Ibid., p. 39.

26. Kulish, "Détente, International Relations, and Military Might," p. 184.

27. "The correlation of forces is not merely a matter of military might, although in the final analysis this factor is decisive" according to Georgy Shakhnazarov, in "The Victory—the World Balance of Strength—Peaceful Coexistence," *New Times* 19 (May 1975): 4-6.

28. N. Lebedev, "Socialism and the Restructuring of International Relations," *International Affairs* 2 (February 1978): 9, quoting a book edited by Richard Rosecrance, *America as an Ordinary Country: U.S. Foreign Policy and the Future* (Ithaca: Cornell University Press, 1976).

29. Ibid., p. 10.

30. Utility, I recognize, is not always what determines whether force is used. We may be reentering a period where the great powers resort to arms more often, quite apart from the solution this provides (or impedes) to the problems supposedly being addressed. In that case the Soviet process of rethinking the place of military power in international politics—a process that has gone quite far in some academic circles—will begin reversing itself.

31. L. Vidyasova and N. Khomutov, "NATO—A Weapon for Imperialist Aggression," *International Affairs* 5 (May 1979): 35.

32. Rather typically, Soviet writers will explore in detail adjustments in U.S. military policy, particularly strategic doctrine, implying these are of great political significance, only to offer the following: In the early 1970s the United States was again struggling with the problem of "what was to be done that [the United States' strategic nuclear power] could be used to

resolve international contradictions without submitting to the threat of 'unacceptable losses in population, cities, and industry?' In other words . . . all attention revolved around . . . the question, What was to be done to make nuclear war 'acceptable'?" The point is taken no further. From R.G. Bogdanov, M.A. Milshtein, and L.S. Semeiko, eds., *SShA: Voenno-strate-gicheskie kontseptsii* (Moscow: Izdatelstvo "Nauka," 1980), p. 206.

33. The point has been made a number of times over the last decade. For a recent illustration, see V. Petrovsky, "Kontseptsii sily i ikh evolyutsiya," *Mirovaya ekonomika i mezhdunarodnye otnosheniya* 4 (April 1979): 36–44. The Soviet argument has a telling vagueness, but so does Harold Brown's comment in the 1980 posture statement: "Without them [strategic nuclear capabilities] the Soviet Union could threaten the extinction of the United States and its allies. With them, our forces become meaningful instruments of military and *political* power." (Emphasis added.)

34. In the early years of postwar U.S. strategy, Henry Trofimenko has recently written, deterrence was directed against a country that "was *physically unable* to directly attack the United States with conventional weapons, and was equally unable to initiate a nuclear strike against the United States because it lacked both nuclear weapons and corresponding delivery vehicles." In this circumstance, he contends, "American deterrence of the Soviet Union thus acquired an offensive rather than a defensive character." For, he goes on, "what was being deterred was not the Soviet military threat to the United States, which should have been the case according to the classical concept of deterrence, but a hypothetical Soviet threat to 'American security interests,' which could mean any set of U.S. foreign policy objectives." (Henry Trofimenko, "Changing Attitudes toward Deterrence," ACIS Working Paper 25, Center for International and Strategic Affairs, University of California at Los Angeles, July 1980, p. 5, emphasis in original.)

35. For only a small but representative sample, see

V. M. Kulakov, *Ideologiya agressii* (Moscow, 1970);

V. I. Lan, *SShA v voennye i poslevoennye gody* (Moscow: "Nauka," 1978);

Yu. M. Melnikov, *Vneshnepoliticheskie doktriny SSha* (Moscow: "Nauka," 1970);

A. A. Toporonin, "Doktrina 'balansa sil' i Vashington," *SShA: Ekonomika, politika, ideologiya* no. 11 (November 1970): 8–20.

36. G.A. Trofimenko, *SShA: Politika, voina, ideologiya* (Moscow: Mysl, 1976).

37. Ibid., p. 157, In reading Trofimenko, one is reminded of a recent little book by Colin Gray, *The Geopolitics of the Nuclear Era: Heartland, Rimlands, and the Technological Revolution* (New York: Crane, Russak, 1977), which applies a similar conceptual framework to the Soviet Union.

38. Remember poor Mrs. Eden, who, Khrushchev would have us believe, made dinner conversation by asking, "Tell me, what sort of missiles do you have? Will they fly a long way?" To which he responded, "Yes, they have a very long range. They could easily reach your island and quite a bit farther." (N.S. Khrushchev, *Khrushchev Remembers* (Boston: Little, Brown, 1970), p. 405. This occurred during his visit to London in spring 1956.) More to the point, Khrushchev vaguely, though explicitly, threatened the British and French with nuclear retaliation in the late stages of the 1956 Suez war, and the NATO countries on several occasions before and after the 1958 Berlin crisis. He himself confessed the game he was playing: "Of course, we tried to derive maximum political advantage from the fact that we were the first to launch our rockets into space. We wanted to exert pressure on American militarists—and also influence the minds of more reasonable politicians—so that the United States would start treating us better." (*Khrushchev Remembers: The Last Testament* (1974), p. 53.) Earlier he says, "It always sounded good to say in public speeches that we could hit a fly at any distance with our missiles" (p. 47).

39. Vadim Kortunov, "The Class Roots of Militarism," *New Times* 32 (August 1979): 5.

40. The 1976 Soviet military encyclopedia, under the entry "Military-technical superiority," says, "Soviet military doctrine . . . gives a program of actions for ensuring military-technical superiority over the armed forces of probable enemies." (Quoted by David Holloway, "Military Power and Political Purpose in Soviet Policy," *Daedalus* (Fall 1980): 30, fn. 22). Soon after, however, the Soviet political leadership began stressing the Soviet Union's commitment not to seek superiority. The first references occurred late in 1976 and in Brezhnev's Tula speech of January 18, 1977. Since then he and his colleagues have often repeated that "the Soviet Union is effectively ensuring its defense capability, but it does not, and will not, seek military superiority over the other wide. We do not seek to upset the approximate equilibrium of military strength existing at present, say, between East and West in Central Europe, or between the USSR and the USA. But in return we insist that no one else should seek to upset it in his favor." (*Pravda*, November 3, 1977.)

    Two points are worth making about nations avowing or disavowing the aim of military superiority: (1) While foreswearing it may be of dubious political consequence, proclaiming the ambition is altogether different. (2) The political impact of one or more countries declaring superiority to be their objective depends greatly on how everyone, particularly the other side or sides, judges the prevailing military balance. If the Soviet leadership, for example, shares the Western perception of a balance that has turned or is turning against NATO and the United States, the effect will be of one kind. If the Soviet leadership genuinely does not, the effect will obviously be quite dissimilar. Other points might be made as well: The political effect also will depend on what a nation does. A nation that declares superiority (or a margin of safety) to be its objective and then does something about it will produce one set of effects; the nation that declares superiority to be its objective and then falters will produce another set.

41. Trofimenko, "Changing Attitudes toward Deterrence," p. 18.

42. "Countering the Soviet Threat," Committee on the Present Danger (May 9, 1980), p. 6.

43. One recent noteworthy exception is Barry M. Blechman and Stephen S. Kaplan, *Force without War* (Washington, D.C.: The Brookings Institution, 1978). The reader will not be surprised to learn that it is a very widely cited source among Soviet authors. A forthcoming companion volume on the Soviet uses of force, edited by Kaplan, presumably will be given less attention.

44. One exceptionally able commentator who does deal with this side of Soviet foreign policy is Seweryn Bialer, *Stalin's Successors: Leadership, Stability, and Change in the Soviet Union* (New York: Cambridge University Press, 1980), pp. 233–39. See also Harry Gelman's chapter in this volume.

45. This does not mean that Soviet observers fail to recognize the many other forms of U.S. power, in particular, economic power. Nor does it mean that they refuse to acknowledge their own country's dependency on military power, which, given the United States' lead in these other respects, derives from "the law of comparative advantage." (David Holloway uses the phrase in "Military Power and Political Purpose in Soviet Policy," p. 17.)

46. Lev Semeiko and others consistently described doctrinal changes like the James Schlesinger notion of "limited nuclear options" and new programs like the MK12A, Trident II, and MX as merely harbingers of a more intense effort to realize the kind of disarming first-strike capability U.S. leaders had never despaired of achieving. (See Bogdanov et al., *SShA: Voenno-strategicheskie kontseptsii*, pp. 169–215.)

His colleague Mikhail Milshtein has been more discriminating. (See M.A. Milshtein, "Nekotorye kharakternye cherty sovremennoi voennoi doktriny SShA," *SShA: Ekonomika, politika, ideologiya* 5 (May 1980): 9–18.) He stresses the changes taking place in American thinking. The increasing accuracy of U.S. systems and the increasing numbers of warheads make it possible for the Americans to indulge the old habit "of seeking to make nuclear arms useful and their application acceptable." At one point he then says of Presidential Directive 59, "the new conception envisaging the use of strategic offensive forces chiefly against military objectives in essence can be *potentially* (my emphasis) regarded as one of a disarming first strike, for the uninterrupted aspiring to greater accuracy and the acquisition of invulnerable mobile systems leads to the material achievement of the conception." (p. 15).

47. Trofimenko, "Changing Attitudes toward Deterrence," p. 25. For an interesting compatible analysis, see A.G. Arbatov, "Strategicheskii paritet i politika administratsii Kartera," *SShA: Ekonomika, politika, ideologiya* 11 (November 1980): 29–40.

48. Ibid., pp. 20–21.

49. The book is *SShA i mezhdunarodno-politicheskie krizisy*, cited earlier. Zhurkin notes the neglect in his introduction, a neglect others must also have noted, because his book was given a highly favorable review in *Pravda*, April 8, 1975.

50. Ibid., p. 27.

51. Zhurkin reviews in detail the growth of the U.S. ability to project force during the 1960s, ibid., pp. 48–57.

52. Indeed, with the repudiation of the doctrine of massive retaliation, according to the Soviet view, an essential purpose of strategic doctrine had become the preservation of U.S. military options at lower levels, or, as Georgy Arbatov puts it, "to give the U.S.A. a free hand to fight 'local' wars in different parts of the world." See his *Ideologicheskaya borba v sovremennykh mezhdunarodnykh otnosheniyakh*, cited earlier, p. 302.

53. Milshtein, "Nekotorye kharakternye cherty sovremennoi voennoi doktriny SShA," p. 15.

54. Khrushchev, *Khrushchev Remembers*, pp. 367–73.

55. Ibid., pp. 368–69. It is worth noting that Khrushchev still thought so seventeen years after the event and after he was out of power.

56. Not only can this be inferred without great difficulty from conversations with Soviet commentators, it does not take much reading between the lines to see the same thing in the more thoughtful Soviet accounts of Afghan developments. See, in particular, V. Sidenko, "Two Years of the Afghan Revolution," *New Times* 17 (April 1980): 18–25.

57. Martin, "The Role of Military Force in the Nuclear Age," p. 23.

58. Kulish, *Voennaya sila i mezhdunarodnye otnosheniya*, p. 24.

59. Ibid.

60. See the chapter written by A.M. Dudin and Yu. N. Listvinov ibid.

61. For this part of the Gorshkov exhortation, see Michael MccGwire and John McDonnell, eds., *Soviet Naval Influence: Domestic and Foreign Dimensions* (New York: Praeger, 1977); James M. McConnell and Bradford Dismukes, "Soviet Diplomacy of Force in the Third World," *Problems of Communism* (January–February 1979): 14–27; and by the same authors, *Soviet Naval Diplomacy* (New York: Pergamon Press, 1979). Gorshkov comes back to the issue most recently in "Slavnoe detishche sovetskogo naroda," *Kommunist* 3 (February 1980): 43–56.

62. General A.A. Yepishev, "Istoricheskaya missiya armii sotsialisticheskogo gosudarstva," *Kommunist* 7 (May 1972): 66.

63. For a recent example, see Barry R. Posen and Stephen W. Van Evera, "Overarming and Underwhelming," *Foreign Policy* (Fall 1980): 99–118. In addition Stansfield Turner, "The Naval Balance: Not Just a Numbers Game," *Foreign Affairs* (January 1977): 339–54; Michael T. Klare, "Superpower Rivalry at Sea," *Foreign Policy* (Winter 1975–76): 86–96; and the earlier cited book by MccGwire and McDonnell. Though now changing, there can be no dispute that the Soviet Union came to have enhanced force projection capability as a function of force improvements for the European and Asian theaters. At the same time the fact that Soviet force projection capabilities are incomplete and unbalanced does not diminish their increasing formidableness. Nor, of course, does it mean that capabilities developed for other missions cannot come to have a new set of missions far from Eurasia.

64. S.I. Filinov, "Vooruzhennaya borba i okeanskie kommunikatsii," *Morskoi sbornik* (March 1965), pp. 33, 38–41, as quoted in Steve F. Kime, *A Soviet Navy for the Nuclear Age* (Washington, D.C.: National Defense University, 1980), p. 16.

65. For a view attributing complex motives to the Soviet Union, see Gerhard Wettig, *East–West Security Relations on the Eurostrategic Level* Berichte des Bundesinstituts für ostwissenschaftliche und internationale Studien, August 1980. See also the chapter by James Martin in this volume.

66. This means building from the ground up; it means returning to the problem of minimally effective conventional defense; and it means abjuring (nuclear) deterrence as a substitute for defense. See Chapter 1 by Philip A. Karber in this volume.

67. See Thomas W. Wolfe, *Soviet Strategy at the Crossroads* (Cambridge: Harvard University Press, 1964), pp. 172–88. See also John Erickson "Soviet Military Posture and Policy in Europe," in *Soviet Strategy in Europe* edited by Richard Pipes (New York: Crane, Russak, 1976), pp. 169–209, and "Soviet Theater-Warfare Capability: Doctrines, Deployments, Capabilities," in *The Future of Soviet Military Power* edited by Lawrence L. Whetten (New York: Crane, Russak, 1976), pp. 117–56. For an elaborate effort to describe the Soviet build-up since 1965 (as reviewed in Chapter 1 of this volume) in terms of a systematic and political pursuit of negating NATO's strategy of flexible response (in effect, though not necessarily only in explicit doctrine) see Phillip A. Karber's Chapter 6 in this volume. See also James Martin's chapter in this volume.

4 THE SOVIET CONCEPTION OF EUROPE AND ARMS NEGOTIATIONS

John van Oudenaren

Soviet propaganda has praised what it calls the "decisive changes" that occurred in international relations in the early seventies. Along with SALT and the U.S.–Soviet détente, these changes included the signing of agreements in Europe ratifying the results of World War II and sealing the division of Germany. The German settlement was followed by the convening of the all-European conference, a dramatic increase in trade and human contacts between East and West, and the general absence of crisis in Europe for the better part of a decade.

Mutual acceptance of the status quo by West Germany and the USSR also paved the way for serious arms control discussion in Europe. Unlike previous attempts at force reduction, which usually had been seen as part of a package designed to settle the "German problem," the talks of the seventies were able to proceed uncomplicated by territorial issues.[1] After the European "settlement" of this period, Soviet spokesmen went even further than their Western counterparts in their assessment of the changes that had occurred. They now claimed that arms limitation had not only become a possibility but was a necessity mandated by the existing political situation, a sentiment echoed in the campaign for military détente as a follow-up to political détente.

Whatever the merits of this propaganda claim, it underscores the link in Soviet thinking between a certain conception of the political

161

status quo in Europe and the Soviet Union's arms control strategy. In the Soviet view the essence of the status quo is its capacity for constant change. Change is of three kinds: political change enhancing Soviet security and the stability of the socialist system; political change seen to further long-term Soviet revolutionary aspirations; and change in the relationship between the superpowers and its effect on Europe. In reality the distinctions between these changes are blurred by Soviet policy, which pursues many objectives—minimal and maximal, political and military, regional and global.

POLITICAL CHANGE AND SOVIET SECURITY

At the time of the European "settlement" observers generally agreed that it represented a considerable triumph for Soviet diplomacy, and for Leonid Brezhnev personally. However, the debate in the West over the ratification of the USSR's wartime territorial gains tended to obscure the extent to which Ostpolitik and Conference on Security and Cooperation in Europe (CSCE) marked a new beginning in, as well as a culmination of, Soviet diplomatic efforts in Europe. Just as the Brandt government accepted the status quo in order to change it, so the Soviets, having attained their minimum territorial requirements vis-à-vis Western Europe, and having stabilized Eastern Europe by military intervention, were ready to accept and work within the Western status quo, the better to influence and ultimately to undermine it. Pierre Hassner for one was quick to recognize that détente meant a new and possibly dangerous engagement by the Soviets in Western Europe and the onset of the "hot peace."[2]

As long as the postwar disposition of Europe remained at least theoretically open, the Soviets could from time to time propose some ambitious scheme aimed at fundamentally transforming the continent to Soviet advantage. Usually this involved isolating West Germany in some way and limiting or expelling the American military presence, which the Soviets had never ceased to regard as "abnormal." 1954 had seen Foreign Minister Molotov propose the first plan for an "all-European security system," 1957 the Rapacki plan for a nuclear-free zone in Central Europe, and the midsixties, prior to the renewal of the NATO treaty, the Warsaw Pact proposal for the simultaneous dissolution of the blocs, or, as a first step, of their military organizations. At the Twenty-third Congress of the CPSU, in 1966, Foreign Minister Gromyko again raised the idea of an all-European conference, without the United States and clearly in opposition to it.

By way of contrast, the 1970s saw no such initiatives aimed at radically transforming the European political landscape. Rather, the basic Soviet line became that Europe *had already been transformed*, by Helsinki and by détente itself, and that what remained to be accomplished was simply the steady "businesslike" implementation of the Helsinki accords and the further development of bilateral relations that had begun with de Gaulle and with Brandt. The message to Europe became that there was nothing fundamentally wrong with the present political order, provided that it continued to move in the near "irreversible" directions laid down by the Helsinki Final Act and the Soviet Union's own policy of détente. The Soviet Union presented itself as not merely resigned to the status quo, but as in fact its greatest protector, claiming that it now had a shared interest with the other European states in upholding and implementing the new order. Meanwhile, the attack on NATO and the American military presence continued but was made in the name of upholding the status quo rather than overturning it. Ostpolitik and CSCE had been possible only because the Soviets did not insist on the breakup of NATO and the withdrawal of American forces as part of a European and German settlement; once these had been achieved, however, the Soviets began to claim that war was being progressively "excluded" from the continent and that as a result NATO was increasingly irrelevant to the new realities in Europe.

The desire to cultivate a positive image in Europe explains the timing of a number of important tactical reversals in Soviet policy in the early seventies. In 1972 Brezhnev declared that it would be possible to establish "some form of business relationship between the inter-state commercial-economic organizations which exist in Europe,"[3] thereby abandoning the long-standing Soviet call for the summary dissolution of the European Economic Community. The second important change was the abandonment, for all practical purposes, of the call for the simultaneous dissolution of NATO and the Warsaw Pact. This standard propaganda item appeared in the peace program of the Twenty-fourth Party Congress (1971), but was left out altogether in the peace program of the next party congress (1976).

The third reversal came in the area of Soviet attitudes toward mutual force reduction talks in Central Europe. In June 1968 when the NATO countries first proposed such talks, the Soviets and their allies failed to respond to the NATO initiative. Instead the East called for an all-European conference to discuss political problems that, while not related to military questions as such, the Soviets contended were central to the issue of European security. By 1971, however, the Soviets agreed, as part of the arrangements to convene CSCE, to open Mutual and Balanced Force Reduction talks (MBFR) one month after the start of an all-European conference.[4]

The reversal on MBFR, although in part the result of Western demands, was characteristic of the other Soviet policy reversals in this period. Initially the Soviet line was that discussions on concrete disarmament made no sense until an overall political settlement had been achieved. Later, however, the Soviet position became that precisely *because* such a political settlement had been reached, concrete military (as well as economic) measures were necessary in order to preserve political détente and to give progressively greater "content" to the formal agreements that had been or were soon to be adopted.

Despite these propaganda claims, in the early MBFR negotiations the Soviets showed little interest in coming to an actual agreement. Faced with a favorable military balance and continuing internal problems in NATO, the Soviets had every incentive to stall. MBFR was merely a forum in which to reiterate their understanding of the political status quo. Many of the early battles about the general principles of the negotiations, the dispute over "balanced" for example, were fought not only to gain potential advantages in the military area but to assure that arms reduction negotiation did not become a roundabout way of once again challenging Soviet hegemony in Eastern Europe.

The image of the USSR as an occupying power, whose presence in Central Europe was, as the Soviets said about the corresponding American forces, "abnormal," had at one time justified the expectation that a drastic improvement in Western Europe's security might come about in the course of a political settlement that would remove these troops. The Soviets had at various times hinted that such a trade-off was at least a possibility. (And as Brezhnev's October 1979 speech indicated, the Soviets are still ready to use the political allure of withdrawal of troops from Eastern Europe—in this case East Germany—to influence West European perceptions).[5] Now however, a political "settlement" had been achieved, but the Soviets were still in the heart of Europe, claiming that their presence had been fully legitimized by the West itself. Getting Soviet soldiers out of Central Europe could no longer be broached in political terms but only in the language of technical arms control: "parity," "balance," "approximate equality," and so on.

Having depoliticized the question of frontiers and the related question of the permanence of socialism in Eastern Europe, the Soviets for the first time agreed that force levels in East Germany and Poland were in principle negotiable provided cuts were made on a mutual basis. The very negotiability presupposed, however, that the West had relinquished the political right to question their presence as such. NATO's initial demand for balanced cuts was unacceptable to the Soviets, not just (and perhaps not primarily) because it had unfavorable implications for the Warsaw Pact in the military sense but because it would repoliticize the issue of Soviet forces in Central Europe. Acknowledgment of geographical asymmetries to the detriment of politicolegal "equality" would have undercut the recently ratified right of the sovereign GDR and of Poland to host Soviet troops on their soil. Attempts to factor in these asymmetries were branded accordingly as attempts to seek one-sided political as well as military advantages.

Another example of how the Soviets used the early MBFR talks to defend their interpretation of the political status quo and to prejudice the future evolution of that status quo was their insistence, underscored by the initial refusal to receive NATO envoy Manlio Brosio, that the negotiations were to take place not on a bloc-to-bloc level, but as discussions in which each nation participated only in its own individual capacity.[6] This insistence carried over into the demand for individual national subceilings on troop strength, which not only had military advantages—most notably by placing a cap on the potential size of the *Bundeswehr*—but which also reflected the USSR's preferred political vision for Europe: that of a collection of nominally sovereign, formally equal states, governed by the Helsinki principles and bound together by multiple agreements on trade, security, and political cooperation. This would leave open the possibility of the eventual formation of some kind of all-European security system, outside of and implicitly in opposition to the bloc structures. At a minimum it would preclude closer West European political and military integration and hinder the link-up of West German military and industrial power with the existing French and British nuclear deterrents.

As this approach to MBFR indicates, for the Soviets the discussion of military balances could not be separated from the existing political situation, nor from Soviet assessments of potential political evolution, either favorable or unfavorable. The purpose of arms limitation for the Soviets was not just enhancement of security, but the encouragement of political change that would abolish insecurity altogether. As a Soviet commentator phrased it, "today it is a matter not of military and political measures to eliminate the threat of aggression, but of political steps to exclude the very emergence of such a threat."[7] The campaign to make détente "irreversible" reflects the same desire.

Some preliminary conclusions about the Soviet approach to arms control are thus: The Soviets prefer what in effect amounts to an apolitical pursuit of political arms limitation, in contrast to the Western preference for a political agreement limited to technical arms control.[8] By technical arms control is meant limiting the possibilities for surprise attack, accidental war, and peacetime intimidation by dealing with deployments regarded as destabilizing. The USSR pursues stability rather than reduction as an end in itself. The Soviet concept of political arms control (they reject the word *control* itself) stresses arms limitation (their preferred term) as an "equal" process whose purpose is to symbolize the formally equal status of the two sides within the context of "normalized" political relations. It does not take account of the intimidating character of Warsaw Pact military power in peacetime. Rather, it seeks to maintain the same military balances and the same force postures but simply at lower levels. Conversely, if the Soviets have fears arising from potential instability on the Western side (for example the case of the forward-based systems, whose vulnerability could tempt first use of nuclear weapons by the West), they show no inclination to negotiate on these matters. Rather, as the SS-20 deployment indicates, the Soviet response seems to be a quest for unilateral deterrence and the ability to dominate the escalation of conflict, rather than peacetime negotiation.[9]

While emphasizing the political symbolism of arms reduction, the Soviets sought to foster the notion that reduction was an apolitical, "businesslike" process following in almost mechanical fashion from the existing political situation. After Helsinki they all but obscured the fact that MBFR and CSCE were originally established as parallel and equal forums for the discussion of East–West issues, with the one originally proposed by NATO (the military one at that), and the other by the Warsaw Pact countries. The USSR increasingly claimed sponsorship of both forums, with MBFR in effect subsumed under CSCE (which in turn was subsumed under the Soviet Union's overall sponsorship of détente.)[10]

This notion of military détente as a mechanical rather than a political process grows out of the Soviet interpretation of the Helsinki final act, which is said to govern the détente process in all Europe. The Soviet concept of détente, in that it focuses on factors that constrain only *imperialist* behavior, does not really allow for political initiative on the Western side. All Western proposals must in one way or another be responses to the Soviet Union's own "consistently peace-loving foreign policy," and as such either realistic or reactionary responses to détente as history's "leading trend."

The campaign for military détente thus proceeded on two tracks, one businesslike and mechanical, the other highly politicized. While relegating the substance of arms limitation to businesslike forums like MBFR where lack of progress was ascribed to the Western side, the Soviets seized the political initiative to foster an illusion of constant movement in East–West relations. Paradoxically, this was accomplished by constantly repoliticizing issues like inviolability of frontiers or nonuse of force, which, in typically circular fashion, the Soviets claimed had been settled and therefore necessitated the nonpolitical pursuit of military détente.

In addition to the treaties with the Federal Republic of Germany, the Soviets sought to include the principles of inviolability of frontiers and nonuse of force in the final act at Helsinki. Once this had been achieved, they reiterated the same principles in bilateral agreements with many of the Helsinki signatories. Alongside these agreements implying nonuse of any force, the Warsaw Pact called for a treaty among the CSCE members that would ban first use of nuclear weapons. Pretending three years later that the West had rejected this proposal on the technical grounds that the East enjoyed conventional superiority, Brezhnev came forward with an even more sweeping proposal, which would include conventional as well as nuclear arms: "something like a non-aggression pact between the members of the all-European conference."[11] Other, less specific proposals, such as Poland's call for an all-European conference on disarmament and the more recent Warsaw Pact proposal for a "world summit" to discuss global tensions are all part of this sustained political offensive.[12]

A measure of the concern felt in Moscow about Western rearmament is the extent to which the Soviets have made concrete concessions in MBFR that undercut elements of their maximal political program. The Warsaw Pact side accepted some form of de facto asymmetrical cuts (although the "data base" discrepancy largely negated the practical effect of this concession), and in its proposal for common bloc ceilings of 900,000 as opposed to national subceilings at least implicitly accepted the bloc-to-bloc character of the talks. These new proposals have been part of a Soviet effort over the last few years to revitalize the MBFR talks, which the Soviets seem to have concluded were a low-risk way of lending credibility to the campaign against major weapons programs, such as the cruise missiles and Pershing IIs, which themselves would have to be discussed outside MBFR.

It is clear, however, that Moscow continues to view security not simply in terms of weapons deployments and manpower but also in the context of political change. If military détente is in part a campaign for concrete disarmament objectives, it is also a lever to expand Soviet influence in Western Europe, to engineer favorable change in Europe "from above" as it were. Already in 1973 Foreign Minister Gromyko told the assembled CSCE delegations from both East and West that the final document would define the norms of peaceful coexistence throughout the continent.[13] Since Helsinki the Soviets have in fact interpreted the final act as a document giving the USSR a formal, quasi-juridical right to be consulted in the affairs of Western Europe and to exercise an influence over the process of economic and political integration in the West.

The Helsinki final act is said to outlaw Western radio broadcasts to the USSR, the Olympic boycott, and the appearance of "anti-Soviet" articles in the Western press.[14] In the security area the Soviets have invoked both the principles of the final act as well as the "spirit of Helsinki" in their efforts to block Western defense efforts. As in the economic and the cultural realms, the thrust of the Soviet line is that under CSCE auspices Western Europe is committed to seeking all-European solutions to problems, which in effect means that East-West talks must take precedence over unilateral actions. As Vadim Zagladin expressed it

> In our view, you see, Soviet security is identical to French, Belgian, or British security. The only way of insuring that security is to pursue the struggle which we have been waging for years.
>
> We must start on the basis of the principles adopted by all the European countries in Helsinki. *We do not want to impose anything on anybody which has not already been accepted in principle.*[15]

As a matter of practical politics spokesmen like Zagladin have shown considerable skill in using their genuinely (or at least seemingly genuine) defensive concerns to lay the groundwork for a Soviet voice in West European affairs—to "bilateralize" to the extent possible the discussion of security in Europe. The USSR would not be a superpower if it had to discuss its security with the Prime Minister of Italy, or even with the Chancellor of West Germany. And yet this is precisely what the Soviet leaders try to do to stir up concern for their "legitimate" security concerns, which can then serve as the pretext for bilateral security consultations between the USSR and the small and medium-sized powers of Europe. The neutron bomb, arms sales to China, theater nuclear forces, and plans to preposition stocks of materiel in Norway have all achieved a prominence in Soviet propaganda and diplomacy, not just for their intrinsic military significance but for their ability to generate concern and debate in the West about the Soviet Union's security.

These concerns and the debate that surrounds them then set the stage for consultations and, in a new development, Soviet requests for "assurances." Both the neutron bomb episode and the flurry of excitement over China's opening to the West saw President Brezhnev send personal letters to the heads of government in the major European countries, seeking reassurance that Soviet interests would be taken into account.

The Schmidt–Brezhnev communiqué of 1978 stated that both sides agreed to "regular consultations."[16] Other Soviet agreements with West European countries also contain passages adumbrating a consultative element in relations, weaker, to be sure, than the clauses in the treaty with Finland or in the various friendship treaties with Third World countries but still basically reflecting the Soviet penchant for regularized consultation on a quasi-legal basis. As far as the subject matter of bilateral relations is concerned, here again the Soviets have made an effort to reach broad agreement on certain principles of security. The agreement with the Federal Republic of Germany, for example, states that "the two sides deem it important that no one should seek military superiority" and concludes that both sides "proceed from the assumption that approximate equality and parity are sufficient to ensure defense."

These security provisions, as well as the economic and more broadly political aspects of the agreement attest, in the Soviet view, to both sides' desire, in the words of the communiqué itself, "to contribute to continued dynamic development begun by the Conference on Security and Cooperation in Europe." In the next section the question of what this "dynamic development" means to the Soviets is addressed.

SOVIET PERSPECTIVES ON CHANGE IN EUROPE

Whatever motivation there may be on the Western side for signing agreements such as the Schmidt–Brezhnev communiqué, the Soviet leadership undoubtedly takes them quite seriously. As Robert Legvold has noted, the Soviets have worked to place all their relations with the major Western countries on the kind of formal, institutional basis reflected in the Brezhnev–Schmidt summit and the accompanying agreements. This "institutionalized bilateralism," as Legvold calls it, includes not only regularized summitry, but also mutually agreed statements of principles governing relations, trade agreements, and standing economic commissions to promote "international cooperation."[17] Brezhnev, a major architect of this policy on the Soviet side, has no doubt staked his domestic prestige on its success.

He explained the rationale behind the policy to a Party gathering in the following terms:

> The salutary changes in the world, which have become especially appreciable in the 1970s, have been called international détente. These changes are tangible and concrete. They consist in recognizing and enacting in international documents a kind of code of rules for honest and fair relations between countries, which erects a legal and moral-political barrier to those given to military gambles. . . . They consist of a ramified network of agreements covering many areas of peaceful cooperation between states with different social systems.[18]

Like other Soviet utterances about relations with the West, Brezhnev's statement emphasizes two elements: On the one hand détente is said to be based on changes that are "tangible and concrete," and on the other that these changes have been "enacted" in East–West agreements of a legal character. Since détente is defined as a process limiting only imperialist options, "law" and "tangible and concrete" Soviet power are regarded as simply different but complementary and reinforcing constraints on imperialism's ability to unleash a war.

The paradox of détente as defined by Brezhnev is that while, to use his terms, it is both concrete and legal, it is strikingly apolitical.

It rejects any notion of international relations as a process of give and take and of mutual adjustment. ("Irreversibility" may be based on power or on law, but it surely does not describe a political relationship.) In doing so it places an inordinate emphasis both on raw military power, particularly strategic parity, and on a patchwork of international "legal" agreements that range in importance from SALT to the most watered-down joint communiqués.

Marxist–Leninist orthodoxy requires that détente be defined as an objective process brought about by increased Soviet might. As Brezhnev phrased it in his report to the Twenty-fifth Congress, "the passage from cold war . . . to détente was largely connected with changes in the correlation of world forces." Perhaps more interesting than the need to ascribe détente to Soviet power, however, is the parallel between this definition of détente as an apolitical process and the more general Brezhnevian tendency to depoliticize domestic as well as international problems. At home the mission of the Communist party is to build a new socialist order; internationally it is to establish a universal and permanent peace throughout the world. In fulfilling both of these tasks, now said to be "organically" linked, the party seeks to displace the autonomous practice of politics. As Marx phrased it, the "administration of things" replaces "government over men." This in part explains the apolitical pursuit of military détente and the curious emphasis the Soviets place on regularized relations and on legalisms of all sorts.

In downplaying overt conflict over values (the difference between the "social systems") and treating political questions as if they were problems of scientific management, the party has developed what it perceives as a method for controlled change. The process has been described in the domestic context as one of "systematic social engineering":

One of the distinguishing characteristics of the present Soviet regime [is] its deliberate use of depoliticization as a strategy for the management of economic and social change. The effort to play down, if not remove from public view altogether, the ideological and conflict-provoking aspects of policy-formation and of intra-elite relations contrasts sharply with what was a quintessential feature of Soviet political life until recently.[19]

Depoliticization is itself an ideology that helps to administer a more efficient and more complex (but less "utopian") Communist society at home, and support a differentiated (less "revolutionary") policy abroad. It captures the essence of a Soviet system that sees itself as expanding in an almost mechanical fashion and that calls upon Western states to join in "international talks" to ratify the latest fait accompli of socialist achievement, be it the occupation of Afghanistan or the Eurostrategic imbalance. It accounts for that peculiar mixture of legalism and brutality that has come to characterize Soviet policy toward the Third World, where "friendship treaties" legitimize Soviet intervention, which is then followed by the imposition, from without, of an indigenous "proletarian" party with the aid of Soviet, Cuban, and East German advisors.

Turning to Soviet policy toward Europe, one sees many of the same notions of change imposed from above via interstate agreements and high-level "implementation" (economic, political, disarmament), always emphasizing the nominal sovereignty of individual states, and shifting the onus of "interference in the affairs of other countries" onto the United States and NATO. The European order under CSCE is now linked with the overall Soviet achievement, which emphasizes adherence to legality, continuity, controlled management of conflict, and a businesslike approach to problems, including those of arms limitation. This linkage is given the highest ideological sanction in the peace programs of the party congresses, and, more important, in the incorporation of the ten principles of the Helsinki final act into the new Brezhnev constitution.

The inclusion of the language of an East–West agreement in the Soviet constitution has a significance beyond its mere propaganda intent. Ideologues working under the direction of Mikhail Suslov have posited a number of organic relationships in Marxist–Leninist theory that link developments in the Soviet Union with the international environment. Within the socialist commonwealth (under socialist internationalism) "solidarity and mutual assistance" are united with "independence, sovereignty, equality, and non-interference"; outside the socialist commonwealth (under peaceful coexistence, which governs relations between states with different social systems), the "international aims of the working class" are said to be organically linked with "national, patriotic interests."[20] By virtue of its ability to comprehend these organic linkages and by virtue of the growing impact of socialist strength on the international system, the Soviet leadership comes close to claiming, as Robert Legvold has noted, that it can "plan" foreign policy and the evolution of international events, much the way it plans the development of the economy and the building of communism at home.[21]

Soviet ideology stresses not only the growing role of Soviet power on the international stage, but the essential character of the socialist system—the moral superiority of the socialist way of life—as a factor in international relations. As a Soviet commentator recently phrased it:

> The fate of world peace is now directly linked with the new socio-political system, with the military and economic might of the Soviet Union and the other fraternal socialist countries and their steadily growing moral and political prestige.
>
> This is behind the increased role played by socialist foreign policy, its transformative revolutionary strength and its impact on the entire course of world affairs.[22]

The link that Soviet author notes is both instrumental, in the sense that Soviet military and economic power is said to deny options to imperialism, and organic, in that there is now a continuum between the USSR's peace-loving essence, its policies of détente, and the "realistic" and peace-loving response to Soviet policy in the West.

The often exclusive emphasis in the West on the "instrumental" use of Soviet military power to expand communism (in Angola, Ethiopia, South Yemen, and Afghanistan) is misleading in that it juxtaposes what are described as the regime's internal failures (the fading allure of the communist ideal—that is, the *absence* of "moral and political prestige," economic problems, dissidence, possible energy crisis, and so on) with its external successes or would-be successes (use of military power to expand influence in the Third World, to intimidate Europe and Japan). It is questionable, however, whether the Soviet leadership juxtaposes success and failure in quite this way. To assume that it does is to underestimate the sheer momentum of an ideological "will to power" that does not allow for the possibility that the Soviet Union will *not* solve its problems. It would be more correct to compare what the regime sees as its internal *successes* (which may not be recognized as such in the West) with its external successes or prospects therefor.

Above all the Brezhnev regime prides itself on having stabilized the system. Since the fall of Khrushchev there has been controlled mobility within the party, stability of cadres, no radical departures in economic planning, a firm commitment to collective leadership, and steady growth of military and economic power. There is a similar sense of pride, expressed in speeches and party reports, in the stabilization and growth of the "world socialist system." Finally, there is stability to the point of institutionalization in relations with the West, particularly Western Europe, and with Third World countries.

There is no reason to expect that the Soviets see this stable system, which in their view they are creating, as stopping at the frontiers of the USSR or at the borders of the "world socialist system." As one observer put it, "the exclusive conceptual framework for all Soviet thought on politics and society dictates the ultimate domination of the world by a single social structure."[23] This is not to suggest that the Soviets are close to achieving "world domination"; it is to suggest, rather, that their exclusive conceptual framework forces them to see other countries as part of a larger system in which all change is tending toward a single, and largely favorable, outcome.

Soviet thinking on change in the international system downplays the role of isolated, cataclysmic revolutionary upheavals and places a new emphasis on steady but "uneven" development throughout the world as a whole. Europe is seen as a system governed by the laws of peaceful coexistence which are said to be embodied in the Helsinki final act. Within this system various countries are at various uneven stages of development in their progression from détente to irreversible détente. Different countries reflect different levels of integration into this emergent all-European order. In the global context Europe as a whole is seen as part of an emergent "peace zone," in which the European powers become in effect junior allies of the USSR in the struggle for détente. References to a Soviet effort to "split" Europe from the United States misperceive the thrust of Soviet policy as reflected in the Soviet Union's own image of itself and its role in Europe. In the preferred Soviet vision of Europe the norms of peaceful coexistence *take precedence over* the Atlantic Alliance. In the Soviet view, then, it is the United States, in attempting to engineer a return to the cold war, that is doing the "splitting," not of the alliance but of the new all-European order.[24]

Soviet thinking about the West European states and the Western communist parties incorporates many of these assumptions about movement within the larger context of uneven historical development. It places success in the "struggle for peace" prior to the success of domestic revolution, rather than after it as in the traditional

Leninist view. This unevenness explains the continued viability of NATO and of the EEC as a "closed economic bloc." NATO in particular is now said to be the work of small "circles" who are increasingly isolated from the broad masses of public opinion in Europe.

The counterpart of the downplaying of "social system" conflict that this policy requires is an exaggeration of the role of U.S. military power, which alone is said to be sustaining a Western system with inevitable tendencies to "take the road to Moscow." Again it is Robert Legvold who has pointed out the instrumentalism that the Soviets see in U.S. military power, which he finds a mirror image of the instrumental way in which the West sees Soviet power.[25] Legvold is surely correct in identifying this instrumentalism, but seems to imply mistakenly that it derives from residual misunderstanding between the two sides, which if cleared up might somehow further the cause of détente. It may be more accurate, however, to conclude that an instrumental view of U.S. power is actually essential to the ideological coherence of Soviet communism's interpretation of détente. Détente as defined by Brezhnev requires a greatly exaggerated view of "Atlanticist" pressures in order to reduce the difference between the social systems to a mere triviality—a result of uneven development rather than failed revolution—which need not have any implications whatsoever for the threat perceptions of the individual Western states.

In a similar fashion previous Soviet attempts to build an all-European security system at one time required an exaggerated view of West German "revanchism," of West German plans to obtain nuclear weapons, of the danger of a National Socialist revival, and so on. In both cases the Soviet objective was to relativize the East–West division in Europe and to replace it with a spurious sense of collective security with the Western states. Anti-Germanism was to replace anti-Sovietism as the main determinant of alignments in Europe; now anti-Americanism is meant to serve the same purpose.

The Soviet need to overstate the role of U.S. military power is more than just a tactical device to split the United States from its allies and to isolate it in the Third World; exaggeration of the U.S. role is in some sense a mirror image of the regime's exaggerated appraisal of its own role in determining the course of history. To the extent that revolutionary change is now seen by the Soviets as a controlled, creeping process that can to some extent be "planned" by the USSR, "reaction," that which frustrates revolutionary change, is increasingly reduced to a single dimension: that of U.S. power and U.S. imperialism, which alone is seen to prevent the Soviet Union from carrying out its historical mission. The "struggle for peace" then in turn becomes one-dimensional, signifying little more than the destruction of U.S. power.

The campaign for military détente in Europe reflects this emphasis in its strongly and almost exclusively anti-American thrust. Two themes, hostility to NATO as a military organization and greater acceptance of everything besides NATO, are mutually reinforcing in Soviet diplomacy and propaganda: Wherever NATO is not, there all-European cooperation will flourish; wherever all-European cooperation is not flourishing, there will be found the hand of NATO. Hence Soviet commentators emphasize the U.S. role in frustrating "progressive" trends within Western countries and in thwarting the development of beneficial cooperation between member countries and the socialist community. The picture that emerges distorts the reality of both economic cooperation and security. According to one Soviet commentator, nuclear weapons are

> a lever to bring pressure on other countries and a means of interfering in international talks. As seen by the Pentagon, the deployment of neutron weapons on the territory of the FRG will increase its influence on that country. Indeed, it is hard not to predict that the Bonn government's freedom of action in many spheres of domestic and foreign policy will be substantially cut if neutron bombs are deployed in the FRG. As a result, a threat would develop to the numerous beneficial changes that are largely due to the accords between the FRG and the socialist countries, and to the European conference in Helsinki.[26]

"Atlanticism" narrows to a subjective meaning in the sense that its main component is anti-Sovietism and not the West European "social system," an almost exclusively military meaning. At the same time, Soviet propaganda ends up transferring to NATO many of those objective factors, such as the military-industrial complexes and certain of the monopolies (and here a distinction is drawn between monopolies producing arms and monopolies which favor East–West trade), which it overlooks in its more benign critique of the very Western social systems that nurture these organizations.

NATO and the Pentagon become figures of speech for vast complexes of forces (mostly subjective and superstructural, to use Marxist terminology): "journalists in the pay of monopoly-owned newspapers, "international Zionists," "so-called Kremlinologists," and so on. This new brand of anti-Americanism qua anti-NATOism leads to the un-Leninist differentiation of the civil side of West European life, which the Soviet Union continues to criticize only mildly, from the military side, about which it grows increasingly shrill. Even military developments, if strictly domestic (such as the SPD's consistent record of high defense spending) are attacked with less vehemence than is NATO, and are attributed to "contradictions" within these societies and to NATO pressure. Less of West European society is subsumed under the rubric of imperialism, which implied in its original Leninist sense a continuity between the social system and aggression against socialism. Whatever about the West remains aggressive is now isolated from the mainstream and ascribed to NATO "circles" that comprise a small numerical minority, "the followers of the cult of strength."

In attributing all domestic anti-Sovietism to NATO and by extension the United States, the Soviets deprive Western Europe of virtually all independent initiative in economic and security matters. This in turn reinforces the Soviet notion of arms control as a businesslike process, in which steady hard work is required to bring the Europeans eventually around to the Soviet position. At the same time this kind of propaganda lends an air of caricature, of unreality to Soviet discussions of security matters. The vacuous bilateral agreements that can be signed precisely because they contain little of substance are said to represent the "real" Western Europe, while NATO is only the product of external pressure. Agreements pledging mutual support for "parity" and "approximate equality" are then contrasted with the deadlock in more substantively important forums such as MBFR and offered as evidence of NATO resistance to military détente.

NATO itself, interestingly, is not regarded by the Soviets as an association of fifteen member states who determine its objectives and capabilities but as a European counterpart to the Pentagon, namely the Brussels headquarters that has seemingly little connection with the actual political and geographic entity Europe. According to *Krasnaya Zvezda*, the Red Army journal, "it has long been noted that NATO is playing an increasingly autonomous role with respect to its members. . . . The policy implemented in the bloc's name by its leading organs frequently differs markedly from the policy proclaimed by any particular state belonging to it."[27]

In this regard the oft cited Soviet desire to obtain a *droit de regard* over the size of the *Bundeswehr* under MBFR is perhaps overstated. The Soviet Union has been remarkably quiet about the size of the

West German army and almost silent on the subject of the territorial forces of the Federal Republic. On the other hand the sustained and noisy campaign against the neutron bomb, which persisted long after plans to deploy had been dropped, indicates that the Soviets can be selective in their emphasis on the military developments that most threaten them. They tend to focus on nuclear questions that inevitably involve the United States, and that tend to shift responsibility for the nuclear threat onto the United States and its role in NATO. At present, for example, the Soviets have stirred up a vigorous propaganda campaign against prepositioned stocks of materiel in Norway, in which they have raised the unrealistic specter of storage of nuclear weapons on Norwegian soil.

While anti-Americanism is an integral part of the Soviet "peace policy" and as such a device for encouraging long-term political change in Europe, the Soviets themselves surely must realize the limits of their peace appeal in the strictly European context. Contrary to many of their more extravagant propaganda claims, anti-Sovietism has its roots in Europe as well as in the United States. The potential for inducing change in Europe by altering threat perceptions is thus limited. The question remains, however, as to whether the USSR can "enforce" change on Europe, not this time by virtue of the attractiveness of its peace appeal in Europe but by virtue of a lack of suitable alternatives in the broader global context.

U.S.–SOVIET "EQUALITY" AND PRESSURE FOR CHANGE IN EUROPE

With strategic parity, the Soviet leadership claimed that it had compelled the United States to recognize the USSR as an equal superpower. In the period since SALT Soviet spokesmen have persistently reminded the West of this newly acquired status, which they have used to assert and to justify a Soviet role in Africa, Asia, and the Middle East. Détente in Europe was thus pursued against a backdrop of at least potentially increased U.S.–USSR conflict in the Third World and, as the dimensions of the Soviet strategic buildup became evident, new superpower mistrust over strategic nuclear forces.

What seemed a paradox in the Western context made perfect sense to the Soviets: Rising Soviet power reinforced rather than undermined Soviet–European détente. Precisely because it was now so powerful, and no longer (as in the Khrushchev era) needed to hold Europe "hostage" as a means of counterbalancing U.S. global and strategic power, the USSR was now in a position to designate Europe as a peace zone off limits to superpower conflict. With the removal of the Berlin and the German questions from the political agenda (but not, significantly from the anxieties of West German political leaders), it was now the United States that was placed in the position of using Europe as a hostage, a base from which to pursue its own frustrated rivalry with the other superpower. The difficulty the United States faced in coping with Soviet activism in the Third World (as well as with Third World chaos in general, as in Iran), and in adjusting to strategic vulnerability (as evidenced by the failure to ratify SALT II), lent a certain credibility to Soviet claims that Europe was indeed a hostage to U.S. policies. Soviet propaganda then went a step further, predictably reducing political and policy differences to the military and instrumental dimension: U.S. global ambitions were causing the United States to turn Europe and especially West Germany into a "launching pad" or *place d'armes* for theater nuclear missiles.

Increased U.S.–USSR tensions did not prevent the Soviets from assuming an increasingly lofty posture as the peaceful protector of Western Europe against a (U.S. inspired) "return to the cold war." Warnings about another cold war thus became a major weapon in the Soviet propaganda arsenal. Whereas in the West the term "cold war" signified a gray period of tensions, Berlin crises, and so on, to the Soviets its meaning is more "scientific" and more ideologically charged. It is identified with U.S. dominance and with U.S. attempts to deal with the Soviet Union from "positions of strength." The lowered tensions of the sixties did not in themselves constitute détente, a term in fact never used at that time. Rather, the transition to détente was closely associated with the international "equality" of the USSR and its recognition by West Germany, by the United States, and by all of Europe at Helsinki.

As with many Soviet concepts the Soviet definition of "equality" has both superficially defensive and other more offensive implications. From the Soviet point of view a contradiction and an injustice are inherent in a situation in which two formally "equal" powers dominate the world—if equality is measured by codification of strategic parity in SALT—but in which one of these powers is largely isolated, diplomatically and economically, while the other enjoys mutual defense treaties with most of the other major industrial countries (two of which are nuclear powers), imports a large percentage of the world's exportable oil, takes in billions of dollars each year from its overseas investments, and most important, has access to numerous military bases, many of them on the periphery of the USSR. Add to this the problem of China, and it can be seen that the world as it is presently constituted is fundamentally unacceptable to the USSR as an equal superpower.

The sense that the United States is unduly privileged is especially acute in the case of Europe. It is only the "abnormal" presence of th United States in Europe that prevents the Soviet Union from enjoying political influence on the continent commensurate with its size and power. Nor is the significance of the U.S.–Europe connection limited in scope to Europe alone. From the Soviet perspective, it is central to the global "correlation of forces" as well: Even as U.S. military power prevents Moscow from enjoying its rightful place in Europe, U.S. power itself, far from resting on the inherent superiority of the U.S. system, is seen to derive in large part from America's worldwide network of historically inherited advantages, the chief of which remains the alliance with Europe.

As relations between the United States and the Soviet Union began to deteriorate, Soviet spokesmen became increasingly blunt in their contention that Europe had an obligation to correct the existing imbalance and to help the USSR achieve more of the benefits of "equality." At a minimum Europe had to refrain from helping the United States to achieve again or reassert its former "positions of strength." This is the crux of the Kremlin's demand that NATO Europe reverse its decision to deploy new theater nuclear force (TNF) missiles. Soviet ambassador to France Stefan Chervonenko, in a speech in Paris that clearly reflected thinking in Moscow, stated in regard to TNF that the United States, in an effort to recover "lost supremacy," was seeking to "attain strategic objectives on the backs of others without exposing the United States to a risk of total destruction."[28]

On one level the Soviets have routinely condemned the TNF decision on the standard grounds that it will disturb an existing balance of European forces. It represents a violation of the joint FRG–USSR pledge of 1978 that "no one should seek military superiority." In support of this interpretation Soviet spokesmen protest that the overall numbers of missiles aimed at Europe have not increased, and that the SS-20 deployment represents a routine modernization of older SS-4s and SS-5s. On another and more important level, however, the one on which the most authoritative warnings to Europe have been formulated, the Soviets have been less at pains to explain away a perceived imbalance in their favor within Europe, and more direct in stating, in effect, that this balance as such is irrelevant and that the essence of the problem is the balance outside Europe.[29] At issue is whether the United States can act with its allies so as to obtain "strategic" advantages (as the Soviets define this, meaning the ability to strike Soviet territory) "on the backs of others." Global equality, in short, can mean de facto regional superiority.

The implications of the Soviet demand for equality are perhaps even more evident in areas less muddied with nuclear controversy and less burdened with conflicting (and ultimately irreconcilable) definitions of the term *strategic*. A case in point is that of Norway, a country that by virtue of its location impinges on the USSR's superpower pretensions, in this case the Soviet navy's access to the Atlantic. Even as it proclaims itself the main defender of the regional status quo, the USSR seems determined to compel recognition of its special status as a superpower. This in turn leads to demands for special regional privilege, as evidenced by infringement on Norwegian territorial waters, naval incidents, and encroachment of Norwegian sovereignty over Svalbard. As in the TNF issue the Soviet attitude is distinguished not so much by an extreme conservatism in the assessment of regional balances, in this case the marked imbalance on the Kola peninsula, as it is by the implication that these balances as such are irrelevant and need to be subordinated to the Soviet Union's global security requirements.

It is one of the paradoxes of détente that the effectiveness of the Soviet demand for greater equality has come to depend not on the degree of American dominance but on increasing American weakness or the perception of it. Precisely at the point at which the U.S. nuclear umbrella is least credible, owing to the rise of Soviet power, does it appear that the United States is not meeting its responsibilities in Europe and that it seeks only privileges. The same is true in the economic realm. Precisely at the point at which the U.S.-dominated system that provided postwar Europe with cheap energy has broken down and the United States itself has become a burden on world energy supplies, the Soviets have come forward with "international cooperation," which includes the provision of petroleum, natural gas, and uranium to Western Europe.

Although a weakening United States did much to place Europe in its current position, it does not necessarily follow that in the term an increase in relative U.S. power would soon improve the situation. It could actually increase Soviet diplomatic and political pressure on Europe by forcing it to choose between détente and support for what is depicted as an increasingly aggressive United States. In the present political climate the Soviet leadership appears to be convinced that circles in the United States are attempting to regain strategic superiority and to reassert American influence in the Middle East and elsewhere. This is seen as a challenge to Soviet gains throughout the world. As a ranking Soviet commentator expressed it, "imperialism has switched to a counter-offensive against peace and the peoples' right which is neither episodic nor regional. West Europe, the Far, Middle and Near East and Africa—all these areas have become zones of American imperialist military–political and economic expansion."[30]

The 1980s may well see an increased Soviet vulnerability to U.S. strategic and naval forces. This in turn could set off a process in which Soviet vulnerability leads to further pressures on its own periphery. U.S. efforts to counter these pressures, whether by placing carriers in the Indian Ocean or missiles in Europe, would then only increase Soviet fears and lead to intensified Soviet efforts to enlist its neighbors in peace zones and security systems directed at the United States.

Something of this process can be seen already in the Soviet response to events in Southwest Asia. The U.S. buildup of naval forces, motivated by a variety of concerns regarding Iran, Afghanistan, and the Persian Gulf states, was labeled by the Soviets as a threat to the USSR's southern regions. In response to this buildup, the Soviets have made certain vague proposals for joint Soviet–West European efforts directed at the U.S. role in the region. According to one Soviet source,

> FRG Chancellor Schmidt, in his recent interview for the journal *Der Spiegel*, stated that the USSR, as a potential purchaser of Near East oil, has a legitimate right of access to its sources. Thus, a definite parallel of interests of all European countries can be seen as far as this issue is concerned.

Therefore, it is quite feasible to include problems of the security of oil communications and equal commercial access to oil sources of the Persian Gulf region in the agenda of the all-European conference on energy, which has been proposed by the Soviet Union. All countries which have signed the Helsinki Final Act could jointly submit to the United Nations proposals concerning appropriate guarantees which would be accepted by this world forum. If the Eastern countries which possess oil agree to this, the United Nations could extend such guarantees to cover the territorial integrity and independence of these countries.[31]

The next few years are likely to see other Soviet efforts, both diplomatic and propagandistic, not only to preserve Europe as an "island of détente," but to enlist active West European support in Soviet-sponsored attempts to resist the U.S. "counteroffensive."

SANCTUARY WAR AND SANCTUARY DIPLOMACY

For the Soviet Union, equality means not only strategic parity but the eventual dismantling of the U.S. forward-based systems. In practical terms the USSR continues to manage its defense and its arms control policies so as to maximize its ability to fight a "sanctuary war," even though technology increasingly militates against physical space as a factor in protection against attack.

Soviet security is now assured by a costly effort to maintain supremacy against all the USSR's neighbors, as well as parity with the United States. Over the long term, however, Soviet security and the advance of socialism would be better served by the establishment of a series of peace zones on the entire periphery of the USSR.

Noteworthy is the Soviet Union's otherwise puzzling insistence—puzzling in that it seems to go so much against Soviet short-term economic and political interest—on a debilitating peace treaty with Japan. In all these regions long-term Soviet thinking points to the replacement of the present systems of alliances with an arc of peace zones in which "national sovereignty" and "noninterference" would be the guiding principles. This would give concrete substance to what in 1956 Khrushchev hailed in largely rhetorical terms as the emergence of a "vast 'peace zone', including both socialist and non-socialist peace-loving states in Europe and Asia."[32]

In attempting to encourage the emergence of such zones the Soviet Union pursues what might be called, to borrow the language of strategic doctrine, a "sanctuary diplomacy." Reaffirming and constantly seeking to recodify its commitment to nonuse of force, refusing to countenance any suggestion that the threat of its own forces can be anything but "totally mythical," and demanding that its continental security glacis be as exempt from international discussion as that of the United States, the Soviet Union busily conducts a security policy aimed solely at reducing the forces on or near its borders.

In negotiations the Soviet Union expects not only special geographical privileges but a special political, ideological, and ultimately moral status. In comments to other communists, the Soviet leaders have no apologies to make for such imbalances as now exist. In response to an Italian Communist party position that a Communist "peace conference" should call for both the defeat of plans for the Pershing II-cruise missile deployments and for removal of the SS-20s, Boris Ponomarev stated: "We only want to warn against the illusion of believing that in putting NATO and the Warsaw Pact on the same level, it will be possible to resolve the problems of war and peace in favor of the latter. These two organizations are diametrically opposed by all their nature and their character."[33]

What is remarkable about these claims is not, given the special claims that Communism makes in regard to peace, that they are made, but rather the extent to which they have succeeded in infecting the West. That they have done so, ironically, is owing not to the force of Marxist–Leninist argument, but to the fear that arises from the Soviet possession of a vast nuclear arsenal. As Richard Pipes has observed,

> Since it acquired nuclear weapons the Soviet Union has succeeded to a surprising extent in persuading foreign opinion that insofar as any conflict between the major powers creates the danger of world destruction, all hostility to the Soviet government and its ideology or any thwarting of its will is *ipso facto* and by definition war-mongering. By this logic, "anti-communism" is equated with "anti-humanism." Like so many weapons of political warfare, this device is double-edged; but it so happens that the other edge is never bared.[34]

Soviet efforts to preserve a moral sanctuary against any responsibility for nuclear war are reflected in the present "détente or doom" scenario that Soviet propaganda is spreading, and in Leonid Brezhnev's table-thumping demands for "international talks" to head off this danger. The word *talks*, as opposed to *negotiation*, for which the Russian language seems to have no precise equivalent, reflects the Soviet insistence that arms control in Europe is a one-way street, in which Western Europe can take no initiative of its own, but can only respond in a businesslike fashion to Soviet proposals.

The difference in meaning between "negotiations" and "talks"—like the difference in interpretation between "control" and "limitation," "stability" and "peace"—points up the difficulty inherent in discussing arms reductions with the Soviet Union. And yet the desirability of arms control for the West remains, bringing with it an obligation to understand more fully the needs and the objectives on the Soviet side. Whether the resulting discussion will remain genuine "negotiation," or will become instead "international talks," the Soviet Communist party leadership will depend not only on Western Europe's commitment to its own security, but also on its ability to understand the Soviet conception of Europe and its ongoing impact on SALT, MBFR, and other East–West discussions.

POSTSCRIPT: SOVIET POLICY IN THE POSTDÉTENTE PERIOD

The second half of the 1970s witnessed a gradual decline in the fortunes of détente. Disillusionment set in first in the United States, where commentators and government officials were quick to criticize Western Europe for its greater attachment to détente. By the beginning of the eighties, however, crises in the third world, the continuing deployment of the SS-20, the intense Soviet campaign to derail NATO's own TNF program, and the threat to Poland all had taken their toll on European as well as superpower détente. Perhaps the clearest signal of the changed mood was the Schmidt–Giscard communiqué of February 1981, which downplayed détente and concentrated instead on the more cautious concept of "stabilization."[35]

The changing mood in Europe naturally raises the question of how Soviet policy is likely to respond. This policy has aimed, at least since Helsinki, at encouraging secular change in Europe. It has done so in part by seeking to convey an impression of relentless progress toward a predetermined goal. For their part, European leaders, while knowing that their own view of change in Europe did not coincide with the Soviet notion of an irreversible détente, have perhaps unwittingly cooperated with Soviet policy by doing little do disabuse their publics of a faith in some kind of progress. Now even this is changing, as West European governments seek to push through the TNF decision against popular opposition, try to deter a Soviet invasion of Poland, and work to head off an even wider rift with Washington.

Against the backdrop of this potentially far-reaching reassessment in Western Europe, there is as yet no sign that the Soviet leadership has opted for a fundamental change in its policy. Even as détente has crumbled, the leadership has avoided major shifts, hoping instead to insulate its West European détente from Poland and from relations with the United States. If anything, the Soviets have sought to portray themselves as still calm and businesslike, and to portray the United States as erratic and a threat to world peace. Brezhnev, for example, traveled to Prague in April and from there reiterated his call for disarmament while downplaying the Polish question.[36] This was at a time when various American officials were changing their assessment of the threat to Poland seemingly from one day to the next. Brezhnev's behavior on this and other occasions fits the general pattern of attending to show concern for the "real" issues of détente and disarmament, in contrast to the United States, which is said to be using the "so-called Afghan affair," the "fuss over Poland," and the "trumped up human rights issue" as pretexts for avoiding the disarmament imperative. In this way the strategy of "depoliticization" continues, despite a more politically charged atmosphere.

Apart from occasionally vicious attacks such as those of Nikolai Portugalov in the less authoritative *Literaturnaya Gazeta*,[37] the Soviet press continues to downplay the importance of conflict between the "social systems." Direct attacks on West European politicians have been selective, and attacks on policy have been couched in the language of arguments heard within the West itself, rather than in that of fundamental ideological conflict between the two social systems. In speaking out against TNF deployment, for example, the Soviet press and those official and unofficial Soviet representatives active in the West European antinuclear movement have simply amplified the charge heard in the SPD that the United States has abandoned the arms control half of the dual TNF decision, thereby undermining the basis for the package as a whole.

The Soviet effort to hold to a steady course reflects both a continued hope that it will be possible to widen the rift between the United States and West European governments and an awareness of the increasing possibilities for exploiting popular anti-NATO and antinuclear sentiments. This can be done by reaching over the heads of the Western governments with the Soviet peace appeal. But while the popular appeal is one of peace, the message to the various governments is a blunt restatement of the Soviet contention that détente is an "objective" historical stage growing out of changes in the global "correlation of forces." Thus a week before Chancellor Schmidt departed for Moscow in June 1980, the CPSU Central Committee Plenum released a resolution on foreign policy stating that "détente is the natural result of the world alignment of forces that has taken shape over the past few decades. The military-strategic balance between the socialist and capitalist parts of the world is an important historical milestone. . . . Any schemes to upset this balance are doomed to failure."[38] As if to underscore the point, throughout 1980 the Soviets stepped up the pace of their SS-20 deployments, thereby positioning themselves favorably for either the mutual freeze on TNF deployments suggested by Brezhnev or for negotiations aimed at their reduction.[39]

The basic continuity of Soviet policy has also been evident in the Soviet approach to the Madrid CSCE follow-up conference, and in the overall interpretation of the Helsinki final act. Here Soviet diplomacy continues with its effort gradually to invest the final act with the status of a blueprint for change, to define the content of this change, and to suggest mechanisms for the businesslike implementation of these changes. While lower ranking officials such as Zagladin have long made the point that the final act implies a priori acceptance by the West of certain Soviet objectives ("we do not want to impose anything on anybody which has not already been accepted in principle"), never has this interpretation received such high-level and transparent endorsement as it did in Brezhnev's speech at the Twenty-sixth Party congress. After referring to various efforts to create "zones of peace" and nuclear-free zones in different parts of the world, Brezhnev went on to state that "the decisions of the European conference are in effect aimed at making all of Europe such a zone."[40]

This long-range objective of making Europe nuclear-free is consistent with the Soviet "sanctuary diplomacy." Along these same lines should also be noted the part in Brezhnev's congress speech in which he agreed that confidence-building measures be extended to the entire European part of the USSR, "on the condition that the Western states make a corresponding extension of the area of measures of trust."[41] Brezhnev's remark was in response to the French proposal, offered at Madrid, to institute confidence-building measures (CBMs) "from the Atlantic to the Urals." Despite the apparent convergence, however in terms of their political content, Brezhnev's "concession" and the French proposal are not parallel but in fact diametrically opposed to each other.[42] The French proposal aims in effect to "repoliticize" arms control in Europe by redirecting attention to the central security problem on the Continent—the fact that the USSR is both a superpower and a power in Europe. By seeking to eliminate the 250 kilometer exception worked out for the Soviet Union at Helsinki, the French proposal would force the Soviets to surrender a superpower prerogative—this exception—as a precondition, in effect, for entry as a "European" power to their proposed conference on disarmament. But this of course is precisely what the Soviets cannot and will not do. In demanding a new concession from the United States (extending CBMs into the Atlantic or more likely to North America itself), for what should simply follow logically from the claim to being a "European" power, Brezhnev is once again "depoliticizing" arms control. He is reiterating the fundamental inviolability of the political status quo and once again interpreting arms control as a process of *quid pro quo* technical measures in each half of a divided Europe in which all political questions have been settled. He is upholding the absolute "equality" of the Soviet Union with the United States, whatever the security implications for Western Europe.

The Madrid conference has also witnessed Soviet efforts to elevate the "legal" status of the Basket Three provisions, as well as to reinterpret these provisions in accordance with Soviet interests. As in their post-Helsinki propaganda and in their post-Helsinki bilateral treaties with several East European states, the Soviets have interpreted the final act not on the basis of the language actually compromised upon by the thirty-five countries at Helsinki, but as if the conference had adopted the original Warsaw Pact country draft proposals.[43] Although the West clearly rejected the Soviet view that the enlargement of human contacts had to be conditional upon—rather than a constituent of—the development of interstate détente, the

Soviets have since reverted to the meaning contained in their original demands:

> It is the level of détente that determines how rapidly the provisions of the Final Act dealing with the broadening of ties in the fields of culture, education and communication are implemented. The higher this level, the more favourable opportunities are created for interstate cooperation in the humanitarian field. Conversely, a worsening of the international situation leads to the scaling down of such cooperation.[44]

Clearly such an interpretation, which East Germany has also made since 1981, is aimed at influencing West Germany with its special interest in contacts between the parts of divided Germany.

Throughout this period of heightened international tensions, then, the Soviets have if anything brought into sharper focus than ever the fundamentally depoliticized nature of the détente between Eastern and Western Europe that they are alone prepared to accept:[44]

- Afghanistan and Poland are entirely intrasocialist matters that are not discussible in international forums. (Although the USSR is willing to discuss the situation "around Afghanistan," as Brezhnev suggested in his congress speech.)

- SS–20s targeted on Western Europe are not comparable to American ground launched cruise missiles and Pershing IIs deployed on European soil. Any agreement to reduce the number of SS–20s will have to be bought at the price of meeting the long-standing Soviet demand to bring *all* American forward-based systems into the negotiations (in effect to acknowledge the "strategic" nature of these weapons).

- CBMs from the Atlantic to the Urals will *not* be permitted to put the USSR, or even the European part of the USSR, on an equal status with the other "European" states, and for this reason will have to be counterbalanced by concessions in North America.

- Finally, East–West human contacts will develop only to the extent that interstate détente develops along the political lines "settled" at Helsinki. Under no circumstances will such human contacts undermine the policies or the goals of the socialist states.

At the same time that it has preempted the political agenda in Europe in this way, Soviet diplomacy has continued to propose new forums, new institutions, new agreements, by which to further the businesslike implementation of détente. In his congress speech Brezhnev ran through the entire list: nuclear-free zones, nonfirst use agreements, CPSU–Social Democratic working groups on disarmament, and the convening of a special committee of experts that would report to the world about the effects of a nuclear war.

In both elements of their policy—seeking to preempt the political agenda, and using propaganda and peace appeals to pressure governments into accepting their agenda—the Soviets have displayed a basic continuity with their policies of the seventies. Whether a full-scale invasion of Poland, should it occur, will force a fundamental rethinking of this policy is as yet an open question. One thing is certain, however. The answer to this question, should one be required, will be determined not so much in Moscow as by the responses of governments and publics in the West itself.

NOTES

1. William B. Prendergast, *Mutual and Balanced Force Reduction: Issues and Prospects* (Washington, D.C.: American Enterprise Institute, 1978), p. 21.
2. Pierre Hassner, "Western Europe as a Constraint on Soviet Power," in *The Political Implications of Soviet Military Power*, edited by Lawrence L. Whetten (New York: Crane, Russak, 1977), p. 58.
3. Quoted in Christopher A.P. Binns, "The Development of the Soviet Policy Response to the EEC," *Co-existence*, 14, no. 2 (1977): 258.
4. For the history of the MBFR negotiations see Prendergast, *Mutual and Balanced Force Reduction*; also J.I. Coffey, *New Approaches to Arms Reduction in Europe*, Adelphi Papers 105 (Summer 1974); Paul J.M. Teunissen, "The Vienna Negotiations on Mutual Reduction of Forces and Armaments and Associated Measures in Central Europe," in *Uncertain Détente* edited by Frans A.M. Alting von Geusau, (Alphen aan den Rijn: Sijthoff and Noordhoff, 1979); Robert Legvold, "The Soviet Union and Current Multilateral Arms Negotiations," in *The Future of Soviet Military Power* edited by Lawrence Whetten (New York: Crane, Russak, 1976); and John Erickson, "MBFR: Force Levels and Security Requirements," *Strategic Review* 1, no. 2 (Summer 1973).
5. In October 1979 Brezhnev offered to withdraw 20,000 men and 1,000 tanks from East Germany. In return Europe would agree to defer a decision on deploying new missiles in Europe, and would enter talks with the USSR.
6. Prendergast, *Mutual and Balanced Force Reduction*, p. 60.

7. V. Matveyev, "Lessons of History and European Security," *International Affairs* (June 1970): 13. Quoted in Melvin Croan, "Soviet Policy," in John Newhouse, *U.S. Troops in Europe* (Washington, D.C.: Brookings, 1971), p. 27.

8. The distinction between these two types of arms control is made by Robin Ranger, "MBFR: Political or Technical Arms Control," *The World Today* 30, no. 10 (October 1974).

9. The term "unilateral deterrence" is John Erikson's. See his "The Chimera of Mutual Deterrence," *Strategic Review* 6, no. 2 (1978). The significance of this concept in the context of Europe is discussed in Uwe Nerlich, "Theatre Nuclear Forces in Europe: Is NATO Running Out of Options?" *The Washington Quarterly* 3, no. 1 (Winter 1980): 113.

10. In their interpretation of the Helsinki agreements, the Soviets often seem to disregard the actual text and revert to their original draft proposals. It is noteworthy that one of the early Soviet approaches to MBFR was to discuss force reductions in a special working committee that would be part of the all-European conference, and subordinate to it. This proposal was rejected by the West.

11. *Pravda*, March 3, 1979.

12. *New York Times*, May 23, 1980.

13. Richard Davy, "Helsinki: Two Concepts of Détente," *The World Today* 29, no. 8 (August 1973).

14. There are numerous examples of the Soviets using the Final Act as a "legal" document with implications for governmental policy in Western Europe. Reacting to reports in the Soviet press about alleged Soviet espionage activity in Switzerland, the Soviet ambassador lodged a protest with the Swiss Department of Foreign Affairs. According to the text of the note, "the Embassy wants to call the attention of the [Department's] press section to the anti-Soviet campaign which the Swiss mass media are systematically conducting. This campaign, which contradicts the spirit and principles of the Final Act of the Conference on Security and Cooperation in Europe, has been joined by the press, television and radio, individual members of Parliament and even official Swiss representatives. . . . In making this statement the Embassy expects the [Department of Foreign Affairs] to take measures to suspend hostile propaganda against the Soviet Union in Switzerland . . . ," *Neue Zürcher Zeitung*, March 20, 1980.

New Times had this to say about the expansion of the EEC and its relationship to potential membership for Spain in NATO: "The desire to use the expansion of the community to stimulate military integration runs overtly counter to the provisions of the Helsinki Conference Final Act and cannot fail to cause serious concern among all peace-loving forces on the continent" (September 21, 1979).

In regard to British Prime Minister Margaret Thatcher's verbal support for an Olympic boycott: "This is a question contained in the Third Basket on international sports relations. . . . How does [Prime Minister Thatcher's support for the boycott] look in connection with the coming conference in Madrid and in connection with the obvious violation of the decisions of this very Third Basket by some Western powers and primarily the U.S." Valentin Zorin on "Studio Nine," Moscow Domestic Television Service in Russian, 1500 GMT, March 29, 1980, in Foreign Broadcast Information Service (FBIS) *Daily Report* (Soviet Union), April 10, 1980.

15.   Interview in *L'Humanite*, November 24, 1979. Emphasis added.

16.   Text of the Soviet–FRG Declaration from TASS, 1800 GMT, May 6, 1978, in FBIS *Daily Report* (Soviet Union), May 8, 1978.

17,   Robert Legvold, "The Soviet Union and Western Europe," in *The Soviet Empire: Expansion and Détente* edited by William E. Griffith (Lexington, Mass.: Lexington Books, 1976), p. 244.

18.   Brezhnev's report on the Sixtieth anniversary of the October Revolution quoted in N.I. Lebedev, *A New State in International Relations* (New York: Pergamon, 1978), p. 89.

19.   Gail Warshofsky Lapidus, "The Brezhnev Regime and Directed Social Change: Depoliticization as Political Strategy," in *The Twenty-fifth Congress of the CPSU* edited by Alexander Dallin (Stanford: Hoover Institution, 1977), pp. 26–27.

Other works have emphasized the tendency toward "depoliticization" of issues under Brezhnev. See the review article by Robert F. Miller, "Whither the Soviet System?" in *Problems of Communism*, March–April 1980. Miller notes the role Soviet interest in "scientific and technical" management plays in encouraging this trend, but subsumes this under a more general hypothesis about Communist politics: "Communist politicians, nurtured in the traditions of democratic centralism, naturally abhor ordinary political competition. Such a possibility should be kept in mind in the search for clues about the future course of Communist systems."

20.   This discussion follows R. Judson Mitchell, "A New Brezhnev Doctrine: The Restructuring of International Relations," *World Politics* 30, no. 3 (April 1978): 374–75. In appealing for disarmament in the West the Soviets challenge Europe (and the United States) to summon the "political will" to come to an agreement with the USSR and its allies. This use of the term "political will" does not contradict the claim made here that the Soviets are trying to encourage a "depoliticized" approach to arms limitation in Europe. An analogy from a different context can perhaps help to illustrate this point: When European leaders urge the United States to cut oil consumption, they are not so much making a political proposal as they are stating an objective fact—that excessive U.S. oil imports tighten world markets, drive up prices, weaken the dollar, and so on. At the same time,

however, the Europeans might call on the U.S. administration to summon the political will to deal with the import problem. In an analogous fashion, the Soviets contend that acceptance of their various arms limitation proposals is not in itself a matter for serious political disagreement, since no one disputes the "fact" that the danger to peace is growing with each day that passes, that "burning issues" are at stake, that enormous sums are being wasted on arms, and so on. European governments must simply summon the political will to deal with the problem of the arms race, which means in effect they must accept the various proposals put forward by the USSR and its allies.

21. "The Soviet Union and Western Europe," p. 244.

22. A. Sovetov, "Leninist Foreign Policy in the World Today," *International Affairs* (March 1980): 5.

23. Mitchell, "A New Brezhnev Doctrine," p. 374.

24. Soviet spokesmen have met the charge of "splitting" head-on. A high-ranking Soviet diplomat in Moscow told Theo Sommer of *Die Zeit*, for example, that "if we, the West European and the socialist countries, do not succeed in stopping Carter, the world will find itself in a dangerous situation. We have many common interests although we belong to different alliances—most of all the common interest in peace. We invite you to be our ally here. If America is using all its strength to destroy the state of peaceful coexistence, then true solidarity would consist in keeping the United States from such activities" (April 4, 1980).

    In a similar vein, *New Times* stated that "the appeal to the West European countries is an appeal to partners in détente. Principled agreement has been reached with some of them that no one should seek military superiority in Europe. Now is the time to recall this, for the plan to deploy the Pentagon's 'Eurostrategic' weapon in the West is aimed at insuring military superiority for NATO," editorial, October 12, 1979.

25. "The Nature of Soviet Power," *Foreign Affairs* 56, no. 1 (October 1977): 64.

26. N. Polyanov, "The Atlantic Moloch," *International Affairs* (May 1978): 46.

27. Colonel M. Ponomarev, on May 27, 1979, reported in FBIS *Daily Report* (Soviet Union), June 1, 1979. This analysis follows the author's *The "Leninist Peace Policy" and Western Europe*, MIT Center for International Studies Monograph, January 1980.

28. Quoted in the *New York Times*, April 16, 1980.

29. Two thorough analyses of Soviet positions on long-range theater nuclear forces are Hannes Adomeit and Christoph Royen, "Die Sowjetische Argumentation zur Modernisierung des in Europa Stationierten Nuklearen Potentials der NATO," *Stiftung Wissenschaft und Politik* (November 1979) and Gerhard Wettig, Die Mittelstreckenproblematik aus sowjetischer

Sicht," *Berichte des Bundesinstituts für ostwissenschaftliche und internationale Studien* 1 (1980).

30. Vitaliy Korionov, "International Review," *Pravda*, March 2, 1980, in FBIS *Daily Report* (Soviet Union), March 5, 1980.

31. Moscow TASS International Service in Russian, 1010 GMT February 29, 1980, in FBIS *Daily Report* (Soviet Union), March 3, 1980.

32. Report to the Central Committee of the CPSU at the Twentieth Party Congress, February 14, 1956, in *The Foreign Policy of the Soviet Union* edited by Alvin Z. Rubinstein (New York: Random House, 1960), p. 382.

33. Quoted in the *New York Times*, April 30, 1980.

34. "Operational Principles of Soviet Foreign Policy," *Survey* 19, no. 2 (Spring 1973).

35. *New York Times*, February 7, 1981.

36. Excerpts of Brezhnev's Prague address appeared in *The New York Times*, April 8, 1981.

37. See his articles of May 14, 1980, and February 18, 1981, for example. See also his interview with *Der Spiegel*, June 9, 1980.

38. *Pravda*, June 24, 1980.

39. The *Washington Star* of February 11, 1981 reported that deployments for 1980 were doubled over the previous year.

40. *Pravda*, February 24, 1981.

41. Ibid.

42. For a view of the French proposal and the thinking that underlies it see the chapter by Jean–Marie Guehenno in Uwe Nerlich, ed., *The Western Panacea: Constraining Soviet Power through Negotiation* (Cambridge, Mass.: Ballinger Publishing Company, 1983).

43. The post-Helsinki treaty between the Soviet Union and East Germany (1975) is a virtual carbon copy of the pre-Helsinki treaty between the Soviet Union and Czechoslovakia (1970).

44. Sh. Sanakoyev, "The Madrid Meeting," *International Affairs* (February 1981): 47. Valuable information about original Soviet and Eastern European draft proposals is contained in Luigi Vittorio Ferraris, *Testimonionze di un Negoziato* (Padua: CEDAM, 1977), and John J. Maresca, To Helsinki: An Account of the Conference on Security and Cooperation in Europe (unpublished manuscript).

5 THE THREAT PERCEIVED? LEVERAGE OF SOVIET MILITARY POWER IN WESTERN EUROPE

Lothar Ruehl

The perception of the political threat of the Soviet Union or of the political deterrence value of predominant Soviet power in Europe and globally can be measured in terms of caution on the Western side of the continent: From 1950–1955 West German rearmament and the European Defense Community (EDC) project were judged in the West on their merits, the reasons invoked against were Western— French resistance, moral issues, hostility to a strong Germany, insecurity about Germany's future (the "national option" in favor of reunification). But Soviet reactions, supposed to be hostile, did not play a great part in Western policymaking. It was assumed that the Soviet Union would react unfavorably and launch a new propaganda campaign, threaten with all sorts of reprisals short of war, but could not do a thing about it. The same was the case with tactical nuclear armaments for NATO forces in Europe. But once the nuclear armament was introduced into the Western forces, the Soviet Union contended with adverse propaganda and proposals for nuclear arms withdrawals and a "denuclearized zone" in the center of Europe (the Rapacki plan of 1956). When the NATO Council decided in 1957 to set up stocks of nuclear arms in Europe and to deploy a nuclear-armed medium-range ballistic missile force to counter the Soviet SS–4 medium-range ballistic missile (MRBM), Soviet hostility was taken for granted and dismissed. What finally prevented the NATO MRBM force, later designated the "multilateral force" or MLF, were

internal political obstacles within and among some Western countries, not fear of Soviet opposition. Even from 1963 to 1965 French
opposition and British lack of interest were invoked against going
forward with the MLF project, not Soviet threats or warnings. It is
true, however, that at this point the U.S. administration already
looked to Moscow for a common policy of arms control and that
General de Gaulle had invoked for the first time Soviet opposition
against West Germany acceding to control of nuclear weapons even
within NATO and under the authority of the U.S. president.

Ten years later French president Giscard d'Estaing did not think
it politically possible or advisable to organize Western Europe's security by common defense, in particular because of Soviet opposition
to any such solution for fear of Western pressure and risk to Soviet
security in Europe. The American–Soviet security partnership for
strategic arms limitations has inhibited America's European allies
who do have to take into account the global relationship and its
requirements for regional security, alliance politics, and arms control.
But this only underscores the loss of European autonomy and the
limits of power and influence for a United Europe. Soviet influence,
based on military more than on economic force, tends to encroach
on Western Europe's and NATO's interests in limiting armaments by
putting pressure on the American partner in negotiation. This is only
classic power politics. But it shows that the impact of Soviet military
power is still and more than ever since 1945 felt on West European
construction and NATO policies.

There is a distinct contrast between European attitudes toward
the USSR since the beginning of the détente period in the mid-1960s
and what used to be the common Western reaction to the Soviet
challenge, when Russia was still looked upon as a menace to the
peace. One of the psychological causes of this change was the ambiguous outcome of the Berlin crisis in 1961, which marked the end of
the Dulles–Adenauer leadership in American–German relations and
announced the political retreat of the Western powers in the stale-
mated contest over Germany. The second obvious cause was the
emergence of the American–Russian superpower bilateralism in international security politics as a predominant force, relegating Western
alliance policies to the second rank of importance and turning the
North Atlantic alliance into an instrument of international East–
West arms control in the persuance of U.S.–Soviet priorities. The
U.S.–Soviet bilateral nonproliferation politics, resulting 1968 in the

Geneva treaty, are a case in point. SALT as a diplomatic process culminated in the Vienna agreements of 1979, which subjugated NATO interests to the bilateral superpower understanding on the general conditions of strategic parity and global security.

De Gaulle had warned as early as 1963 that Western Europe would neglect its own defensè, if American leadership were overbearing and hegemonic. In 1967 he justified French "national independence by national defense" with the argument that nations dependent for their security on foreign power and with their armed forces under foreign control would abdicate as free societies and subject themselves to the will of the strongest power. De Gaulle finally denounced NATO as an "American military protectorate over Western Europe" and advanced the notion of double pressure on Europe by "the two hegemonies," the two superpowers, seeking to dominate by partition and confrontation or by a "condominium," effectively resulting in a "neutralization of Europe."

French opposition to American strategy and political–military control of NATO contributed to aggravate the tensions between American and Western Europe while estranging France's West European partners from their originally intimate and strong French connection. French plans for a West European political confederation in a union of sovereign states with a common European defense outside the NATO military integration framework and an independent international policy to be coordinated with that of the United States and Great Britain paralyzed European efforts in the Atlantic alliance, reduced the value of the American–European partnership, and finally led to a contraction of NATO under a still more vigorous American control with British and West German participation than ever before, while France maintained an ambiguous and tenuous position outside NATO.

French "détente" policies took the initiative for a rapprochement with Soviet Russia after the immediate postcrisis period 1961–1964. By 1966, when de Gaulle went to Moscow, France had inaugurated an entirely new and national approach to the European security problems and the relations with the Soviet Union.

The American and French examples, closely followed and imitated by British policy, led to a general competition in Western Europe for better relations with Moscow.

The disintegration of Western positions and approaches vis-à-vis the Soviet Union in Europe and Eastern Europe as a whole had reached the critical point in 1966-67, when the Harmel report to the North Atlantic Council recommended solidarity and a closed political formation in the strongest diplomatic terms compatible with its mission:

> As sovereign states the Allies are not obliged to subordinate their policies to collective decision. The Alliance affords an effective forum and clearing house for the exchange of information and views; thus, each of the Allies can decide its policy in the light of close knowledge of the problems and objectives of the others. To this end the practice of frank and timely consultations needs to be deepened and improved. Each Ally should play its full part in promoting an improvement in relations with the Soviet Union and the countries of Eastern Europe, bearing in mind that the pursuit of détente must not be allowed to split the Alliance. The chances of success will clearly be greatest if the Allies remain on parallel courses, especially in matters of close concern to them all; their actions will thus be the more effective.[1]

Belgian, Scandinavian, Canadian, and Italian diplomacy had developed as many national approaches to the East as there were national situations, differing one from the other. Danes, Norwegians, Icelanders were more concerned with the "Northern balance" and the special Scandinavian security—including neutral Sweden and Finland in a precarious situation between neutrality and alignment with the Russian hegemonial power of the North and East—than with collective defense of Western Europe. Canadian foreign policy tended to drift in the same vague northeastern direction, where under the dim light of the polar circle a new area of peaceful and effortless cooperation seemed to take form on the horizon. Paul-Henri Spaak, one of the founders of Western Europe's communities and fervent advocate of European supranational unity, had become one of the most eager scouts on the uncertain terrain of East-West rapprochement, reconnoitering the approaches to Moscow; only a few years earlier, in 1961, Spaak, then secretary general of NATO, had warned President Kennedy against the secret yearning of the smaller West European nations for neutrality and the risk of unilateral disarmament of these countries, if America allowed the alliance to dissolve politically or to be weakened militarily by de Gaulle's policies.

The expectations in a "new area of negotiations" instead of confrontation, encouraged by President Nixon in 1970, anticipated the possible results of détente and equated intent with success. Soviet policy was often judged with more understanding than caution

should have permitted, the concept of prompting Eastern concessions by offering Western concessions for compromise gained in all
Western capitals, as if the West held the stronger position and could
afford to leave it. Soviet interest in the détente process was generally
overestimated and explained with Western notions of economic ra-
tionality. The burdens of defense and confrontation were considered
in the West to be equal on both sides or even heavier in the East,
weighing on the scales of decision in Moscow as in Washington or
London and Bonn. A notion of similarity of essential interests in
security, arms control, and peace, of symmetrical economic, demographic, technological, and social constraints to the expansion of
military power in East and West was developed, while the Soviet
Union embarked on the most important and determined effort for
the achievement of military superiority in Europe.

The misreading of the signs visible in the East, the overestimation
of the positive aspects of détente in Europe, the excessive confidence
in the constraining effects of U.S.–Soviet negotiations on strategic
arms limitation and global conditions of international security created the misconception of détente as a lasting reality, offering an
alternative to conflict and confrontation. The cause for the decline
of determination to prepare for conflict and hold out to the Soviet
Union in confrontation against threats has been identified with the
psychological effects of détente. But détente was itself the *result* of
confrontation; the "spirit of détente" was a mixture of goodwill,
peaceful intentions, renewed pacifism, the nostalgia of comfortable
neutrality and growing impatience with the rigors of "Cold War" and
the tensions of political hostility between two armed camps. Years
passed with Europe suffering mentally and emotionally from the
claustrophobia of permanent armed confrontation and the frozen
state of politics.

Détente was above all a mental attitude, a psychological condition
of Western society, not a political reality going deeper than the super-
ficial relaxation of tensions in the East–West conflict. The strategic
and ideological substance of this relative relaxation of relations between two opposed systems, which remain opposed to each other
and incompatible by all standards with little prospect for "convergence" was conveniently overlooked in Western Europe, even when
so-called delimitation and demarcation policies were being enforced
by the East. The fear that the Cold War might reappear out of a
renewed state of tensions, that relations might again freeze and

diplomacy become immobile in Europe, has continued to influence Western attitudes toward Soviet display of military power and demonstration of the readiness to fall back on positions of hostility.

It is in this psychological environment that Western Europe has had and will have to face the growing profile of Soviet military power, perceive the threat that is embodied in offensive capabilities, offering offensive options on the Continent and on the adjoining seas. Military power as an instrument of policy, military strategy as a concept for political action in peace or in conflict short of actual war have been conceptually downgraded if not simply discarded in Western thinking. The assumption that war can no longer serve as the continuation of politics by other means has been disproved many times since 1945 and in particular since the beginning of the East–West détente. Southeast Asia gave the most impressive example with the one decisive military victory, determining the outcome of a protracted conflict after thirty years, conquering an entire territory, destroying a state in *debellatio* (the classic total defeat ending in political and juridical annihilation in terms of international public law) and reunifying a nation while establishing a regional predominance by the use of military power in offensive action and for the occupation of foreign countries. The contention that "no military solution" could "end the war," has been entirely and dramatically refuted and shown for what it always has been: an illusion of the weak and the undecided.

The Soviet Union had the opportunity to use the Vietnam War and the conflict in Indochina to tie down American military power while the Soviet strategic and naval armaments drive was pursued with an investment higher than the amount of capital the United States could invest in strategic forces from 1965 until 1972. The Vietnam War turned out to be a valuable ally of the Soviet Union in its power challenge to America, since American society was demoralized and the use of military power discredited in the United States and in Western Europe.

The infamous end of the American involvement in this war, when the last Americans took off from the roofs of Saigon, leaving their doomed allies to their certain fate, two years after the political capitulation of the United States hardly veiled by the armistice agreement of Paris, made a deep impression on the people of the West and the Orient. A world power had lost face, and it remained paralyzed for several years, inhibited in political strife by a unique orgy of self-mutilation. American impotence gave the Soviet power-projection force a free ride to Africa from Angola to Mozambique and Ethiopia, where every single mile of airlift, every nautical mile of steaming bore all the marks of a high-risk operation for Soviet forces through potentially hostile space.

The coincidence between the rise of Soviet Russia to world power—still constrained for global expansion, still exposed to considerable risks in offensive action, still landlocked along its coasts in spite of the new fleet and maritime strategy—and the decline of American power aggravated the political consequences of the state Western Europe had slipped into during the seemingly easy years of détente. The "Finlandization of Europe" is the expression of a historical possibility, not of an actual reality. The West European countries will give the answer to the question, whether Europe prefers accommodation with the interests of the dominant power in the East or whether Western Europe can be a force of its own, holding its own, allied with North America, defending its vital interests in the world even if the North–South conflict were to be dominated by the East–West conflict and military action became inevitable to enforce free access to the sources of energy and to protect the lines of communication across the seas.

The evidence of the years between the Soviet occupation of Czechoslovakia in 1968 and the Soviet invasion of Afghanistan in 1979–80 is not clear. Western Europe has not given in to Soviet demands during the security negotiations on Mutual and Balanced Force Reduction and in the CSCE. Only the political–territorial status quo of postwar Europe has been formally recognized. However, the political contents of this status quo in Eastern Europe cannot be fixed once and for all by international recognition and détente has contributed to the beginning of the unraveling of the fabric of power in the Communist party states. The risk of political destabilization of the East has been greater than that of the West or the South of Europe. The evidence of destabilization in Poland has brought to the attention of Europe that in a crisis the use of or at least the threat with military power remains the *ultima ratio regis* in the East, that the Soviet army can be used to maintain the imperial control of Poland and keep the Polish Communists in government.

This evidence, underlined by the concentration of Soviet forces close to the Eastern border of Poland at the end of November 1980 and by demonstrative security measures in the Soviet garrison state of East Germany, sealing off Poland from the West, contributes to the fallacious concept according to which the Soviet army has above all a "defensive" mission as a military police: to control the Soviet glacis in Eastern Europe as it did in 1968 in Czechoslovakia. There is no doubt that control of Eastern Europe is one of the main missions of the Soviet armed forces, in particular of the army and of the KGB forces. But the domination of the European situation in a crisis beyond Eastern Europe would seem to be a major reason for the continuing build-up and upgrading of the Soviet armed forces since the mid-1960s, while the "process of détente" was slowly developing. Domination of the situation around the Soviet Union presupposes that the prospective theaters of conflict can be dominated by military force. To create and deploy the forces required for such domination has been obviously the reason of Soviet military policy and the armaments programs related to the European situation: on the ground, in the air, and on the seas, with conventional and nuclear weapons, with short, medium, and continental range delivery systems. All foreseeable contingencies must be covered by appropriate military options, including the capability for a limited theater nuclear war. Redundancy of military means has to be prepared in order to make up for losses and failures; reserves have to be held ready in order to replace spent arms and forces or to exploit success. The geopolitical environment of the European continent must be subject to Soviet offensive moves in order to separate Europe from its overseas communications, to interdict supplies and reinforcements.

Western Europe has been exposed to the threat of a Soviet land attack ever since 1945, a threat of varying substance and changing probability. Western Europe, an agglomerate of peninsulas and islands on the periphery of Eurasia, a coastline territory with a long land frontier from the Baltic to the Adriatic, is also exposed to Soviet naval offensives and seaborne nuclear threats as well as amphibious attacks from the East. Seapower can be used short of war to blockade and disrupt, to disturb maritime commerce and shipping on the high seas, to disorganize highly vulnerable industrial economies, dependent on undisturbed international trade and traffic. Western Europe is thus confronted with a serious strategic problem by all aspects of Soviet armament, for example, by the Backfire long-range combat aircraft in a conventional antishipping or maritime reconnaissance and seaspace control mission as much as in a "continental-strategic" nuclear mission.

For the West European countries in NATO the first priority is to determine the function of arms control concepts related to defense requirements and credible deterrence. It is in this field of setting priorities and defining criteria for optimal combinations of military and diplomatic means to assure security that threat perception must serve political decisions. As long as Soviet military power is looked upon as outdated, unusable, defensive, or introverted, the capabilities will be underrated and explained away with assumptions made on Soviet intentions and on the effectiveness of international constraints such as "MBFR a confidence-building measure in itself" or the "CSCE a guarantee for restraint of all participants" that "depend on détente" or would not "risk détente." The problem with Soviet military power is precisely that the Soviet Union, while depending on détente as long as it can count on Western economic-technological transfers of values to aid the Soviet economy or to contribute to the maintaining of the Socialist order in Eastern Europe, has the means to risk détente in a major contingency such as the breakdown of the Socialist order in Poland or the national secession of one of the East European countries from the Russian empire.

Since 1968 Western Europe has been reluctant to invest more than a minimum of its resources in military defense and in particular in effective military options in war, either defensive or offensive. The indecision over the neutron weapon and the difficulties with the NATO program for long-range theater nuclear force (LRTNF) systems modernization for the deployment of modern continental nuclear delivery systems show that Western Europe looks with concern to the East, before or while arming against an increased threat. The esoteric dispute over the respective significance of "capabilities and intentions" in the West betrays a lack not of insight into the nature of the problem but rather of the courage to face its consequences.

In this way the Soviet deployments of new arms in Europe (or European-oriented in the USSR) have been said to represent defensive purposes in spite of their range and obvious target areas in Western Europe. Yet to deploy a counterthreat of medium or intermediate missiles as delivery systems for nuclear arms, targeted on Soviet territory in order to enhance deterrence in the face of an increased threat to NATO, has proven to be a difficult political choice for the Western allies. "Not to provoke" has become the adage of conventional political wisdom in Western Europe when dealing with the Soviet Union. Soviet military power as an instrument of Soviet policies of domination, coercion, and persuasion has made a deep impression on the peoples of the West. This psychological impact, causing a tendency toward enforced accommodation with Soviet interests in Europe, has created a state of mind for political decisions resembling self-inhibition. Governments have to correct this latent disposition whenever they have to counter the change in the balance of forces, shifting to the East's advantage, by increased military expenditure or measures of preparedness.

Soviet policy and propaganda try to play on the sensibilities of Western consciences and feelings toward military force and the risk of war. This is standard Soviet/Communist procedure and has been so for a long time. In the past, West European policy of military cooperation, common defense and armaments, and regional security has by and large ignored the threats and warnings from the East. But in recent times the propaganda effect and the results of Soviet diplomacy have exercised the inhibiting influence on Western decisions, which have always been the aim of Soviet dealings with the West. Most NATO programs have been adopted all the same but with a growing force of resistance in some West European countries. For example participation of German troops in allied manoeuvers in Norway was the object of strong Soviet protests and warnings (echoed and amplified in Scandinavian ears by the voice of Finland) and was finally reduced to military medical personnel. Stockpiling of conventional arms and equipments for U.S. rapid deployment forces in Norway was first agreed upon between Norway and the NATO authorities but later postponed for fear of domestic protest and Soviet reactions.

In this general perspective of reluctance on the West European side to deal effectively with the military security issue either by active policies within NATO or by European additional organizations and programs—for example, for naval forces to be used in the defense of European interests overseas and outside the geographical limits of the Treaty of Washington—the national French and British nuclear programs for the upgrading of their strategic offensive capabilities (and for tactical nuclear arms in the French case) stand out to break the pattern of indecisiveness prevailing in the rest of Western Europe. Strengthening the deterrence value of the British and French forces can only enhance overall deterrence on the Western side. But both efforts, while European and potentially useful to all of Western Europe, cannot improve the position of the West European NATO partners as a group nor the political coherence of Western Europe as an emerging political community.

Other factors impede the process of political unification of Western Europe. The pressure from the oil-producing countries on West European economies, the divisive impact of inflation and distortion of currency exchange rates in the monetary relations, the scarceness of capital for investment and growing unemployment in industrial economies without real growth tend to block the engine of economic integration within the framework of the Common Market. The lack of a comprehensive and coherent West European energy supply policy aggravates the vulnerability to exterior pressures and international accidents such as the Gulf War or the Iranian Revolution. But the single most dangerous risk is that caused by the massive increase of Soviet military power and by the increased political use of this power in demonstration as against Poland or for actual intervention as in Afghanistan. The growing dependence of Western Europe on undisturbed international relations for the sake of its international trade and supply with raw materials, on U.S. protection and on Soviet goodwill has become the critical factor of West European independence and security.

NOTE

1. Report of the Council on The Future Tasks Of The Alliance, adopted December 14, 1967, in Brussels by the fifteen foreign ministers. (Reprinted in NATO Facts and Figures (Brussels: 1971), p. 366.)

6 THE BATTLE OF UNENGAGED MILITARY STRATEGIES

Phillip A. Karber

In the accelerating arms race in Central Europe since 1965 the West is falling behind in quantity while the Eastern bloc has caught up in quality. Driving the armament buildup is the military machine of the Soviet Union, whose force expansion has far outdistanced its rival superpower's. The Soviet Union alone has added more conventional weapons in Central Europe than all of its Warsaw Pact allies and more than twice as many as the combined NATO forces. The obvious question is why? What political dividend do the Soviets hope to reap from the military investment? The inner workings of Soviet political-military decisionmaking are sufficiently opaque as to prohibit empirical observation. But there are other important questions as well: Has the Eastern bloc gained militarily significant options as a result of its conventional buildup, and if so do they undermine NATO's strategy of flexible response adopted in 1967? Why has arms control failed to halt, slow or stabilize the conventional armament competition? After 15 years of force modernization and expansion, is the Warsaw Pact any closer to winning the arms race in Central Europe than before? The answers to these questions reflect the returns the Soviet Union may have anticipated from its massive capital investment.

The interaction in an armament competition is seldom limited to the quantitative and qualitative balance of weaponry. Rather, political and military elites on both sides tend to focus on how and with what options this force could be employed. Military strategy in peacetime, when the scenario for initiating war is at best uncertain (even the operating locale and opponent may be ambiguous), consists of a series of general contingency plans explicating the application of military operations in the event of hostilities. This may take the form of explicit doctrine or it may be implied by the views of military leadership, the limits of force structure, and the nature of military training.

Between 1965 and 1980 only one explicit declaration was issued by either of the two blocs competing in Central Europe. In 1967 after several years of intense discussion and much political persuasion from the United States, NATO formally adopted the strategy of *flexible response*. This strategy specified three defense requirements necessary to deter any Soviet-led Warsaw Pact attack on NATO territory. The first, *direct defense*, called for the maintenance of adequate ground, air, and naval forces in a high state of peacetime readiness to meet any likely contingency. The primary change in doctrine was to emphasize having sufficient conventional forces to meet a major attack. If unable to defeat a massive attack, NATO troops must at least be able to hold it at bay while defending as far forward as possible until the optimum level of response for the next defense phase is decided.

The second requirement of flexible response was *deliberate escalation*, a nuclear strike to symbolize the seriousness with which NATO viewed the aggression. The scope, magnitude, and duration of the deliberate escalation phase have never been defined. Rather, NATO defense planners have assumed its ambiguity will keep Soviet military and political elites uncertain as to its application and thus be a deterrent. Implied is that deliberate escalation is unlikely to be exercised until the collapse of NATO's conventional defense or the loss of significant territory is imminent.

After this transitory phase, should the situation continue to deteriorate, NATO would initiate a *general nuclear response*. This large-scale nuclear strike would not only be delivered against Eastern Europe but also against critical military targets in the USSR. Implementation could either precede or be exercised simultaneously with the unleashing of U.S. intercontinental strikes.

Flexible response was widely viewed in the West as a significant step in stabilizing the Central European military balance, decreasing the risks of nuclear escalation in the event of hostilities, and leading to a political environment of interbloc cooperation and exploration of arms control options. These perceived advantages were not unrealistic. The mid-1960s conventional force balance in Central Europe was the best it had been in the postwar competition. The forces of the Warsaw Pact deployed in Central Europe had less than a 50 percent advantage over NATO in conventional weaponry and in level of technological capability and combined arms force structure design they were decidedly inferior to the quality of Western forces. Without large-scale mobilization and reinforcement the success of an Eastern bloc conventional attack would have been improbable. The level of readiness of even the forward-deployed Soviet units, their insufficiency in conventional fire support and logistics, and the interceptor orientation and severe range and payload limitations of frontal aviation combined to make the prospect of a nonnuclear surprise attack remote.

The flexible response reduced both the automaticity and escalatory level of the resort to nuclear first use. It provided time to determine the intent and magnitude of an attack, time for Eastern bloc political elites to reassess the strength of Western political resolve and military resistance, time for careful NATO consideration of nuclear options. Any conflict in Central Europe would be fraught with enormous danger but this is in inverse proportion to time between the onset of hostilities and the nuclear response. Developing the flexible response doctrine gave NATO decisionmakers an opportunity to reassess the military balance in Central Europe and demonstrated the attractiveness of negotiating arms control.

In retrospect the West's adoption of the flexible response strategy appears to have served unwittingly as a stimulus for the resultant Soviet-led Warsaw Pact military buildup. The new NATO doctrine was based on several conditions implicitly expected to remain constant throughout the life of the strategy: First, political competition between the blocs appeared to be growing less confrontational, the prospect of a military crisis seemed remote, and a drastic change in the situation would permit NATO to take advantage of defensive preparations. Second, NATO's significant lead in the technological development of new conventional weaponry favored direct defense over an Eastern offensive—a qualitative advantage that was expected to continue to offset quantitative imbalance. Third, NATO was expected to retain significant superiority in tactical battlefield nuclear weapons that would convey military advantage in deliberate escalation to first use of nuclear weapons, and while the Eastern bloc might have an advantage in longer-range theater nuclear systems, the superior U.S. strategic force component of general nuclear response was expected to continue to dominate the top end of the ladder of nuclear threats and more than compensate for Soviet theater systems.

Neutralization of any of these assumptions by the Warsaw Pact would have cast doubt on the credibility of flexible response, but should all three assumptions be negated, it would mean nullification of the doctrine—a symbolic victory in a peacetime arms race. The three dependent conditions of flexible response thus became pressure points vulnerable to reaction. The Soviet-led Warsaw Pact could be content with the military and political status quo in Central Europe. Or they could undertake a heavy investment in military assets and technology with the hope of surpassing the West. They could invalidate NATO's new doctrine, thereby opening new avenues of political maneuver and thus achieving for the USSR the deferential status of preeminent military power in Europe, a status the Soviets felt had been unjustly denied them after 1945.

The success of their reacting to unintended challenge posed by flexible response was far from assured. It required an enormous commitment of resources that could succeed only if the West failed to compete and it had to be supported by a diplomatic offensive well orchestrated and fine-tuned to Western longing for détente and belief in the utility of arms control. The military problem faced by the Warsaw Pact was not limited to a large-scale buildup and modernization of their conventional armament simultaneously with the theater and strategic nuclear forces, although this was a requisite, but even more fundamentally it demanded a radical alteration in their own doctrine for theater conflict in Central Europe.

Throughout the late 1950s and early 1960s the Soviets believed that the strong prospect of nuclear weapons being used on the battlefield made a linear positional defense operationally untenable; the defender would be forced either to disperse or face certain destruction. Under such conditions maneuver was viewed as the key to operational success. Movement of the ground battle onto the territory of the defender meant that it would be the homeland where most of the nuclear destruction would take place. Knowing where to go the attacker could unleash nuclear salvos in the direction and on the flanks of the advance. If concentrated, the defense would be destroyed; if the defense was dispersed, the attacker could be confident of freedom of maneuver. High rates of maneuver offered the prospect of deep penetration and quick interpositioning of forces so that the effectiveness of the defenders' use of nuclear weapons was likely to be undermined by concern over troop safety and the cohesion of the rear area. The massing of combat formations, a historical characteristic of Soviet operations, was viewed as a critical vulnerability and the concept of concentrating for a breakthrough was abandoned in favor of dispersed multiple axes of advance across the breadth of the front.

Since any European conflict was assumed to be nuclear from the outset, conventional artillery assets and supporting structures for sustained conventional combat were cut drastically between 1958 and 1965. The primary role for nuclear delivery was transferred from aircraft to surface-to-surface missiles, with frontal aviation being heavily oriented to a role of defending Warsaw Pact air space against NATO's nuclear strike aircraft. With the expectation of a short, intense conflict engaging widely dispersed or heavily suppressed defenses, even greater emphasis was placed upon the tank as a mobile firing platform with high survivability within that environment, and an extensive effort was made to achieve full mechanization for infantry.

By the mid-1960s the Soviets began to consider a *conventional variant* to their theater warfare doctrine, recognizing that political conditions might preclude the immediate use of nuclear weapons. The Soviet adoption of a conventional variant to their theater warfare doctrine should not be confused with NATO's doctrine of flexible response. Where the latter strategy calls for a prolonged conventional defense for as long as possible and presumes that the initiation of nuclear fire will be at NATO's discretion and to its advantage, the Soviet concept is quite asymmetrical. The Soviet conventional variant presumes that the nonnuclear stage of the conflict will not be a substitute but a precursor to nuclear initiation. If the attack is succeeding, the defender is likely to initiate nuclear first use; on the other hand if the defense holds and the attack has a high prospect of becoming bogged down in a protracted conflict, it will be the Soviets who initiate nuclear fire in order to force the defender to disperse and open up the battlefield to offensive maneuver. Contrary to NATO's faith in the defensive value of tactical nuclear weapons, the Soviets clearly believe that the initiation of nuclear fire by either side merely ensures their offensive success by maximizing high rates of advance deep into NATO's rear area.

Adoption of a conventional variant in the late 1960s presented the Soviets with some fundamental problems. Because of the realization that a conflict might turn nuclear at any moment, the requirement to suppress NATO's nuclear delivery systems during the conventional phase of battle took highest priority. A long period of mobilization would provide the West with time to disperse its warheads and delivery systems, and, even if these could be acquired, the inaccuracies of conventionally armed surface-to-surface rockets and the inherent limited range and payload of frontal aviation interceptors provided little prospect of degrading NATO's nuclear capability during the conventional stage of conflict. The forward-deployed Warsaw Pact ground forces were clearly insufficient in conventional firepower and logistical sustainability to engage in prolonged nonnuclear hostilities. While massive mobilization and reinforcement of Soviet forces from the western USSR could provide additional mass needed to break through mobilized NATO defenses, the tactical concentration required would render them maximally vulnerable to NATO's first use of nuclear fire.

The upsurge in the Central European arms race is a product of the Soviet-led Eastern bloc implementing correctives to make their undeclared strategic concept of a conventional variant operationally viable. To the extent that NATO's doctrine of flexible response has served as stimulant, one can only grudgingly admire the audaciousness and tenacity of the Soviet decisionmaking elite, not only for the Spartan approach to military resource allocation, but also their determined commitment as long-term competitors. However, to the extent that they have succeeded in eroding the strategic foundations of flexible response, Central Europe has become a more dangerous place to live.

The change in the conventional military balance between 1965 and 1980 produced a dramatically different operational environment, a new range of offensive options for the Warsaw Pact, and a series of defensive problems for NATO out of proportion to the quantitative and qualitative shifts that occurred within individual armament categories. The new conditions produced by the conventional imbalance cut across the spectrum of potential conflict: They greatly increase the likely instability associated with an interalliance crisis; they have given the Eastern bloc the capability to implement new and more threatening offensive operational concepts, and they significantly decrease the credibility of NATO's nuclear deterrent.

Crisis Stability

In the mid-1960s the dominant conventional military threat posed to NATO was the contingency of massive Warsaw Pact mobilization. The Eastern bloc was perceived as being able to field within a month of mobilization a force of ninety divisions on the Central Front—reinforcing Soviet, East German, Czechoslovakia and Polish forward-deployed units with a 55 percent increase in conventional weaponry by the redeployment of formations located in the western USSR, the Baltic, Belorussia, and Carpathian military districts. With sparse local reserves and limited capacity to ship reinforcements overseas from the United States in several weeks, NATO could augment its conventional weaponry by less than 20 percent. Thus in a Guns of August scenario the West, already outnumbered 1.5 to 1 in forward-deployed conventional weapons, would over thirty days mobilization be forced to watch as the Warsaw Pact added five weapons to each one activated by NATO—the result being an unfavorable Central Theater imbalance of 2 to 1. While the West could utilize the extended Eastern bloc period of mobilization to deploy its own forces to the border and prepare defensive positions, once hostilities began it would be only a matter of time before the echelons of Warsaw Pact armies massed for local breakthroughs and penetrated the defending line. NATO's forces already stretched thin to cover the front, with minimal operational reserves and no means of replacing heavy unit losses, would face a slowly developing but irresistible penetration of their forward defense (see Table 6-1).

It is ironic that over the last 15 years the respective sides have employed determined but asymmetrical measures to alter the material bases of the mid-1960s mobilization scenario. NATO focused its effort on improving its reserve and reinforcement capability, expanding the conventional assets available in 1980 after countermobilization by 50 percent over what it could have fielded in 1965. This has been achieved by doubling the quantity of U.S. prepositioned (but unmanned) equipment stored in the Federal Republic of Germany, by an expanded air transport capacity to ferry men and combat aircraft to Europe rapidly, the growth of West German territorial defense units, the rebuilding of the French army deployed adjacent to Central Europe, and incremental improvements in Dutch reserve mobilization units. The good news is that today, unlike the mid-

Table 6-1. Expansion of Forward Deployed and Mobilization
Conventional Weapons, 1965-80.

		Forward Deployed	Mobilization	Combined Total
		(Central European Active Operational Units)	(External Reinforcement and Central European Reserves after 30 days)	(Forward Deployed and Mobilization)
1965	NATO	25,000	3,000	28,000
	Warsaw Pact	38,000	18,000	56,000
	Ratio (Warsaw Pact/ NATO)	1.5: 1	6: 1	2: 1
1980	NATO	31,000	11,000	42,000
	Warsaw Pact	62,000	26,000	88,000
	Ratio (Warsaw Pact/ NATO	2: 1	2.4: 1	2.1: 1

1960s, over the course of an extended thirty days mobilization the interbloc force ratio does not get worse for NATO. The bad news is that, after years of concentrated effort by NATO, the ratio in conventional weaponry upon mobilization is still 2 to 1 in favor of the Warsaw Pact, and even more significantly, the ratio in conventional weaponry prior to mobilization—armament in forward-deployed active units—has increased to NATO's disfavor from 1.5 to 2 to 1.

In contrast to NATO's priority of building up reserve and reinforcement vis-à-vis active unit expansion, the Warsaw Pact conventional buildup has been focused on the expansion and modernization of operational forward-deployed forces without sacrificing potent reinforcement capability. By 1980 the Warsaw Pact active units in Central Europe had strengthened their inventory of conventional weaponry to the point that their premobilization strength exceeded the total quantity of systems available in 1965 after 30 days of mobilization and the reinforcement of over 30 divisions. Through its methodical buildup the Eastern bloc has altered the Central European military balance more significantly than had they reinforced the forward-deployed forces by over 30 divisions in 1965, yet without triggering a countermobilization by NATO.

If in the mid-1960s the Warsaw Pact had perceived the necessity of conducting a conventional campaign against the West on the central front, they had no choice but to mobilize and reinforce. The reason was not limited to quantitative ratios of conventional weaponry but driven by the low state of readiness of forward forces, lack of combined arms integration at the level of maneuver units, disparate mobility of artillery and air defense units to keep pace with mechanized formations, a tactical air force with insufficient range and payload to pose a nonnuclear offensive threat, inadequate logistics and transport to keep pace with fast rates of advance or high-intensity combat. In 1965 extended preparation time and massed concentration offered the only means of compensating for these deficiencies. By 1980, however, the Warsaw Pact not only had the necessary mass forward deployed, but, because of qualitative improvements in all combat arms and supporting elements and with significantly increased unit readiness, they no longer needed the time traditionally associated with extended mobilization and reinforcement in order to field a potent offensive threat.

In 1965 NATO could comfortably delay a reaction to early warning for at least a week so that further intelligence could be collected, allied political elites could calibrate response options to the situation, and Eastern bloc intentions could be diplomatically probed before military mobilization was undertaken. In the 1980s a political crisis carrying even the portent of heightened military activity within the Eastern bloc will necessitate the immediate calling of military alerts; quick and visible deployment of the majority of NATO forces to their border defense positions; initiation of large-scale reinforcement from the United States with transatlantic movement of 1,000 combat aircraft; dispersal of nuclear warheads located in Central Europe; and full European mobilization—call-up of reservists, commandeering of civilian support assets, militarization of transportation and telecommunications infrastructures—all as economically disruptive as they are militarily essential.

This drift toward a hair trigger military imbalance is very disturbing. While the political environment in Europe is much more cooperative than in previous decades and historical flashpoints (such as Berlin) appear dormant, the interests of the respective sides today compete not on a regional but a global stage. A clash of wills elsewhere, one not even involving European political issues could escalate horizontally to the only place on the globe where troops of the two superpowers face each other across a common border. In this type of crisis the West's military vulnerability on the Central front could be viewed by the Warsaw Pact as a means of political leverage for even a remote flank. The Eastern bloc's acquisition of a forward-deployed offensive capability expands their ability for coercion. NATO today faces a broad range of threats, from short-warning attack to extended massive mobilization, which not only greatly increases the complexity and cost of defense on the central front but opens up multiple new avenues for arms competition. The Eastern bloc's material expansion of forward-deployed units would not be nearly so disturbing if they were not so actively developing new offensive operational concepts to take advantage of the new reality of a changed military balance in Central Europe.

The most trenchant implication of the Warsaw Pact conventional buildup is that in a crisis, NATO must respond to ambiguous warning in hours rather than weeks. Such action cannot help but appear provocative but unless it is fast and full, the opportunity for avoiding a decisive defeat will depend upon the political magnanimity of the Eastern bloc, not the military capability of NATO. Western forces in place in Central Europe, while not unformidable, are extremely vulnerable to a short-warning attack, unless they have had a minimum period of preparation and reaction time—for a forward defense 96 hours are essential. But sufficient Warsaw Pact forward-deployed forces are at a high enough state of peacetime readiness that they could launch a successful offensive within 96 hours after receiving campaign orders.

The problem is that these respective time windows, while both approximate to four days, are not symmetrical in either opening or closure. At the beginning of a crisis as Eastern bloc units are deploying to dispersed positions and forward assembly areas NATO forces will still be waiting for intelligence indicators to be accessed, assessed, and acted upon by the alliance political decisionmaking process. With as little as 48 hours lead time, elements of Warsaw Pact assault formations are likely to be in position for an imminent border crossing before the majority of NATO units have even left their kasserns. This will present an extremely dangerous military situation. Over the next several days the Eastern bloc high command will be in a position to implement their conventional variant with probable success—NATO forces will be at their maximum vulnerability and the fact that this is a temporarily limited opportunity will exacerbate incentives to capitalize on it. Thus the visible and labored process of NATO deployment will offer attractive incentives for both military preemption or political pressure.

Whether the Eastern bloc would actually attempt to exploit this crisis of asymmetrical readiness is unknowable. What is clear is that it is a capability for the 1980s that did not exist before—a capability not accidently acquired but intentionally and methodically procured.

Primacy of the Offensive

Under flexible response, the concept of forward direct defense poses the most formidable challenge for conventional forces. Its primary requirement is that NATO's ground forces currently deployed in Central Europe must be able to meet and stop a Soviet-led Warsaw Pact attack under a wide variety of potential contingencies, with success measured by the length of time they can hold (practically, a matter of weeks) and the amount of territory that can be defended (as much of West Germany as possible, but not infrequently measured in terms of permitting no penetration deeper than fifty kilometers from the border). The potentialities of new weapons technology have raised the hope that an innovative combination of technology and tactics will usher in a new era of defensive supremacy in land warfare.

Throughout the 1970s military analysts of both NATO and the Warsaw Pact discussed and even debated the growing prospect that the combined impact of newly developing conventional technology could produce a fundamental alteration between offense and defense on the modern battlefield. It was observed that fire power and maneuver are related. In an era when the latter is ascendent, it provides a clear advantage to the attacker, in that the inherent advantage of the initiative (being able to choose the time, place, means, and method of attack) results in the defense being quickly penetrated and rapidly overrun. On the other hand when fire power is dominant (as in World War I), maneuver is reduced to a crawl, exposure during an attack results in high attrition, and the inherent stability of the defense produces a stalemate. With only few exceptions the most new military technology is oriented to antimaneuver fire power. No simple wonder weapon has been invented, but when the newer systems are employed in an orchestrated manner they have the potential of creating a combined arms maelstrom that greatly enhances the stability of the defense against mechanized assault.

Thus, for example, the introduction of advanced sensor technology and the creation of true all-source fusion centers may give NATO ground forces the time that they need to deploy forward, select optimal firing positions, dig in, lay minefields, and bring up sufficient reserves of ammunition. Realizing that a short-warning attack is insufficient against a NATO defense that is prepared, the Soviet military will be forced to bring up substantial reinforcements, which in turn will buy NATO more time—time to prepare a truly effective defense that is linear, dense, and deployed in depth. Success in the attack, as the Soviets well realize, is not merely a function of high force ratios in concentrated sectors but is equally affected by density—the ratio of force to space. Since there is a finite amount of area between the Baltic and the Bavarian Alps, once NATO has closed the gaps of its defensive line every battalion that can be added from the mobilization of reserves or the introduction of reinforcements is worth several times its number on the opposing side. Facing deployed defenses, the Warsaw Pact forces must mass and accept enormous attrition in the hope of punching a hole through NATO's defense; an echelonment that can only be conducted simultaneously on several narrow and widely separated sectors.

This is a situation for which much of the new technology is applicable. The slow rate of advance during the breakthrough process and the highly perceptible signatures emanated will not only permit the new generation of tactical sensors real-time target acquisition but also allow the defense to deploy rapidly in threatened sectors. It is against massed armored targets that the new generation of stand-off air and artillery area munitions are optimized. Although unlikely to produce high attrition in and of themselves, the effect of scatterable mines, DPICM bomblets, and fuel-air explosives will slow down significantly the momentum of the attack by creating disorganization in the assault elements, suppression of their concentrated fire support, and disruption of the closure rate of the second echelon. Reducing the tempo of attack would give NATO's infantry and armor time to service the targets presented. By taking maximum advantage of terrain, they can reduce their own vulnerability to direct fire while producing a highly disproportionate attrition of the attacker, who in order to succeed must move over exposed ground despite a relative disadvantage in visibility and far less fire effectiveness. In this environment the antiarmor capability of infantry and tanks, when used in combination, greatly enhance each other's capabilities. The long range and highly accurate fires of the heavy antitank guided missiles (ATGMs) can pick off the initial elements of the attacking force before their weapons are in effective range, forcing the attacker to slow down and disperse. As the assault closes on the defensive positions, the high rate of fire of the tank guns and the proliferation of large quantitites of concealed portable ATGMs create a heavy concentration of fire. The effects of highly lethal improved conventional munition (ICM) prevent the attacking infantry from dismounting and keep the armored vehicles buttoned up, while scatterable mines fired into the middle of the assault echelons immobilize their remaining armored vehicles and inhibit their reassembly. Laser-guided cannon-launched, guided projectiles (CLGPs) and the surge capability of helicopter-mounted long-range ATGMs can turn a disorganized attack into a rout.

The increased survivability provided to the defending tanks by the new armor, combined with the maneuverability and base of fire provided by mechanized infantry combat vehicles mounting rapid-fire guns, would permit the defending forces to hold their positions longer, thus inflicting higher attrition. When pressed, they would not have to risk the loss of unit integrity by being overrun, but instead can withdraw a kilometer or two to the next terrain feature, under the cover of the long-range ATGMs mounted on armor vehicles and repeat the whole process. There is a critical point in tactical battle when, as the result of unequal attrition and disorganization, the attack becomes overextended; it is during these few minutes that a well-organized defense using the high maneuverability and suppressive fires of tanks and mechanized infantry combat vehicles can, through audacious counterattack on the attacker's exposed flanks, not only retake the terrain so dearly lost, but also envelop and overrun isolated formations that can then be reduced piecemeal and at leisure.

The success of this ground scenario presumes that overhead NATO's tactical air forces, reinforced by 1,000 aircraft redeployed from the United States, have retained their freedom to intervene decisively and can keep Eastern bloc fighter bombers off by intercepting them in the air and attacking the infrastructure of their air bases. It means holding the Warsaw Pact second echelon at risk by reconnoitering their approach, interdicting their rate of forward deployment, breaking their logistic flow, and striking concentrations at key choke points and assembly areas. It means too supporting NATO counterattacks by saturation attack, patroling of open flanks, and suppressing opposing air defenses.

In the situation just described, the effect of this combined arms battle, when replicated over and over across the breadth of the Central European front, is to make forward defense viable not only as a means of securing the territorial integrity of NATO but also as the mechanism of a strong conventional deterrent. Unfortunately this dream has more than an equal likelihood of turning into a nightmare.

There are several fundamental problems for NATO in assuming an inherent defensive advantage is conveyed with the new generation of armament. First, technology is neutral. Although a given weapon or group of systems may be clearly defensive on the tactical level, when combined with surprise, quantity, and innovative doctrinal orchestration, the same technology can be decisively offensive at the operational or theater levels and the Eastern bloc now has access to this advanced weaponry. For example, the new armor that increases the survivability of NATO tanks correspondingly when mounted on Eastern bloc tanks greatly reduces their vulnerability to defending anti-tank warheads. The vehicle-mounted ATGM can provide protective fire support to a high-speed mechanized assault and also be used defensively for flank protection in a breakthrough so that assaulting armored assets can remain concentrated throughout the depth of an attack. Artillery-fired antimaneuver submunitions prevent the very tactical movement upon which the cohesion of the active defense depends, likewise multiple rocket launchers (MRL) and air-delivered scatterable mines can forestall the timely arrival of NATO reserves. Attack helicopters can leapfrog and outflank the ground defenses and add momentum to the exploitation of a breakthrough. Fighters armed with all-aspect air-to-air missiles and overlapping air-defense gun and surface-to-air missile envelopes can prevent NATO close air support aircraft from intervening in a critical ground battle. Warsaw Pact fighter bombers armed with the same type of advanced air-to-surface munitions as NATO depends upon for its defensive interdiction campaign can seriously impede Western air base sorties as well as ambush the forward deployment of NATO brigades caught out of position at the start of hostilities.

Even advanced intelligence-gathering technology—satellite photography, aerial side-looking radar, infrared detection, and electronic communications intercept—can be used offensively to identify the location of exploitable gaps in the defenders' line. This was one of the lessons from the defeat of the Egyptian army in 1973 which Eastern bloc commentaries noted with particular interest. Depending on how the new conventional technology is employed and the operating environment in which it is used, virtually all of the new tactically "defensive" fire power could significantly increase the lethality of the assaulting formations, increase the speed of penetration and rate of advance for mechanized warfare, and increase the paralyzing shock effects of the modern combined arms offensive.

A second problem with assuming inherent defensive gains from new high technology is that in order to take advantage of the new fire power in stabilizing forward defense over the course of a campaign a stable defense forward is needed at the beginning of a campaign. Doubtless fully mobilized and prepositioned prepared defense can inflict with modern weapons a favorably disproportionate level of attrition on an attacker even if the latter has the same level of technological sophistication. This raises the question of whether a 2 to 1 overall theater force ratio is a sufficient margin of superiority for the attacker to initiate offensive operations with an uninhibiting level of confidence. Historically, for battalion tactical level engagements strategists have prescribed a minimum of a 3 to 1 attack/defense force ratio. Today on comparable terrain and with an equal level of defense preparation a successful force ratio would likely require the double the assaulting forces, a ratio of 6 to 1. Given the offensive advantage of the initiative, the high mobility of modern formations, and the concept of echeloned assault, however, an overall theater force ratio in conventional weaponry of 2 to 1 is sufficient to give an attacker the necessary level of force generation for multiple simultaneous corps or army breakthrough assaults across the breadth of a front the width of Central Europe. Lest this be doubted, it should be remembered that in the 1940 campaign in France the Germans attacked a defense that had been in position for nine months at theater level odds of less than 1 to 1 in total quantity of armament (including an inferiority in tanks) and in the process established the blitzkrieg as a new measure for offensive success. Moreover, the entire

German force had fewer armored vehicles than just one of today's Soviet tank armies.

Whatever validity force ratio assessments have as predictators of battle outcome it is neither at the theater level nor in contingencies where the defender has not established a continuous and dense defense in depth. The longer the defending forces are deployed in wartime positions prior to the outbreak of hostilities, the more they can substitute terrain preparation (minefields, demolition, wire, entrenchments, and alternate firing positions) for tactical density, thus adding depth with the residual units.

With at least four days of reaction to intelligence warning, NATO has sufficient forces to provide a continuous front along the interbloc border, however, because of the peacetime maldeployment of forces, few units will have occupied their positions long enough to undertake serious terrain preparation and the only reserves will be those still in transit. An attacking force of 56 divisions with a theater 2 to 1 advantage in conventional armament would likely pose a serious threat to the cohesiveness of the defense within several days of combat. With several additional days reaction period NATO forces would more than double their forward resiliance. With three weeks or more, even facing a full Warsaw Pact reinforced threat of 90 divisions and a theater force ratio of 2 to 1, the NATO defenders would have a dense defense with in-depth reserves that the battle would be one dominated by attrition where high-technology fire power would give a disproportionate level of losses to the attacker, half of whose force could not be committed at one time due to the saturation of the available frontage.

At the other end of the spectrum, that is with less than 72 hours of reaction time, no matter how frenetic the effort, NATO could not field even a continuous defense. With major gaps across the front, with single battalions stretched to cover key axes of advance where an entire division is required, with half of NATO's units still drawing ammunition, or strung out in road march, maneuver would reign supreme. Under these conditions a Warsaw Pact attack, even one limited in the initial border crossing to only 30 divisions, with a marginal force ratio of 1 to 1, would be a disaster for NATO. There would be regimental and division size penetrations across the breadth of the front, many of them facing only weak resistance, some proceeding into the depths of the defense virtually unopposed. Where NATO brigades attempted to stand and fight with exposed flanks they would quickly be enveloped, to be reduced by follow-on East European armies. Those NATO units still in forward movement would have to engage the attacker in a continual series of meeting engagements unable to make use of the inherent defensive advantages of terrain. There would be no front line or FEBA, only disconnected defensive pockets separated by red tentacles—forward detachments pulling the Soviet offensive toward the Rhine. Confusion throughout NATO's rear area, heightened by Soviet air attack and assault helicopter landings, would be rife. In this situation high-technology fire power is not an answer to maneuver but rather its victim. Quality does not offset quantity but favors the side whose forces are ready— the side that seizes the initiative first.

That the foregoing description cannot be dismissed as sheer fantasy is the third problem in assuming the ascendence of high-technology defensive fire power. The Eastern bloc has been developing conventional offensive operational concepts uniquely designed for short-warning attack. Virtually an entire generation of Western Sovietologists have built their careers on the theory of an innate Russian proclivity for minimized risk. Unfortunately they have not convinced the Soviet general staff and the high command of the Warsaw Pact. Since the end of the Second World War the Soviets have consistently emphasized an offensive strategy in the event of hostilities on the central front. However, even an offensive strategy would not be so destabilizing if as in the 1950s the Soviets still demanded a minimum 3 to 1 theater superiority for an attack or as in the 1960s they still presumed that massive nuclear attacks were a prerequisite. Unfortunately, there is a direct correlation between the Soviet-led Warsaw Pact buildup of conventional forces and the Soviet-led adoption of new conventional air and ground operational concepts.

The Soviet conventional variant strategy remains dissimilar to NATO's doctrine of flexible response because they still do not view a conventional campaign as alternative to theater nuclear warfare but, rather, as an opportunity to conduct nuclear denial under conventional conditions. Thus in the early 1970s the Soviets introduced the concept of an air offensive, a multistaged sequential attack to be launched in the first hours of a campaign. This operation envisaged first the orchestrated employment of nearly 2,000 aircraft, including frontal aviation fighters, medium bombers, and "strategic" bombers from long-range aviation, in a set of concentrated strikes against NATO's main operating air bases, command and communications infrastructure, and ground-based nuclear assets. Given the mission and target structure, a conventional air offensive would have to be initiated under as close an approximation to surprise conditions as possible. With warning and mobilization NATO would have time to disperse its nuclear warheads from their peacetime centralized storage sites; a higher percentage of nuclear delivery aircraft would be vectored to alternate fields and placed on quick reaction alert. Surface-to-surface missile launchers and tactical nuclear artillery would be hard to acquire once deployed in the field. Western command and release communications would be harder to degrade and more redundant. NATO's peacetime posture makes each of these components lucrative and efficient targets, but they must be attacked as a synergistic set and with minimal defensive reaction time.

By 1980 the marriage of concept and capability had matured to the point where under short warning conditions the Soviet-led air offensive not only would endanger NATO's nuclear forces but in the process would seriously degrade Western conventional capability as well. Today Western air commanders view the air offensive as the most serious threat. They have tracked the Soviets' acquisition of the platforms and munitions with which to implement it and witnessed the command and training exercises by which it is practiced. Even if the air offensive fails in its primary mission, the sheer magnitude of the attack will preoccupy Western aerial assets to the point that they will have minimal impact on the ground campaign for the first several days of conflict—the very time they are needed most. If the air offensive meets Soviet expectations, however, by the end of the first day at least half of NATO's main operating air bases in Central Europe will be effectively shut down and others will have significantly reduced sortie generation capacity, there will be a number of large corridors cut through the former NIKE/HAWK SAM air defense belt and the ground-based early warning radar net will be nonexistent, critical command communication nodes will be destroyed and the major nuclear storage depots prevented from dispersing their warheads. The second and third days would include expanded attacks against air bases and nuclear sites as well as strikes against key logistic and lines of communication targets.

The significance of a conventional air offensive for NATO strategy is threefold. First, over the last decade every year has witnessed a growth in Warsaw Pact capability relative to NATO's capacity to counter it. Second, advances in weapons technology have not only been essential to the implementation of the concept but have clearly favored the attacker over the defender. Third, the successful implementation of the air offensive is directly correlated with a short-warning attack. Indeed the latter is a prerequisite for the Warsaw Pact achieving the primary mission of nuclear denial during the conventional period of hostilities.

During the 1970s the Eastern bloc also adopted new offensive operational concepts for the ground forces. Its pattern of development and implementation was quite different from that of the air offensive. Whereas the concept was introduced first and then the capability enhanced throughout the 1970s for the air force, for the Warsaw Pact armies the new operational methods followed a decade of force maturation. For the air the new capability almost exclusively involved qualitative improvement—one-for-one replacement of aerial platforms, new munitions, more sophisticated training—while for the ground forces much of the growth in capability was quantitative. For the air the basic premise was to employ the air offensive in a new mission as a means to exploit a NATO vulnerability; for the ground forces the mission remained the same as before, however—penetrate NATO defenses and seize Central Europe as rapidly as possible. The problem was to reduce the vulnerability of Eastern bloc armies to NATO's initiation of tactical nuclear strikes, a threat that would be both most likely and most effective at the very point where Warsaw Pact forces generated the necessary conventional mass to break through a prepared defense. In fact, the Soviets had since the early 1960s developed the basic operational concept to solve this problem of vulnerability by replacing the breakthrough via multiple, rapid simultaneous axes of advance with disciplined dispersal down to battallion level. But this operational concept assumed that nuclear weapons would be employed on the battlefield from the start of a campaign, that the defender would also be dispersed out of fear of a nuclear strike, that the front would be granular and discontinuous rather than a prepared forward defense. In essence the fire power of nuclear weapons would so dominate tactical engagement that linear conventional battle would be negated, thus providing an environment optimized for maneuver. But with the shift in strategy to a conventional variant and the perceived necessity to fight in the initial period of war without nuclear weapons, yet continuously anticipating their imminent introduction, forced a fundamental reappraisal of Warsaw Pact operational concepts for ground warfare.

Following the 1973 Middle East War, there was a considerable tactical discussion anticipating the potential impact of new technology in stabilizing a prepared defense under conventional conditions and a number of alternative options were examined with the most innovative emphasis being on such concepts as "deep envelopment," "daring thrusts" and "strategic highway raids." However, it was not until the 1979 implementation of the Soviet theater force reorganization, as extensive and fundamental as the one conducted in the late 1950s, which also coincided with a radical change in strategy, that it became evident that the new operational environment for ground forces placed an even greater requirement for a "maneuver offensive."

Although new methods of assault are now being formally introduced and the formation of the new combined arms regimental level maneuver groups is well underway, nevertheless the new threat posed by "daring thrust" type concepts is neither in tactical innovation nor structural implementation but instead in the redefinition of the battlefield scenario. The Eastern bloc ground forces are not expected to gnaw their way through a prepared defense because the maneuver offensive presumed that the attack will be initiated before the defense is prepared. The problem for the Warsaw Pact is less one of creating gaps in the front via the massed breakthrough than exploiting gaps where a contiguous front does not exist due to the conditions of a short-warning attack.

Although the new air and ground offensive concepts were neither introduced simultaneously nor implemented similarly, the operational problem posed to NATO in the 1980s lies not in Warsaw Pact doctrinal developmental differences but rather, in a convergency of capability. Both the air and ground concepts are inherently offensive. They are designed to seize the initiative at the beginning of hostilities and maintain it throughout the conventional campaign by exacerbating and exploiting NATO's inherent vulnerabilities. Both heavily depend upon the assumption of a short-warning environment for their success. The risk in employing these new operational methods is less dependent upon the ratio of forces than it is upon the level of the defenders' readiness—mobilization, deployment, and reinforcement—at the outbreak of a conflict. The air and ground offensives complement each other. A by-product of the air offensive is that it greatly reduces and impedes the intervention of NATO's air forces in the ground campaign. Likewise a maneuver offensive that rapidly penetrates the ground defense will complicate the defenders' initiation of nuclear battlefield strikes by the confusion associated with an unstable and fluid front; the difficulty of targeting fast moving formations intermingled in the depths of the defense; and the over-running of the very tactical delivery systems, nuclear artillery and surface-to-surface missiles, deployed where the penetrations are most critical.

Thus the new air and ground offensive concepts present NATO's strategy of forward conventional defense with a lethal combination for which it has no doctrinal antidote. For NATO to defend forward requires that the defenses be deployed forward at the initiation of hostilities, an implicit assumption of flexible response that Soviet strategists have not taken for granted. Thus while NATO has under-taken a number of conventional force improvements, solving its vul-nerability to air attack and its unit maldeployment have not been among them.

Demise of Flexible Response

As the outlines and objectives of the Warsaw Pact's new offensive operational concepts become less opaque it also becomes more ob-vious that with NATO's adoption of flexible response the Eastern bloc has been engaged in a conscious and concentrated effort to negate the premises upon which the continued viability of the West's strategy depends. The three tiers of NATO's doctrine—direct defense, deliberate escalation, and general nuclear response—reflect a strategy of action based on four interrelated but differentiable levels of mili-tary balance. At one end of the spectrum the anticipated effective-ness of direct defense could be measured by the balance of the respective alliances' conventional forces deployed or committed to Central Europe while at the other end of the spectrum general nu-clear response could be equated to the correlation of intercontinental nuclear strategic forces between the rival superpowers. Between these end points on a continuum of violence deliberate escalation served as a crucial military and political link.

Direct defense represented an undesirable condition, warfare in Europe, executed with traditional means, conventional forces. Gen-eral nuclear response represented a desirable condition, deterrence, with unacceptable means, strategic nuclear exchange. Through the mechanism of "escalatory dominance" NATO strategists attempted to combine usable defense with an unusable deterrent in the hope that the former would make the latter credible and that the latter would prevent the former from being tested. Escalation dominance presumes that in an interactive process of ever-increasing violence, the side with the military advantage at the last point before the means of warfare produce unacceptable ends possesses a degree of coercive leverage conducive to termination of conflict on favorable terms. This introduced two intervening levels of force correlation. Between direct defense and deliberate escalation was the tactical number balance—nuclear weapons, most of which depended upon dual-capable conventional systems for delivery, that could be employed to influence the operational battlefield on the central front. Between deliberate escalation and general nuclear response was the theater nuclear balance—nuclear weapons, most of which resembled intercontinental systems in method of delivery and destructive yields, that could strike deep behind the battlefield and hold European political–economic targets hostage to strategic coercion.

Thus the flexible response strategy was based on four overlapping and escalating military balances, each competitive force element representing an expansion in the intensity and depth of violence. In the 1960s NATO recognized that its forces were quantitatively inferior in the conventional balance, particularly after a prolonged mobilization; however, it also realized that the West had a decided advantage in both quantity and quality in the tactical nuclear balance, which, if the conventional defenses were sufficient to force the Warsaw Pact armies to mass, could be employed to disrupt a concentrated attack. Given an initially viable forward defense, nuclear weapons could thus be introduced on the battlefield with decisive military impact and maximum political symbolic effect yet limited in intensity, geography, and collateral damage. For the Eastern bloc to respond they would have to escalate to theater nuclear strikes, which would not only mean self-defeating destruction but trigger the American intercontinental strategic force against the entire USSR target set. Thus with U.S. strategic nuclear superiority offsetting Soviet theater nuclear superiority the last point of clear escalatory dominance was in the realm of tactical nuclear weapons—where NATO had a significant advantage and any incentive to use it first.

Today this paradigm has changed radically from top to bottom. American intercontinental nuclear forces are offset by the Soviet achievement of strategic parity and the Eastern bloc has continued superiority in the theater nuclear balance. NATO has lost its vaunted superiority in the tactical nuclear balance, and, if the nuclear denial functions of the Warsaw Pact conventional variant strategy can be achieved, the West will be inferior on the battlefield whether the campaign is conventional or nuclear. Thus escalation dominance has not ceased to be a relevant concept for NATO but has changed polarity. Instead of being a credible means of NATO's military deterrence, it threatens to become the mechanism of its political defeat by the Warsaw Pact.

What makes the Eastern bloc's challenge to NATO's strategy so dangerous is that is has been developed against both the conventional defense and nuclear deterrent elements of flexible response simultaneously. The Eastern bloc conventional buildup in forward-deployed forces has presented new contingency options that significantly alter the significance of an altered conventional balance. One can argue whether the political decisionmaking elite of the Eastern bloc would in fact undertake the risks inherent in exploiting crisis instability, but it is undeniable that compared to 1965 they have achieved a new option of a short-warning attack. The Eastern bloc nuclear buildup in tactical, theater, and strategic forces effectively negates NATO's concept of escalation dominance. One can argue whether a residual uncertainty remains vis-à-vis the West's willingness to conduct a nihilistic act for which no military or political advantage would accrue once executed, but it is certain that the credibility of its nuclear linkage has been substantially reduced since 1965. What is most telling regarding Eastern bloc motives is that neither the conventional short-warning attack option nor denial of nuclear escalatory dominance were accidental. For the 1980s, unless there is a radical shift in the current trends in the Central European military balance, either through unilateral NATO force improvement or mutually agreed arms control, NATO strategy will have become a fatal victim of the Eastern bloc's peacetime competitive success and flexible response a decaying corpse waiting only for the onset of an inopportune crisis to be buried forever.

SOVIET MILITARY POWER
The Context of Restraint

7 SUSTAINING THE BURDEN OF SOVIET DEFENSE
Retrospect and Prospect

Abraham S. Becker

Soviet economic growth has been declining since about 1960, from average annual rates of 6 or 7 percent in the 1950s to 5 percent in the 1960s under 4 percent in the 1970s, and to less than 2 percent in the early 1980s.

Over the same two decades the Soviet Union has been engaged in building up its military forces without letup, although with some fluctuation in pace. At the conservative estimate of 4 to 5 percent average growth per year, total Soviet military expenditures must have increased between 2.2 and 2.7 times over the 20 years.

The future prospects of the Soviet economy must embarrass a regime for whom growth has been an element of legitimation, a regime that viewed itself in basic economic competition with the capitalist industrial nations. More important, the growth problem threatens political dangers through the creation of intensification of conflict among claimants on the national product as the annual increases in their allocations continue to shrink. It is a reasonable hypothesis that the high level and uninterrupted growth of military spending have been major factors in the deceleration of economic growth. Soviet leaders are doubtless aware that the military buildup has taken a toll on the economy and that reduction of military spending would yield resources badly needed for civilian development. The reasons for the persistence of the military buildup over so prolonged a period and on such an impressive scale as well as into

233

the likelihood of future change in this pattern are explored in this chapter.

EXTERNAL VS. INTERNAL DETERMINANTS OF SOVIET MILITARY EXPENDITURE

External Threat

The very purpose of a military force leads to a focus on the external threat as the explanation for the size and trend of expenditures to raise and maintain that force. A substantial literature has grown up, developing in theoretical-abstract, empirical or just descriptive terms the theme of functional relation between a state's military effort and the external threat. These efforts have not been conspicuously successful, despite the intuitively obvious nature of the relation. One reason is that national defense budgets have domestic functions—economic, political, or social—more or less unrelated to external developments. A more important reason is that mathematical-statistical treatment naturally attempts to isolate the foreign influence from domestic factors affecting the state's response, in what have come to be known as action–reaction models of international arms competitions.[1] However, the distinction between foreign and domestic influence is not always obvious, because they are linked by what may be called "operative" images. Foreign affairs are perceived by particular persons in a particular milieu. The point is a commonplace, but it is worth restating the corollary, that the determinants of foreign policy are in a significant sense entirely domestic: The meaning and implications of external events are perceived through prisms of domestic manufacture.

The foreign and domestic spheres are sometimes viewed as competing frameworks of explanation, whereas they should be considered as complements.[2] In any case, it is a remarkable fact of the literature on arms race modeling in the twentieth century that it took many years before the unique emphasis on adversary levels of expenditure as the independent variable was replaced by a more differentiated effort to link internal structural–institutional factors or perceptions of threat with expenditure dynamics.[3]

This is also an important reason why the dominant Western rationalizations of Soviet policymaking have come to grief. In the early

1960s one could imagine that in response to perceived weakness relative to the USSR's main adversaries, the Soviet military budget would be molded chiefly by evaluation of the NATO (and Chinese) threat. But if the initiation of a Soviet military buildup could thus be projected, it would also have been natural to forecast a diminution of the effort as "parity" was approached or achieved. As we know, the effort has not yet diminished.

It is true that no less an authority than Nikita Khrushchev implied that the Soviet defense budget in his time was largely dictated by U.S. military activities.[4] Eisenhower once complained to him that U.S. military leaders "keep grabbing for more" money to prevent falling behind the USSR, and he asked Khrushchev, "How is it with you?" "It's just the same," Khrushchev responded:

> Some people from our military department come and say "Comrade Khrushchev, look at this! The Americans are developing such and such a system. We could develop the same system, but it would cost such and such." I tell them there's no money; it's all been allotted already. So they say, "If we don't get the money we need and if there's a war, then the enemy will have superiority over us." So we discuss it some more and I end up giving them the money they ask for.

However, there are reasons to doubt that the anecdote fully describes actual Soviet practice under either Khrushchev or his successors. The Soviets have evolved a distinctive style of military development far from a carbon copy of the American. Nor can it be shown that the level or trend of Soviet military outlays has moved in tandem with that of the United States.

A three-way defense expenditure interaction model—USSR, United States, and People's Republic of China—was constructed by Despres and Dhrymes. The model was reviewed, revised, and fitted with revised CIA estimates for the Soviet Union by Shishko, who found that U.S. and Chinese defense expenditure were of little help in explaining changes in Soviet military outlays. The USSR level of a given year was primarily determined by Soviet military expenditures and GNP in the previous year. Shishko concluded that existing models were probably too crude to capture any interaction process that did exist.[5]

Figure 7–1 shows the relation of Chinese, Soviet, and U.S. defense spending, using CIA unclassified estimates and compilations for the period 1968–1978. These data indicate that from 1968 (the high-

Figure 7-1. Comparative Growth of U.S., Soviet, and Chinese Military Outlays, 1968–1978 (*1970 = 100*).

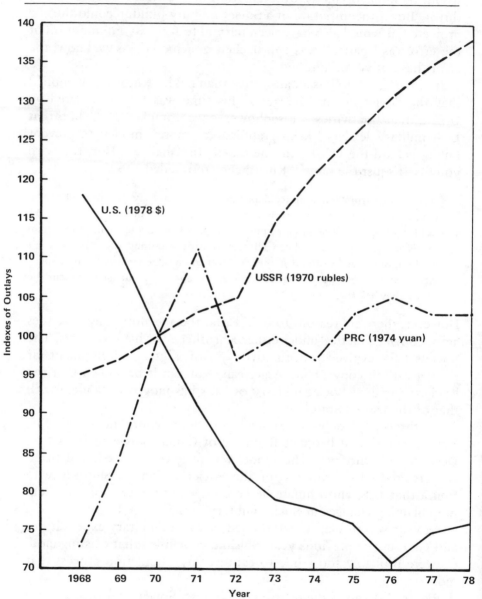

spending point of the Vietnam war) to 1976, the real value of U.S. defense outlays declined without interruption, while Soviet military spending at constant ruble prices is estimated to have grown without interruption; Chinese military expenditure in constant yuan rose 1.5 times in three years but leveled off thereafter at little over the 1970 mark.[6] Note that the U.S. expenditure curve in Figure 7–1 also describes the path of the ratio of U.S. spending to the dollar value of Soviet activities—from about 1.4 to 1 in 1968 to 0.7 to 1 in 1975–1978.

The data on outlays at constant prices are the best measure of the change in military activity. However, we do not know whether Soviet images of U.S. actions and intentions are influenced by this indicator or by others. Perhaps Soviet planners are more inclined to monitor other U.S. budgetary measures, such as obligational authority or funds available, or to introduce time lags and leads into their calculations. Still, these indicators are not likely to diverge substantially from the movement of expenditure as long as account is taken of price inflation. If Moscow is inclined to ignore the effects of inflation,[7] it could derive a sharply different picture of the trend in the U.S. military budget: At current prices, U.S. outlays on national defense (excluding veterans' benefits but including atomic energy and other defense-related activities) almost tripled between 1960 and 1980; deflated for price change, however, 1980 outlays were below those of 1960.[8]

Since the Kremlin may have been more impressed by other indicators of U.S. intentions—for example, statements by congressional or administration figures—it is not possible to refute the hypothesis of Soviet reaction to U.S. action conclusively. Moreover, no account has been taken here of non-U.S. NATO and non-Soviet Warsaw Pact expenditures. In general, then, to explain the overall Soviet military buildup in relation to the actions of its major adversaries would require a far more complex model. Failing that, the simple best predictor of Soviet military expenditure has been past expenditure.[9] At the same time, because simple action–reaction models do not explain the expenditure trends, the data do suggest the desirability of examining Soviet leadership perceptions and their decisionmaking environment.

Economic Size as Determinant

"[T]he expense both of preparing this military force in time of peace, and of employing it in time of war, is very different in the different states of society, in the different periods of improvement," wrote Adam Smith.[10]

Efforts have been made to explain levels of spending on defense in various countries by cross-national and intertemporal regression analysis emphasizing major macroeconomic variables. Pryor examined the available data for NATO and Warsaw Pact countries (revalued in a single currency) and found that at any point in time within both groupings the defense share of GNP tended to be related to the absolute level of GNP, but not to GNP per capita.[11] The negative finding was also an important result of Benoit's research with regard to developing countries. Benoit discovered a strong, positive correlation between the defense share of GNP and rates of growth of GNP and therefore raised the possibility of an income effect—that rapid growth made possible high allocations to defense. But the absence of any significant correlation between defense as a proportion of GNP and GNP per capita and the fact that "in multiple regression analysis, economic growth did not emerge as a significant determinant of the defense burden" caused him to reject the hypothesis.[12]

The notion that defense spending is significantly related to GNP or other aggregate output measures in the *short run* seems counterintuitive. It is implausible to expect a nation's year-to-year military efforts to vary directly with its economic fortunes. To the extent that decisions are made with some reference to external events, domestic economics will generally be expected to adjust to perceptions of foreign threat.

Adjusted for inflation, U.S. defense outlays dropped monotonically between 1968 and 1976 while GNP increased. Total Soviet military expenditures are estimated to have declined both right after World War II and in the mid-1950s. Explanations will not reflect a concern for keeping a constant relation between total military effort and aggregate national output.[13] With regard to the developing countries he studied, Benoit concluded that

> the main determinant of the size of the defense burden was the expectation of political and military leaders of the need for forces to deter, to threaten, or to engage in combat. Basically the defense burden was high in areas where combat had occurred or threatened to occur or which were on the boundaries between rival power blocs. (p. 275)

Over the middle term, especially with stabilization of the (perceived) external threat, greater regularity in the relation between defense and general economic activity may be expected. CIA has estimated that between the mid-1960s and the late 1970s, Soviet defense expenditures rose at approximately the same rate as GNP. It would hardly be appropriate to conclude that the Politburo adjusts the annual defense budget to the planned level of national output, even allowing for the fact that Soviet planners do their national accounting in terms of material product, which excludes most services, and not Western GNP. To begin with, the trend noted is an average; the CIA estimates of both GNP and military expenditure show year-to-year fluctuations, not necessarily of the same relative size. Moreover, the expenditure estimates are believed to be more accurate as to trend than as to annual values. Third, the CIA estimates are compiled in 1970 prices. There is no evidence that Soviet planners use that price set as their framework of weights for analysis of time change. It is much more likely that they use the data available to them—for example, industrial production indexes that use linked weights for five- or ten-year intervals.

Over most of the Brezhnev period military spending remained within bounds that, by Western measurement, correspond roughly to the overall growth of the economy in that period. However, the rate of aggregate economic growth was slower in the 1970s than in the 1960s, especially in the last half of the 1970s. So far there is no indication that Soviet military expenditure plans are taking account of that fact.

In the long term the level of development must bear considerably on the observed scale and quality of military activity. Not every indicator of scale will be equally affected as can be seen from the fact that the Tsar mobilized an army in World War I about the same size as that raised by the Soviets in World War II.[14] Between these two dates military technology changed considerably, but the effect of the rapid economic development over those decades may also be seen in the sharp changes in the magnitude and quality of support facilities—communication, transport, supply, military medicine, etc.

Defense capability is not just arms and men, forces in being, but capacity of the economy to sustain the waging of war. That development is of great importance in this respect is traditionally emphasized by Soviet writers. The guarantee of deterrence of imperialist attack on the socialist states, Marshal Grechko wrote, lay in strengthening the economic and defense might of the USSR and of all the states of the socialist commonwealth."[15]

The importance of the economic base is underscored in an era of "military–technical revolution."[16] The demands on the national economy for military preparedness are vastly enlarged by the sophistication and costliness of modern weapons,[17] while the possible scale and intensity of general nuclear war make it dangerous to count on building up military potential once hostilities have begun.[18] The Soviets have thus understood from the beginning that a powerful modern economy is the foundation of a strong military establishment, and their emphasis on the expansion of heavy industry, transportation, and communication—later, on research and development in high technology areas—as a path to developing armed might is too well known to require elaboration.[19]

This is the permissive side of the coin. The other is constraint. Over the long haul, stage and level of development also place limits on military activity, although such limits must be understood broadly, as Benoit showed. Anwar Sadat mortgaged the future for his 1973 gamble, but mortgage size depends on asset value and the loan must eventually be repaid. Except in the very short term, guns versus butter is a real dilemma for most real economies. Also, it is a characteristic of the trade-off between consumption and arms production that after a point the more a state wishes to buy of the one, the more it has to sacrifice of the other, as diminishing returns to increases of inputs in the expanding sector set in. This dictum, which economists know as the diminishing marginal rate of transformation, is a short or medium-run formulation. Even in the long run, it is not possible to have prolonged high rates of growth of military outlays and continued rapid expansion of the civil economy without equally rapid technological progress or substantial help from others. Not surprisingly, however, no hard and fast rules can be suggested to supply concrete meaning for "prolonged," "continued," "high," and "rapid."

Summary

Where then, do we stand, in the search for explanations of the prolonged Soviet military buildup?

1. If Soviet military spending over the past two decades has been a response to U.S. (or even NATO plus Chinese) military outlays, the models portraying that phenomenon have not yet been devel-

oped. The role of the external threat in Soviet resource allocation decisions must be reviewed in terms of decisionmakers' perceptions and the institutional context in which decisions are taken.

2. The growth and modernization of the Soviet economy have constituted the foundation for the development of Soviet military power, but it hardly seems likely that the military budget has been tailored to the Central Statistical Administration's national income statements. In the last few years, rates of military spending are being maintained despite marked slowdown in overall economic growth.

3. Nevertheless, economic constraints are real even when they are disregarded. In the pursuit of the political utility derived from military programs, policymakers may pay high and growing opportunity costs. The point of crisis surely depends on particular circumstances.

Clearly it is necessary to peer more closely at the Soviet particular circumstances: What domestic political conditions and forces stimulated or protected the buildup?

THE POLITICAL-INSTITUTIONAL CONTEXT

Generals the world over, it is said, picture the external threat in worst form scenarios and press for high defense budgets. "Soldiers will be soldiers," Khrushchev grumbled in his retirement: "They always want a bigger and stronger army. They always insist on having the very latest weapons and on attaining quantitative as well as qualitative superiority over the enemy." They were, of course, heroes, ready to sacrifice their lives for the motherland. Nevertheless,

> leaders must be careful not to look at the world through the eyeglasses of the military. Otherwise the picture will appear terribly gloomy; the government will start spending all its money and the best energies of the people on armaments.[20]

Yet the Soviet leaders went a long way in that direction, despite a generally falling rate of economic growth. Was there no opposition? Do the military control the polity? It is a commonplace that ultimate power resides in the Party hierarchy, and it is not professional officers who dominate the Politburo.[21]

Evidently, the military had the required political support for its claims on national resources. The nature of that support and the process by which it is generated and sustained are the keys to understanding the persistence of Soviet military buildup over the better part of two decades. In a society that still prefers to conceal its mode of operation, the heaviest cloak protects the deliberations at the apex of the hierarchy. Mechanisms at various subnational levels of decisionmaking complement and guarantee the implementation of top-level policy choices.

Alexander Dallin has offered the assumption that

> the stability of a given Soviet policy orientation tends to be greatest when there is a reinforcement or cumulation of (a) perceived national interest at the top; (b) self-serving interest on the part of multiple subnational groups and actors; and (c) a network of bureaucratic politics that creates vested interest in the status quo.[22]

Perceived National Interest

In private conversations Soviet representatives often point to "objective" factors in the geopolitical situation of the USSR that make for a high level of security mindedness in Moscow: long and topographically open frontiers, poor internal transportation, extreme weather conditions, the two-front threat of China and NATO, and the instability of the regions immediately to the south of the USSR in the Middle East and South Asia. Do Soviet leaders then view Soviet military activities as a burden on the society and economy undertaken to cope with these objective, geopolitical security problems? Recall that the idea that defense constitutes a burden on the national economy depends on two assumptions: that defense has an opportunity cost and also that like government administration, it is at best a means, undesirable in itself, to a worthier end. Because investment too may be looked on as socially useful only by virtue of its contribution to future benefits, consumption alone would be regarded as an ultimate good.

Despite the classification of defense as a nonproductive activity in Marxian accounting, this is *not* the way Soviet leaders have tended to view the matter. The USSR is not a modern-day Sparta,[23] but the role of military preparedness in the leaders' "utility functions" is much more than that of an instrument to achieve other social ends. For Stalin, the self-perceived man of steel, that product was not just an input to other industries but closer to a final good. Military power and the economic base that underlies it were clearly ends in themselves.[24] The value of power probably still ranks high on the preference scale of the present top leadership. An analysis of this question would involve an examination of the basic security concepts of the Soviet leadership and the relation of these concepts to Soviet political culture.[25]

The dominant American notion of national security is essentially static defensive. It is primarily concerned to ensure that the external world not become an unfriendly place in which to operate, which might redound to the detriment of life in the United States itself. To this has been added the post-1945 conviction that nuclear weapons fundamentally changed the nature of war and therefore the foundations of national security. American strategic nuclear conceptions have focused on the level of punishment, in terms of economic damage and population fatalities, that could be credibly promised to deter a potential aggressor from an act that could destroy the world.

In contrast, the view of national security held by the Soviet political–military leadership appears fundamentally dynamic and outward thrusting. The apparent Soviet commitment to develop a broad-based set of military capabilities across the spectrum of war-fighting situations may be ascribed in part to what Lambeth called "classical principles of military thought," to prudent, old-fashioned military logic.[26] Recently, Western observers have highlighted the conceptual distinctions and the differences in force posture implications between American notions of deterrence, based on "mutual hostage" relations of the superpowers in the nuclear era, and Soviet concepts of deterrence, concerned with the requirements for surviving and winning wars should they occur.[27] However, one envisions the scenario of central war in Europe, it seems clear that the USSR will not again have the luxury of selling space for time, of evacuation to the Urals, to begin a posthostilities buildup of military production and forces. Moreover, frantic mobilization efforts in crisis periods are enormously costly. To prevail in future war, Moscow sees the necessity for superior forces at the inception of the conflict. Gradual but steady accretion of a large, broad-spectrum force structure accords with this perception of needs and realities. It also leads to open-ended demands (over time) on the military budget.

From the moment of seizure of power, the threat to the survival of the social–political system was one of the salient features of Soviet self-definition with regard to the outside world. It gave rise to a particular form of linkage between foreign and domestic policy; the primacy of the USSR's national interest, especially defense, over its foreign and international revolutionary involvement.[28]

Several generations of Soviet leadership attempted to use foreign policy as a vehicle for the concealment, protection, and liquidation of Soviet vulnerabilities. As Dallin once remarked, from Stalin to Khrushchev foreign policy was directed at securing "a maximal gain of time," which would be used to build up economic, political, and military strength. And from Brest Litovsk to Nixon's Moscow visit in 1972, after the mining of Haiphong harbor and the bombing of Hanoi, Moscow made internally wrenching foreign accommodations in the consciousness of the weakness of Soviet posture.[29]

With the rise of the USSR's strategic nuclear power came growing self-confidence in its military strength. The last half of the 1970s also saw an increasing Soviet activism in third areas, which has been interpreted as arising from that enhanced self-confidence. However, it may be that in the popular mind and even in that of the leadership the confidence is shadowed by fear of the potential inherent in a billion Chinese jointed to Western technology. Now, too, as over centuries past, geography and history condition inhabitants of the Russian land mass to suspect the ambitions of their neighbors or their neighbors' allies. But the expansion of the Russian state frontiers simultaneously created the space that constituted the foundation of Russia's defense and the enduring hostility of the nations on the fringes. When he upbraided the Czech leaders for the actions that precipitated the Warsaw Pact invasion in the summer of 1968, Brezhnev reminded them that Soviet blood had been spilled to free Czechs from Hitler's yoke.[30] A similar theme is sounded in Poland. Thus, defense and offense may be inextricably linked in Soviet perceptions as they were in those of Imperial households.

In addition to this defensive-offensive security orientation, the world view of many Tsarist Russian leaders incorporated impulses to perfect the more accessible parts of the world. The pure Leninist ideology of foreign policy is globally evangelical and, of course, far more engaged with an explicit philosophy of history. Its perception of international affairs is based on a belief in systemic conflict regulated by historical forces that find in the Soviet Union a willing tool and helpmate. Through the fog of events and the complexity of institutions, the catechism maintains, the party of scientific socialism perceives the underlying reality. There is a capitalist system and a socialist system and the struggle between the two is historically inevitable, because the objectives of the two are opposite and irreconcilable.[31] Systemic hostility—the fact of imperialism—proves that a potential for aggressive attack against the socialist commonwealth will always remain.[32] The intersystem tension simultaneously legitimates the defense of the socialist world and its outward thrusts. Therefore, the constant improvement of Soviet defense capability is an objective necessity. At the same time, the Soviet Union cannot be a bystander in the historic drama that must end with the world victory of socialism, the more so that imperialism, in its panic, seeks to ward off the inevitable by attempting to crush the revolutionary impulse as it appears in the weaker developing nations.

One suspects that few Soviet leaders subscribe in full to all parts of this catechism;[33] not many actions of Soviet foreign policy can be explained in this framework alone. The apparent turn to greater economic interdependence with the West seems to presuppose, in Dallin's view, "implicit elements of mutual benefit, symbiosis and recognition that the Soviet Union stands to gain from closer ties with the presumably contagious and dangerous opponent."[34] There is considerable evidence of ferment in the views of the outside world held by Soviet academics and policy intellectuals—that is, those whose studies of the non-Soviet world are published in the Soviet specialized journals or in scholarly monographs and books.[35] Moreover, it has been argued that the growing sophistication of view observed among Soviet academics extends to high ranks of the Party central apparatus:

> Many of the most fundamental propositions about the evolution of the outside world and about the way the outside world *should* evolve have become the subject of heated debate in the Soviet Union; only a part of this debate has been permitted to surface in print. It extends deep into the Central Committee apparatus.[36]

Nevertheless, the prevailing view in the Soviet leadership seems to be as Bialer puts it: The advancement of socialism is a historical process; peaceful coexistence is a political strategy.[37]

Military power appears to be a more basic element of the Soviet self-perception than is the case in Western states. The change in the Soviet Union's place in the world that is so common a feature of Soviet discussions of international relations in the last decade is attributed to the change in the "correlation of forces." This term incorporates economic, social, and political elements too, but there is little question that the military element is primary. Military competition is the arena in which the USSR seems to have been the most successful in recent years—indeed, perhaps the only arena of unambiguous success, which may reinforce the importance of military power in the Soviet self-image.

These considerations support the belief that the continued modernization and expansion of Soviet forces, resulting in a steadily growing level of military outlays, were rooted in leadership convictions that basic national interests were at issue.[38] But the questions of Soviet military power were not the only national interests being weighed in the Kremlin. The Politburo was clearly aware of the deceleration of Soviet economic growth that had been taking place since the late 1950s. How long could the leadership tolerate this "scissors" pattern—upward thrust of military expenditure, downward slide of economic growth?

Western perceptions of the Soviet approach to détente encouraged the hope that Soviet economic problems would restrain the expansionist impulses in Soviet foreign policy and thus slow the pace of military buildup. One strand of thinking suggested that economic difficulties alone would lead to unilateral cuts in Soviet military spending. The more common argument, however, was that Soviet leaders had come to recognize the difficulty or even impossibility of resolving the USSR's economic difficulties unaided. Their desire to secure Western technology as a means of boosting Soviet industrial productivity would, it was presumed, counsel prudence in foreign policy so as not to endanger the continuity of this valued contact. Soviet domestic weakness was seen as having led to a conscious Soviet decision to accept dependence on technology transfer from the West; this was then presumed to imply a constraint on Soviet foreign involvement and on Soviet military spending and may have led the USSR to agree to the Strategic Arms Limitation Treaty (SALT).[39] But SALT I certainly did not result in a reduction of the level of Soviet military spending, not even in its rate of growth or in the proportion of total output allocated to the military.

Indeed it is difficult to show that anything like the hypothetical linkage of domestic economic need and military restraint was manifested in Soviet policy in the 1970s. Apart from maintaining the Soviet military buildup, Soviet leaders continued to insist that détente dealt only with the central area of East–West relations. At the Twenty-fifth Party Congress, Brezhnev set out the basic propositions:

> It is quite clear that détente and peaceful coexistence are concerned with interstate relations. This means primarily that quarrels and conflicts between countries should not be decided by means of war, use of force or the threats of force. Détente does not in the slightest way abolish, and cannot abolish the laws of the class struggle. No one can count, in conditions of détente, on communists becoming reconciled to capitalist exploitation or of monopolists becoming partisans of revolution. But the strict observance of the principle of non-interference in the affairs of other states, respect for their independence and sovereignty, is one of the immutable conditions for détente.
>
> We do not conceal the fact that we see détente as a way toward the creation of more favorable conditions for peaceful socialist and communist construction. This merely confirms that peace and socialism are indivisible.[40]

The record of actual Soviet involvement in Third World conflict in the last half of the 1970s, starting with Angola and ending with the Christmas 1979 invasion of Afghanistan, is familiar. The West has come to recognize that Soviet outlays for military purposes have been increasing year after year for two decades.

Thus the logical chain of much Western thinking in the 1970s was faulty. The connection between Soviet economic development problems and the reaching out for Western aid through technology transfer is clear enough. But the next set of links has proved to be imaginary. There was little or no evidence of the political constraints that economic weakness and dependence were supposed to create. If there was a Soviet vulnerability on this account, the West was unable or unwilling to exploit it.

Interest Group Conflict and Concord[41]

Were the USSR a rigidly controlled totalitarian society, perhaps the single-plane depiction of national interest might suffice to explain the record of military buildup, but the totalitarian model provides a poor fit for the Brezhnev regime in the 1960s and 1970s. In any polity, resource allocation at the macro level is not just a subject of economic analysis but an issue of power: Changes in the status quo have the potential for major influence on the balance of political forces in the society. Even under Stalin, personal and factional conflict could be discerned that in some cases related to resource allocation (the case of N. A. Voznesenskii). With Stalin's demise, resource allocation, centering on the appropriate weight to be accorded to military preparedness, became an important generator of leadership conflict— between Malenkov and Khrushchev in 1954–55, between Khrushev and much of the military around 1960, within the post-Khrushchev oligarchy in the mid-1960s. The evident Soviet hesitation in deciding whether to enter SALT talks with the United States and the long delay in making public the ninth five-year plan (1971–1975) have also been linked to guns-vs.-butter discussions. The involvement of top leadership in conflict generated by resource allocation is the more likely because of the direct links, operating in either direction, between domestic and foreign policy. Struggle for control over resources is, however, no longer limited to individuals or factions. The progressive differentiation of post-Stalin Soviet society has meant multiplication and increasing complexity of ethnic–national, regional, and social–economic group conflict in the USSR; at the same time, the conflicts are more visible to the external observer. Yet military spending has grown uninterruptedly and substantially during the Brezhnev regime. Evidently, other interest groups have not been able to rein in military demands effectively.

It is surely necessary to begin a discussion of the relevance of interest groups to the military budget with the Communist Party. Has it been among the ineffective opposed interest groups or has it been a powerful supporter of the military? What has been the Party's conception of the role of the military in a socialist society? With their unique awareness of the history of European revolutions, Bolshevik leaders were sensitive to the latent danger of Bonapartism in Soviet politics. Khrushchev cited this as the basic reason for the removal of Marshal Zhukov from power in 1957,[42] although the validity of the charge is in serious doubt.[43] Nevertheless, such concerns have not led to a political ideology of separatism between military and civil spheres. According to the Polish sociologist J. J. Wiatr, speaking about socialist societies, "in place of the formal legal subordination by the civil power of an army which is a distinct, isolated environment, we have to do with the conscious striving for organic union of the civil and military spheres of life."[44] The impulse to union is fundamentally political rather than professional–military; it seeks a politicization of the armed forces, rather than complete militarization of the society. Perhaps this may be associated in part with the values of mobilization, discipline, and sacrifice that are the salient features of the Party's most memorable experiences—1917, the Civil War, industrialization and collectivization, World War II, and postwar reconstruction. In part too, the impulse to union should be understood as flowing out of the Marxist–Leninist concepts of war.

A significant feature of Soviet discussions of war is the emphasis on the integral links of war and society. Far from being an isolated feature of social organization and policy, war is seen by Soviet "military science" as rooted in politics. The aspect of this concept familiar to Western public discussions is the adaptation of Clausewitz's dictum that "war is an extension of politics by other means." Less well known is the belief that war is a test of the viability of a society in all its aspects—economic, technological, ideological, social, and political.[45] These notions are linked to the anticapitalist ideology of the USSR, providing the conceptual (and emotional) framework within which the subordination of purely civil to military interests becomes institutionalized.

The harmonization of party and military interests has become more apparent with the growing conservatism of the former in the Brezhnev period. In his conflict with some military leaders, Khrushchev seemed to be engaged in a liberalizing, reformist struggle, in a direct line of connection to the subordination of the secret police to the party after Stalin's death. In the 1970s, however, the party appeared a bastion of conservatism—concerned with order, against the seditious influence of alien ideas, and idealizing the past (collectivization, World War II) and therefore a natural ally of the armed forces. From the latter's viewpoint, an increasingly conservative party guarantees the military an honored place in the society.

Rigby has suggested that there are several pillars of patronage relationships in political or bureaucratic systems, in addition to the act of appointment itself: shared loyalties and attitudes based on common background, ties based on prior joint service, and shared ideas.[46] The foundation for the alliance of military and civilian spheres in the USSR is the common perceptions of the party and military leaders, the sharing of a particular mind set partly described earlier.

A second factor for mutual understanding among political and military elites is common background and prior joint service. Several members of the present political leadership, including Brezhnev, had extensive military experience as political officers during World War II.[47]

The organizational interconnectedness between the Party and the military begins with military unit Party membership. Almost 90 percent of the armed forces are enrolled in the Party or the Komsomol, and in the upper levels of the officer corps, Party membership is universal.[48] At lower levels, many officers have influential positions in regional and local party organizations, while regional party leaders are also coopted into the administration of the military district.[49] At least five military district commanders serve on the bureaus of republic central committees (the republic counterparts of the Politburo), in Uzbekistan, Latvia, Kazakhstan, Georgia, and Belorussia. Currently, twenty-four military representatives, most of the key people in the defense ministry and armed forces, are full members of the Party Central Committee; an additional thirteen are candidate members.[50] With respect to the early 1970s, it was found that "Central Committee rank and military rank are interlinked; all Marshals of the Soviet Union, almost all generals of the Army, and a few Colonel-Generals are full members of the Central Committee; candidate members and members of the [Central Auditing Commission] are with few exceptions Colonel–Generals or the equivalent."[51]

The organizational links between the Party and the military extend to the government apparatus. Thus, every military district commander is also a member of the Supreme Soviet (as are commanders of the four Groups of Forces in Eastern Europe); every military member of the Party Central Committee or its Central Auditing Commission is also a member of the Supreme Soviet.[52] This is particularly true if the scope of the term military is broadened to include military–industrial activities.[53] An observer concludes that "it is a common occurrence among the top military and defense industry leadership for the same individual to fill a functional role in the military, hold a seat in the more ceremonial Supreme Soviet, and also fill an important Party position in the Central Committee, the Secretariat, or the Politburo."[54] In view of the foregoing, it is hardly surprising that Party organs within the armed forces behave, in Colton's words, "as an integral part of the Soviet military establishment, sharing its aspirations and faults."[55] Brzezinski has pointed to the "enhance[ment of] the domestic importance of the military. The military is thus increasingly becoming the major repository of the state tradition and an alternative unifying symbol."[56]

Yet there *has* been conflict between Party and military in the past. The major chronicler of that conflict, Kolkowicz, has stressed the military's defense of (1) its "traditional values, self-images, and beliefs of the profession" against the Party's effort to politicize (Communize) the officer corps, and (2) its aspirations to professional autonomy and institutional independence in planning, management and policy implementation, against the Party's insistence on intrusion into their spheres.[57] This perspective has had its critics, particularly Odom and Colton.[58] The evidence of Party–military conflict tends to disappear after the ouster of Khrushchev, and relations between the two groups seem to have stabilized under Brezhnev. More likely, as interests develop on given issues they cut across institutions.[59]

The Brezhnev regime has provided a sharp contrast to Khrushchev's. Military preparedness has not been sacrificed to achieve "goulash communism" on the cheap. Military preparedness now seems to mean what the bulk of the military leadership wanted it to mean—balanced forces within the strategic nuclear realm and across the spectrum of possible conflicts. Anti-Stalinism, with its overtones (to military ears, at least) of pacifism, has vanished entirely. According to Brzezinski "today, the military are in a more symbiotic relationship with the ruling party, and are thus more directly influential on policy matters, than at any point in Soviet political history."[60]

The question of what other interest groups play a significant role in macro-level resource allocation decisions is not easy to answer. The Skilling and Griffiths collection, a basic work, deals with industrial managers, economists, writers, and jurists, in addition to the Party and the military.[61] But whether economists and writers, or even managers, can be viewed on the same plane with Party *apparatchiki* is highly doubtful. Moreover "Soviet "interest groups" are not the kind of independent private pressure groups of a pluralist society originally subjected to this particular analysis, but correspond more to the competing functional interests discernible within the governmental bureaucracy of a non-Communist country," as Daniels has pointed out.[62]

Skilling acknowledged "that every occupational group is divided into opinion groups and that 'reformists' and 'conservatives' are to be found in all of them, except perhaps the security police."[63] And "Unlike the virtual free-for-all of U.S. politics, its Soviet analog— while real—is bound to reserve greater authority to the ultimate decisionmaking body . . . ,"[64] especially on the size of the military budget.

This does not mean that the military, with the Party and the military industry, always have their way. The fact that defense spending has risen monotonically for twenty years should not be taken to mean that all military demands were fully met, only that Soviet politics has not provided the structure and opportunities for institutional pressures that could more effectively constrain the military buildup.

The Decisionmaking Apparatus

The chief feature of Soviet decisionmaking is its centralized hierarchical structure.[65] Hierarchy is, of course, characteristic of the entire Soviet bureaucracy, and that of other countries as well. Centralization and the command principle implicit in hierarchy are, however, particularly marked in the military sphere and are powerfully reinforced by the extreme secrecy that attaches to military matters in the USSR.

1. The base of the hierarchy is the ministerial bureaucracies—the Ministry of Defense and the military–industry ministries. The scope for policyforming inputs from other ministries seems small.

2. The materials from which military program choice decisions are made—requirements analyses, supporting data, policy recommendations, and the like—originate in interrelations largely among the Ministry of Defense, the State Planning Committee (Gosplan), the military–industry ministries, the department for military industry of the Party Central Committee, and the Military Industrial Commission. The last is also the major coordinating, troubleshooting body overseeing the defense industrial establishment.

3. The general size of the military program for any planning period is surely reviewed and confirmed at the highest political level, the Politburo. Some have speculated that, except in unusual circumstances, where the issue is contentious, Politburo action may only ratify decisions taken within the framework of the Defense Council. The latter organ is still shrouded in mystery, although officially

acknowledged since the mid-1970s. The 1977 constitution provides for its appointment by the Presidium of the Supreme Soviet, which suggests that the Council includes at least some government representatives. Garthoff named Grechko, Kosygin, Podgorny, and Ustinov (then the Central Committee secretary in charge of military matters), in addition to the acknowledged chairman, Brezhnev, as members in the early or mid-1970s.

The foregoing sketch indicates how self-contained military decisionmaking is. Particularly noteworthy is the apparent insulation of military economic policy from control by the government (as contrasted with the Party) "cabinet," the Presidium of the Council of Ministers, despite the Prime Minister's probable membership in the Defense Council.

The high-level coordinating and policyforming layer was probably fashioned in the middle or late 1960s, part of a general effort under Brezhnev leadership to increase military efficiency. This concentration and centralization of management and policymaking functions in the military sphere was probably in part a reaction to Khrushchev's free-wheeling decisionmaking and a response to the growing recognition of the severe requirements for command and control in the nuclear era. In the mid-1960s a number of Soviet military writers expressed the need for the creation of a military–political leadership system along the lines of the World War II apparatus that would enable rapid transition to wartime organization.[66] However, military requirements for simplicity and clarity, which tend to maximize centralization, conflict with political fears of granting excessive power to one man or one institution. If the Defense Council, supported by the Ministry of Defense and General Staff on one side and the Military–Industrial Commission on the other, is a response to the felt needs of the military, it is apparently also designed to ensure ultimate party control.

The picture of the military decisionmaking system presented here provides a basis for evaluation of one of the chief Western hypotheses explaining the Soviet military buildup, what may be called technological automatism, a notion that harks back to Robert McNamara, who spoke of the "mad momentum intrinsic to the development of all nuclear weaponry" whereby "if a weapon system works—and works well—there is strong pressure from many directions to proceed and deploy the weapons all out of proportion to the prudent level required."[67] McNamara's nightmare applies particularly well to the Soviet system of weapons acquisition because of the organizational and funding stability of the network of design-development institutions and the insulation of the system from pressures by competing claimants for resources.

It would be a mistake to picture the military decisionmaking process as one in which major budget priorities and development alternatives are being constantly weighed and decided at the highest levels.

> It is probable that the great bulk of [political–military consultations at the top level] is concerned with incremental decisions—that is with the management of ongoing enterprises. . . . We suffer from a professional penchant for thinking of military policy in terms of large-scale programs and global strategies.[68]

It is likely that policymaking, even at the apex, most often focuses on marginal changes—except for the periodic long-term decisions required in the five-year plan cycle—thus keeping alive programs that would not survive a general higher order review.

The military decisionmaking system also has the significant characteristic of sharply limiting access by other groups in the society. Military strategy, force requirements, and force development are exclusively the province of military professionals, perhaps under the general political supervision of the Politburo subgroup that provides the core of the Defense Council. There is no parallel to the U.S. practice of placing civilians, with their ties to other groups in the society, in key military development and policy positions.[69] A striking feature of the Soviet system is the absence of any competence on Soviet military policy outside the professional military. The very few analysts in the Academy of Sciences—in the Institute on the USA and Canada or the Institute of World Economics and International Relations—concerned with military matters are in fact dealing with the policies of other countries, not their own.[70] Nothing remotely resembling the American military analysis and arms control communities has been allowed to develop in the Soviet Union. Soviet writings in this area are almost entirely by military professionals or by uniformed political officers. Individual initiative by civilian scholars and analysts in the form of contributions to central policy discussions is frowned upon. Even invited papers by civilian specialists are handicapped by denial of access to classified information on existing or future weapons.[71] Of course, questions of national security policy are not subject to even the restricted forms of debate that may appear in the Soviet press on economic issues.

Numerous questions bearing on resource allocation are settled in bargaining between departments.[72] What prevents this process from impinging on defense resource allocation, as Hough acknowledges, is the obedience to the rule of military priority.

Leadership Perceptions of Burden

This does not mean that human welfare can be or is ignored. Even in wartime there are irreducible consumption and investment needs: "There is a limit below which civilian production and consumption cannot be decreased without imperiling the whole economy."[73] Even in the good times during the past thirty years, various consumer goods and services were in short supply; retail prices generally failed to clear the market, resulting in queues and gray markets. At the same time, consumers were aware that the military siphoned off a large share of the national income.

We do not know how the Kremlin has perceived the size and trend of the burden. The subject is taboo for the ordinary channels of communication—the scholarly journals and the mass media—visible to the outside world. Moreover, the picture presented to even high Soviet leaders may be different from that forming in the West. Concepts of national accounting are different, basic production time series are computed with different weights, and the Soviet price system has known and suspected deficiencies that could distort comparisons and analysis based on prevailing prices. However, it is impossible to believe that Soviet leaders in the know failed to recognize that the USSR's military effort absorbed a large share of national output by contemporary world standards and that the resources allocated to the military sector had valuable alternative uses in the civil economy.

At the same time, at least until the last few years, the military could have been conscious of having made substantial contributions to the state without ignoring consumer interests. In World War II the armed forces met and overcame the greatest challenge to Russia since the Mongol invasion. As nuclear parity with the United States was attained, the Soviet armed forces probably credited themselves with having made possible real security for the Soviet state for the first time since the Bolshevik Revolution. Military weakness, the uniformed officer might argue, made possible the humiliation of the 1962 Cuban missile crisis; growing military capability enabled the USSR to protect the revolutions in Angola, Ethiopia, and Afghanistan, and to refuse to submit to the United States in Cuba in 1979. The increasing armed might of the USSR forced the developed capitalist world to recognize the change in the real balance of forces with the socialist camp. This opened up not only a number of political opportunities, but even economic ones; the change in the correlation of forces brought capitalist representatives to Moscow eager to deal on favorable terms and kept the West Europeans and Japanese from fully joining in American measures of economic warfare in the wake of the Soviet incursion into Afghanistan.

As for the costs to the economy, the generals might point out that more than one-third of all gross fixed investment was being allocated to agriculture and agricultural-related industry. For twenty-five years after the death of Stalin agricultural output increased annually at a rate of about 3.5 percent, while population was growing at barely 1.4 percent per year.[74] Per capita consumption rose even more rapidly than per capita agricultural output, closer to 4 percent.[75] Defense was the first priority, but it had left enough in the resource allocation pot to secure an uninterruptedly rising standard of living.

At least this was true until the mid- and late 1970s. Then the problems of continuing the advance in living standards were sharply aggravated. The very maintenance of existing levels came into question, with acute food shortages and even scattered ad hoc rationing. The daily search for food supplies seems to have become a powerful, mass preoccupation. The USSR seemed to be entering a time of troubles that would require reconsideration of basic assumptions and future policy options.

PROSPECTS

Dilemmas and Options

The 1980s confront the Soviet policymakers with several clear, unavoidable challenges. The single most important external factor bearing on the defense budget is the impending buildup of the U.S.

armed forces, accompanied by a more militant American foreign policy around the world. Internally, two characteristics of the policy environment are likely to be dominant: leadership change and economic downturn.

Undoubtedly the 1980s will see new opportunities for Soviet exploitation of the instabilities of the Third World. In Europe Moscow can manipulate to its advantage differences among the NATO allies on trade and security policies. However, the Kremlin fears that a formidable external challenge is in the making. A crisis of détente was brewing considerably before the invasion of Afghanistan and even before the battle over U.S. ratification of the SALT II treaty, perhaps since the 1973 Middle East War. The monotonic downturn in real U.S. defense spending ended in 1976 and the trend has been moderately up since then. Now a new American administration is intent on sharply accelerating that upturn. Around the globe the Kremlin sees an American hand everywhere in rising threats to Soviet security. The renewed American effort to contain if not reverse further Soviet expansion in the Third World involves setting up a chain of bases in the Middle East, from Egypt to the Indian Ocean. In Moscow's perception the first steps in the forging of a Sino–American military alliance have been taken, while Japan is being pressured to step up its military spending and the nations of Southeast Asia are incited against communist Vietnam.[76] The Polish crisis raises major questions about the stability and reliability of the Warsaw Pact, the guardian of the USSR's western flank, at a time when the Reagan administration is pushing hard for the modernization of NATO's (European) theater nuclear forces. American strategic nuclear arms are also to be strengthened, while Washington appears to be ambivalent about renewing SALT negotiations. The United States seems increasingly less likely to behave in the 1980s as Moscow had expected in the halcyon days of SALT I.

On the domestic side perhaps the greatest influence on the policy environment will be leadership change. Because of Brezhnev's age and poor health, the question of the succession to the top leadership has been a subject of considerable interest in the West for the better part of the past decade. But it is not only Brezhnev who is showing his years: The USSR is ruled by a gerontocracy. The retirement, then death, of Kosygin in the fall of 1980 and his replacement by a man one year younger make vivid the likelihood of a wholesale change of leaders at the top within the next few years. The average age of the second and third echelons of the leadership is only somewhat lower, and a number of observers have forecast a generational change in the system's directors during the 1980s.[77]

The forthcoming succession appears unique in Soviet history because the longevity of the post-Khrushchev regime, the advanced age of a large part of its leadership, and the stability of elites under the top level that has been a deliberate policy of the Brezhnev oligarchy all point to considerable turnover in important policy and administrative positions even in the first half of the 1980s.

The retardation of economic growth that has been a fact of Soviet life about as long as the current military buildup has intensified in recent years. Prospects for the 1980s are as bad or worse: Natural increments to the population of working age are diminishing sharply as a second-wave echo of World War II human losses and because of decline in postwar birth rates; oil production seems to be reaching its peak and will probably decline soon thereafter, perhaps even at a rapid rate; costs of other raw material production are climbing as the centers of exploration and extraction move east and north; stable growth in agricultural production is still out of the policymakers' reach, primarily because of bad weather but also aided by organizational rigidity. Unfortunately for the Brezhnev successors, their options for coping with these problems will be essentially the same as his. The new team will probably find the choices even less palatable.

The Soviet economy may be viewed as confronting a growth dilemma arising from the simultaneous retardation in the growth of inputs and in the productivity of use of inputs. Productivity was never a major factor in Soviet growth, but in the good old days it could be slighted because labor and capital flows were expanding rapidly. According to CIA estimates, rates of increase of total inputs have been falling almost steadily since the middle 1960s, from about 4.5 percent per year then to about 2–3 percent now. At the same time, growth of total factor productivity (output per unit of combined inputs) has been low even in good years—a modest 1 percent per year average in the 1960s; it has been negative in every year but one since 1973.[78]

Acceleration of Soviet economic growth in the traditional fashion would require a higher rate of input increase. However, demographic constraints on growth of the labor force are increasingly severe; raising the rate of investment to intensify the substitution of capital for labor would mean sacrificing the interests of either the military or the consumers. Moreover, high and growing capital-output ratios reflect diminishing yields for increases in the rate of investment, requiring even larger sacrifices on the part of consumption or defense.

The problem of high capital-output ratios points to the other horn of the dilemma, involving faltering productivity growth. Instead of attempting to continue the policy of feeding ever larger capital and labor inputs into the "growth machine," the regime could concentrate on improving the efficiency with which inputs are combined. However, the changes in trade policy or internal economic organization required to significantly improve productivity are probably unacceptable to the Kremlin on political-ideological grounds.

To augment the volume of resources allocated annually to civil economic growth and consumption, the Brezhnev regime could have cut back on military spending. That approach was never taken—possibly, not even considered. Perhaps the arms control agreements to which the USSR was a party, from the Limited Nuclear Test Ban treaty through SALT I and the SALT II negotiations, helped prevent the military budget from growing still more rapidly, although that is probably not demonstrable. But there was no apparent easing in the pace of the Soviet military buildup in the heyday of détente. As long as the economic problem seemed manageable, it is hardly surprising that the military budget remained intact.

Instead, in the first decade of its rule, the Brezhnev regime pursued successively two different routes to higher productivity. The leadership first chose the path of economic reform. The much heralded 1965 reform proved to be of restricted scope even in its inception; hostile or indifferent implementation drained it of much of its limited significance.[79] A new reform program was announced in July 1979. So far most observers in the West have been skeptical of the reform's prospects or usefulness. Nimitz, one of the few who does see merit in it, is cautious in setting forth its presumed benefits.[80]

In the early and mid-1970s, an attempt was made to import the solution from the West. Because Soviet industry seemed incapable of generating and sustaining a rate of innovation that would raise the faltering rate of productivity growth, it appeared that the Soviet Union would have to import the augmentation in productivity in the form of Western advanced technology. Scholars are still at odds about how much stimulus to Soviet economic growth actually resulted.[81] It is clear that the same structural deficiences of organization and incentive that help account for the slow pace of technical progress, at least as measured in productivity calculations, also constitute a major barrier to diffusion of the imported technological innovation.[82]

If radical economic reform is politically unacceptable and technology imports are inadequate, the only other policy for coping with the sharp decline in productivity appears to be neo-Stalinism, which is used here to designate any of several forms of reactionary impulse, whatever their ideology and political coloration. The justification for lumping these various tendencies together, despite their different sociopolitical character, is a common orientation in political economy. The common denominator is indeed reaction—against markets, the actual ones of the "second economy" and the theoretical ones of the market socialist reformers, against corruption and bribery, against "speculators" and "parasites," and back to the purer forms of a bygone Golden Age. To neo-Stalinists, the essence of the national economic problem is indiscipline, and the key to national economic regeneration is restoration of discipline. Its adherents may offer neo-Stalinism as the only way to meet the increasingly serious external threat compounded by the internal danger of economic degeneration and collapse of morale.

Many observers have noted that as popular frustrations rise, the memory of Stalin is refurbished. One reason this alternative has not seemed feasible until now is that a real *Vozhd* ("boss"), an iron hand at the helm, was a precondition. Without it, an attempt to reverse course could backfire, leading to disruption of the present elements of growth-sustaining initiative and to Schweikian implementation of central directives. According to Yanov, prominent individuals, institutions, and groups have developed vested interests in détente in both its foreign and domestic aspects.[83] Although the power of these forces is difficult to assess, the Brezhnev consensus could have been threatened from this flank as well as the other. Apparently the conservative forces were not sufficiently strong to crush the opposition.

The Brezhnev regime has often been described as one in which authority derives not from terror and charisma but from a balance of coalitions based on consensus. Radical policy change, whether to the right or the left, constitutes a threat to the survival of a regime whose "dominant political tendency . . . is defence of the *status quo*—a desire for predictability, stability, and security of tenure, and the avoidance of fundamental political change either in a radical reformist direction or in a Stalinist direction."[84] Accordingly, the Brezhnev leadership has found refuge so far in the economics and politics of "muddling through." Economically, such a policy is anchored in the acceptance of lower growth rates, a factor that has often been overlooked by Western observers.[85] A major element has been small-scale reform—frequent tinkering with organizational mechanisms, planning indicators, or incentive systems. It is not clear whether this effort to reform without really reforming has helped slow down the deceleration of productivity or has been dysfunctional on balance. In any case it has been a significant feature of recent Soviet economic history. Another has been considerably greater dependence on foreign trade—grain and technology imports paid for by exports of gold and fuel, to simplify the complex reality—than most Western observers ever considered likely. Muddling through also relies heavily on exhortation, witness the extraordinary "Letter to the Soviet People" issued by the CPSU Central Committee, the USSR Council of Ministers, the Trade Union Central Committee and the Central Committee of the Komosomol in *Pravda*, January 14, 1978.[86] It may also have included an effort to hold down the *growth* of military expenditure, because Soviet leaders are certainly conscious of the burgeoning costs of new military technology.

Succession and the Outlook for Change

Because the succession process in the Soviet Union has not been institutionalized and standardized, it carries a degree of unpredictability that "opens up the [political] system to initiatives for change in basic policies which would be unthinkable or very difficult to institute in normal times. The succession period is conducive to sudden switches in policy," according to Bialer.[87] Change is needed because tough choices have been avoided for too long.

The difficulty with this argument is that it ignores the reasons why policy boldness has been avoided under Brezhnev. It can hardly be said that the regime has been blind to the growing economic problems, to the pervasive indifference and cynicism of large parts of the population, to the ethnic-national frictions, and so on. The regime has been well aware of these and other difficulties and has devoted a considerable amount of leadership and expert attention to their study. However, the solutions, such as they are, have involved the sacrifice of interests of the most powerful groups of the oligarchical system. No matter how the succession develops, it will not see the sudden submergence of these groups; their influence will probably remain dominant and their interests preeminent. If major change in the pattern of satisfaction of interests is to take place, it will have to come from deliberate self-denial within these groups.

The prospects for such a sharp policy change depend on a perception that muddling through has exhausted its potential for contributing to the national welfare and has become instead a clear and present danger. Under the most favorable circumstances Soviet economic growth prospects through the late 1980s are worse than at any time since World War II. Bad luck—several harvest failures, more rapid than expected depletion of currently exploited oil fields, difficult winters with a resultant extra strain on overburdened transportation facilities—could turn a difficult problem into a major crisis. Similar pressures on the diminishing increments of output could result from such a magnification of the external threat (in Moscow's perception, of course) that the Soviet leadership was convinced its military efforts must be intensified significantly.

As a policy for the future, "muddling through" in the 1970s manner imposed additional costs that conservatives must take into account. Among them are the threat to future military capabilities and the political costs of a policy relying heavily on trade with the Western world.[88] Prolonged restraint on capital formation, even with preference for heavy industry retained and even if such a limitation is partly intended to help weed out unproductive investment, must risk reduced capability to satisfy future military demand, particularly if the need should arise for crash buildups.

Moscow's attempt during the 1970s to enlist the aid of the Western world in the solution of the Soviet economic dilemma created a new predicament. Importation of Western technology was designed to boost productivity where internal efforts yielded indifferent success. The reason was the persistence of systemic barriers to domestic innovation and diffusion of new technology, whose removal would apparently require thoroughgoing and politically distasteful reform. Thus conservatives could initially be in favor of seeking wider trade relations or at least could recognize the economic attraction of this course. Tried on a small scale, however, the policy cannot work miracles, because the known problems of diffusing new technology in the Soviet economy also make it improbable that small injections of foreign knowhow, in embodied or disembodied form, will have significant multiplier effects. Pursued on a substantial scale, the policy would create important dependencies on the West, foreshadowed in imports of grain and particular classes of machinery, as well as in the need for Western credits to finance large volumes of technology imports. Despite the loopholes in the Carter administration's embargos after the Soviet invasion of Afghanistan, Soviet leaders in 1980 were painfully reminded of the costs of dependency.[89]

Is the next generation of Soviet leaders more likely to reconsider the twenty-year commitment to a sustained rate of military modernization and expansion? Might they slow down the growth of Soviet military outlays from its fifteen-year annual average of 4–5 percent? If they did, what economic effects might be expected?

Most Western simulations of transfers from the military to civilian needs that use statistical–mathematical models of the Soviet economy indicate some improvement in levels of consumption but negligible effects on production growth, either by branch or in aggregate.[90] This is because the savings from cutting back on defense spending constitute relatively small increases in the stock of aggregate inputs to production. If the cutback were taken entirely out of procurement and construction, the investment component of defense, the stimulus to output growth would probably be larger. However, the military outlay change would have to be substantial to effect a significant increase in total output even within the medium term, five years: The rate of growth of military expenditure would have to be driven down to zero or even to negative levels.

Cuts in military spending of this magnitude would hardly be welcome in the party–military–industrial complex. It is conceivable that reductions at the margin—stretching out some programs stretchouts and postponing others—although yielding correspondingly smaller savings, would be undertaken to ease particular civilian bottlenecks and prevent more general deterioration. Perhaps the leadership recognizes that a reduction of procurement growth even to zero would still keep additions to existing hardware stocks flowing at a rate that must, for a number of weapon systems, continue to surpass U.S. levels for several years to come. However, all that we have learned about the political context of Soviet defense decisionmaking suggests that the idea of drastic cuts would be abhorrent to the leadership. It probably does not believe that its military capabilities are adequate to the demands of preparing for the contingency of war across the broad range of conflict possibilities. It is most likely becoming increasingly concerned about the growth of the external threat posed by the American buildup and would be fearful of the signals that would be conveyed to its allies and adversaries by significant cutbacks. All in all, it would probably take an economic crisis and the perceived threat of internal political–social unrest for the Kremlin to weigh so drastic a policy reversal.

Some Implications for U.S. Policy

If the Reagan administration persists in its present course of rebuilding American forces at an accelerating tempo and of attempting to mount credible challenges to Soviet power around the globe, some elements of the leadership are likely to perceive the vigorously pursued U.S. policy of arms racing and foreign policy militancy as unacceptably intensifying the threat to Soviet security. If these elements persuade the Politburo to step up Soviet military spending, the effect on the economy and society could be severe. The prospects for significant economic reform would certainly be reduced. More likely, the tensions generated by the resource shifts in favor of the military would strengthen the tendencies to neo-Stalinism. Of course, the external face of Soviet policy would become even more hostile.

On economic and social–political grounds alone, therefore, the Kremlin might resist the internal calls for a military effort to match the renewed American challenge. These pressures *might* be resisted even on political–military grounds. The "peace program" of the Twenty-fourth Party Congress in 1971—the Soviet notion of détente—represented in part a strategy for curbing American activism and restraining the growth of American military power through relaxation of tensions, arms control agreements, and cultural-economic–political interchange. Such a policy reflected a realization of the dangers of unrestricted military competition with the United States. These dangers will certainly continue to be weighed in Moscow, which still respects the medium- and long-term mobilization capability of the American economy. The Kremlin could, therefore, continue to seek means to restrain the American buildup rather than attempt to match or surpass it. Apart from any direct efforts to persuade the Reagan administration to slow down its military effort and to moderate its global activism, Moscow will probably continue to see opportunities to constrain the growth of the U.S. threat by affecting the perceptions of Washington's NATO allies, who are receptive to evidence that Soviet intentions are moderating. There is already a considerable Soviet effort to convince Europeans of the importance of maintaining détente, negotiating on theater nuclear forces, canceling NATO plans for deployment of cruise and Persing-II missiles, and desisting from joining the United States in economic sanctions or long-term measures of resource denial to the Soviet bloc. Given the great dangers and high costs of the alternative policy, the Kremlin will very likely continue to pursue a "peace" campaign to reduce the security threat posed by the policies of the new American administration *as long as that option holds out any hope of success.*

This suggests that U.S. government policy has an important role to play in influencing Soviet policy, to hold the Kremlin to a peace campaign rather than impel it in the direction of a military budget response or even, as some Western analysts have warned, military action to exploit a limited "window of opportunity." If U.S. policy can offer persistence in rebuilding American military power as well as prudence in the enunciation of U.S. political–military objectives and in the use of American military forces, if Washington can make clear its recognition of the necessity of both arms expansion and arms control, then it may be possible to keep Soviet reaction from escalating dangerously.

NOTES

1. The best known of these is the class of Richardson models, in which changes in the military expenditures of two states are explained by the levels of their own and the other state's military outlays.

2. The role of external considerations, even understood as crucially shaped by perceptions, has been sharply downgraded by the behavioral revolution in social science. Traditional political science was criticized for excessive faith in rational actors seeking to maximize national interest. The new credo was that state decisions arise through the clash of men and organizations in the pursuit of particular interests. It is not facts of the outside world or even the perceptions of these "facts" that determine decisions but the result of internal conflict, institutional and personal.

    As was perhaps only to be expected, the pendulum seems to have swung too far, and efforts are being made to attain a new balance, one in which the conflicting viewpoints may find at least partial reconciliation. I find the synthetic approaches more congenial than either the thesis or anti-thesis alone.

3. For a review of the literature, see Kenneth D. Moll and Gregory M. Lueb-bert, "Arms Race and Military Expenditure Models," *Journal of Conflict Resolution* 24, no. 1 (March 1980): 153–85. The authors note with regret that "the increasingly sophisticated mathematical models of the 1970s have not shown insights in proportion to their complexity" (p. 156).

4. Nikita S. Khrushchev, *Khrushchev Remembers. The Last Testament*, ed-ited and translated by Strobe Talbott (Boston: Little, Brown, 1970), p. 572, and 1974 edition, pp. 411–12.

5. In a double sense: First, a certain amount of political respectability ex-plain very poorly the past course of the military competition" (p. 10), and second, "each expenditure level may imply vastly different combinations of force size and force deployment; at the same cost, smaller forces in a forward deployment may appear more threatening than larger forces sta-tioned at a distance. Military expenditures alone may hide too much to be the principal variable in a model of military competition" (p. 11). (Robert Shishko, Defense Budget Interactions Revisited, The Rand Corporation, P–5882, June 1977.)

6. The sharp rise in Chinese military expenditure followed a Soviet buildup on the Sino–Soviet border; the largest increases came in 1969–70, follow-ing actual armed clashes on the frontier.

7. As it may occasionally do for propaganda purposes: see, for example, V.P. Konobeev, "Voennyi buidznet SShA," *SShA: Ekonomika, politica, ideo-logia* 3 (1981): 122–27, esp. pp. 123, 126.

8. U.S. Bureau of the Census, *Statistical Abstract of the United States: 1980* (Washington, D.C.: U.S. Government Printing Office, 1980).

9. See also H. Rattinger, "Armaments, Détente and Bureaucracy: The Case of the Arms Race in Europe," *Journal of Conflict Resolution* 19, no. 4 (De-cember 1975): 571–95.

    The concept of reactive military growth has been applied in relation to the advance of military technology, when perceived on the adversary's side or observed in one's own laboratories and development plants. In the lat-ter case, the action–reaction cycle is totally self-generated.

10. *The Wealth of Nations* (New York: Modern Library, 1937), book 5, ch. 5, part 1.

11. Frederic L. Pryor, *Public Expenditures in Communist and Capitalist Na-tions* (Homewood, Ill.: Richard D. Irwin, 1968).

    GNP per capita is found to be one of the determinants of nonpersonnel military expenditures per military person. See also L. Hollist, "Alternative Explanations of Competitive Arms Processes: Tests on Four Pairs of Na-tions," *American Journal of Political Science* 21, no. 2 (May 1977): 313–40. Hollist speaks of "technology" but seems to mean only GNP. The absence of any relation between the defense share of GNP and GNP per capita seems to undercut the hypothesis derived from Lenin's theory of imperialism that "as the per capita GNP increases, capitalist nations must resort to ever-increasing relative levels of defense expenditures, in order to stave off the general crisis of capitalism." (Pryor, *Public Expenditures*, pp. 89, 93). See also Gavin Kennedy, *The Economics of Defense* (Totowa, N.J.: Rowman and Littlefield, 1975), pp. 74–78. Another writer comes to the same conclusion on the basis of data for fifteen "advanced capitalist" countries at three dates over a twenty-year period. He suggests, instead: "The alternative approach is that the functions of military expenditure [in capitalist states] were not primarily to maintain demand, and that its economic consequences may have been contradictory—expenditure necessary for strategic reasons had economic consequences which, in fact, undermined the system it was intended to support," pp. 66, 69 in R.P. Smith, "Military Expenditure and Capitalism," *Cambridge Journal of Economics* 1, no. 1 (March 1977): 61–76. For further discussion of this article, see the September 1978 number of the same journal.

12. Emile Benoit, "Growth and Defense in Developing Countries," *Economic Development and Cultural Change* 26, no. 2 (January 1978): 271–80.

Arthur Westing found that military expenditures were "moderately" closely correlated with GNP for the entire population of 159 de facto nations in the world of 1975 ($r = 0.777$). However the correlation was considerably higher among the group of 89 "poor" nations ($r = 0.943$) than among the group of "wealthy" nations ($r = 0.758$). (Military Expenditures and Their Reduction," *Bulletin of Peace Proposals*, Stockholm, 9, no. 1 (1978): 24–29.) Westing concluded, however: "The military expenditures of many poor nations can be expected to increase as they become wealthier in the years to come, barring dramatic changes in the world order" (p. 27).

13. In part, the difficulty arises from the crudity of the measurement: "It is commonly assumed that resource constraints must be reflected in models. . . . But measuring the sheer size of the economy . . . on the health of the currency . . . implies simplistic notions about how resource constraints impact on armaments." Moll and Luebbert, 1980, p. 171.

14. R. Ernest Dupuy and Trevor N. Dupuy, *The Encyclopedia of Military History from 3500 B.C. to the Present* (New York: Harper & Row, 1970); and *Pravda*, January 15, 1960. The intervening variable is evidently size of population, as Pryor pointed out.

15. A.A. Grechko, *Vooruzhennye sily Sovetskogo gosudarstva*, 2nd ed. (Moscow: Voenizdat, 1975), p. 7.

16. P.V. Sokolov, ed., *1974 Politicheskaia ekonomiia. Sotsializm—pervaiia faza kommunisticheskogo sposoba proizvodstva* (Moscow: Voenizdat, 1974), pp. 7–8.

17. The demands are not only in terms of technologically more advanced capital but also for more highly skilled labor. The mass production of military industry in World War II in the USSR was accomplished largely with unskilled labor. A.F. Khavin, "Novyi moguchi pod" em tiazheloi promyshlennosti SSSR v. 1946–1950 gg.," *Istoriia SSSR* 1 (1963): 22–47.

18. "In a possible missile-nuclear war, the economy will determine [the war's] course and outcome first of all and mostly by what it is able to give for the war before the war begins, in peacetime, in the process of military construction." P. Trifonenkov, "Ob" ektivnye zakony voiny i printsipy voennogo iskusstva," *Kommunist vooruzhennykh sil* 1, (1966): 8–16.

19. Military power depends not only on quantities of resources but also their utilization. Here the Soviets have traditionally claimed an advantage over their adversaries through the superiority of the socialist system (Sokolov, *Politicheskaia ekonomiia*, p. 88). The relative efficiency of the Soviet and U.S. defense establishments is still a contentious issue, but whatever the verdict, it seems doubtful that it will depend on the differences between socialism and capitalism.

20. *Khrushchev Remembers*, 1974 ed., p. 540.

21. No military representative sat on the Politburo between 1957 (the dismissal of Marshal Zhukov) and 1973 (the appointment of Marshal Grechko). The defense minister has been a member since 1973, but since 1976 the post has been held by Dmitri Ustinov, who, although a marshal of the Soviet Union, is an industrial specialist rather than a professional officer. At the same time, other members of the Politburo speak directly for the concerns of the economy and society as a whole, for example, the chairman of the Council of Ministers or the secretary of the Party central committee concerned with agricultural questions.

22. Alexander Dallin, "The Domestic Sources of Soviet Foreign Policy," in *The Domestic Context of Soviet Foreign Policy*, edited by Seweryn Bialer (Boulder, Colo.: Westview Press, 1981), pp. 335–408.

23. See, however, Richard Pipes, "Militarism and the Soviet State," *Daedalus* (Fall 1980): 1–12. The subject of Pipes's article is Soviet "militarism," but he does not define the term. He calls it the "principal instrumentality" of militancy ("a commitment to violence and coercion") and the two are "as central to Soviet communism as the pursuit of profit is to societies with market-oriented economies . . . for sound reasons derived from Russian history, the ideology of communism, and the Soviet view of the nature of future war" (p. 1). There is much truth in his development of these three sources of Soviet militarism. However, the logic of the argument leads to extreme conclusions: e.g., "in the Soviet Union . . . industrialism is a by-product of militarism" (p. 1) and "the philosophy of economic determinism, as reinforced by the experiences of World War I and World War II, has tended to erase in the consciousness of Soviet leaders the line separat-

ing the military and civilian sectors, with *the civilian sector being increasingly regarded as an ancilla of the military*" (p. 10; italics added). For a contrasting view, see David Holloway, "Military Power and Political Purpose in Soviet Policy," *Daedalus* (Fall 1980): 13–30.

24.   In Bialer's view military development was the sole goal of Soviet economic expansion under Stalin, p. 426 of "Soviet Foreign Policy: Sources, Perceptions, Trends," in *The Domestic Context of Soviet Foreign Policy*, edited by Bialer (Boulder, Colo.: Westview Press, 1981), pp. 409–41).

25.   One definition of political culture is "the subjective perceptions of history and politics, the fundamental beliefs and values, the foci of identification and loyalty, and the political knowledge and expectations which are the product of the specific historical experience of nations and groups" (p. 1 of A.H. Brown, "Introduction," in *Political Culture and Political Change in Communist States*, edited by Archie Brown and Jack Gray (London: Macmillan, 1977), pp. 1–24.

26.   Benjamin Lambeth, *Soviet Strategic Conduct and the Prospects for Stability*, Rand Corporation, R–2579–AF, December 1980. Cf. Barry Posen, "the only way to be certain of one's security is to know all there is to know about the most important military technology, and to exploit this knowledge in a way that minimizes the possibility of being surprised by the adversary. Nuclear arms racing is simultaneous, mutual balancing behavior in a sovereignless, bipolar system where high costs accrue to wrong guesses. States have an incentive to be conservative in their military force planning," (book review, in *Survival* 21, no. 4 (July–August 1979): 186).

27.   Lambeth suggests that the Soviet military's views on the role of strategic power are "reinforced by a pervasive fear that the denial of the possibility of victory would entail a fundamental rejection of the legitimacy of military institutions, with eventual defeatism and moral decay the inevitable results" (ibid).

28.   Article 28 of the present (1977) Soviet constitution lists "insuring international conditions for the building of communism in the USSR" first in the list of Soviet foreign policy goals.

29.   The decision to hold the Summit may have reflected the Politburo's self-control and adherence to a scale of priorities, but it may also have been associated with a leadership crisis, the purging of Piotr Shelest. Hedrick Smith, *The Russians* (New York: Quadrangle, 1976), p. 349; Roy Medvedev, *The Observer* July 29, 1979, p. 9; and Dallin, "Domestic Sources of Soviet Foreign Policy," p. 367.

30.   Kenneth D. Moll and Gregory M. Luebbert, "Arms Race and Military Expenditure Models," *Journal of Conflict Resolution*, 24: 1, March, pp. 153–185. I am grateful to Jiri Valenta for identifying this source.

31.   Party propaganda warned that détente should never be understood as promising eventual reconciliation between the two systems. "Communists

would cease to be communists if they did this" (V. Stepanov, "Peaceful Coexistence Is Not Class Peace," *Sovetskaia Kirgiziaa*, December 13, 1974, p. 2 cited in Morton Schwartz, *Soviet Perceptions of the United States* (Berkeley and Los Angeles: University of California Press, 1978), p. 150).

32.   Even the chief Americanist, Georgii Arbatov, found it necessary to say that "in analyzing imperialist policy, its assessment as 'friendly' or 'hostile' cannot be used as a point of departure. This policy will always be intrinsically anti-socialist" (*Ideologicheskaia bor'ba v sovremennykh mezhdunarodnykh otnosheniiakh* (Moscow: Politizdat, 1970), p. 269). Elsewhere, he also stated: "One cannot doubt that any change in the correlation of forces in favor of imperialism would have led not to a relaxation but an increase in tension, whipping up the aggressive aspirations of reactionary circles" (p. 9). "Sobytie vazhnogo mezhdunarodnogo znacheniia," *SShA: Ekonomika, politika, ideologiia*, 8 (1972): 3-12. The quotations are cited in Schwartz, *Soviet Perceptions of the United States* on pp. 149 and 141, respectively.

33.   Although its operative significance need not necessarily be diminished by cynical exploitation. Hannes Adomeit suggested the analogy of a tribal medicine man: Even if he were a complete cynic about the rituals he practiced, he would have an interest in maintaining unquestioning belief in the myth among the members of his tribe and, indeed, of spreading the myth to other tribes, pp. 19-20 of "Soviet Foreign Policy Making: The Internal Mechanism of Global Commitment," in *Foreign Policy Making in Communist Countries*, edited by Hannes Adomeit and Robert Boardman (Farnsborough, England: Saxon House, 1979), pp. 15-48. Oleg Penkovskiy (*The Penkovskiy Papers* (New York: Doubleday, 1965), pp. 55, 318-321) accused the higher officers as a group of cynicism, money-grubbing, personal corruption and immorality. Yet, he maintained, a Soviet general was bound to arrive at different conclusions from the objective data of contemporary war than would his American or English counterpart, "because, first of all, he [the Soviet] begins from a completely different set of basic premises and preconceived ideas, namely the Marxian concepts of the structure of society and the course of history." (p. 252). Other reasons were Soviet use of Marxist dialectic logic, differences in moral laws and differences in objectives between the societies.

34.   Dallin, "Domestic Sources of Soviet Foreign Policy," p. 352.

35.   For Western appraisals of this ferment, see, for example, Schwartz, *Soviet Perceptions of the United States*, and Jerry Hough, "The Evolution of the Soviet World View," *World Politics* 32, no. 4 (July 1980): 509-530.

36.   Hough, ibid., p. 529.

37.   To David Holloway the conclusion emerging from a survey of "Foreign and Defense Policy," was: "*détente* as a continuation of the East–West conflict by other means" (p. 72 in "Foreign and Defense Policy," in *The*

Soviet Union since the Fall of Krushchev (New York: The Free Press, 1975), pp. 49-76.

38. This is not to deny that Soviet force structure is the outcome of a process that involves bargaining, maneuvering, and conflict among elements of the military. (See, for example, Edward Warner, III, *The Military in Contemporary Soviet Politics: An Institutional Analysis* (New York: Praeger, 1977).) However, (1) it would be inaccurate to place all emphasis on political and ignore bureaucratic processes of decisionmaking; (2) to the extent that decisions are explicitly made on how much to spend on defense in aggregate, rather than on what weapons to buy in particular, the more ideological considerations outlined here must come into play more fully; but (3) these considerations probably also form a common denominator of the mindsets of most of the important actors in the complex of bureaucratic-political processes of decisionmaking in this sphere.

39. See Raymond L. Garthoff, "SALT and the Soviet Military," *Problems of Communism* 24, no. 1 (January-February 1975): 21-37.

40. *Pravda*, February 25, 1976.

41. The existence and nature of interest groups in the USSR has been the subject of some controversy. The classic work is H. Gordon Skilling and Franklyn Griffiths, eds., *Interest Groups in Soviet Politics* (Princeton, N.J.: Princeton University Press, 1971).

   The major critic is William Odom; see his "A Dissenting View on the Group Approach to Soviet Politics," *World Politics* 28, no. 4 (July 1976): 542-67. For a skeptical review of the literature see David Powell, "In Pursuit of Interest Groups in the USSR," *Soviet Union* 6 pt. I (1979): 99-124.

42. *Khruschev Remembers*, 1974 ed., p. 14

43. Timothy J. Colton, "The Zhukov Affair Reconsidered," *Soviet Studies* 29, no. 2 (April 1977): 185-213.

44. Cited on p. 1 of David Holloway "Technology Management and the Soviet Military Establishment," *Adelphi Paper* 76 (1971).

45. See pp. 42-46 of Christopher D. Jones, 1975. "Just Wars and Limited Wars: Restraints on the Use of the Soviet Armed Forces," *World Politics* 28, no. 1 (October 1975): 44-68.

46. See p. 23 of T.H. Rigby, "The Soviet Regional Leadrship: The Brezhnev Generation," *Slavic Review* 37, no. 1 (March 1978): 1-24.

47. Brezhnev extended his contacts with the military after the war in service with the Ministry of Defense and as a secretary of the Central Committee. Among the others, Suslov was a political officer in the North Caucasus during the war and the head of the Stavropol partisans; Kirilenko was trained in an aviation institute and was the State Defense Committee's representative at an aviation plant during the war as well as a member of

an army political council. Solomentsev was an executive in a Chelyabinsk armaments plant during the war; and after the war, Romanov worked briefly as a designer in the shipbuilding industry after graduating from the Leningrad Shipbuilding Institute (Jerry Hough and Merle Fainsod, *How the Soviet Union Is Governed* (Cambridge, Mass.: Harvard University Press, 1979), pp. 241–47; p. 103 of John McDonnell, "The Soviet Defense Industry as a Pressure Group," in *Soviet Naval Policy. Objectives and Constraints*, edited by M. MccGwire, K. Booth, and J. McDonnell, (New York: Praeger, 1975): pp. 87–122.

48.   Hough and Fainsod, *How the Soviet Union Is Governed*, p. 393.

49.   The military district is "essentially an interlocking military-party-administrative directorate disposing of military and civilian resources alike: the Military Council (*Voennyi Sovet*) presided over by the District commander, includes the chief of staff, area and service commanders together with the First Secretary of the local Republic or *oblast* party organizations— all collectively charged with insuring that Party, government and Defense Ministry instructions are strictly carried out. The Military Council is, therefore, an important body responsible for coordinating the work of the military command and regional Party leadership." (p. 257 of John Erickson's comments in *Regional Development in the USSR: Trends and Prospects*, edited by the Economics and Information Directorates of NATO (Newtonville, Mass.: Oriental Research Partners, 1979).

50.   Peter Kruzhin, "Military Representation in the Leading Organs of the CPSU Following the Twenty-Sixth Congress," *Radio Liberty Research Bulletin*, RL 116/81, March 16, 1981.

51.   See p. 89 of Michael J. Deane, *Political Control of the Soviet Armed Forces* (Crane Russak, New York, 1977).

52.   Gerald A. Nolan, *USSR: The Unity and Integration of Soviet Political, Military and Defense Industry Leadership*, Defense Intelligence Agency, ODI–2250–17–77, Washington, D.C., March 1977, p. 21.

53.   The interlocking membership and activities of local Party organs, military district and military industry are depicted in Ellen Jones, "Soviet Civil-Military Relations: A Focus on the Military District," prepared for the Workshop on Soviet Military Manpower: the Military District Model, Airlie House, Va. April 9–11, 1979.

   The armed forces and the leadership of military industry get to know each other well because administrators in defense industry have had a remarkable record of long tenure in office and in the profession. See pp. 107–68 of Karl F. Spielmann, *Prospects for a Soviet Strategy of Controlled Nuclear War: An Assessment of Some Key Indicators*, Institute for Defense Analysis, P–1236, March 1976.

54.   Nolan, *USSR*, 1977. Although not nearly as prevalent as during the war, there is a widespread practice of military ranks and designations for leading civilian cadres, particularly, of course, in military industry and R&D.

The uniforms and titles are the symbols of the interdependency between Party, military, and significant parts of the industrial–scientific elite.

55. Colton, "The Zhukov Affair Reconsidered," p. 213.

56. See p. 351 of Zbigniew Brzezinski, "Soviet Politics: From the Future to the Past," in *The Dynamics of Soviet Politics*, edited by Paul Cocks, Robert V. Daniels, and Nancy Heer (Cambridge, Mass.: Harvard University Press, 1976), pp. 337–51.

57. Roman Kolkowicz, *The Soviet Military and the Communist Party* (Princeton, N.J.: Princeton University Press, 1967); "The Military," in *Interest Groups in Soviet Politics*, edited by H.G. Skillings and F. Griffiths (Princeton, N.J.: Princeton University Press, 1971); and "Interest Groups in Soviet Politics: The Case of the Military," in *Civil–Military Relations in Communist Systems* edited by Dale R. Herspring and Ivan Volgyes (Boulder, Colo.: Westview Press, 1978).

58. William E. Odom, "Who Controls Whom in Moscow?" *Foreign Policy* 14 (Summer 1975): 109–23; "A Dissenting View on the Group Approach to Soviet Politics," *World Politics* 28 no. 4 (July 1976): 542–67; "The 'Militarization' of Soviet Society," *Problems of Communism* 25, no. 5 (September–October 1976): 34–51.

Timothy J. Colton, "The Zhukov Affair Reconsidered"; "The Party–Military Connection: A Participatory Model," in Herspring and Volgyes, eds., *Civil–Military Relations in Communist Systems*, pp. 53–75; *Commissars, Commanders and Civilian Authority: The Structure of Soviet Military Politics* (Cambridge, Mass.: Harvard University Press, 1979).

59. "The conflicts of interests and opinions which comprise the decisionmaking process in national security affairs mirror not only differences between party, governmental, and military institutions, but more often reflect differences between inter-institutional coalitions formed on the basis of a community of interests. It would constitute a major analytical error to perceive conflicts of interests along institutional lines exclusively." Kenneth A. Myers and Dimitri Simes, *Soviet Decisionmaking, Strategic Policy and SALT*, Center for Strategic and International Studies, Georgetown University, Washington, D.C., December 1974, p. 22. See also Colton: "When conflict does occur, it rarely divides Army and Party into neatly juxtaposed categories. Issues and loyalties cut across formal occupational and institutional boundaries" ("The Zhukov Affair Reconsidered," p. 212).

60. Brzezinski, "Soviet Politics," p. 351.

61. *Interest Groups in Soviet Politics.*

62. "Office Holding and Elite Status," pp. 94–95.

63. Gordon H. Skilling, "Group Conflict in Soviet Politics: Some Conclusions," pp. 379–416 in Skilling and Griffiths, eds., *Interest Groups in Soviet Politics.*

64. Dallin, "Domestic Sources of Soviet Foreign Policy," p. 342.

274 SOVIET MILITARY POWER

65. Information on this subject is still scanty but the Western literature is becoming substantial. See Arthur J. Alexander, "Decision-Making in Soviet Weapons Procurement," *Adelphi Paper* 147/8 (Winter 1978–79); Thomas W. Wolfe, *Military Power and Soviet Policy*, Rand Corporation, P–5388, March 1975, ch. 3; Michael Checinski, *A Comparison of the Polish and Soviet Armaments Decisionmaking Systems*, Rand Corporation, R–2662–AF, January 1981); and also the previously cited work by McDonnell, by Jones, and by Warner.

66. Spielmann, *Soviet Strategy of Controlled Nuclear War*, pp. 89–90; Jones, "Soviet Civil–Military Relations," p. 5.

67. *The New York Times*, September 19, 1967.

68. See p. 53 of Matthew P. Gallagher, "The Military Role in Soviet Decision-Making," in *Soviet Naval Policy. Objectives and Constraints*, edited by M. MccGwire, K. Nooth, and J. McDonnell (New York: Praeger, 1975), pp. 40–58.

69. There seems to be no department in the Central Committee charged with overseeing military policy and military operations, as distinct from military industry or military appointments (the Administrative Organs department). The autonomy of the armed forces in this sphere is limited in principle, to the degree that grand strategy, what the Soviets call "military doctrine," is the prerogative of the political authority; the province of the military is "military art."

70. The *instituchiki*, a few of whom are former officers, may advise the political leadership directly on issues connected with their areas of research. However, according to a senior staff member of the group, they have been allowed no direct connection to the General Staff and the Ministry of Defense. A Soviet writer claims that scientists and "economic specialists" are often invited to attend Politburo meetings: "they take an active part in discussion of issues under review and express competent judgments" (p. 35 of A. Vodolazskii, "Vysshii printsip partiinogo rukovodstva," *Kommunist* 12 (1979): 30–41. The context suggests that the "issues under review" relate to civil not military policy.

71. Igor S. Glagolev, "The Soviet Decision-Making Process in Arms Control Negotiations," *Orbis* 21, no. 4 (Winter 1978): 767–76.

72. Hough and Fainsod, *How the Soviet Union Is Governed*, pp. 445–46.

73. Sokolev, *Politicheskaia ekonomiia*, p. 86.

74. Pp. 28–30, 40, and 49 of Douglas B. Diamond and W. Lee Davis, "Comparative Growth in Output and Productivity in U.S. and U.S.S.R. Agriculture," and pp. 61–64 of David W. Carey and Joseph F. Havelka, "Soviet Agriculture: Progress and Problems," both in *Soviet Economy in a Time of Change*, vol. 2, Joint Economic Committee, U.S. Congress, Washington, D.C., 1979.

75. Gertrude Schroeder and Elizabeth Denton, *An Index of Consumption in the USSR*, forthcoming.

76. For further discussion of the problems of Soviet–American relations seen from Moscow, see Harry Gelman, *Reconstructing the Soviet Perspective on U.S. Global Policy*, in this volume.

77. Seweryn Bialer, "Succession and Turnover of Soviet Elites," *Journal of International Affairs* 32, no. 2 (Fall/Winter 1978): 181–200.

78. CIA, *Handbook of Economic Statistics 1980*, ER–80–10452, October 1980, p. 59, and *Handbook of Economic Statistics 1981*, NF HES 81-001, November 1981, p. 60.

79. Gertrude Schroeder, "The Soviet Economy on a Treadmill of 'Reforms,' " in *Soviet Economy in a Time of Change*, vol. 1, Joint Economic Committee, U.S. Congress, Washington, D.C., 1979, pp. 312–40; Nancy Nimitz apparently believes that the 1965 reform was a net loss and asserts that "by the end of 1969, disillusion with the 1965 reform was total, and party opinion was divided on whether to move forward or backward" ("Reform and Technological Innovation in the Eleventh Five-Year Plan," Paper prepared for the "Conference on the 26th Party Congress of the CPSU," April 23–25, 1981).

80. Nimitz, ibid.

81. Philip Hanson, "Western Technology in the Soviet Economy," *Problems of Communism*, 27 (November–December 1978): 20–30; Martin L. Weitzman, Donald W. Green, and Yasushi Toda, Three articles on technology transfer to the USSR, in the *Journal of Comparative Economics* 3, no. 2 (June 1979): 167–94.

82. Thane Gustafson, *Selling the Russians the Rope? Soviet Technology Policy and U.S. Export Controls*, Rand Corporation, R–2649–ARPA, July 1981.

83. Alexander Yanov, *Détente after Brezhnev: The Domestic Roots of Soviet Foreign Policy*, Institute of International Studies, University of California, Berkeley, 1977.

84. See p. 232 of A.H. (Archie) Brown, "Political Developments: Some Conclusions and an Interpretation," in *The Soviet Union since the Fall of Khrushchev*, edited by Archie Brown and Michael Kaser (New York: The Free Press, 1975): pp. 218–75.

85. The common Western view of the Soviet growth dilemma probably errs with respect to a major assumption—that Soviet policymakers aim at restoring growth rates to the level of the 1950s or even the 1960s. Two decades of lower economic growth have now been experienced and one may doubt whether the pre-1970 record continues to be viewed as the norm. If the trend to be extrapolated is based on a more recent period embodying less utopian assumptions, the gap between aspiration and reality, and hence also the acuteness of the growth problems, may be less than is commonly perceived in the West. Moreover, a poorer Western record of late means less of a challenge to the Soviet self-image.

86. The watchwords of that document are "socialist emulation," organization, and discipline as the means to increasing efficiency. The document con-

cludes with appeals to each segment of the society: to "the heroic working class, to continue to be in the vanguard of nationwide socialist competition"; to "our glorious kolkhoz peasantry, all rural toilers: actively join the movement to achieve the highest yield of agricultural crops and productivity in stockbreeding"; to "the Soviet intelligentsia . . . strive to accelerate scientific–technical progress"; even to "dear Soviet women: Your work in the factory, your maternal concerns for the family and the upbringing of children have won universal gratitude and respect! Participate even more actively in public life and creative work!"

87. "Succession and Turnover of Soviet Elites," p. 188.

88. Another consideration is the self-image of the regime. Traditionally, Moscow has viewed the rate of economic growth as an indicator of the state of competition between the two systems. Khrushchev made much of this in the 1950s. Little is heard of this theme now, but the rate of expansion of the Soviet economy relative to that of the major capitalist states is still seen as a measure of the progress of the socialist world in its historical conflict with capitalism. More rapid and uninterrupted socialist growth is supposedly both a visible indicator of the inherent superiority of a socialist order and a beacon attracting the new states of the Third World to the socialist side.

89. The Polish crisis may have similar effects, because the Soviets probably blame Warsaw's industrial modernization drive of the 1970s, financed by heavy borrowing abroad, for the erosion of Communist power in Poland.

90. Daniel L. Bond and Herbert S. Levine, "The Soviet Economy Toward the Year 2000: An Overview," paper prepared for the conference on "The Soviet Economy Toward the Year 2000," held October 23–25, 1980, and "The 11th Five-Year Plan, 1981-1985," revised version of a paper prepared for the "Conference on the 26th Congress of the CPSU," sponsored by The Rand Corporation and Columbia University, held April 23–25, 1981; also CIA, *SOVSIM: A Model of the Soviet Economy*, ER–79–10001, February 1979, and *Simulations of Soviet Growth Options to 1985*, ER–79–10131, March 1979.

8 RECONSTRUCTING THE SOVIET PERSPECTIVE ON U.S. GLOBAL POLICY

Harry Gelman

The aging and ailing Soviet leadership now perceives itself to be undergoing a broad "counterattack" by its chief opponent.[1] Public use of this term by a Politburo member in this context is somewhat unusual in that it implies acknowledgment of a preceding, equally broad and hostile Soviet stimulus. But Brezhnev's putative heir-apparents, in thus characterizing U.S. policy toward the USSR at the outset of the new decade, as usual did not elaborate on his hint that a long-existing Soviet offensive posture toward the U.S. position in the world may have cumulatively helped to precipitate the U.S. response to Afghanistan. Instead, Kirilenko depicted the United States as seeking, in its efforts to isolate the Soviet Union, to rebel against objective, self-propelled phenomena that are incrementally and inevitably eroding U.S. influence and in the process advancing that of the Soviet Union. In reacting against "the profound consequences of détente and the objective process of progressive social change taking place in the world," the United States is vainly seeking to turn back "the laws of history," which, Kirilenko implied, both necessitate and legitimize Soviet advances.[2]

Moreover, in so doing, the U.S. leadership has given vent to "whim, caprice, emotional outbursts."[3] These are alleged to contradict genuine U.S. self-interest, which requires graceful adjustment rather than foolish resistance to historical necessity. Soviet pronouncements on this subject are calculated to impress upon foreign audiences—and to some degree may genuinely reflect—a certain anger and contempt at this amateurish yielding to emotion; but the Politburo has no intention of doing the same.[4]

The first imperative for the Party leadership under such an attack is to respond vigorously,[5] yet appropriately, without allowing itself to be "provoked" into abandoning the mixture of policies seen as optimizing Soviet interests.[6] "No one will succeed in provoking us."[7] "No one will push us off this course."[8]

In the world seen from the Politburo, pugnacious struggle so shaped and channeled has the dual advantage of continuing and even intensifying that universal offensive against U.S. influence so much resented by unrealistic circles in the United States, while earning whatever political rewards may accrue from professed moderation toward others.

Accordingly, with the Soviet–U.S. bilateral relationship at a standstill, the keynote of Soviet competitive strategies for dealing with the United States in the world arena today remains their continuity with the past. An initial overview of the interacting spheres of Soviet concern today will suggest the nature of the offensive and defensive tactics developed over the last decade, as adapted to the new challenge.

The Capitalist Industrial World. By appealing to the perceived self-interest of the allies of the United States in the preservation of their separate economic and security relationships with the USSR; by pressing on the lines of cleavage opened up by the multiple disparities revealed among Western interests; by encouraging and playing upon spontaneous allied reactions to U.S. policy as dangerously unpredictable, immoderate, and inconsistent; and by attacking the domestic base of those individuals and groups most supportive of the United States, the Soviet leadership seeks to escape the isolation sought for it by Washington and to isolate the United States in its turn.

China. Confronted with an alarming acceleration of Sino–U.S. alignment against them since Afghanistan, the Soviet leaders remain determined to pay no significant price to either antagonist to end it. The Politburo therefore persists in what are thus far unsuccessful efforts to split the weaker opponent from the stronger one. It therefore offers China improvement in selected aspects of the bilateral relationship without relaxing those competitive assaults on Chinese geopolitical interests around the periphery of the People's Republic of China that continuously refuel Chinese antagonism.

Its Own Sphere. While pursuing the uninhibited military consolidation of its position in Afghanistan and as a corollary to its continued cultivation of West Europe, the Soviet leadership assures the nervous East Europeans that it has no intention of curtailing their dealings with the West. At the same time, the Politburo struggles with the grave new threat the ongoing Polish crisis poses for its European policies, striving to contain popular pressures in Poland without resorting to punitive measures so drastic as to undermine its strategy toward Western Europe, yet preparing to pay that price should it become necessary. Meanwhile, the Politburo accelerates the consolidation of its position at home against what it has long regarded as Western-sponsored subversion. To this end, since the invasion of Afghanistan, it has adopted measures against Sakharov and other dissidents that were long delayed by concern over the Western response, thus creating *faits accomplis* to be incorporated into the revised definition of détente.

The Third World. By adjusting and modulating what was already a highly variegated set of policies to meet both defensive needs and offensive opportunities created by the new U.S. posture, the Soviet leadership perseveres in the long-term process of extending the Soviet political presence into previously Western-oriented nooks and crannies throughout the world: exploring avenues of opportunity as they are opened up to Politburo view by the interaction of complex variables and accepting major setbacks as inevitable incidents in the process of advance on a gradual broadening front through the enemy's hinterland. A few representative examples will suggest the flavor of the whole:

- To Iran, to African and Latin American radicals, to the Arab rejectionists, and even to moderate Arab states unhappy with the Camp David agreement, the Soviets stress the transcendant importance of the grievances each has against the United States. The Soviet leadership thereby seeks to persuade each audience that the Soviet offenses committed in Afghanistan are much less important to its private interests.

- While using various diplomatic expedients to reassure audiences that merit soothing, such as India and the Arabs, that the invasion of Afghanistan has no threatening implications for them, the Soviets seek tacitly to convey the opposite impression to those audiences for whom intimidation is thought useful—for example, Pakistan and China.

- While playing upon the misgivings of states such as India and Kuwait over reactive U.S. efforts to strengthen its local military presence and capabilities, they quietly take steps to enhance the USSR's own naval presence in the Indian Ocean and its military readiness in the Caucasus.

- While intensifying efforts to defend and consolidate those political and military bridgeheads achieved through a Soviet security relationship over several years (in Angola, Ethiopia, South Yemen, and Indochina), they adjust to what they hope will prove only transitory recent disappointments in other areas, such as Zimbabwe.

- Meanwhile, they seek to preserve and develop a nascent arms-supply relationship with a hitherto Western-oriented African state (Zimbabwe's neighbor Zambia) by redoubling efforts to play upon Zambian fears of South Africa. At the same time they begin cautious development of a new relationship with Nicaragua, on the main enemy's decaying periphery, while awaiting and loudly applauding the imminent fall of further fruit in El Salvador.

- Finally they continue quietly to expand the multiple military and political uses they have found for their earliest consolidated bridgehead in the Third World, in Cuba. They seek to pacify Castro's annoyance at the Afghanistan embarrassment and to encourage him to repair the damage done by Afghanistan to Soviet and Cuban interests in the nonaligned movement and thus, gradually, to help revive the temporarily diminished intensity of anti-U.S. sentiment in the movement.

This brief tour of the Soviet world horizon suggests that the leadership's strategy toward the United States has become both defensive and coercive. The defensive aspect of Soviet behavior responds to what the Soviets see as unprecedented U.S. efforts to isolate and surround them. The coercive core of the Politburo's policies reflects the Soviet hope to so shape the international environment as to compel the United States eventually to restore those elements of the bilateral relationship still deemed useful to the Soviet Union, but on terms favorable to accelerated Soviet exploitation of competitive advantages.

Viewing the world as a single, interrelated, many-faceted battlefield, the Soviet leaders have for many years regarded the management of their bilateral relationship with the United States as but one aspect, albeit a very important one, of a much broader, indeed universal interaction with the United States, involving a multitude of engagements, sometimes open and sometimes hidden, sometimes sharp and sometimes subdued, between interests that are in most cases assumed to be incompatible. Although, as we shall see, the Politburo's priorities across this wide canvas have shifted with changing circumstances, a very large proportion of the Soviet energies devoted to coping with the United States have always been channeled through Soviet dealings with others. Since 1974 this proportion has steadily grown. With the virtual dissolution of the remnants of the bilateral relationship in 1980, the competitive thrust of the Politburo's policies affecting the United States, long dominant in Soviet thinking, has become all-embracing.

This does not mean that the increasingly decrepit members of the Politburo have in their eleventh hour at last acquired a master plan for further advance in the world at U.S. expense, capable of magically anticipating the interaction of all the myriad variables they had been unable to anticipate before. On the contrary, despite the obligatory obeisance all Soviet institutions must make to paper plans, the practical decisionmaking horizon of the Soviet leadership, particularly in foreign affairs, is remarkably short.

Instead of a blueprint the Soviet leaders have a consistent world view centered on the unblinking expectation of lasting struggle with the main antagonist, furnishing a sense of self-justification in all circumstances, and providing a stable framework from which to assign priorities in that struggle as decisions and events emerge. They are totally isolated within a network of advice and information strongly predisposed to confirm this attitude of pugnacious righteousness. Under the Brezhnev regime there has been an expansion in the size of the foreign policy elite surrounding the leadership and probably some increase in the diversity of views privately held within that elite, but there is little evidence to suggest that heretical notions about the assumptions underlying Soviet policy are exposed to the policymakers. On the contrary, the record of Soviet conduct strongly suggests that this elite in no case provides the Politburo with advisors who have the treasonous temerity to interpret ambiguous phenomena in a fashion likely to challenge the fundamental preconceptions of these old men. In the military sphere, where the general staff and a few closely associated functionaries enjoy an unchallenged monopoly of esoteric information and advisory rights (through de facto Politburo subcommittee known as the Defense Council), the voiceable view of Soviet needs and interests is even more closely circumscribed.

From this vantage point, thus informed and supported, the members of the Politburo explore their avenues of opportunity as they come into sight, forming tentative expectations and discarding them with great dexterity, sometimes blundering, but always subordinating this shuffling of expedients to a central purpose.[9]

THE ELUSIVE CORRELATION OF FORCES

The Soviets now say that the United States is attempting to reverse the trend of the world "correlation of forces." This is implied to be illegitimate.

The Two Sides of the Ledger

Within this amorphous concept the Soviets subsume, in extremely vague fashion, all the political, social, economic, and military factors they perceive to be involved to some degree in their worldwide competition with their chief antagonists. In this melange the Soviet attainment of a growing edge in ICBM throw-weight has a certain place, but so do such considerations as the successive humiliations of the United States in Vietnam and Iran, the baneful effect of the OPEC cartel upon Western economies, the successful Soviet–Cuban operations in Africa, the internal political and economic disarray in the United States, and the decline of moderating Yugoslav influence and rise of that of Cuba in the Nonaligned Movement. Thus all trends are relevant, nonmilitary fully as much as military, that affect the relative status of the United States and the Soviet Union. Moreover, events that further weaken the antagonist may be as important as Soviet victories.

The Soviet leaders are well aware of the opposite side of the ledger. Among the negative trends in the correlation of forces, an objective Soviet observer would list, above all, such factors as the fragile, dangerous, and unreliable Soviet relationship with Poland; the grave and growing Soviet economic difficulties and the long-term decline in the rate at which the Soviet economy has been overhauling that of the United States; the growing costs of the Soviet empire, both in East Europe and elsewhere; Chinese implacable hostility and the growing Sino–U.S. military association; the negative reaction in the Moslem world to the invasion of Afghanistan; and, most worrisome, the possibility of a revival of military expenditures and deployments in the West.

The tension between the two sets of phenomena causes the Soviet leadership to be at the same time confident and increasingly assertive in exploitation of opportunities created by favorable trends, and indignant and defensive about threats to Soviet interests evoked by the reaction to that exploitation.

The Emotional Effects of U.S. Disasters

There is in Moscow no standard by which to weight the factors just listed, and different Soviets almost certainly balance them differently. But although the frequent complacent assertions of Soviet propaganda must to a certain extent be discounted,[10] it is probably true that most Soviet leaders have seen favorable trends as considerably outweighing unfavorable ones over the last decade and now see the United States as frantically seeking to reverse this ratio.

Events of recent years have assured the Soviet leadership that notwithstanding many particular Soviet defeats, difficulties, and dangers, underlying trends have on balance been working in Soviet favor. The members of the Politburo, no less than the leaders and populace of the United States, are sensitive to the emotional effects of symbolic events. The replacement of Batista by Castro has been followed two decades later by the replacement of Haile Selassie with Mengistu; the humiliating U.S. flight from Saigon has been followed by Soviet entry into Cam Ranh Bay; the Shah of Iran and Somoza have fallen.

Again, these images are counterbalanced to a considerable degree in the Soviet mind by the misadventures and worries affecting Soviet policy, particularly by the crisis in Poland. But despite these and other grave concerns, the Soviet leaders are unlikely to have serious doubts, on balance, as to who has been in retreat over the last decade and who has been pressing ahead.[11]

Soviet assumptions on this score are strongly reinforced by Soviet perceptions of the opinions of others. The Soviet leaders surely agree with commonly expressed Western judgments that the last decade has been characterized by increasing Soviet emergence as an actor on the world scene. They are well aware of the widespread view, both in Western Europe and in the United States, that U.S. leverage and influence in Europe has been eroding over the last few years, partly because of leadership personality differences and different perceptions of national interest, but also to some extent because of underlying secular shifts in relative economic strength.[12] And they are equally well aware of the common U.S. perception that the last few years have been characterized by a succession of far-reaching U.S. disasters in the Third World, beginning with the humiliating flight from Saigon.[13]

The Soviet leaders regard this worldwide train of U.S. misfortunes as invigorating to observe and important to encourage not only for its own sake, but also because of the possibilities thereby opened up for the implantation of Soviet influence. The Politburo takes for granted that such influence, particularly in areas not contiguous to the Soviet Union, may be relative, conditional, possibly ephemeral. The leadership discounts this fact. Painfully aware that not every U.S. loss produces an immediate Soviet gain and that not every Soviet gain endures, the Soviet leaders share a perspective that renders these realities patiently supportable. If given trends are not immediately and obviously zero-sum in their effects, there is reason to believe that they will eventually be so.

The Enemy's Weakness, Frivolity, or Sloth

Side by side with the contraction of U.S. influence and the emergence of unprecedented Soviet power projection opportunities abroad, the Soviet leaders have lived through a decade of favorable changes in the relative Soviet position in the three chief military arenas: the strategic matchup with the United States and the regional confrontations with NATO and China. In the Soviet view these modifications in military balances were facilitated not merely by the energy and determination of the Soviet Union, but equally by the various social or economic weaknesses of the USSR's antagonists. These weaknesses have diluted and delayed efforts to compete, again testifying to a changing correlation of forces.

Among some Soviets with an institutional vested interest in the pursuit of maximum advantage in the arms competition, this heady experience has diminished even the traditional Soviet awe of the superior size, technological level, and productive potential of U.S. industry. As one Soviet writer asserted, in heavy industry the U.S. advantage is rapidly dwindling; in fact, he suggests that it has almost vanished. The United States fritters its undoubted economic advantages away in self-indulgence:

> In the USA the production of such items as objects of luxury, means for advertising, automobiles, household appliances, etc., which cannot be converted in practice to satisfy military needs or have limited significance in this area, makes up a significant proportion of total industrial output. If industrial production in the USSR currently constitutes more than 75 percent of the American level (in 1950 it constituted less than one-third of the USA level), the quantity of production of means of production is not less than 90 percent of comparable production in the USA. It is clear that this has not only tremendous general-economic but also military-economic significance. . . . The coefficient of superiority of the socialist commonwealth over the aggressive imperialist bloc in the area of assuring the material needs of military construction is currently considerably more weighty than the corresponding index of the USSR in comparison with Hitlerite Germany during the past war.

Although these assertions are probably regarded as one-sided and tendentious even by other Soviets,[14] this hint of a certain contempt for the lagging and frivolous behavior of the competitor is probably reflected to some degree in Kremlin attitudes.

It is not for the sake of our blue eyes, as a Soviet leader might say, that the Americans froze their ICBM and sea-launched ballistic missile (SLBM) launcher totals for a decade while we rushed past them, relying instead upon qualitative advantages that we have now also largely eliminated. Nor is it considered a matter of goodwill that the West has failed to attempt to compensate for the Eastern preponderance of tanks in Europe and had no deployment programs in train to anticipate and compensate for the SS–22 as it emerged. Certainly it was not because of Chinese goodwill that the pace of modernization of Chinese conventional forces facing the USSR has fallen behind the rate at which the Soviet Union has continued to strengthen its forces on the Chinese border. These historic omissions are the result of specific deficiencies in the Politburo's antagonists: In the U.S. case they reflect the enervating effects of the Vietnam War upon the U.S. will to compete, even in weapons production; in the NATO case, the extreme reluctance of the alliance members to make sacrifices commensurate with Soviet force improvements and their inability to agree on any countermeasures until long after the particular Soviet stimulus has materialized; and in the Chinese case profound and enduring economic and technological weakness. All this is surely very encouraging to the Politburo.

And yet, a note of less than complete assurance about the continuity of these phenomena is detectable in much of Soviet comment. The prospect of large new U.S. military programs, of European theater nuclear deployments, and of U.S. transfers of military technology to China undoubtedly creates a Soviet sense of accumulating new dangers that the leadership will have to fight to overcome as it enters a prolonged period of increasing economic stringency. The revival of American nationalism, the threat of heightened encirclement, and the extreme volatility of the Third World forces the leadership sought to manipulate in the 1970s multiply the latent uncertainties with which the Politburo must contend.

THE OFFENSIVE ESSENCE OF SOVIET DEFENSIVE CONCERNS

Throughout the Soviet public and private reaction to the U.S. response to Afghanistan is a note of righteous grievance. The Americans, it is implied, are unreasonably trying to deprive the Soviet Union of what rightfully belongs to it by virtue of geopolitical achievement and historic mission.

The Expandable Empire

The Politburo must defend the legitimacy of its determination to ensure the "irreversibility" of its authority—defined as "socialist gains"—in its own sphere. The leadership sees this right as valid not only inside the Soviet Union and in Eastern Europe, but also in such other areas, particularly adjacent to the USSR, as history and the balance of forces may from time to time reveal. In defending this dual claim, the Soviets tend to appeal for empathy with the Politburo's right to maintain internal stability within the imperial boundaries previously staked out. At the same time, they demand respect for those natural changes dictated by geography—that is, for what are intimated to be the Soviet Union's natural gravitational rights as a great power.

The Politburo thus expects from its adversaries both tacit acquiescence in its right to use force if deemed necessary to preserve Soviet domination over Poland and acceptance of a similar right to use force to consolidate and extend Soviet domination over Afghanistan.

An Expanding (Supplanting) World Role

The Politburo must also defend the legitimacy of its intention to make incremental use of emerging opportunities and capabilities to become a fully global actor.

The Right to Emulate.   This is generally defended by Soviet spokesmen as the Soviet right to play a role the United States had previously reserved for itself. Particularly in private conversation, this argument is sometimes supplemented with the accurate observation that the Soviet Union even now has not yet achieved either the far-flung political presence or the distant power-projection capabilities long enjoyed by the United States. U.S. objections to Soviet overseas operations are therefore said to be reflections of a continuing hypocritical U.S. refusal to accept the Soviet Union as a real equal. Some sympathetic non-Soviet observers see this tendency as exacerbating historical Russian feelings of inferiority and wounding the Politburo's *amour-propre*, thus encouraging bad Soviet behavior (which is therefore, at root, the fault of the United States).

This line of justification and self-justification generally ignores the fact that the global U.S. role is widely perceived as gradually diminishing and that the Politburo sees the USSR's efforts to expand its own role as heavily dependent on this trend. The corollary is that the Soviet leadership in fact seeks not merely to match but to erode and to supplant U.S. presence and influence.

To the Soviet leadership, the decisive test of the antagonist's readiness to accept the inevitability and legitimacy of the emerging Soviet

role is his willingness to maintain a mutually profitable bilateral relationship with the USSR while the supplanting process is going on.
The Politburo regards the United States as never having fully accepted the necessity of maintaining this wall between Soviet-U.S.
dealings and Soviet policy affecting the United States elsewhere,
and as having finally rejected it in 1980, seizing on the invasion of
Afghanistan as a pretext.

You Do the Same to Us.   Soviet representatives privately say this,
again, is hypocritical because, in their view, the United States has
never ceased to attempt to damage Soviet interests abroad. Examples
sometimes cited include the Middle East, where the United States
helped facilitate a major reduction in Soviet influence after the 1973
war, and China, with whom the United States is seen as constructing
a security relationship to "encircle" the Soviet Union.

It is possible that some members of the Soviet leadership may
indeed find additional justification in these terms for what they have
felt impelled to do in any case. The Politburo, however, has an asymmetrical view of these matters. Although the leadership insists on the
isolation of the bilateral relationship from the effects of their competitive operations against U.S. interests in the Third World,[16] it maintains another standard regarding U.S. association with China against
Soviet interests. It does not agree that this association can also be
insulated from U.S.–Soviet dealings. On the contrary, over the years
the Soviet leadership has responded to the unfolding of the U.S.–
Chinese relationship with repeated warnings that it could have major
effects upon U.S.–Soviet bilaterals, including arms control negotiations. Here they have professed to believe in "linkage."

More fundamentally, the Politburo has never provided reason to
believe that it was prepared to offer reciprocal concessions to the
United States in the Third World. It has not shown willingness to
reciprocate for major U.S. concessions to Soviet interests in areas of
relative Soviet weakness—such as those the United States momen-
tarily seemed ready to extend to Moscow at the time of the October
1977 Soviet-U.S. communiqué on the Middle East—with comparable great Soviet concessions to U.S. interests elsewhere, in areas of
relative U.S. weakness. Still less has the Soviet leadership indicated
readiness to respond to such U.S. concessions with a general relaxation of the Soviet offensive posture against the United States in the
Third World. In obedience to the taboo against unprincipled funda-

mental concessions constricting the Party's freedom of maneuver and its room for future advance,[17] the present Soviet leadership recognizes no region of the world—and no country within any region—as a legitimate U.S. sphere of influence exempt from Soviet efforts to eliminate and supplant U.S. ascendancy.[18] The Soviets are, indeed, indignant at the notion that they might be asked to provide such an exemption.[19]

The Compulsion To Attack. Thus universal attacking essence of Soviet policy toward the U.S. position in the world is the central underlying reality the Politburo wishes the United States to accept as compatible with détente. Such spectacular events of the last decade as the deployment of Soviet or Cuban forces for combat (in Africa or Southwest Asia) or the use of Soviet geopolitical weight to underwrite agression by others (in Southeast Asia) are therefore not isolated aberrations in the Soviet interpretation of détente but, rather, special manifestations of a continuous flow of policy. Although particular kinds of Soviet behavior may or may not be repeated, depending on circumstances, the propensity to seek to supplant, which drives the whole, is unabating and uncompromisable.

The requirements of the attacking compulsion are thus insatiable; they appear to be incompatible with acceptance of any final equilibrium with the United States. Periods of pause and retreat are disturbing anomalies that must be justified as consolidating interludes within some broader framework of unabated offensive. It is for this reason that Brezhnev felt obliged to reassure some militant followers privately in the spring of 1973 that the improvement of bilateral relations with the West was a stratagem intended to enable the Soviet Union to improve its relative position to the point where by 1985 it could deal with the West more forthrightly.[20]

When advantages are at hand, they must be pursued.[21] It was not enough that the post-Shah regime in Iran sought to perpetuate Iranian hostility toward the United States by seizing U.S. diplomats. The Soviet leadership, lacking a good opening to that regime, had to seek one by fanning the flames of that hostility by praising and justifying the takeover of the U.S. embassy, at first explicitly and thereafter implicitly.

It is not enough that the United States was ignominiously expelled from Vietnam with the aid of Soviet-supplied material. To consolidate a position of advantage, the Politburo diverted Vietnam from pursuing a nonmilitary solution to its border problems with Pol Pot's Cambodia that could reduce Vietnam's need for the Soviet Union. To that end it had to make feasible a military solution—the conquest of Cambodia—that could perpetuate Vietnamese dependence on the USSR. It is not enough that the United States has been forced to accept the permanence of a Soviet military alliance with and military presence in a close neighbor of the United States. The Cubans must be encouraged and discreetly assisted to seize emerging opportunities to erode the U.S. position further in the Caribbean and Central America.[22]

The unspoken assumption in all such behavior is that if the Soviet Union does not press to advance in the universal struggle against the United States, it may fall back. In view of past Soviet experience and the economic pulling power of the West, the Soviet leaders are acutely aware of the potential fragility of their influence on noncontiguous clients, whatever their ideological makeup (or, indeed, on contiguous ones, except when the Soviet hold can be enforced by military occupation, as Tito, Mao, Kim Il-sung, Ceaucescu, Dubcek, and Amin have variously shown). Precisely because the permanence of both gains and opportunities must be considered uncertain, despite all favorable trends, consolidation can be sought only by pressing on.[23]

In sum, the Soviet offensive posture is dictated by a confluence of judgments, assumptions, and emotions: the sense of beckoning opportunities created by U.S. misfortunes and a changing "correlation of forces," the Leninist compulsion to pursue potential gains to the limit of prudence, awareness of the emergence of strategic parity and of the growth of Soviet force-projection capabilities, the rationalization that the United States behaves similarly, and the fear that the gains of recent years may be reversed if not reinforced with others.

Asymmetrical Security

Closer to home Soviet leaders sense themselves to be defending certain favorable asymmetries in their security relationships with their antagonists that have evolved over the years and are now also under attack. These the Soviets have come to regard as prescriptive rights genuinely essential to the defense. Although the Soviets do not usually spell out the claim, the common denominator in different contexts appears to be the conviction that because of geography and other unique geopolitical burdens, the Soviet Union requires greater force levels in each arena than its antagonists to end up with "equal security," or "equilibrium."

The overall size of the Soviet armed forces in comparison with those of the United States is publicly justified on the grounds that the Soviets must defend on two fronts, against China as well as Europe.[24] What is not acknowledged is an apparently equally strong conviction of a Soviet need to maintain a continuously updated local advantage in each of these theaters.

In the case of China the Soviets maintain what they consider sufficient local forces and fire power to overmatch the Chinese at every step up the escalatory ladder, with the measurement of sufficiency heavily influenced by the need to offset Soviet dependence upon a long rail line for reinforcement. By the standards of most Western observers, they have greatly overcompensated even for the defensive needs created by this handicap. The Chinese therefore see the stationing of these powerful forces in Siberia and Mongolia as intended simply to intimidate them. The Soviets, however, see this as justifiable insurance through superiority, particularly because these forces can also be used to exert geopolitical leverage on Chinese behavior elsewhere, as in Indochina. The Politburo is accordingly indignant at the possibility that the United States might provide China the wherewithal even to dilute this superiority.

The Politburo's underlying attitudes regarding sufficiency appear roughly similar in Europe. Although the Soviets have offered no justification for the Warsaw Pact's sizable advantages in manpower and tanks (since they do not admit these exist), it is conceivable that they may at one time have regarded them as necessary to compensate on the one hand for the uncertain reliability of some East European troops and on the other hand for the once important NATO advantage in tactical nuclear weapons. Despite the reduction of the latter handicap in recent years, the Soviets cling to their very large advantage in tanks, unwilling to forgo the measure of extra military insurance it confers, the bargaining advantage it presents in arms control forums, or the intimidating weight it gives the Politburo in dealings with West European states and populations.

In addition, having sought and failed in SALT I and II to secure compensation from the United States for the so-called forward-based systems,[25] the Politburo has produced and deployed systems[26] in Western Russia that again, in the Western view, greatly overcompensate for this Soviet handicap. The Soviets profess to believe that these systems have merely restored an equilibrium and profess to be indignant that the West plans to deploy in reply theater nuclear systems capable of reaching the Soviet Union. Having established a unilateral, nonnegotiated *fait accompli*, they insist on a right to participate in the determination of the Western response and have indicated their intention to make additional deployments, in advance of the arrival of the new Western systems, in reaction to the Western refusal to halt deployment pending negotiations. Once again the Soviet leaders regard the United States as the chief cause of the Western failure to accept the legitimacy of the asymmetrical security established with the advent of the SS-20.

Finally in the strategic sphere Soviet vital interests appear to the Soviet leadership to require pursuit of a war-fighting capability that is supplementary and additional to that required merely to deter the United States from attack. The quest for this additional capability is evidently regarded as a search for insurance against the possibility that deterrence might fail[27] and thus as legitimate reinforcement of the Soviet sense of security, like the unacknowledged advantage in tanks and manpower maintained in Europe. At the same time, just as they are unwilling to acknowledge the degree of insecurity created in the West by their pursuit of maximum security for themselves in Europe, so the Soviets are unwilling to come to grips with the U.S. perception of menace to *its* deterrent—and thus to U.S. security—created by Soviet strategic overinsurance. Because the Soviets are unwilling to accept any formulation that would cast doubt on the legitimacy of this overinsurance, during the SALT negotiations they explicitly rejected the principle of mutual assured destruction.[28] They have thus, in effect, disowned any responsibility on their part for the preservation of the U.S. deterrent.

They have sought to compensate for this refusal with a variety of statements claiming the existence of a strategic parity of equilibrium and vigorously denying any intention to upset this alleged equilibrium or to seek superiority.[29] These statements bear a strong resemblance to the analogous Soviet assertions that the advent of the SS-20 has brought about an equilibrium in Europe. Because such general reassurances do not address the destabilizing capabilities created by the trend of Soviet weapons deployments in question, they do not remove the insecurity created by Soviet actions.

The Family of Defensive-Offensive Concerns

A family resemblance in Politburo attitudes thus exists in diverse spheres of Soviet policy. Determination to ensure adequate defense of Soviet interests is seen as simultaneously requiring and justifying the forcible addition of Afghanistan to the inner sphere of Soviet control, the continuous outward pressure against the U.S. position in the world, the vigilant preservation of unequal security balances in regional theaters, and the pursuit of a strategic war-fighting capability against the United States.

The adverse implications of these attitudes for others appear to be legitimized in Politburo thinking by the underlying assumption that Soviet interests can be adequately defended only at the expense of the antagonist and are fundamentally incompatible with his interests. It is thus taken for granted that if the Politburo allows constraints to be placed on its behavior by foolishly accepting the possibility of a real and lasting middle ground, this can only give unilateral advantage to the opponent.

FACTORS IN THE EVOLVING SOVIET POLICY MIX

Within the framework created by this strong Politburo compulsion to maximize gains to the limits of prudence, there is reason to believe that the leadership's evaluation of disparate alternative advantages fluctuates somewhat with changing circumstances. Several interacting factors have to some degree affected the evolving Soviet calculation of costs and benefits.

The Scope of Third World Opportunities. Certainly the single most important factor has been the scope of evolving opportunities in the Third World. This is itself the product of both the shifting situation on the ground, in specific Third World arenas, the changing Soviet and U.S. political and military capabilities.

The Scope of Alternative Benefits from Détente. Despite all Soviet rhetoric about the impossibility of linkage, the Soviet leadership has never been indifferent to the size of the prospective payoff in bilateral benefits that might flow from hypothetical selective acts of restraint calculated to conciliate the U.S. elite. In practice, however, the rewards for restraint that have seemed likely to materialize have at no stage seemed commensurate with the alternative gains offered to Soviet competitive appetites. In retrospect, it is possible that none of the benefits originally sought by the Soviet leaders from the détente relationship would have constrained Soviet behavior in the Third World. Since the mid-1970s, the Soviet leadership has contemptuously dismissed periodic U.S. attempts to hold other aspects of the Soviet–U.S. leadership—such as arms control agreements—hostage to better Soviet behavior.

The Tolerable Price of Averting Sino–U.S. Collaboration.   Ever since the 1969 Soviet military clashes with China on the Sino–Soviet border, the Politburo has feared that the United States would use Soviet vulnerability over the China issue as a lever on Soviet policy. From the moment that Sino–U.S. normalization surfaced in 1971, the Soviet leadership has increasingly seen the United States as attempting to apply such leverage, disregarding U.S. disclaimers it (correctly) assumed were not seriously intended.[30] In the earliest stages Politburo concerns about China were sufficiently great that the Soviet Union was in fact willing to make certain concessions to the United States in an effort to ensure U.S. neutrality and, if possible, some degree of alignment with the USSR against China. Thereafter and particularly since 1974–75 when the Soviet leadership became simultaneously disappointed with the practical fruits of détente and enticed by new opportunities for gain at U.S. expense in the Third World, the Politburo has been adamant in its determination to avoid making further such concessions. What was seen in one context as a wise tactical adjustment to unfavorable circumstances has now become, in another context, unprincipled yielding to pressure, allowing the Party to be "used" by the enemy.[31]

In the last few years, the Soviet leadership has therefore responded to a growing Sino–U.S. alignment against the USSR with a combination of vague and inadequate threats to the major opponent (the United States), and equally vague and inadequate inducements to the secondary one (China). Although the Politburo became increasingly alarmed at the Sino–U.S. combination against it, it has evidently refused to acknowledge, even to itself, that its offensive policy of maximizing gains against the geopolitical interests of both adversaries has been largely responsible for driving them together. Instead, the Soviet leaders appear to have ascribed these unwelcome phenomena to the blind, autonomous, and ultimately unappeasable malevolence of particular individuals: Zbigniew Brzezinski in the United States and Deng Xiaoping in China. Such a Soviet view leads to the rationalizing conclusion that the enemy's propensity to follow this baneful line will only be encouraged by concessions and is better met by opposing pressures,[32] an assumption that meshes well with the Politburo's seeming need to avoid such concessions and to maintain an offensive posture in any case. This pattern of Soviet thought has been facilitated by the continuing ambiguity of ultimate U.S. aims regarding China, an ambiguity that is itself the product of a lack of U.S. consensus on how to calibrate U.S. policies toward China and the USSR.

The Balance of Personal and Institutional Interests.   The fourth factor, the internal dimension, is of a different order. It does not concern any crude juxtaposition of mythical Politburo "hawks" and "doves" in the determination of policy toward the United States. Rather, it involves the interplay of subtle shadings of differences among leaders and institutions regarding the balance of Soviet interests, as events moved that informal Politburo consensus to which all have felt it wise to conform in a direction more highly prized by some than by others.

Over time the growing confidence of the Politburo in the political rewards to be obtained through the military instrument has influenced the relationships among the institutions surrounding the Politburo. Above all, the prestige of the Soviet military establishment and its leaders, already greatly enhanced by the political effects of growing Soviet strategic strength, rose further with successive demonstrations of what Soviet power-projection capabilities could add to the Soviet political position in the Third World. And it appears likely that Soviet military leaders, particularly Marshal Grechko, were important participants in the political coalition that favored increasing Soviet engagement in Third World enterprises regardless of the effect on U.S. attitudes.

The point is not, of course, that the military could dictate to the Party. Rather, the total political environment, inside and outside the Soviet Union, gradually impelled Party leaders toward the consensus that this line of policy was in the net Soviet interest. Each Politburo member therefore was increasingly inclined to assume, in marginal situations, that it was in his personal political interest to lean in the direction favored by military endorsement. One symptom of this changing political atmosphere as the decade progressed was the readiness of the party leadership to authorize Soviet military spokesmen to make increasingly explicit references to the legitimacy of the Soviet overseas combat role.[33]

A subtler symptom was an apparent upgrading of the importance of military considerations against countervailing political ones in Soviet decisionmaking, even in some cases when the predictable result would play into the hands of the United States. The decision to proceed with the invasion of Afghanistan may possibly have been such a case, although the extent of the negative political consequences to be weighed against the powerful imperatives to act may have been underestimated. A clearer example was the decision late in the decade not merely to adhere to the adamant Soviet refusal to discuss the Japanese claim to the southern Kuriles but also greatly to enlarge the garrisoning and fortification of those islands in a highly visible manner. Although there are probably important military reasons for this conduct (the desire to deny U.S. wartime entry to the Sea of Okhotsk and to ensure Soviet egress), the price paid—in terms of increasing Japanese hostility toward the Soviet Union and the Japanese propensity to increase military expenditures, as desired by the United States—seemed to many outside observers to be disproportionate, and almost certainly foreseeable.[34]

Aside from the military, the most important single Soviet institution supporting the more forward line in the Third World as it unfolded in the 1970s may have been the Central Committee apparatus, particularly its International Department under party secretary and candidate Politburo member B.N. Ponomarev. In what has evidently been an ongoing rivalry with the Foreign Ministry over the management of different aspects of Soviet foreign policy and the rendering of policy advice to the Politburo, this department has probably enjoyed some advantages over the Ministry in dealings with certain portions of the Third World. It has had frequently publicized, ongoing contacts, which the Foreign Ministry bureaucracy has evidently lacked, with leaders of so-called national liberation movements not yet in power.[35] This circumstance may have played some role in the watershed Soviet decision to take decisive action on behalf of the

MPLA during the civil war in Angola in 1975–76, despite the angry U.S. reaction.

It is conceivable that some sections of the Foreign Ministry and some of the leaders of advisory foreign policy institutes may have been initially unenthusiastic about the priorities displayed in this trend of Soviet policy, privately resentful of the attitudes and influence of the Defense Ministry, and somewhat more concerned than other sections of the foreign policy elite about the effect upon the Soviet bilateral relationship with the United States. If so, this lower level lack of enthusiasm had no effect on the Politburo.[36] Foreign Minister Gromyko's speeches and travel and contacts patterns suggest that he always gave dealings with the United States and Europe much more personal attention, and a higher priority, than he gave most of the underdeveloped world. But if he shared any of the misgivings, his reactions probably were increasingly submerged in the general hardening of Soviet policy as relations with the United States decayed.

Finally, although the vested interest of large sections of the Soviet elite on the preservation of those personal economic advantages that the "New Class" derives from détente[37] are real enough, they nevertheless have had little effect on those Soviet policies that have eroded the Soviet–U.S. relationship over the last decade. This has evidently been so for two reasons.

First, the advantages that members of the elite derive from the greater opportunity for contacts and travel and the greater access to Western consumer goods associated with détente have not yet been severely curtailed by the cooling of U.S.–Soviet relations. This is partly because considerable intercourse with the United States still goes on but largely because détente with Western Europe has thus far been affected only marginally.

Second, even if that were not the case, the posture of the regime is well calculated to deflect elite resentment over the demise of détente. As noted earlier, the Soviet regime has never ceased to assert its support for the notion of improved economic and political relations with the United States, while simultaneously insisting that Soviet actions elsewhere in the world must be isolated from the bilateral relationship. The United States has thus, in effect, been forced to assume immediate responsibility for the decay by insisting that a good bilateral relationship is not compatible with recent Soviet patterns of behavior in the Third World. It is much more difficult for the elite generally to hold the regime responsible for this indirect culpability than would be the case if Moscow refused to do business with the United States.

The Mix of Future Soviet Policies

The precedent of Afghanistan has undoubtedly increased the Politburo's awareness of the geopolitical advantages obtainable through the uninhibited use of Soviet military force on the USSR's periphery and perhaps whetted its appetite for more such gains. Soviet attitudes on this subject are almost certainly equivocal, however. In addition to the frustrating difficulties encountered in the process of subduing the Afghans, the Politburo is by no means indifferent to the political costs attached to its behavior in Afghanistan. It probably judges certain of these costs to be much more important than others.

- Some costs—such as the reaction in Europe—may be regarded as easily tolerable, and indeed offset by favorable secondary effects, such as the fissures created in the Western alliance.

- Others—such as the reaction in the Moslem world—may be seen as surmountable but still somewhat uncertain in their ultimate effects.

- Still other costs are probably considered to be potentially quite serious for the Soviet Union, although also not yet final. One of these is the long-term effect of Afghanistan upon the U.S. propensity to increase arms spending; another is the ultimate effect upon the Sino–U.S. relationship.

The Politburo's sense of the balance of profit and loss among such disparate factors is thus probably tentative and likely to be continuously revised. The desirability of first obtaining a more secure political base in the next target country than was available in Afghanistan may temper the appetite for further gains.

The Effects of a Repetition upon
Other Soviet Clients

The Politburo probably also senses that the potential advantages of further such uninhibited use of Soviet force to establish clearcut Soviet control of Third World countries will have to be weighed against the possibility of counterproductive effects upon relationships with clients that the USSR has achieved through more carefully circumscribed use of military power for geopolitical ends over the last decade. This is not a trivial consideration.

We have seen that the Soviets during the 1970s became increasingly active in dispatching Soviet and proxy forces at the invitation and service of sympathetic Third World regimes. Until Afghanistan, the appeal for Soviet assistance and the services rendered to the Third World client were in every case genuine, as such varied clients as Le Duan, Nasser, Sadat, Asad, Neto, Mengistu, and Nkomo could testify. In no case did acceptance of this Soviet assistance bring loss of effective political control of the client's own regime. This was, to be sure, in many cases not for want of Soviet trying. The fact remains, however, that although several states (particularly Cuba and South Yemen) have an exceptionally close relationship with Moscow because of a perceived commonality of interests, there are still no noncontiguous Soviet puppets in the world today.[38] Soviet presence and influence has, on the whole, expanded considerably in the Third World since the late 1960s. Thus far, Soviet control has not.

The Politburo is well aware that its clients and prospective clients in the Third World are generally sensitive to this distinction and that the Soviet success in advancing the Soviet presence in the Third World has been conditioned by a client assumption that the USSR would be unable to extract control as the price of its services. Afghanistan was a radical departure from this pattern and a challenge to this assumption. Afghanistan was a parody of previous Soviet ventures precisely because the alleged invitation to the Soviets to intervene was generally perceived, inside and outside the country, as a fictitious justification for the violent assertion of Soviet control. If Soviet clients such as the Syrians, Angolans, and Ethiopians are thus far not greatly disturbed by this precedent, it is largely because of their continuing overriding need for Soviet services; but it is partly also because they see Soviet behavior in Afghanistan as an isolated and nonthreatening instance.

The USSR will no doubt vigorously pursue its efforts to expand its political and military presence in the Third World, on the pattern successfully practiced in Africa, when and if suitable new clients in need of Soviet security assistance emerge. The Soviets are likely to consider relationships of less than complete control, with sympathetic regimes heavily dependent on the USSR, as in Ethiopia and South Yemen, to be on balance more advantageous than any more Afghanistans. The profitability of their past and present joint operations with the Cubans and the fact that the Cubans have up to now been widely perceived by clients as less threatening also suggest that, other things being equal, the Soviet leadership will continue to emphasize the use of such proxies to the extent feasible.

Possible More Dangerous Alternatives

A major caveat, however, is that such Politburo preferences, even if considered in Moscow to represent the balance of Soviet interests in the abstract, may easily be sidetracked by the spontaneous evolution of short-lived opportunities in circumstances where the ultimate political costs are initially ambiguous. The Soviet leaders have established two sets of disquieting precedents in the last decade that could entice them to override cautionary considerations.

First, they have three times assisted client regimes to conquer rivals across established boundaries (in India's attack on Pakistan in 1971, in Hanoi's attack across the seventeenth parallel beginning in 1972, and in Hanoi's onslaught against Cambodia in 1978). They could therefore be led to do this again and in some circumstances to play a larger and more independent military role.

Second, they have been willing to accept thinly supported conspiratorial coups as sufficient pretext to establish security relationships with the resulting unpopular regimes. Despite any present misgivings, they will be under temptation to do so again should such coups materialize in places that are both important to the Soviet Union and within the geographical range of Soviet effective power-projection capabilities. Within this radius, they may therefore be readier than heretofore to intervene in civil wars in which such regimes are involved, even in cases where the possibility of a U.S. military reaction is not ruled out. Indeed, on their immediate periphery they are now more likely than before to seize on any pretext offered by U.S. conduct to justify such Soviet intervention in a civil war as a response to a U.S. initiative. Finally, they could also be tempted, given the appropriate combination of circumstances, to seek to stimulate coups in nearby states in order to establish the political base for a subsequent military presence.

NOTES

1. Kirilenko address to Twelfth Hungarian Party Congress, *Pravda*, March 25, 1980.
2. Ibid.
3. Brezhnev TASS interview, *Pravda*, January 13, 1980.
4. Nathan Leites, The Rand Corporation, *The Operational Code of the Politburo*, (New York: McGraw-Hill, 1951), p. 31.
5. Ibid., p. 78.
6. Ibid., pp. 42–43.
7. Brezhnev election speech, *Pravda*, February 22, 1980.
8. Brezhnev TASS interview, *Pravda*, January 13, 1980.
9. This central purpose has been defined succinctly by Galina Orionova, a recent defector who has worked in the Moscow Institute of the USA, as determination "to extend Soviet power, by détente or any other means, wherever or whenever such expansion is neither too costly nor too dangerous." See Nora Beloff, "Escape from Boredom: A Defector's Story," *Atlantic Monthly*, November 1980.
10. Soviet media have over the years very commonly proclaimed a changing correlation of forces, in periods of Soviet good fortune and bad fortune alike, including periods (such as that of the illusory missile gap) when the Politburo has wished to convey a misleading impression of its strength. The manipulation of this concept is, in fact, an instrument of Soviet political warfare. This does not mean that the Politburo does not believe in its underlying reality.
11. The capitalist world is in a fever. . . . Among the many signs of an exacerbation of the general crisis of capitalism, particular importance is being assumed by the obvious decline of the neocolonialist system.

    (M. A. Suslov, speech to Polish party congress, Moscow radio, February 12, 1980.)

    The source [of U.S. policy] is U.S. reactionary imperialist circles' discontent with the strengthening of the socialist community, the growth of revolutionary processes and the upsurge of the anti-imperialist struggle. The very course of world events does not suit them.

    (A. P. Kirilenko election speech, *Pravda*, February 20, 1980.)
12. L. Vidyasova, "U.S. Imperialist Foreign Policy and the Modern World," *International Affairs* (January 1980).
13. Ibid.
14. V. Rut'kov, "The Military Economic Might of the Socialist Countries— A Factor in the Security of Nations," *Kommunist Voruzhenikh Sil* (Communist of the Armed Forces) 23 (December 1974): 19–20.
15. The presentation cited was clearly meant as an argument for maximum Soviet perseverance in allocating resources in the desired direction and for

avoiding temptations to fall into the U.S. consumerist trap. Some Soviets today would disagree with certain of its assumptions, especially the tacit suggestion that military industry and heavy industry in the USSR do not compete for resources, or that the U.S. standard of living has no significant effect upon the world correlation of forces.

16.   Those operations are generally justified in lofty terms, as reflecting the unalterable and inevitable Soviet duty to come to the aid of "revolutionary and national liberation movements." This justification is taken much more seriously by some Western observers than by the Soviet leaders. The Politburo has a highly selective sense of this obligation, which is measured in practice almost exclusively in terms of *realpolitik* and the net Soviet advantage in the worldwide struggle with its main antagonists. Even the ideological leanings of a given movement are significant to the Soviets only to the extent that they promise to serve the larger geopolitical interests of the USSR. Although the Marxist MPLA in Angola and the less radical ZAPU of Zimbabwe were deemed worthy of Soviet support in the last decade, ZAPU's more radical (but Chinese-contaminated) rival ZANU was not, nor were assorted Kurds in Iraq, Eritreans in Ethiopia, and Biafrans in Nigeria (to say nothing of the Afghan tribesmen and the Cambodian ultra-Marxists).

17.   *Code*, p. 90.

18.   To take an extreme example: The Soviet media in recent years have given increased support to a long-established Cuban campaign of denunciation, conducted in the UN and elsewhere, of the U.S. relationship with Puerto Rico. On December 18, 1979, less than two weeks before the invasion of Afghanistan, *Pravda* depicted the United States as having hastily dispatched military forces to this island "in recent days" to put down "the Puerto Rican people's protracted struggle" and to safeguard the use of the island's "advantageous strategic location in the Caribbean." *Pravda* condemned in advance the results of any new plebiscite the United States might hold in Puerto Rico, depicting any such vote, regardless of the outcome, as intended "to perpetuate the present situation." In view of the obvious parallels between this largely fictitious representation of the U.S. position in Puerto Rico and the actual Soviet position at that moment in Afghanistan, it is conceivable that the timing of the article was not fortuitous and may have been intended to imply that U.S. complaints about Soviet actions in Afghanistan could only be hypocritical. Whatever the tactical purpose, however, the article is striking testimony to Soviet attitudes regarding the legitimacy of a U.S. sphere.

19.   Such an understanding, they argue, would be equivalent to translating détente into the "preservation of the status quo," whereby "imperialism could continue unhindered its tyranny in the areas remaining in its sphere

of influence." B. Pyadyshev, "Opponents of Détente from Miami," *Za Rubezham* 45 (October 30, 1975): 15–16. This Soviet position is also asymmetrical; the Soviets argue the opposite case when defending on geopolitical and security grounds their inherent right to insure continuation of a friendly regime in Kabul.

20. A credible account of this incident appeared in *New York Times*, September 17, 1973.

21. *Code*, pp. 66, 75.

22. For a decade the Soviet leadership has urged Soviet foreign policy institutions and organizations to work to reduce the U.S. special advantage in Latin America. Immediately after the fall of Somoza the Soviet press exulted in unusually strong terms, asserting that U.S. influence over Latin America was decaying rapidly and that Cuban influence was growing, as demonstrated by the U.S. inability to get support from the Organization of American States to head off a Sandinista victory, as well as by the "ever-increasing participation of Latin American countries in the nonaligned movement." The Soviets expressed gratification that "the Americans are feeling increasingly uncomfortable in their "internal security zone." " *Sovetskaya Rossiya*, July 20, 1979.

23. *Code*, p. 79. Alluding to Soviet policy of the last decade in the Third World, the former USA Institute staff member Galina Orionova thus comments that "the Soviet government behaves like any ordinary Soviet consumer. He grabs anything which happens to be on the counter, even if he doesn't need it, knowing that tomorrow it may no longer be available." See Beloff, "Escape from Boredom."

24. See, for example, statements by Ponomarev on April 25, 1978 (TASS, April 25, 1978) and Kirilenko on February 27, 1979 (*Pravda*, February 28, 1979).

25. The USSR probably received tacit, partial, and temporary compensation for the French and British nuclear delivery systems and the U.S. land- and carrier-based nuclear weapons in the European theater in the U.S. acceptance and legitimization of unequal SLBM ceilings in SALT I. This was obviously considered inadequate, however, particularly because those ceilings were to be rendered moot in the broader framework of the SALT II agreement, which permitted both sides to mix and match disparate systems to common ceilings.

26. The SS–20 IRBM and the Backfire bomber.

27. An alternative view is that the Soviet leaders regard a strategic war-fighting capability as itself an essential part of the Soviet deterrent and that the leadership has come to believe that the United States will never be sufficiently deterred to satisfy Moscow until the United States is persuaded that the Soviet Union can fight and win a war against it.

28. See Thomas A. Wolfe, *The SALT Experience*, (Cambridge, Mass.: Ballinger Publishing Company, 1979), pp. 107, 111.

29. L.I. Brezhnev, "The Great October Revolution and the Progress of Mankind," Radio Moscow, November 2, 1977; and *Pravda*, November 3, 1977, cited in Raymond L. Garthoff, "Mutual Deterrence and Strategic Arms Limitation in Soviet Policy," *International Security* 3, no. 1 (Summer 1978). Garthoff cites a number of other such Soviet assertions of recent years.

30. See Henry Kissinger, *White House Years*, (Boston: Little Brown, 1979), pp. 179, 187, 836, 1053.

31. *Code*, pp. 82–84, 41–42. "To seek unilateral concessions from the Soviet Union by pressing as hard as possible on the 'Chinese lever,'" one leading Soviet specialist insisted in the fall of 1979, "is completely unrealistic." V.B. Lukin, "Washington-Beijing: Quasi Allies?'" *USA: Economics, Politics, Ideology* 12 (1979).

32. *Code*, p. 75.

33. Beginning with Marshal Grechko's statement at the twenty-fourth Party Congress in 1971 (see *Pravda*, April 3, 1971) this progression of assertions continued without interruption through the era of détente (see A.A. Grechko, "The Leading Role of the CPSU in Building the Army of a Developed Socialist Society," *Voprosy Istorii KPSS* (May 1974), emerging at the other side at the close of the decade in extraordinarily defiant form (see *Red Star*, March 15, 1980).

34. Some observers suggest that Soviet calculations of their political interests in this instance did not oppose but reinforced Soviet military motives, and that Soviet decisionmakers assumed a policy of intensifying pressure upon Japan through such deployments would eventually be profitable. Some sentiment of this kind undoubtedly exists in important Soviet circles. The Soviet leadership consensus cannot have felt high confidence in this thesis, however, or have been unaware of the possibility of seriously adverse effects upon Japanese attitudes regarding rearmament. Professional military views as to Soviet force disposition needs were therefore probably decisive.

35. This bureaucratic or operational advantage probably was more important in influencing Soviet policy toward so-called "liberation movements" in the Third World than the more obvious fact that Gromyko since 1973 has been a full member of the Politburo, while Ponomarev is merely a candidate member. More generally, the Central Committee apparatus probably possesses a more direct channel of influence to the Politburo than does the Foreign Ministry, although this fact is probably outweighed by the personal stature of the Foreign Minister in those policy areas in which he has primary operational responsibility, such as dealings with the capitalist industrialized world.

36.   The earlier mentioned defector Orionova emphasizes that the USA Institute as such has no direct effect on Soviet policy and that even the personal influence of Institute director Arbatov had apparently declined after 1975 with the decline of détente.

37.   As elaborated, in particular, by Alexander Yanov. See his *Détente after Brezhnev: The Domestic Roots of Soviet Foreign Policy*, Institute of International Studies, University of California, Berkeley, 1977.

38.   Some observers may think that South Yemen already belongs in this category; I disagree, and would draw attention to the widespread mistaken belief in 1971 that the enormous Soviet military presence in Egypt, including the stationing of advisers in key positions down to battalion level, had then given the USSR such control in Egypt.

9 PROSPECTS AND REQUIREMENTS FOR THE CONTAINMENT OF MATURED SOVIET MILITARY POWER

Fritz W. Ermarth

For its survival and the defense of the West the United States requires a new strategy to meet the challenge of Soviet power. Likely to be long-lasting, this severe challenge is not solely military in character or origin, hence it cannot be addressed with military measures alone. Nevertheless, adequate military response to a predominantly military challenge is the minimum essential for dealing with the other important dimensions of the contest.

The principal objective of U.S. strategy toward the USSR and the main criterion for assessing the effectiveness of U.S. military power clearly has to be containment or something akin to it. The term suggests a return to policies of the 1940s and 1950s. Yet contemporary conditions are very different from those of the past. The spectacular shift in the East–West power balance that compels reassertion of the objective of containment also makes its attainability questionable. At issue besides the feasibility of containment today is its sufficiency as a goal for the future. These are the most central questions before Western governments today. The magnitude of the Soviet challenge and the fragility of the larger international environment give the utmost urgency to finding answers.

THE STRATEGIC REVOLUTION

According to public comment a return to the Cold War in East–West relations is taking place or is threatened. However one chooses to characterize the Cold War that began after World War II, the notion that we are returning to it is fundamentally mistaken. Conventional views on the comings and goings of the Cold War are almost entirely a function of fluctuating opinion in the United States and in Europe about the need to resist the chief engine of the Cold War, which has never been shut down—that is, the efforts of the USSR to expand its power at Western expense.

Resurgent concern about the challenge of Soviet power confronts circumstances much changed from those that defined the period usually labeled the Cold War, extending from the late 1940s into the 1960s. The USSR, Western Europe, and Japan have long since recovered from the war-inflicted devastation that assured the geopolitical supremacy of the United States for more than two decades. In all but small pockets of the Third World the processes of building nations and modernizing economic and social conditions have conclusively supplanted the politics of decolonization.

Most dramatic has been the changed military relationship between the USSR and its adversaries. As Kissinger has noted, modern history does not record an equally pronounced shift in military power balances without war, and most remarkably, with the more or less voluntary acquiescence of the disadvantaged parties.

Until the mid-1960s the USSR confronted decisive American strategic nuclear superiority that canceled out its numerical force preponderance in Europe. Until the onset of the military buildup opposite China after 1964, its military dispositions in the Far East were quite limited. Because of both American nuclear superiority and its own very limited naval and air capabilities, the USSR lacked a credible capability to project military power beyond its borders, even to the south. The superiority of U.S. military technology in almost all sectors was taken for granted.

Although much of the foregoing is more evident with hindsight than it was at the time, East–West military relationships clearly have changed dramatically. Rather than totaling up hardware and manpower, it is important to understand this strategic revolution in terms of its results in theaters and sectors of activity. Whether the USSR has become "Number One" can be left to the pundits and commentators. The conclusion from examining all aspects of the strategic revolution of recent years is that the relative position of the USSR to serve its purposes in the world through military means has improved substantially. The relative position of the United States and its military allies to meet their strategic requirements and defend their strategic interests has declined below tolerable levels in all theaters. That political factors outside the control of either superpower or its main allies have played some role in determining or qualifying these trends, for example, the reorientation of China's foreign policy and the fall of the Shah of Iran, should not blind one to the fundamental conclusion that dramatic shifts in strategic power have taken place.

Some contend that a very rough parity now prevails between the United States and the USSR in strategic nuclear power. Yet much of the "roughness," the uncertainty and unpleasantness, applies more to the U.S. side. The intercontinental ballistic missile (ICBM) leg of its strategic triad will remain vulnerable into the late 1980s. The survivability of the bomber leg rests upon timely strategic and tactical warning as well as upon other crucial command-and-control functions. The possible vulnerabilities of U.S. strategic command, control, and communications systems (C^3) have been brought to public attention. The USSR has deployed extensive air defenses; those of the United States are very minimal. Although their effectiveness may be arguable, the civil defense programs of the USSR are extensive whereas those of the United States are only on paper. The USSR must be presumed more likely to survive some forms of central nuclear conflict.

By analyzing the strategic nuclear balance in operational terms, it is possible to make a case that, were it to strike first during a crisis, the USSR might *win* a central nuclear conflict. It is more difficult to make the argument that the U.S. could win such an exchange, except perhaps by attacking from the blue, a totally incredible proposition. The political impact of rough parity perceived this way lies in the reduced capacity of the United States to offer credible nuclear guarantees of others and also to withstand the pressures of intense military crisis.

Soviet and Warsaw Pact force modernization in Europe, both nuclear and conventional, has given the Eastern side credible military preponderance. To put it most simply, the Soviets would have, and themselves perceive, a better than even chance of winning the fast-paced offensive war in Europe that their plans and force posture call for. NATO's escalation to nuclear use against such an attack would raise its cost for both the attacker and the victims but would probably not alter its outcome. NATO's force improvements have not served to restore defensive or deterrent adequacy, because Soviet modernization and force expansion have kept pace. At most NATO may claim that its efforts have prevented an adverse situation from deteriorating more rapidly.

The strategic shifts that have taken place in the USSR's Far Eastern theater have been dramatic and paradoxical. Where a quarter century ago the USSR enjoyed what was thought to be a major ideological and military ally, today it faces a deeply hostile, nuclear-armed, and potentially very formidable adversary in the People's Republic of China (PRC). The costs to the USSR of fielding the military forces it has chosen to deploy against China since the mid-1960s have been variously estimated at from 10 to 25 percent of total Soviet military expenditures in that period. Without question, the Sino–Soviet rivalry and the growth of Sino–American amity, around a core of undeniably (if perhaps not permanently) common strategic interests, represent an awesome debit relative to the geopolitical and military situation the USSR might have enjoyed had the Sino–Soviet rift not occurred.

Sino–Soviet military rivalry has now existed longer than the decade of public Sino–Soviet military cooperation, which itself shrouded several years of growing tension between these communist states. The soviets now have successful military superiority over the PRC that would permit the USSR to drive the PRC out of a major war and to occupy significant peripheral territory from Manchuria to Central Asia. Moreover, the naval, air, and missile components of the Soviet Far Eastern military buildup, although motivated in large part by the Sino–Soviet rivalry, have improved the relative capability of the USSR against Japan and increasingly strained the Western Pacific forces of the United States. Soviet military superiority over the PRC, along with extensive materiel assistance to the regime in Hanoi, procured the USSR an important base in Vietnam as well.

From the withdrawal of British power to the Soviet invasion of Afghanistan a long train of developments has created a third major Eurasian theater of strategic engagement in Southwest Asia, centered on the Persian Gulf. In strictly military terms, the USSR enjoys preponderance in this theater by virtue of its large standing and mobilizable land forces and its land-based air power available for use in offensive operations southward without redeployment of forces from Europe or the Far East. Given the weakness of indigenous local forces throughout the area and the great difficulties faced by the United States in the timely deployment of adequate countering forces, it is primarily the threat of nuclear escalation from the United States, made credible by the enormity of the stakes in the region, that imparts a psychological element of strategic balance to this theater. Nonetheless, even as the United States is seeking to build capabilities for rapid force deployment to Southwest Asia, the Soviets are upgrading the quality of their own, hitherto lower priority, forces opposite this theater.

Although the U.S. navy might be judged still to be superior to the Soviet navy in any head-to-head comparison, the modernization and expansion of the Soviet navy has given the USSR new capabilities that are critically significant in a geostrategic sense. The most important are (1) strategic nuclear strike capabilities based at sea, (2) the ability to maintain a secure strategic nuclear reserve at sea during a major conflict, (3) the ability to disrupt the projection of American military power onto the Eurasian land mass in a variety of conflict scenarios, and (4) its own ability to project power overseas at a distance from the USSR.

A generation ago Soviet military power was regarded as massive but technologically primitive. U.S. technological superiority was assessed to provide a large portion of the margin of safety Americans and their allies presumed to enjoy. The USSR has not become the equal of the United States nor of its advanced allies in technical virtuosity across the spectrum of military technologies. Yet Soviet military technology is broadly competitive; the USSR tends to deploy its military–technological innovations more systematically into its forces, combining quantity and quality in its forces in ways that may overwhelm dwindling U.S. technological advantages and limited force size.

The height of the Cold War in the mid-1950s found Moscow taking its first hesitant steps into the business of projecting political influence via military instrumentalities in the Third World. Today Soviet arms exports rival those of the West in volume. Soviet naval forces show the flag in distant waters. Soviet-sponsored multinational military and security contingents operate in several troublespots of Africa and Asia, their Cuban component drawing most of the attention. Cuba itself has become a base for paramilitary and revolutionary operations throughout the Caribbean basin.

Clearly the world we associated with the Cold War no longer exists. The economic, military, and political power of the United States relative to the USSR, its allies, and the Third World has declined. The overall power of the USSR has markedly increased. The character of the Soviet role in the world has also altered in some important respects. During the Cold War, Soviet behavior went through at least two distinguishable phases. The Stalinist phase was essentially defensive and isolationist, intended to protect a totalitarian system deeply wounded by war and to consolidate the achievements of victory. Khrushchev's behavior was more mixed. His actions in Berlin and Cuba, although they precipitated crises, were responses to Soviet perceptions of vulnerability. His outreach into the Third World was ideologically ambitious, but it lacked military, economic, or political staying power. Similarly, his erratic forays into the diplomacy of détente rested on too weak a power base to influence Western behavior deeply. His most important achievements were to build up the USSR's military–industrial base, whose products were to emerge after him, and to implant the political principle that the international system had to accommodate the USSR despite its revolutionary aspirations, its military ambitions, and its political aggressiveness.

The political and strategic outreach of the USSR in the present period is more ambitious, more sustained, and more securely based on military power. The USSR has become a global actor as well as a nuclear superpower, notwithstanding its considerable internal weaknesses and the limitations of its political appeal. Simultaneously, it remains a revolutionary state, that is, committed to radical transformations of the international system. The task of responding to the challenge of Soviet power in the 1980s and 1990s is bound to be more taxing and dangerous than during the Cold War.

IS CONTAINMENT NECESSARY?

The objectives of containment policy in the current period must be to prevent the expansion of the USSR's political influence and control and to reverse the shift of the East–West military balance that is providing the USSR with opportunities and instruments for such expansion. A number of concerns must be addressed if a strong political consensus behind a containment policy, however defined, is to be created in the United States and within the North Atlantic community.

Little doubt remains in the West or in much of the Third World that the leaders of the Soviet Union want and actively seek to extend their hegemonic power in the world. Even the more amiable facets of Soviet foreign policy—for example, Soviet proposals about arms control and détente in Europe—are perceived by a majority of observers as intended *by the Soviets* to serve as instruments for extending their political influence and strategic power at the expense of the United States.

Broad consensus on the desires and intentions of Soviet leaders, however, does not lead automatically to consensus on the necessity for effective containment policies, much less on their priority or nature. Several persistent doubts and contrary beliefs must be dealt with.

One argument that continually thwarted the development of effective containment policies in the recent past was that the Soviets could not maintain permanent control or influence in the more distant outposts of their would-be imperium. Were not the Soviets thrown out of several client countries in the 1960s (Ghana, Indonesia) and the 1970s (Egypt, Somalia)? Local nationalism and insistence upon independence would sooner or later, according to this view, assure that Soviet imperialism would be no more lasting than the older Western variety.

There are several obvious flaws in this line of argument, especially as a rationalization for passivity today in the face of Soviet expansionism. The setbacks suffered by the Soviets in the 1960s occurred because Soviet political pretentions reached far beyond Soviet military power. Today the USSR is much better able to match its pretentions with real power to exert control at a distance from home. The setbacks in the 1970s yield a more complex diagnosis. The Soviets were thrown out of Egypt, in the final analysis, because the United States came into a unique position to displace them. They left Somalia as a consequence of shifting their attention to a more promising opening in Ethiopia. The fact that they came to be detested in all these places was a necessary but insufficient condition to explain their departure.

A more significant point is that, with the growth of Soviet military power-projection capabilities, especially on their own Eurasian periphery, the Soviets have increased their capacity to sustain influence and control in client states. The pattern of the 1960s and 1970s is unlikely to repeat itself in the 1980s, for example in South Yeman, Ethiopia, Libya, or Angola, not to mention in Afghanistan, Vietnam, or Cuba. Strong external pressure will be required, at a minimum, to remove them.

The most important point is that, in all the locations where the transience or permanence of Soviet influence is of interest, the West can no more afford transient Soviet influence or even a failed Soviet effort to acquire control than it can tolerate a permanent extension of Soviet hegemony. This is because all such adventures now have more pronounced ripple effects beyond their immediate location (e.g., extension of Soviet control in the Yemens), imperil Western equities even where the Soviets might fail to establish full control (e.g., physical access to oil), or present the highest probability of a major conflict after such a Soviet thrust has begun and created investments the Soviets must then protect.

The history of the 1960s and 1970s itself demonstrates that we cannot afford and will be denied by the dynamics of events the luxury of a bystander role as the staying power of Soviet imperialism is tested. The question is merely whether we actively engage in this historic contest early, when prospects for successfully defending our interests at tolerable cost and risk may exist, or get dragged into it later, when the costs and risks are much higher. The anguish of the present predicament arises precisely because past passivity has now driven the stakes and costs of the contest to alarming heights while denying us the option of not becoming much more actively engaged.

A second argument often used to challenge the necessity of active containment policies is that troubles within the Soviet bloc and within the USSR itself will act to constrain Soviet expansionist capabilities and energies. Declining economic growth rates, social stresses, and nationalism within the USSR and pressures for liberalization in East Europe are cited in this context. The contrary argument immediately springs forth, namely, that stresses within the Soviet system are more likely to stimulate aggressive external behavior than they are to constrain it within limits tolerable to the West. The Soviet thirst for fresh energy sources, the historic Russian propensity to expand frontiers steadily as a means of stabilizing new acquisitions, and the need of the Soviet system to enhance its increasingly challenged internal legitimacy through external demonstrations of power can be summoned to this case.

This is a controversy of enormous historic importance. It will have to be addressed systematically by Western leaders and scholars in order to inform the content of containment policies toward the USSR, particularly policies oriented toward promoting change within the Soviet system. it will be resolved, however, not by analysis and argument, but by history. In the meantime, we cannot afford to count on internal constraints on Soviet expansionism as a substitute for countervailing external forces. Soviet history as well as the specific character of problems within the Soviet system strongly suggest that internal constraints will not be powerful enough to spare us very dangerous Soviet pressures in the next decade. More important, the matter is simply uncertain; and a passive Western role based on expected internal constraints is too risky.

IS CONTAINMENT POSSIBLE?

Were trends inherent in the development of East–West power relationships during the late 1970s to continue through the 1980s, at least two and possibly all three of the following would result: (1) The Soviets would acquire effective control of the Persian Gulf region and its physical resources. (2) Under the political pressure of its superior military position, the USSR would induce most of Western Europe to accept a separate détente and a predominant Soviet role in European security affairs as the price of peace in Europe. The United States would withdraw, and NATO would dissolve. (3) Feeling the weight of increasing Soviet military superiority and perceiving as inadequate its own and U.S. ability to counterbalance it, the PRC would accept a limited but significant rapprochement with the USSR.

Were all these developments to occur the USSR would be much more than a global superpower. It would be the hegemonic power of Eurasia, with decisive control over the security affairs of all Eurasia and increased political influence over the internal affairs of key noncommunist states. As events proceeded toward this result, there would inevitably occur a period in which general nuclear conflict between the Soviet Union and the United States would be highly probable.

To ask whether containment is possible is to ask whether these developments can be thwarted at acceptable cost and risk. The leader must answer affirmatively, and sound confident in doing so. The scholar is permitted a more equivocal answer. Successful containment of Soviet expansionism in the 1980s is possible but by no means certain. One strain in the American political tradition assumes correct policies pursued with maximum effort must be successful policies. If they do not seem to guarantee success, they must be the wrong policies. There is little room in American political thinking for the notion that even the right or optimal policy might prove unsuccessful because of simply too little power or time to effect the desired result. This notion is uncomfortably relevant to our present situation.

Moreover, as in the ecological realm, the unknown and, in some sense, unknowable interactions of political forces in world affairs make it inevitable that some courses of action will have perverse effects quite different from those intended. Thus, to put the matter simply, but not oversimply, the pursuit of détente and arms control objectives in policies toward the USSR in the 1960s and 1970s demonstrably increased the probability of war in the 1980s. It will not do to argue that the fault lay with inadequate Western defense policies rather than détente policies, because the two were intimately and, for many actors involved, purposely connected. After all, the achievement of this perverse political effect within the West was one of the principal objectives of the USSR's détente policy, despite its ideologically rooted awareness that the objective danger of war would increase as the "correlation of forces" steadily shifted to Soviet advantage.

The inevitability of perverse or undesired effects perceived to result from some policy actions (but who knows which?) induces a constant quest for moderation, balance, and nuance on the part of policymakers. Where a high degree of governmental discipline and constancy is possible, these qualities can sometimes be achieved. But in open societies where foreign policy is highly politicized, the search for balance and nuance most often produces confusion about priorities and the adoption of simultaneous conflicting courses of action. This predicament is vividly apparent in the dialogue between the Reagan administration and its European allies about the balance to be struck between rearmament and containment policies on one hand and arms control policies on the other.

Decisionmakers on both sides of the Atlantic must face, as must their publics, the hard reality that the near term outlook for arms control is very unpromising. To expect that negotiations can produce meaningful relief to Western security problems is to indulge in fantasy. The Soviets have no incentive whatsoever to grant such relief under current strategic conditions. They have every incentive to play on the pietism that has grown up around arms control in America and more recently in Europe, however. Their objectives have always been to stall NATO military programs and to divide the allies at least cost to themselves.

Today NATO's TNF deployment program serves as the best target of opportunity. The Soviets' real aim is to undermine the Atlantic alliance's unity and capacity for politically controversial action on all matters relating to military posture and policy toward the East. While they would like to stop the deployment of Pershing II and ground-launched cruise missiles (GLCMs), that modest arsenal is militarily not so worrisome to them as all the other things NATO might be capable of doing, especially in the modernization of its overall nuclear resources and doctrines, once it has struggled successfully through the TNF episode. For the Soviets to agree to a theater nuclear arms control regime that renders NATO's TNF program even sufficient, much less superfluous, to restoring theater nuclear balance in Europe would represent an abject failure of their foreign policy that neither political nor military circumstances oblige them to accept. It is simply an illusion to expect the Soviets to assist NATO, through serious arms control agreements, in recovering from the strategic revolution that the Soviets have accomplished at considerable cost to themselves.

Even were the Soviets more receptive to genuine arms control remedies on behalf of European security, NATO lacks the doctrinal framework for determining what arms control remedies would be helpful, tolerable, and long-lasting. Until NATO has developed comprehensive doctrines for judging both military programs and arms control possibilities, the active conduct of negotiations will simply generate confusion while institutionalizing Soviet codetermination of NATO's defense policies.

The main danger is that we may fail to come to early and firm agreement on the absolute primacy of rearmament and containment policies. Achieving consensus on that priority will determine whether containment policies are likely to succeed. Balancing such policies with policies that pursue détente and arms control goals that are in current conditions entirely chimerical will be worse than self-defeating; it will ultimately increase the probability of military conflict with the USSR. This will be all the more the case if confusion over priorities occurs because governments must defer to domestic political sentiment about relations with the USSR that is, and is known to be, entirely unrealistic. Such deference will only cause the Soviets to persist in their belief that the West can be demoralized into making concessions by the right combinations of intensified threats and peaceful blandishments. This belief could encourage the USSR to try various forms of brinkmanship in dealings with the West, and it would be very dangerous in a crisis that came about for any reason.

It is precisely at this time in the history of the East–West contest that political clarity on the absolute primacy of containment and re-armament objectives is a vital necessity. Not only is it required to sustain the necessary resource allocations and cooperation within the Atlantic alliance, it is needed to convince the USSR that it dare not count on lack of political resolve within and among NATO govern-ments to limit the risks it faces in exploiting Soviet strategic advan-tages that it suspects will only be temporary. Thus the time for more balanced policies, which combine containment and rearmament with exploration of the possibilities for relaxation and for genuine arms control, is not at the beginning but, rather, later in a period of stra-tegic restoration. At the beginning of the effort to contain the USSR and to keep the peace, the West will be trading more on nerve and less on strength than might be wished and should scrupulously avoid policies that convey a lack of nerve or could have the practical politi-cal effects of undermining nerve for the competition.

The first condition, therefore, that can make successful contain-ment possible is an unqualified political commitment to this task within the Atlantic community and especially within the United States. The first test as to whether we can meet that condition has, unfortunately, to be our ability to lay aside purposely cultivated illu-sions about what we can actually achieve through arms control nego-tiations with the Soviets. The second condition is to formulate and begin action on a comprehensive plan for strategic restoration.

STRATEGIC RESTORATION

A number of major themes of a political and doctrinal character must be addressed in determining the military requirements of containment in the 1980s. Through its sustained military buildup and the lack of an adequate Western response, the USSR has acquired effective strategic preponderance in Eurasia. In the geographic and geopolitical context from which it operates, the totality of its military capabilities, including strategic intercontinental and regional military forces, places the USSR in a markedly better position to extend its hegemony in Eurasia than the military position of the USSR's adversaries allows them to defend themselves and to thwart Soviet political purposes. To employ a modification of a euphemism that once played an unhappy role in all of this, the Soviets have, in a sense, acquired "essential superiority," having passed through the phase of "essential equivalence" sometime in the late 1960s or early 1970s. This is not a judgment on the quantitative and qualitative relationship of U.S. and Soviet, or NATO and Warsaw Pact, arsenals as such, but rather a judgment on the relationship of military means to political ends in an historical and geopolitical setting.

The military tasks of an effective containment policy will involve depriving the Soviets of this essential superiority, restoring the essential military superiority of the Atlantic democracies and other states associated with them for the purpose of political and military defense, and, while so doing, preventing the current disequilibrium from being aggressively exploited by the Soviets or from collapsing into a major conflict unintended by either side.

It is obvious that this effort will require a considerable increase in the resources that capable NATO allies and Japan devote to security purposes. It will require unprecedented degrees of political and military cooperation. It will require major increases in security assistance to key countries in the Third World, especially in Southwest Asia, and deft management of political relationships with them in what will inevitably remain a qualified partnership. It will also require doctrinal innovation, because mere acceleration of security activity along previously established lines is likely to produce inadequate or perverse results.

Urgency

The most immediate problem the West faces is the very immediacy of the problem. Our bureaucractic, technological, and economic resources for restoring the strategic equilibrium are geared to lethargic responses. We cannot effectively restore the strategic balance until sometime toward the end of the decade, at the earliest. Yet we face the distinct possibility of direct military challenge much earlier. This possibility arises most obviously in Southwest Asia out of the instability of Iran, the vulnerability of vital Western interests in the Gulf region, and the determination of the USSR to extend its influence over the region's security regime and its resources. The danger may lie less in outright Soviet military aggression, although this cannot be excluded, than in a process of aggressive Soviet political involvement, in Iran or on the Arabian peninsula, that leads to a military confrontation from which the United States and its allies cannot retreat and the Soviets, by virtue of superior local forces, need not retreat.

In terms of resources, planning effort, and political management, Southwest Asia and the Persian Gulf represent the most demanding potential flashpoint. It is not the only one. The prospect of Soviet military intervention in Poland is even more immediate; and there is some, although probably smaller, risk that the ensuing violence and political trauma throughout Europe could lead to a military crisis. Other troublespots around the world, from El Salvador to Indochina, could easily produce crises that become direct East–West tests of strength and resolve, requiring forceful engagement but avoidance of distraction from the main strategic theaters.

The Carter administration made some progress in defining a policy framework for defending U.S. security interests in Southwest Asia. It made inadequate progress in mobilizing political commitment and resources for it. Carrying this effort forward is a priority task of the Reagan administration. Its key military features must be (1) accelerated creation of rapidly deployable military forces capable of facing Soviet forces (as well as other threats) with serious opposition; (2) creation of physical and political environments that permit timely introduction of U.S. forces into the region if needed and the permanent presence of some U.S. forces on land in the region; and (3) rapid improvement of the military forces of Turkey, Pakistan, and Egypt.

Although the rapid deployment joint task force and Persian Gulf defense problems are properly the focus of the most urgent concerns, it should be kept in mind by Western strategists that a direct U.S.–Soviet confrontation there would present the threat of escalation elsewhere, even in Europe. Because it is locally weak in Southwest Asia, U.S. leaders have hinted at the possibility of responding elsewhere to Soviet military moves there. This "horizontal escalation" may or may not be a credible deterrent. Perhaps more to the point, because it is strong in all three Eurasian theaters the USSR might have recourse to military pressures elsewhere, particularly in Europe, to fragment Western political and military capabilities and to help it win decisively and cheaply a local contest for the Gulf region. The prospect that a military confrontation in one vulnerable region might present the threat or reality of conflict elsewhere, a phenomenon Wohlstetter has called "virtual war," means that the entire spectrum of U.S. and allied military capabilities must receive immediate attention.

Division of Labor versus Burden-Sharing

The first political requirement of the NATO allies and Japan is to establish firm consensus on the primacy of rearmament and containment policies. The second most urgent political task is to define viable formulas for sharing the burdens of security management in the three linked Eurasian theaters of common security concern.

Again the theater of most immediate concern is Southwest Asia, although unity of action in other troubled areas, such as Latin America and Africa, is of vital importance. Ways must be found to engage European allies and Japan directly in all the security-related tasks of defending this theater. Undoubtedly the United States will bear the main political, military, and financial burdens. European and Japanese defense efforts will remain focused in their own regions. But their direct participation in the military defense of the Third Theater is also required because the burden of restoring balance in this theater will be too much for the United States alone while it attends to all its other demanding military responsibilities.

Equally important, a division of labor that spares Europe and Japan direct military responsibility in a theater where their interests are maximally involved and the greatest danger of conflict is presented will be politically intolerable in the United States. The resultant political stresses would almost certainly wreck the alliance structure that is the basis of American commitment to Eurasian security. By the same token the political difficulty of defining workable forms of European and Japanese engagement in Southwest Asian military tasks cannot be underestimated. Improperly conducted, an American effort to elicit such engagement could also wreck the alliance structure. Nevertheless, the effort must be made. Its success is vital to defense of the region and also to deterrence of aggressive Soviet behavior.

The most viable approach to conducting this effort is probably to build upon patterns of collaboration among the allies that have already begun to emerge, in areas of political and military contingency planning, joint exercises, security assistance, and intelligence sharing. Such collaboration can be substantially expanded without impinging on the formal scope of alliance commitments.

The potential role of Turkey in Southwest Asian security presents both a valuable opportunity and a knotty problem for NATO deserving of special attention. For the foreseeable future any strategy for defending the Persian Gulf against a Soviet attack through Iran, the most severe if not necessarily the most probable threat to the region, will depend heavily on the ability of U.S., Turkish, and other allies' air forces to conduct operations from Turkish bases. Operations from other areas will be important, but those out of Turkey will be vital because it lies adjacent to the most important Soviet avenues of approach.

The certain involvement of Turkey in defense of the Gulf would act as a powerful deterrent to Soviet military action or political behavior that might elicit military action. The Soviets would have to consider the costs of striking against air bases in Turkey that would generate opposition to their advance through Iran and possibly attacks on their own bases in the Transcaucasus. Striking the Turkish bases would engage the entire NATO alliance in the conflict with unpredictable consequences likely to outweigh immediate Soviet stakes in the Gulf region.

Here is a telling case in which strong political nerves can magnify the value of otherwise inadequate military capabilities, at least for a time. Military distaste for reliance on air bases so close to the enemy's main strength and the political difficulties of orchestrating Turkey's explicit involvement in Southwest Asian defense strategy have so far inhibited taking full advantage of Turkey's potential role. The Turks have been understandably hesitant to move too explicitly into the role suggested because their experience with the United States and the deteriorated condition of their military forces generate fears of being left politically and militarily exposed. This legacy must be rapidly overcome. With the participation of all the allies, Turkey's armed forces must be much more speedily modernized. The Turkish air-base and related support structure must be rapidly put in condition to accept substantial U.S. and other allied tactical air power for use in a Persian Gulf contingency. The Turks must be persuaded to adopt an explicit role in Persian Gulf defense as characterized above, and be explicitly supported in this role by NATO's accepting the implication that an attack on Turkey arising out of its involvement in such a conflict would constitute an attack on NATO.

The important thing is to take practical actions in Turkey that communicate a new strategic reality to the Soviets and the collective NATO resolve that goes with it. A reluctance to state plainly what the adversary should perceive detracts from the appearance of resolve. A credible and collective political–military program to exploit Turkey's potential role in Southwest Asian strategy is probably the single most important burden-sharing opportunity available to NATO in the immediate future.

Strategy and Doctrine

Assuming that the near term danger of a military confrontation over the Persian Gulf can somehow be contained without political concessions that fundamentally alter the international system, the military dimension of effective containment over the longer term will require new strategic concepts to guide the development of adequate military forces and strategies for their possible use. The conceptual foundations of Western defense will have to be reexamined and in some respects revised. To be sure, U.S. and NATO strategic concepts have been evolving and changing in recent years. But this process has been disjointed, uneven, and incomplete in its scope.

The core difficulty is the classical problem of the defensive alliance. On what basis can a collection of states, varyingly endowed with resources, differentially vulnerable, committed to common security interests in varying degrees (when one includes partners not formally allied), and genuinely sovereign in political and strategic action, defend themselves against a single very powerful adversary determined to alter the conditions of their security by the implicit threat of force if not its actual use? As the leading and most powerful member of this loose collective, the United States must find how to achieve "extended containment" (a notion that combines the content of "extended deterrence" and "forward defense") when its own survival is potentially at stake in any test of strength and it must engage in multiple forward theaters, possibly at the same time. Paradoxically the combined potential resources and strengths of those who oppose Soviet expansion far exceed Soviet power, but at the same time are susceptible to defeat in detail where local defeats can radically undermine security conditions for those at a far remove. To escape this paradox the United States will have to define and create for itself, in the context of alliance resources and commitments, a new form of strategic superiority.

One task is to overcome the now deeply ingrained abhorrence of otherwise sensible people toward this term. From the realistic appreciation that the USSR could not be kept forever abjectly inferior to the United States in intercontinental offensive nuclear weapons there arose in the 1960s the conviction, persisting to this day, that the United States cannot ever reacquire strategic superiority. This conviction evolved further into two starkly contradictory but simultaneously held beliefs that strategic superiority has no real use but that its pursuit will lead to unlimited arms competition and, quite possibly, to war. The notion of superiority thus came to be equated in American thinking with insecurity, in contrast to Soviet thinking, which sees security as proportional to military superiority.

Part of the problem arises from a doctrinal tendency to compartmentalize U.S. strategic responsibility. The ultimate challenge to American security is thought to be the threat of an intercontinental nuclear attack by the Soviet Union on the United States. Although such an attack might occur as the result of war in Europe that began with conventional conflict, the end game is seen as a duel between two intercontinental arsenals, unrelated to what might be going on in other theaters with other forces. Once intercontinental war begins, according to this scenario, theater war would be over or irrelevant. A similar tendency treats conventional and nuclear conflict within theaters in separate categories.

Some steps toward correction of this doctrinal compartmentalization have been taken in that attention has been given to the possible role of strategic intercontinental weapons in theater defense. This attention has arisen in the context of limited nuclear options, not in the context of an unrestrained central exchange.

As Soviet strategy has recognized for years, the ultimate problem for deterrence and defense is not the strategic intercontinental exchange, but *general war* in which use of strategic nuclear weapons would be a part, along with nuclear and conventional operations in theaters, war at sea, homeland survival measures, intelligence operations, and so on. The antagonists in a general war might well observe limitations on the manner and extent to which they used nuclear weapons to elicit restraint on the opponent's part, to conserve forces, or to preserve valued territory from destruction. Limitations as to what countries or theaters were brought into the conflict might be observed for the same reasons. Assuming that an intercontinental exchange began in such a way as to leave both sides' essential C^3 structures intact, which is by no means a certainty, each side might have the raw military capability of inflicting such awesome damage on the other as to deprive any outcome of the conflict of military or political meaning. This is what is meant by assured destruction. The trouble is that it is not assured and, in any case, bears no relationship to the interests of either antagonist in the event.

General war thus must be recognized to engage all the war-making potential of nations and alliances, either actively, virtually, or as reserves. It has a time dimension of some unknown magnitude, which may permit maneuver and mobilization. It has an aftermath. The successive rungs of the escalatory process by which a general war might occur will remain linked.

It may be necessary today to credit the USSR with essential superiority in the context of general war. Soviet objectives would be (1) to provide for the survival of the USSR as a national entity having reserve military capabilities, (2) to eliminate hostile forces from continental Europe either by occupation or destruction, (3) to make it physically impossible for the United States to remain in or to get back into Europe militarily. Ancillary objectives might be (4) to neutralize the PRC by intimidation or destruction and (5) to occupy the Persian Gulf region. Direct attack on the United States is a means to these ends, a particularly dramatic form of long-range artillery support, not an end in itself.

The USSR's principal assets for the conduct of general war are formidable "damage-limiting" capabilities against U.S. strategic forces, C^3, and force projection bases; strategic reserves; large land armies capable of fighting in nuclear and chemical environments; active and civil defenses of the homeland; and the oceans that the United States must cross to reinforce in Eurasia. These assets place the Soviet Union in a better position to wage general war than the

United States, especially if given the operational initiative and restraint in the use of nuclear weapons is observed.

The security of the West requires that the USSR be denied this kind of superiority as it relates to the conduct of general war with the key objectives of Eurasian position and national survival. How is this to be achieved in terms of fundamental doctrine?

Reversion to an "assured destruction/unacceptable damage" strategy, even if combined with more credible limited nuclear options, is not a viable approach. Its lack of credibility risks collapse in a crisis and progressive demoralization under the pressures of peacetime power politics.

Is forward defense a viable approach? Undoubtedly an effective containment posture will require substantial improvement of U.S. and allied general-purpose and nuclear forces for forward defense in Europe. In addition to the current TNF initiative, the entire theater and battlefield nuclear posture of the Atlantic alliance needs to be reassessed and updated, particularly to provide for survivability and efficiency in employment against advancing ground forces. It is of the greatest importance that NATO general-purpose forces be substantially improved in their capability to fight in chemical and nuclear conditions.

In the final analysis, however, even substantially improved forward defense backed by assured destruction plus limited nuclear options, which is an idealized way of characterizing NATO's present strategy, do not represent a strategic approach in which we could place lasting confidence. The basic problem is that forward defenses against a formidable continental adversary are bound to be uncertain in the best of circumstances. Moreover, the USSR cannot with this combination be deprived of the nuclear capability to threaten or inflict such destruction on Europe as to make forward defense appear irrelevant to the Europeans. If the Soviets were unable to occupy Western Europe it would remain in their interest to so damage NATO countries as to prevent their being a locus of hostile power. European interest in self-defense could collapse as soon as a war began, a possibility that has bedeviled alliance strategy since the Soviets reached nuclear parity. The United States could not enforce forward defense without them, however.

This leads to the proposition that a kind of strategic superiority relevant to the general war problem must be acquired by the United States. In the past, strategic superiority has been defined as some combination of offensive counterforce (especially counter-ICBM) and strategic defense (air defense, ballistic missile defense, and anti-submarine warfare) capabilities effective enough to limit the retaliatory damage of which the opponent is capable to so low a level as to permit deliberate initiation of intercontinental attack. The United States probably enjoyed this kind of damage-limiting strategic superiority well into the early 1960s. It provided the basis of European security in the persistent absence of reliable local defenses. The buildup of Soviet strategic forces eliminated this kind of U. S. strategic superiority. Because advancing technology promised to make strategic offensive forces relatively invulnerable to preemptive attack while leaving the ultimate targets of "unacceptable damage," namely cities, relatively vulnerable to attack, this kind of superiority came to be viewed as no longer available to either side and as a quixotic, even dangerous goal if actually pursued.

This view may retain some abstract (therefore irrelevant) validity as it applies to intercontinental attack forces and their city targets alone. In the context of general war, the context in which the actual use of strategic nuclear weapons is most likely to occur and in which deterrence operates because it dominates Soviet strategy, other possibilities arise. In this context the Soviets may have possibilities for achieving militarily and politically meaningful victory. By the same token strategies and military capabilities may in principle be available that permit the United States to deny the Soviets such a victory on terms consistent with its own survival. A posture that represents a credible capability to do this is clearly vital to deterrence generally and to European security in particular against a robust Soviet opponent whose strategy is clearly oriented toward the conduct of general war.

The Carter administration took a number of limited steps in the direction of this posture, among them, Harold Brown's effort to define a "countervailing strategy," heightened attention to the survivability of strategic command and control, recognition of the role of civil defense capabilities in the strategic balance, and reassessment of central targeting priorities. Over the last two years of the Carter administration, these shifts were recorded in a series of presidential directives, the last and most comprehensive of which was the much publicized but never published PD-59.

Unfortunately, no comprehensive doctrine enjoying broad support within that administration emerged to integrate these evolutionary developments. Insufficient resources and bureaucratic support were provided to give them real substance. The Reagan administration had the task of salvaging the worthwhile innovations of the recent past, adding some of its own, and creating a comprehensive doctrine that can integrate and guide the strategic recovery effort over the next decade. The hallmarks of the required doctrine are as follows:

- The minimum objectives of U.S. strategy in a general war would be (1) to assure the survival of the United States as a functioning and militarily capable national entity and (2) to prevent the forces of the USSR from occupying adjacent Eurasian areas. The two are intimately related.

- Considerably improved active and civil defense of the United States, as well as improved counterforce capabilities, are clearly required. As the relevant technology matures, area antiballistic missile (ABM) capabilities will have to be soberly reassessed against the requirements of general war strategy, rather than the doctrinal precepts underlying the SALT I ABM agreement.

- Strategic forces must not only be able to survive rapid massive attack, they must endure in protracted engagements, be susceptible to recovery and reconstitution, and able to stand in reserve. They must also be susceptible to flexible and precise employment in large and small raids. The possibility of combining long-range strategic delivery systems with new types of nonnuclear weapons, not only for limited contingencies but for general conflict ought to be carefully examined. These requirements should be addressed to the entire spectrum of strategic force improvement programs now underway, M–X, Trident, and air-launched cruise missiles. They are especially relevant, however, to defining the character and role of new strategic bomber forces.

- Strategic capabilities to locate and target enemy mobile strategic strike and projection forces are clearly at a high premium.

- As the Soviet doctrine recognized almost two decades ago, general war strategy places the greatest significance upon technologies and organizational structures for accomplishing command, control, communications, and intelligence (C^3I) functions during extended operations and while under attack. Until effective ABM technologies are ready for deployment, strategic C^3I enhancements will be the cutting edge of doctrinal reform and posture improvement.

- In support of C^3I functions the United States must develop and enforce its dominance in the military use of space.

- U.S. general-purpose forces and logistic structures must be adapted to operations in a chemical and nuclear environment. This applies to all the military services.

Besides these doctrinal revisions, the United States urgently needs to increase and redirect defense research and development, expand the defense industrial base, fulfill expanded manpower requirements, improve intelligence efforts, and modernize the forces of friendly states.

It is not safe to ignore the imperatives of a general war strategy, for it is ultimately general war, not an exchange of strategic arsenals, that is the fundamental problem of deterrence. It is the virtual war lurking at the top of the escalation ladder and the ultimate risk that Soviet decisionmakers explicitly or subconsciously weigh in calculating their actions against U.S. interests. Not only local Soviet strengths, local instabilities, and local Western exposure, but also the absence of reliable deterrence at this level make the future dangerous.

BEYOND CONTAINMENT

By adopting a general war strategy and meeting its force posture requirements, the alliance has a chance to restore viable conditions of deterrence in Europe. If successful, we would achieve a form of strategic superiority for defense or for denial of victory, resting on a U.S. national-survival capability and the operational coupling of U.S. strategic forces to strengthened European defenses.

In pursuing such a course, we must squarely face the prospect, indeed the strong likelihood, that the Soviets will increase their own efforts to retain and increase their strategic advantages for the conduct of general war focused on Eurasian objectives. There is no chance whatsoever that they can be dissuaded by arms control negotiations from pursuing such advantages, at least until they become persuaded by the actions of the West that such advantages will be denied them in any case and will eventually shift to the Western side. Therefore an intensification of the arms competition, at least through most of the 1980s, is a certainty. This is the case not because of present Western choices but because of past Western laxity. Failure to engage in this contest now will not enhance the prospect for arms control solutions to the present security problems. Rather, such failure will only allow Soviet advantages to grow, leading either to radical new political arrangements in Eurasia or to war, and possibly both.

Equally, there can be no guarantee that a new Western commitment to restoring the military equilibrium and the structure of containment will not itself lead, because of past neglect, to confrontation and conflict. This risk is genuine. The risk is less, however, than that involved in a failure to respond. The Soviets seek to pocket the rewards of military preponderance at lowest cost and risk to themselves. They prefer to advance their interests through intimidation, demoralization, and confusion of their victims and adversaries. They show great patience and some resourcefulness in doing this. In both their internal and their international behavior, they nevertheless display a readiness to delay, recalculate, and retreat when confronted with resolute opposition even on the part of those who are objectively weak. This quality of the Soviet system is the most important factor allowing the West to restore the conditions of containment. Only when such conditions have been restored, will it be possible for a new combination of pressures and inducements to persuade a new generation of leaders in Moscow to adopt policies that help reconcile the security of the Soviet or Russian state with the security of its neighbors on this globe. We must also recognize that this will require changes to the Soviet system itself, however long they may be in coming.

The ultimate source of our peril lies, we must finally admit, in the nature of the Soviet political system itself, in its hunger to acquire absolute control as far as it can reach, in its inability to accept security on terms other than control over others. Beyond containment, therefore, we face the dual but mutually reinforcing tasks of, first, combatively engaging the Soviets at significant points of test so as to deny them confidence in progress through our demoralization, and, second, facing the Soviet system with such unremitting pressures and failures as to render it politically nonviable and, hence, open to fundamental change.

10 ALLIANCE STRATEGY IN THE 1980s AND THE POLITICAL APPROACH TO SOVIET POWER

Uwe Nerlich

THE CONTEXT: AN OMINOUS ABSENCE OF WESTERN GRAND STRATEGY

For years the Atlantic alliance has been without a common strategy or indeed any strategy for coping with Soviet power or for exploiting Soviet weaknesses. Throughout the 1950s NATO's military strategy toward the Soviet Union was linked to prerequisites for political order in Europe. The combination of the Paris summit in 1960, the Soviet–East German "friendship treaty," the Berlin wall, and the Cuban missile crisis eliminated issues of political order from the European agenda and stressed Soviet–American bilateralism in ways that increasingly led Western elites to consider military stability a substitute for political order.

The disappearance of achievable political order in Europe deprived military strategy of its genuine role in East–West relations: to support foreign policy by denying disruptive actions by the other side. In the 1960s the principal task in the pursuit of military strategy was the structuring of appropriate relations between foes and allies. In the name of stability and with expectations of reciprocity the West hoped to persuade the Soviet Union to accept a state of military affairs sufficiently stable to allow for increasing self-restraint and co-operativeness in East–West relations. Then followed the only phase since 1945 that saw the West and notably the United States gaining diplomatic initiative vis-à-vis the Soviet Union—with instant geostrategic and political advances in many areas as well as with some perspective for structural change in Western relations with the Soviet Union. But the combination of Watergate, the Yom Kippur war of 1973, and the economic crisis following the oil price rises discontinued this promising train of developments and left the West with the worst of both worlds: Military strategy continued to be crippled in order to encourage Soviet self-restraint (especially in SALT), even though the shadows of Soviet military power began to loom larger and larger, whereas the scope for meaningful arms control disappeared simply because there was less and less to be bargained away. At the same time the notion of pursuing peace by political conflict resolution (as evidenced through the Berlin agreement) with some perspective on building new political incentive structures, which might eventually have reopened avenues toward European order, quickly appeared invalidated again as a result of inappropriate efforts on both sides of the Atlantic to capitalize on early successes for domestic purposes. In fact the political instrumentalities of economic cooperation with the Soviet Union faded again because of a combination of domestically imposed restraints (most noticeably the Church, Stevenson, and Jackson/Vanick amendments in the United States) and also because of lack of governmental leverage (because of industrial opportunism), souring Western markets for Eastern products, intra-Western competition, and Eastern apprehensions about increasingly intrusive effects of cooperation, as evidenced by the implications of Giereck's policy.

The net result of all of this was that the West continued to give overriding priority to the "process of détente" but saw itself increasingly deprived of the means and policies for achieving any structural results in the course of this process. Business, even business as usual under extreme circumstances, and political primacy for arms control with almost no bargaining leverage left vis-à-vis the Soviet Union are the dominant features of Western Europe's approach to the Soviet Union. Neither is related to any policy for structuring political relations with the Soviet Union or any strategy for coping with increasing Soviet military power on the Continent.

This Western, or at least West European, inclination not to opt out of a process that is bound to leave Western Europe without any option to participate actively in the shaping of its future, meets any definition of decline and decadence, and it may be hard to discover political resources in Western Europe that would suffice to turn this trend around. What is worse, Western Europe tends to discourage unilateral American efforts to rebuild a sustainable base for coping with Soviet power. By the same token it forgoes any chance to provide a sense of direction to American policies that would more unambiguously serve West European interests. The dogged effort to push the United States into the intermediate nuclear forces (INF) negotiations contained whatever ultimate ironies there are in the present situation.

It is in this context that the West begins to discover again the need to rethink profoundly its military strategy toward the Soviet Union. No comprehensive, let alone common policy in the West toward the Soviet Union exists to which it could be linked, but there is a continued commitment in Western Europe to stay in a process that tends to reduce the political distance from the Soviet Union and to increase the distance from the United States. A continued political primacy of arms control in Western Europe increases doggedly over both efforts to rebuild the means to check Soviet military power (and thus rebuild the base for meaningful arms control) and policies of disarmament that do not forgo demands for substantive Soviet reciprocity. The alliance is increasingly seen in parts of Western Europe as a framework for the gradual transformation of European East–West relations through the arms control process, whereas in the United States quite understandably, however disastrous for Western Europe, frustration over Western Europe increasingly breeds a kind of unilateralism that not only will result in American impatience with and even disregard for NATO (a kind of conservative Mansfield syndrome, only much more difficult to manage) but will eventually increase existing dangers for Western Europe while depriving it of the remaining means to influence American policies.

THE RESULT: THE FADING OF NATO's MILITARY STRATEGY

What then are the options left? There is no way the Atlantic alliance can simply continue the way it is. Without major changes in capabilities, strategy and policy its very rationale will be eliminated and its political fabric torn apart. Adenauer and de Gaulle recognized a fundamental need for changing the alliance in the late 1950s. The European solution was more sharing of control with continued emphasis on nuclear deterrence; the American was more centralized control with reduced dependence on nuclear deterrence. Neither solution was achieved. When NATO eventually agreed on the doctrine that had been part of the earlier American solution (embodied in MC 14/3), the scope for a broader range of conventional options and thus for reduced dependence on nuclear responses had been destroyed (largely upon West European insistence), and the strategic flexibility required for NATO's escalatory posture was almost ignored at the time in Western target planning as it was ignored in Western nuclear weapons modernization. What flexible response meant under the circumstances was for all practical purposes delayed massive retaliation.

It was only in the mid-1970s that a more systematic effort unfolded both to broaden the range of conventional options[1] and to introduce more strategic flexibility through postural changes in doctrine, weaponry, and supporting elements like command and control capacities—which had become even more imperative under conditions of strategic parity than it had been earlier. The need to decrease the West's dependence on nuclear responses was recognized in the Schlesinger era to be all the more important in view of the widening range of plausible conflict scenarios involving Soviet military power that simply did not lend themselves to reliance on nuclear weapons (especially contingencies outside Europe with instant bearing on Western Europe's viability as in the Persian Gulf).

Originally, dependence on nuclear response was meant to offset Soviet conventional superiority without turning Western societies into garrison states, without building a huge mobilization base, yet with a kind of superiority tolerant of error that is needed in Western democracies, and within budgetary confines expected to be compatible with other needs.[2] By the mid-1970s the Western strategic problem had become neutralizing Soviet nuclear first strike options along with maintaining or regaining some Western control of escalation.

A comprehensive nuclear modernization program for NATO was worked out at the time that could have helped to regain some strategic flexibility, and efforts began to bear fruit that were designed to reduce the West's dependence on nuclear weapons while recognizing the need for a more coherent employment doctrine for nuclear and nonnuclear capabilities, especially in view of a Soviet posture build around combined arms operations. At this stage political changes in the United States as well as in Europe discontinued these defense improvement programs, however, and thus ruled out the kind of strategic flexibility so badly needed in order at least to increase Soviet uncertainty again over what risks the Soviet Union might incur in a serious crisis—which is what deterrence is about. The advent of the Carter administration and the rediscovery of domestic political utilities of détente policies in some West European countries created a confluence of restraints, political inhibitions, deliberate diffusion of defense programs, and determined efforts to polarize electorates over nuclear issues that turned out to have profound effects in the West. While some programs for conventional defense improvement survived in the new long-term defense program (LTDP)—even with some further elaboration—yet with reduced political priority the nuclear modernization program by and large failed to survive these changes except for isolated but highly politicized elements, first the enhanced radiation weapon (ERW) and then the long-range theater nuclear force (LRTNF) programs. Moreover, after the seemingly promising NATO summit in London in spring 1977, unspecified arms control objectives took political priority over defense improvement programs. The philosophy emerged that the implementation of defense programs would occur only to the degree arms control would fail to eliminate the requirements. A clear tendency also emerged to adapt defense requirements to the diminishing scope of arms control rather than to provide some leverage for arms control through procurements and deployments.

Eventually the Carter administration returned to some aspects of the strategic need for strategic flexibility (however driven by domestic considerations), but Western Europe, or at least "Protestant Europe," now turned to an arms control-first-or-only approach which in retrospect may be seen as the most self-defeating foreign policy trend in Europe since 1945. This came into the open when the incoming Reagan administration somewhat incoherently, yet with a clear sense of the priority restoring Western defense, continued to support some of the defense improvement programs, especially in the LRTNF category.

Political responses in a number of West European countries, including West Germany, in effect called for the end of either the doctrine of flexible response or the abdication of nuclear deterrence altogether. Despite more recent backlash in the direction of soberer approaches within moderately leftist parties and the churches,[3] the media appear to be dominated by persons whose attitudes are out-rightly hostile toward any effort to restore deterrence and indeed toward the United States as the very backbone of deterrence. Iron-ically the elements in this "debate" who advocate preserving nuclear deterrence at least for the forseeable future often do so by stressing the need for some nuclear balance or even by emphasizing the re-quirements for deterrence in such a way that what their pledge implies spells again a massive retaliation posture in its crudest terms and under the most unlikely circumstances. Strategically it is virtu-ally meaningless under conditions of rough strategic parity (with a strong momentum pointing toward Soviet strategic advantages), and politically West European near hostility toward the United States is likely to destroy the most precious element of NATO solidarity, while massive retaliation simply is irreconcilable with viable political relationships between Western Europe and the United States.[4]

The NATO posture thus is constantly eroding, and there is no way the security of the West will be maintained by virtual American unilateralism. If the American society should find itself burdened with all the penalties of defense and all the risks in case deterrence fails, its response is easy to predict, especially if the fate of Reagan's economic policy should necessitate what large segments of the West European published opinion astonishingly demand anyway: lowered American defense efforts. Moreover, unlike recent times when close U.S.-West German cooperation in NATO appeared not only funda-mental but even potentially excessive, alienation in U.S.-German relations has progressed on both sides and West German rediscovery of their dependence on American protection and their vital inter-est in intimate cooperation may come too late for the American public.

Given these circumstances there is no chance for free rides on the part of other West European countries, especially of the Scandilux variety, and what has been called Hollanditis simply is one more boost to yet another and most probably final European self-destruc-tion. All societies within the Atlantic alliance will have to decide in the 1980s either to pull resources together in order to protect a viable political order in the West or to escape from this responsibility in the name of narrowly conceived nationalisms or of moral condem-nations of particular deterrence means or of priorities that are left-overs from more affluent societies. All would result in the loss of whatever European destiny may be left.

REDEFINING POLITICAL PURPOSES OF
NATO's MILITARY STRATEGY

The West thus must agree on a more viable military strategy in order to cope with a widening range of contingencies, most importantly those relating to serious disruptions of Middle Eastern oil supplies by hostile change or extended Soviet control. Yet the political consensus for even keeping the Atlantic alliance alive is in serious jeopardy. The only way for the alliance to work out and maybe even adopt a military strategy more commensurate with challenges of the future will be by agreeing on a new broad approach toward the Soviet Union. In spite of a long history of dilemmas of Western deterrence policy—derived from Western conceptions of deterrence rather than from genuine limitations of what the West can do in order to check Soviet power—the problem never was to design response options, although this too does require hard work on concepts, technology, and organization. The problem always was and was always seen to be one of political will, which time and again turned out to be a scarce commodity.

The obvious loss of political will was more or less unavoidable as was the demise of a notion of what kind of relationship the West wants to create with the Soviet Union and what purposes its military strategy should serve in this process. What happened was that Western approaches toward the Soviet Union became more fragmented, deterrence policy becoming one basic approach and détente another. Polarization of political supporters of what ought to have been the two basic elements of a comprehensive approach in the West resulted in competing domestic constituencies and more recently into a polarization between some West European countries and the United States over how to deal with the Soviet Union, with neither side having a version appropriate to the task.

As understanding faded about what political purposes Western military strategy was meant to serve, the West's military efforts began to appear to many more as a liability than a resource. Not only did this fail to generate political will, but it led to growing apprehensions in the West about the consequences of a failure of deterrence. Paradoxically public views in the West began to follow a bizarre logic: Improving the West's deterrence, which is designed to cope with a Soviet initiation of military conflict under conditions of Soviet conventional superiority, is seen to make this initiation (the outbreak of war) more rather than less likely. By the same token the improvement of deterrence is expected to magnify the devastating consequences of a failure of deterrence. In this perspective no conceivable rationale for improving nuclear deterrence is likely to escape the verdict of the new opposition. What is at stake thus is nothing less than the principle of deterrence.

What supporters and opponents of deterrence have in common is the lack of a conception of the kind of relationship they want to develop with the Soviet Union. Either side essentially entertains rather abstract notions—of a stable military balance or of a process as an end in itself. For responsible governments the principal task in the years ahead is to establish a conceptual framework to structure long-term relations with the Soviet Union. Within the framework, military strategy and a Western deterrence posture would be designed to make a positive outcome more likely. Linking military strategy to political objectives, which is commonplace in Soviet thinking, would thus help to replace misconceptions widely entertained in Western publics, like the notion of seemingly endless arms races that continue almost independently of political influence. As Samuel P. Huntington points out, "the current phase requires not only new strategic ideas but a new role for strategy itself."[5]

This would allow the West to escape an awkward situation: On the one side Soviet military efforts systematically take away one Western response option after another while widening the range of contingencies with which the West would have to cope, whereas on the other any effort to regain response options at least on a modest scale is denounced in the West (of course strongly reinforced by Soviet propaganda) as a mindless continuation of an endless arms spiral. The redefinition of military strategy thus requires a much broader set of considerations than can be derived from current or projected military realities. It has to rediscover European order as the basic issue of European security. This context would be conducive to restoring the principle of deterrence in Western security policy. It would also serve to minimize domestic and intraalliance polarization over how to deal with the Soviet Union. The goal is to reduce Soviet opportunities to play on a keyboard of West European politics, at the same time facilitating a broader and more stable political base for future alliance policy.

COPING WITH SOVIET POWER:
A DUAL APPROACH FOR THE WEST

It is outside the scope of this chapter to describe in detail the essential features of a comprehensive approach toward the Soviet Union.[6] The point of departure would be this: Unlike the past when for the West military stability as an end in itself and Western recognition of the Soviet imperial structure in Eastern Europe combined so as to turn the Soviet Union into a black box for all practical purposes and to take stability of the Soviet power structure as a given, it becomes obvious that alternative futures are conceivable for the Soviet empire and that the course of events may not be largely indifferent to the way the West approaches the Soviet Union.

Ever since the 1950s confrontation has been seen by the Soviet Union as well as by the West as a suitable framework for the solution of internal structural problems. The Soviet Union never forgot this though, while in the name of détente this instrumentality of confrontation tended to become blurred for both Western Europe and the United States. Yet the Soviet Union incurs ever more problems (as in Poland or in the development of Siberia) that it cannot hope to solve within a confrontationist framework and without Western cooperation, nor is Western solidarity likely to derive from confrontationist policies. The solution to Western economic and societal problems is even more difficult to achieve than it would be anyhow if it must be found under conditions of either dominance of the Soviet threat or accommodation to Soviet power. For both sides to be able to focus on internal problems is of tantamount importance, and for the Soviet Union to gain the kind of broad assistance envisaged in the early 1970s is still as crucial as is responsible deemphasis on Soviet military power on the Continent for the West.

While this is a plausible description of either side's needs, it is not by itself a description of *perceived* interests: In the West there is a widespread readiness to forgo confrontationist policies even to the point where Soviet realities tend to be systematically ignored. The Soviet Union may hope to muddle through internally and at the same time have the cake and eat it as far as Western cooperation is concerned. In other words, without facing tough choices in the West the Soviet Union is likely to capitalize on economic relations with the West without exercising any degree of self-restraint as a result.[7]

What is needed is a kind of dual approach to the Soviet Union. However, unlike the Soviet dual approach to the West—display of power plus pursuit of détente—which is not conceived in terms of alternatives but of synergism, a Western dual approach would have to be seen in terms of two possible and distinctly alternative strategic offers by the West between which the Soviet Union could choose. The choice could be made during a testing phase of several years against the background of its increasing internal difficulties as well as of the political succession process in the Kremlin. It would be a choice between, first, a broad yet instrumentalized Western offer to cooperate in the solution of Soviet internal problems within an emerging framework of effectively reduced military threats and, second, a systematic effort in the West to rebuild military strength in case the Soviet Union eventually rejects a broad cooperative relationship.

Given the time factors involved in such an approach and given current trends in the West, the Soviet Union may recognize a need for more dramatic change in the face of increasing internal difficulties but may do so by looking for a quick fix or a breakout (e.g., gaining military control over oil supplies from the Gulf) by exploiting favorable military balances and political disarray in the West. One possible illustration would be a Soviet effort to forgo the prize for Western cooperativeness by trying to extend Soviet control over crucial parts of the Persian Gulf region.

These considerations lead to three purposes military strategy would have to serve in this context: (1) to *deter and discourage Soviet breakouts* in order to impose the tough choice on the Soviet Union between conditioned cooperation along with effective disarmament and effective military counterveiling efforts with cooperation reduced to the lowest possible level; (2) to *stabilize a kind of military holding pattern* as part of an emerging less-confrontationist structure in East–West relations; and (3) to *meet the Soviet challenge* in case the Soviet Union opts against such a structure.

As a corollary, arms control as it was pursued throughout the 1970s would cease to play a role in this context. If the Soviet Union chooses to opt for cooperation, what is required is substantive disarmament rather than symbolic arms limitation (as is reflected in the American concept of START), whereas in Western Europe political primacy of arms control as a rule combines with a policy of "not asking too much" from the Soviet Union.[8] If the USSR takes its chances and leaves the West with the option to rearm effectively, there is no room for arms control either.

Another corollary would be that unless the Soviets explicitly choose to opt for outright arms competition, military measures would not be seen as part of an arms race with a dynamics of its own. Military competition would lose its centrality in East–West relations. Military measures would become recognizable again as something to be evaluated in terms of whether it supports broader political objectives or not. Arms control would serve simply as an auxiliary to make military measures commensurate with those political objectives.

NOTES

1. Unlike the early 1960s, however, new conventional technologies and improved readiness and reinforcement capabilities were emphasized rather than increased manpower.
2. See especially Eisenhower's budget ceilings as part of his rationale for depending more heavily on nuclear weapons.
3. See the memorandum issued by the Council of the Evangelical Church in Germany, November 1981.
4. As a corollary a number of West European governments have long embarked on a bargaining-chip policy in their justification of the deployment part of the LRTNF package: As the ominous "zero-solution" displays, military or, rather, strategic rationales no longer play much of a role in this context, even though the most visible defense decision is at stake.
5. Samuel P. Huntington, "The Renewal of Strategy," in S. Huntington, ed., *The Strategic Imperative: New Policies for American Security* (Cambridge, Mass.: Ballinger Publishing Company, 1982), ch. 1, p. 50.
6. See Huntington, "The Renewal of Strategy."
7. The usual short answer to this is in the West "linkage." But linkage is a tactical concept, whereas what is at stake is the basic strategic approach of the West.
8. However, stabilizing measures that at times have occurred on arms control agendas would be part and parcel of such a scheme. The more reinforcement becomes a strategic necessity prior to any major military move as a consequence of effective reductions or withdrawals, the more important is the potential functional value of stabilizing measures.

LIST OF ABBREVIATIONS

ABM	Antiballistic Missile
ACE	Allied Command Europe
ACR	Armored Cavalry Regiment
ADM	Atomic Demolition Means
ALCM	Air-Launched Cruise Missile
ATGM	Antitank Guided Missile
AWACS	Airborne Warning and Control System
BMP	Bronevaja Mašina Pechoty (Soviet infantry fighting vehicle)
BTR	Brone Transporter (Soviet armored transporter)
C^3	Command, Control, and Communication
C^3I	Command, Control, Communication, and Intelligence
CBM	Confidence-Building Measures
CDE	Conference on Disarmament in Europe
CENTAG	Central Army Group in NATO
CSCE	Conference on Security and Cooperation in Europe
CSFG	Camp of Soviet Forces in Germany
ECM	Electronic Countermeasures
EMT	Equivalent Megatonnage
EPC	European Political Cooperation (of the Common Market member states)
ER/RB Weapons	Enhanced Radiation/Reduced Blast Weapons ("neutron weapons")

343

FBIS	Foreign Broadcast Information Service
FBS	Forward-Based Systems
GLCM	Ground-Launched Cruise Missile
GSRS	General Support Rocket System
ICBM	Intercontinental Ballistic Missile
ICM	Improved Conventional Munition
IFF	Identification Friend/Foe
IFV	Infantry Fighting Vehicle
IISS	International Institute for Strategic Studies (London)
INF	Intermediate-Range Nuclear Forces
IRBM	Intermediate-Range Ballistic Missile
LRTNF	Long-Range Theater Nuclear Forces
MAD	Mutual Assured Destruction
MBFR	Mutual Balanced Force Reductions
MC	Military Committee (in NATO)
MIRV	Multiple Independently Targetable Re-entry Vehicle
MLF	Multilateral Force
MPLA	Movimento Popular de Liberacao de Angola
MRBM	Medium-Range Ballistic Missile
MRCA	Multi-Role Combat Aircraft
MSBS	Mer-Sol-Ballistiques Strategiques (French)
NADGE	NATO Air Defense Ground Environment
NGA	National Guidelines Area—area for MBFR: East Germany, Poland, Czechoslovakia, and West Germany, and the Benelux countries
NORTHAG	Northern Army Group (in NATO)
NPT	Nonproliferation Treaty
OPEC	Organization of Petroleum-Exporting Countries
PD	Presidential Directive
PGM	Precision-Guided Munition
POMCUS	Prepositioning of Material Configured to Unit Sets
QRA	Quick Reaction Alert
RAP	Rocket Assisted Projectiles
SACEUR	Supreme Allied Commander Europe
SACLANT	Supreme Allied Commander Atlantic
SALT	Strategic Arms Limitation Talks
SAM	Surface-to-Air Missile

SLAR	Side-Looking Airborne Radar
SLBM	Sea-Launched Ballistic Missile
SLCM	Sea-Launched Cruise Missile
SSBN	Sub-Surface Ballistic Nuclear
START	Strategic Arms Reduction Talks
TNF	Theater Nuclear Forces
TOW	Tube-Launched, Optically Tracked, Wire-Guided Antitank Missile
VG	Variable Geometry
WEU	West European Union

INDEX

Adenauer, Konrad, 196, 333
Afghanistan, 10, 139–44 *passim*, 173, 189, 201, 247, 256, 257, 263, 277, 283, 286–88, 293, 296, 298, 310, 314
Africa, 178, 182, 201, 279, 282, 289, 299, 312; defense of, 321
Airborne Warning and Control System (AWACS), 76
Aircraft, combat, 59–60
Aircraft, high technology, 64
Aircraft, multimission, 64–67
Aircraft sheltering program, 75
Aircraft, tactical, 40–42, 59; British, 62, 67, 96; French, 64, 96; NATO, 61–62, 64–67, 75–76, 93–97, 102; nuclear warheads for, 93–96; Soviet/ Warsaw Pact, 61, 63–66, 76, 81, 85, 96, 97, 219–20; technical obsolescence of, 59; U.S., 62, 64, 66, 85, 96, 309; West German, 62, 67
Air defense systems, 38, 39, 40–42, 69–70, 220; Airborne Warning and Control System, 76; artillery, 70; early warning radar, 73, 224; fleet, 92; NATO, 66, 69–76; Soviet, 38, 39, 65, 75, 87, 309; U.S., 87, 309; Warsaw Pact, 69–76
Air-delivered munitions, 64, 218
Air-launched cruise missiles, 328

Air offensive, 224
Air-to-air intercept missiles (AIM), 65, 220
Air-to-ground missiles (ATGMs); British, 50–51; NATO, 49–53, 77, 78, 87; Soviet/Warsaw Pact, 49–53, 78, 85, 87; U.S., 50, 85, 87; West German, 50
Allied Command Europe (ACE), 112
Alsace–Lorraine, 1
Angola, 16, 136, 314; civil war in, 140, 297; and the Soviet Union, 141, 143, 144, 173, 201, 247, 256, 280, 299
Antiair systems, 147
Anti-Americanism, 178
Antiarmor systems, 38, 39, 40, 49, 77, 219; balance of power, 49–53; NATO, 49–53; Soviet/Warsaw Pact, 38, 39, 49–53
Antiballistic missiles (ABMs), 328
Anti-communism, 184
Anti-NATO sentiment, 187
Antinuclear movement, 186, 187
Anti-Sovietism, 176–78
Antitank guided missiles (ATGMs), 40, 42, 49, 52, 219, 220; guidance system, 52; limitations, 50–53; technology, 50

Antitank guns, Soviet/Warsaw Pact, 52, 87
Arab states, 279–80
Arabian Peninsula, 320
Arbatov, Georgy, 129
Argentina, 16
Armament, 40–42; categories of, 79; levels in Central Europe, 40, 85–88; NATO, 195, 211; Soviet/Warsaw Pact, 87; technology, 220–22; U.S., 87
Armor, 38, 39, 45; balance of power, 46; Soviet/Warsaw Pact, 38, 39, 147
Armored personnel carriers (APCs), 40, 41, 46–47; balance of power, 46; British, 46; Dutch, 46; French, 46; NATO, 46–47, 52; Soviet/ Warsaw Pact, 46–47; U.S., 46, 48–49, 85; West German, 46
Armor-penetrating fin-stabilized discarding sabot, 44
Arms control, 6–7, 149–50, 188, 199, 209, 229, 315–16, 332–33, 335, 341; agreements, 259, 294; and defense, 203; and East–West relations, 20, 196, 333; in Europe, 188, 341; future of, 316–17; INF negotiations, 333; mutual and balanced force reduction talks, 164; mutual force reduction talks, 163–64; and NATO, 317; negotiations, 12, 22, 25, 89, 98, 106, 125, 161, 209, 288, 329; political, 166; and security, 329; and the Soviet Union, 8, 22, 91, 106, 162, 166, 177, 183, 185, 196, 291–92, 294, 313; technical, 166; and the United States, 6–7, 186; and the Western alliance, 31
Arms limitation, 161, 166, 167, 172, 196; negotiations, 199
Arms race, 19, 24, 31–32, 207–08, 212, 216, 264, 285, 329, 241; action-reaction models of, 234, 237; conventional, 41, 76; defined, 32; reason for, 76–77; unlimited, 324
Arms reduction negotiations, 164
Artillery, 38, 40–42, 218, 220; air defense, 70; antiarmor, 57; antitank capability, 56; balance of power, 53–59; British, 54; delivery systems, 54; Dutch, 72; East German, 57–58; fire control capability, 54, 57;

French, 54, 72, 87, 155; lethality of, 54–55; NATO, 54, 57–59, 97; nuclear, 93, 224; self-propelled, 54, 57, 83, 87, 147; Soviet/Warsaw Pact, 38, 54, 57–59, 72–73, 81, 87, 96, 147; towed systems, 54, 58; U.S., 54, 56, 57, 70, 72, 87; West German, 54, 72, 87
Asia, 178, 183, 312
Assured destruction, 325, 326
Atlantic alliance, 198, 318, 333–34, 336; and arms control, 8, 196; defense policy, 8–9, 197; military strategy, 337; nuclear posture, 326; security policy, 10–11; and the Soviet Union, 21, 174, 317, 331; and the United States, 334; and Western security threats, 17
Attack: air, 98; chemical, 98; echeloned, 221; nuclear, 98; preemptive, 327; short-warning, 216, 223–26, 229; surprise, 209. See also War/warfare
Austria, 1

Balance of power: aerial, 59–69, 76; air defense, 69–76; antiarmor, 49–53; artillery, 53–59; conventional, 24, 32, 34–42, 228–29; Eurostrategic, 149, 172; military, 1, 6, 9–10, 11, 19, 20, 77, 124, 125, 127, 129, 130–36, 166, 179–83, 208–09, 213–17, 227, 284–85, 292, 307, 329, 338; military-conventional, 212; military-strategic, 187; Northern, 198; nuclear-strategic, 135, 309, 319–20, 327; tactical nuclear, 228; theater nuclear, 24, 90, 91–92, 98–99, 106, 107, 112, 228, 317; theory, 130
Ballistic missile submarines (SSBNs), 96, 101
Ballistic missiles, Soviet/Warsaw Pact, 10, 97, 181, 195, 285; SS–20, 10, 93, 96, 148, 149, 166, 181, 184, 185, 187, 189, 292
Basket Three provisions, 188
Batista, Juan, 283
Belgium, 37, 39, 84, 198
Benoit, Emile, 238, 240
Berlin, 312
Berlin agreement, 332

Berlin crises, 138, 145, 196
Berlin wall, 331
Blitzkrieg, 221
Bolshevism, 248; Bolshevik Revolution, 256
Bombers: NATO, 102; Soviet/Warsaw Pact, 93, 96, 97, 98, 102, 202; U.S., 328
Bonapartism, 248
Brandt, Willy, 162, 163
Brezhnev, Leonid, 139, 162, 163, 164, 167, 169–70, 187–88, 244, 249, 253, 257, 258, 260–61, 289; on Afghanistan, 189; and arms control, 188; Brezhnev Doctrine, 142; constitution, 172; defense spending, 239, 248; on détente, 175, 185, 247, 260; and disarmament, 186; policy-making, 261; successors to, 258
Brigades, 82–84
Britain, 37, 39, 165, 310; brigades, 84; British Army on the Rhine, 37, 84; and multilateral force project, 196; and NATO, 197; nuclear program, 204
British Army on the Rhine, 37, 84
Bronevaja Mašina Pechoty (BMP), 47–49, 87
Brosio, Manlio, 165
Brzezinski, Zbigniew, 250, 251, 295
Bundeswehr, 165, 177

Cambodia, 290, 300
Camp David agreement, 279
Camp of Soviet Forces in Germany (CSFG), 39
Canada, 37, 198
Capitalism/capitalist, 187, 244–45; anticapitalism, 249
Caribbean, 21, 290, 312
Carter, Jimmy, 133–34, 263, 320, 327, 335; Presidential Directive, 59, 134, 327
Castro, Fidel, 280, 283
Central America, 290
Central Army Camp (CENTAG), 37
Central Auditing Commission, 250
Central Committee, 245, 250, 261
Central Committee Plenum, 187
Central Europe: armament levels in, 40, 85–88; arms race in, 31–33; as denuclearized zone, 195; and

flexible response, 212; geographic parameters, 32; military balance in, 34–42; nuclear weapons of, 32; Soviet military power in, 145, 164–65; war in, 209
Chervonenko, Stefan, 180
China, 140, 180, 242, 280, 283, 308; defense spending, 235–37; force modernization, 285–86; foreign policy, 309; Soviet arms sales to, 169; strategic doctrine, 133; and the United States, 257, 283, 288, 294–95, 298, 310
CIA, 235, 258
Civil defense, 101, 327, 328
Clausewitz, Karl von, 128, 249
Cold War, 10, 132, 171, 174, 179, 199, 308, 311–12
Colton, Timothy J., 250, 251
Combat capability, 34–35
Combined arms integration, 82–83, 104, 218, 221, 226, 334
Combined arms offensive: NATO, 209; Soviet/Warsaw Pact, 104, 147, 148, 209
Command, control, and communications (C^3) systems, 89, 98, 101, 309, 328–29
Common-launched guided projectiles (CLGPs), 219
Common Market, 145, 205
Communist party/communism, 171, 173, 174, 201, 247, 248, 249; and détente, 175; Italian, 184; membership profile, 250–51; and the military, 249–51; Soviet, 185, 241, 245, 249–50, 295–96
Conference on Security and Cooperation in Europe (CSCE), 162, 163, 164, 170, 172, 187, 201, 203
Confidence-building measures (CBMs), 188–89, 203
Containment, 24, 133, 307, 321, 329; extended, 323–24; military requirements of, 318–19; necessity for, 313–15, objectives of, 312; possibility of, 315–18; and rearmament, 316–18
Conventional technology, 226
Correlation of forces, 30, 130–31, 139, 180, 228, 245–46, 282–83, 290, 316

Countervailing strategy, 327
Crechko, A.A., 239
Crisis diplomacy, 138, 140
Crisis initiatives, 135
Crisis policy, 138
Crisis stability, 127, 150, 213–17
Cruise missiles: NATO, 265; Soviet/
  Warsaw Pact, 149
Cuba, 136, 144, 256, 280, 282, 289,
  290, 299–300, 312, 314; Cuban
  missile crisis, 256, 331
Czechoslovakia, 37–38, 42, 45, 58,
  244; artillery, 87; ground forces, 83;
  and the Soviet Union, 63, 201–02

Dallin, Alexander, 242, 244, 245
Deep engagement/strike, 57, 59, 147,
  211, 226
Defense spending, Soviet, 177,
  233–34, 240–41, 246, 254;
  Brezhnev period, 239; CIA estimates
  of, 235, 239; economic size as determinant of, 237–40; external threat
  as determinant of, 234–37, 238–39,
  241, 259, 264; and GNP, 235, 239;
  interest groups as determinant of,
  247–52; Kruschev period, 235, 241;
  military demands on, 252; national
  interest as determinant of, 242–47;
  and U.S. defense budget, 240; and
  U.S. military activities, 235; and
  U.S. military buildup, 256–57
Defense spending, U.S., 6, 235–37,
  240, 257; and inflation, 238
de Gaulle, Charles, 163, 196, 197,
  198, 333
Delimitation/demarcation policies,
  197
Delivery vehicles: British, 112;
  defined, 109; NATO, 104, 112;
  Soviet/Warsaw Pact, 96
Denmark, 198
Denuclearized zone, 195
Depoliticization, 171–72, 186, 188
Détente, 8, 24, 129–30, 130–31, 134,
  162, 163, 166, 178, 181, 185–90,
  199, 200, 210, 259, 260, 265, 332,
  335, 337; and communism, 175;
  defined, 170–71; demise of, 297;
  depoliticized, 189; or doom scenario,
  184–85; European, 178, 183; international, 170; irreversible, 174, 186;
  military, 166, 168, 171, 176;

political, 164; results of, 198; Soviet,
  163, 166, 170–71, 172, 178,
  184–85, 187, 189, 199, 203,
  246–47, 260, 264, 279, 289,
  293–94, 313, 315–16, 340; U.S.,
  197, 277, 339; U.S.-Soviet, 161,
  185
Deterrence, 133, 138, 203–04, 239,
  243, 329, 335, 336, 337–38;
  extended, 126, 324; failure of,
  337–38; intrawar, 127; military, 6;
  mutual, 137, 150; nuclear, 2, 12, 15,
  23, 127, 334; Soviet, 106, 243, 327;
  theory, 126, 133, 134; unilateral,
  137, 166
Deterrence policy: Soviet, 106, 243,
  327; Western/U.S., 15, 23, 25, 125,
  132, 243
Direct defense, 208, 217, 227, 228
Disarmament, 12, 186, 188, 190, 198,
  340
Disarming first strike, 137
Dubcek, Alexander, 37
Dulles, John Foster, 196

Early warning radar (NADGE), 73,
  75, 224
Eastern Europe: force modernization,
  39; military power of, 19; political
  change in, 22; socialism in, 203; and
  the Soviet Union, 1, 20, 133, 146,
  162, 164, 188, 197–98, 202, 279,
  283, 314; as target for war, 101, 208
East–West relations, 15–16, 20, 22,
  125, 167, 168, 170, 185, 196, 199,
  247, 308, 315, 331, 333, 340–41
East–West trade, 176
East Germany, 165, 189
ECM platforms, 76
Egypt, 313, 320
Eisenhower, Dwight D., 144, 235
El Salvador, 280, 320
Ermath, Fritz, 148
Escalation, 100–101, 102, 105–06,
  138, 166, 311, 325; deliberate, 208,
  227, 228; dominance, 105–06, 127,
  227–28; horizontal, 321; by NATO,
  227–28, 310; threat of, 320
Ethiopia, 141, 143, 173, 201, 256,
  280, 299–300, 314
Eurasia, 319, 325–26, 329–30;
  security of, 321

Europe: arms control in, 188; change in, 170–78, 185–86; defense of by U.S., 105; defense policy, 321, 326–27; as denuclearized zone, 195; and détente, 178, 183; European–Soviet relations, 2; Left, 130; military change in, 21–23; military power in, 17; neutralization of, 197; nuclear arms in, 195; peace in, 2, 3, 13, 14, 15, 21, 315; as "peace zone," 174, 179, 183, 187; political developments in, 5, 21–23; political integration in, 2–3; political order in, 18, 163; security system, 3–4, 18, 162, 165, 175, 317, 327; security threats to, 17, 169, 197; and the Soviet Union, 180, 182, 195, 196–98, 326; and the United States, 181–82, 284; war in, 13, 16, 21, 89, 99, 100, 101, 179, 220–21, 243, 324
European Defense Community (EDC), 195
European Economic Community (EEC), 163, 175

Falkland Islands, 16
Far East, 182, 308, 310–11
Finland, 169, 198, 204
Fire control capability/systems, 54, 57, 58
First strike, 137, 309, 334
First use of nuclear weapons, 9, 100, 103, 106, 136, 137, 166, 167, 208–11; by NATO, 225; nonfirst use agreements, 190
Fixed-site early warning radar, 75
Flexible response, 132–33, 138, 335; demise of, 227–29; and direct defense, 217; and military balances, 228; NATO doctrine of, 62, 100, 207–10, 212–13, 223, 227–29; and the Soviet Union, 3, 210
Force ratio, 221
Forward-based systems (FBS), 6, 166, 183, 189
Forward defense, 324, 326
Forward-looking infrared guidance, 52
France, 165, 188, 195, 197, 213, 221; defense policy, 8; Eastern policy, 7; French–Soviet relations, 197; ground forces in Central Europe, 37, 39, 84; military buildup, 1; and

multilateral force project, 196; nuclear program, 204

General support rocket systems (GSRS), 59
Geneva summit, 10
Geneva treaty, 197
Germany, 19, 161, 195, 221–22, 285; and arms control, 6–7; German–U.S. relations, 6–8, 196, 336; ground forces in Central Europe, 37; military buildup, 1; and NATO, 204; nuclear weapons of, 176
Ghana, 313
Giscard d'Estaing, V., 196
Gross national product, 235, 238
Gorshkov, Sergei, 143
Grechko, A.A., 253, 295
Greece, 145
Gromyko, Andrei, 162–63, 168, 297
Ground-launched cruise missiles, 149, 189; Pershing I (NATO), 168; Pershing II (NATO), 96, 97, 102, 103, 104, 184, 189, 265, 317; U.S., 48–49, 189
Ground laser locator designator, 56
Guatemala, 138
Guidance systems, 50. 52
Guns vs. butter, 240, 248

Hamilton, Alexander, 134
Harmel report, 198
Hassner, Pierre, 162
HEAT warheads, 45, 48, 56
Helicopters: armed attack (AAHs), 60–61, 67–69, 77–78, 87; attack, 40–42, 220; ATGM-equipped, 68; guidance systems on, 69; technology, 67–69
Helsinki accords, 163, 165, 176, 179, 188, 189
Helsinki Final Act, 163, 167, 168, 172, 174, 183, 187, 188–89
High technology, 221–23, 262
Howard, Michael, 126
Huntington, Samuel P., 338

Iceland, 198
Improved conventional munition (ICM), 219
Il-sung, Kim, 140, 290
Imperialism, 128, 143, 170, 173, 176, 177, 239, 245

India, 280, 300
Indochina, 280, 291, 320
Indonesia, 313
Infantry fighting vehicles (IFVs), 42, 47–49, 83; Dutch, 47, 87; French, 47; NATO, 47–49, 53; Soviet/Warsaw Pact, 47, 49, 85; U.S., 47–48, 85, 87; West German, 47, 48
Inflation, 237, 238
Intelligence-gathering technology, 221
Intercontinental ballistic missiles (ICBMs): Soviet/Warsaw Pact, 93; U.S., 285, 309
Intermediate nuclear forces (INF) negotiations, 333
Inter-range ballistic missiles (IRBMs): French, 96, 103; NATO, 102; Soviet/Warsaw Pact, 96, 102
International Institute for Strategic Studies (IISS), 92, 109, 112
International politics, 130, 137, 172
Interventionism, 139
Iran, 16, 179, 279, 282, 289, 320, 322
Iranian Revolution, 205
Iraq, 16
Israel, 16, 48
Italy, 1, 198; Communist party, 184

Jackson/Vanick amendments, 332
Japan, 173, 183, 256, 257, 296, 308, 310, 319; rearmament policy, 321

Kampuchea, 140
Kennedy, John F., 144, 198
Khruschev, Nikita, 135, 139–40, 145, 173, 179, 183, 244, 248, 249, 253; defense spending, 235, 241; and Third World, 312
Kirilenko, A.P., 277
Kissinger, Henry, 5, 308
Kolkowicz, Roman, 251
Korea, 140
Korean War, 139
Kortunov, Vadim, 135
Kosygin, Aleksei, 253, 257
Kulish, V.M., 142
Kurile Islands, 296
Kuwait, 280

Lambeth, Benjamin, 243
Latin America, 279, 321
Lebanon, 16

Legvold, Robert, 172–73
Lenin, 175, 244
Libya, 314
Limited Nuclear Test Ban treaty, 259
Long-range cruise missiles, 7
Long-term defense program (LTDP), 335
Look-down/shoot-down radar, 66
Low-altitude air defense system (LOADs), 65

McNamara, Robert, 253–54
Madrid CSCE conference, 145, 187, 188
Malenkov, Giorgi M., 248
Maneuver regiments: NATO, 82–83; Soviet/Warsaw Pact, 82–83
Martin, Laurence, 128
Marx/Marxism, 171, 176, 242
Marxism–Leninism, 129, 171, 172, 184
Massive retaliation strategy, 101, 132–33, 138
Media and communications, 4–6, 335–36
Medium-range ballistic missiles (MRBMs), 195–96
Mengistu, Haile Mariam, 283
Middle East, 16, 21, 139, 178, 182, 242, 257, 288, 337
Middle East War (1967), 62
Middle East War (1973), 48, 50, 62, 72, 74, 226, 257, 288
Military power/force, 34–35, 207–08, 328; and foreign policy, 136–37; instrumentality of, 136–41; nonuse of, 167, 184; and politics, 15, 131; role of, 123–27, 133, 140; Soviet view of, 136–37; trends in, 129–36; use of, 132, 136, 138–40, 141–44, 149, 247, 298–99; and war, 200
Military strategy, 331, 340; crisis stability, 213–17; primacy of offensive, 217–27. See also specific countries
Military superiority, 135, 137
Military-technical superiority, 135
Military technology, 239, 308
Missile, all-aspect, 65, 67
Missile technology, 65
Mobilization, 213–15, 249
Mobilization units, Dutch, 213

Molotov, Vyacheslav, 162
Mongolia, 291
Moslem states, 298
Mozambique, 201
Multiple rocket launchers (MRLs),
40–42, 58, 220; NATO, 59; Soviet/
Warsaw Pact, 58, 59, 85, 87; U.S.,
59, 85, 87; West German, 59, 87
Multirole combat aircraft (MRCAs),
66
Munitions, Soviet/Warsaw Pact, 65
Mutual and balanced force reduction
talks (MBFR), 7, 20. 31, 34, 164,
165–70, 177, 185, 201, 203
Mutual force reduction talks, 163–64
Mutual assured destruction (MAD),
100, 101, 150, 292

National Socialism, 175
NATO; air offensive strategy, 224–27;
armor units, 218–19; and arms
control, 317; combat capabilities,
35, 37–38; command, control, and
communications system, 104,
105–08; containment policy, 321;
defense budget, 237; defense
options/strategy, 145, 218, 227–28,
335; defensive advantage, 220–22;
dissolution of, 163; and escalation,
227–28, 310; first use doctrine, 103,
106, 212; flexible response doctrine,
62, 100, 207–10, 212–13, 223,
227–29, 334; force development,
35, 227; force expansion, 38; force
modernization, 229, 309–10, 317,
334. See also NATO, TNF modernization. force reductions, 37; force
structure and design, 80–84; ground
forces in Central Europe, 34–37,
82–84; ground offensive disadvantage, 226–27; High Level Group,
90, 93; infantry units, 49, 218–19;
massive retaliation strategy, 101; and
military détente, 177; and military
force, 32; military options, 147,
334; military strategy, 226, 227,
323–29, 333–38; military vulnerability, 216–17; mobilization
potential, 213–15, 216–17; multilateral force, 195–96; nuclear
capability, 212, 291; nuclear options,
64, 89, 100–101, 102, 106, 146,
147–48, 209, 227–28; and nuclear
war, 90–91, 105, 225; and the
Persian Gulf, 322; and public
opinion in Europe, 175; rearmament
policy, 321; Special Consultative
Group, 90; and the Soviet Union,
124, 145–46, 163, 176–77, 284,
286, 317, 331; summit, 335; tactical
nuclear advantage, 291; technical
capabilities, 209; technology, 77–80;
TNF capabilities, 90; TNF data
sources, 108–16; TNF deployments
program, 317; TNF inferiority, 229;
TNF inventory, 90–99; TNF modernization, 93–99, 185, 203, 257;
TNF posture, 89, 105–08; TNF
strike options, 103; theater nuclear
operational concepts, 99–105;
theater targeting, 102; treaty, 162;
and the United States, 87, 178, 333;
and war, 90–91, 105, 225, 147; war
capabilities, 106; war strategy, 101,
warheads, 104; and Warsaw Pact, 31,
89, 91, 100, 184, 208; weapons. See
specific weapons. and Western
Europe, 125, 204
Near East, 16, 21, 182
Netherlands, 7, 46, 47, 84, 213
Neutron bomb, 9, 178
Neutron bomb episode, 169
Nicaragua, 280
Nixon, Richard M., 198, 244
Nonaligned Movement (Cuba), 282
Nonproliferation politics, 196–97
North Atlantic Council, 198
North Korea, 139–40
Northern Army Group (NORTHAG),
37, 38
Norway, 169, 178, 181, 198, 204
Nuclear-chemical environment, 89,
99, 325–26, 329
Nuclear weapons, 82, 100, 131, 132,
136, 148, 202, 225, 228, 243,
253–54, 327; first use of, 9, 100,
103, 106, 136, 137, 166, 167,
208–11; limitation of, 15; preemp-
tive strikes, 89, 327; Soviet view of,
176; theater, 146, 148
Nuclear warheads, 92, 103; British,
112; defined, 109; NATO/U.S., 112
Nuclear codetermination, 7
Nuclear diplomacy, 135

Nuclear-free zones, 187, 190
Nuclear freeze, 9, 187
Nuclear linkage, 229
Nuclear options: limited, 100, 133, 324, 326; of NATO, 64, 89, 100-101, 102, 106, 146, 147-48, 209, 227-28; selective, 132-33
Nuclear responses: general, 208, 227, 334; second-strike, 101; theater, 228
Nuclear war. *See* War/warfare
Nuclear war scenarios, 213

Offensive counterforce, 327
Ogaden War, 140
Oil, 182, 314, 337
OPEC cartel, 282
Option III, 7
Osgood, Robert, 126
Ostpolitik, 162, 163

Pakistan, 140, 280, 300, 320
Palestine, 16
Paris summit, 331
Peace movement, 7, 9, 14
Peace research, 13
Peace zones, 174, 179, 183, 187
Peaceful coexistence, 245, 247
Persian Gulf, 17, 139, 144, 182-83, 310, 320, 334; defense of, 320-23; Gulf War, 205; and the Soviet Union, 11, 315, 325, 340
Phased-array radar system, 74
Pipes, Richard, 184
Poland, 38, 45, 63, 165, 185, 186, 189, 190, 201-02, 205; crisis, 257, 279, 283; and disarmament, 167; ground forces, 83; socialism in, 203; and the Soviet Union, 244, 257, 279, 283, 287, 320
Political action, 4-5
Political restraint, 15
Ponomarev, Boris N., 184, 296
Portugal, 145
Portugalov, Nikolai, 186
Pot, Pol, 290
Precision-guided munitions (PGM), 56, 64
Preemption, defined, 118, note 2
Preemptive attack/strikes, 89, 327
Pryor, Frederic L., 238

Radar systems, 66, 73, 74, 75, 224
Rapacki Plan, 162, 195

Rapid Deployment Force, 143
Rapid deployment joint task force, 320
Reagan, Ronald, 6, 7, 264, 316, 320, 328, 335, 336
Revolution, 140; and war, 129
Rhee, Syngman, 140
Rigby, T.H., 249
Rocket-assisted projectiles (RAPs), 58

Sadat, Anwar, 240, 299
SALT (Strategic Arms Limitation Talks), 98, 161, 171, 178, 179, 185, 197; negotiations, 248, 257, 292; and the Soviet Union, 246; U.S. position on, 6
SALT I, 246, 257, 259, 291, 328
SALT II, 179, 257, 259, 291
Sanctuary diplomacy, 184-85, 187
Sanctuary war, 183-85
Scandinavia, 125-26, 198
Scatterable mines, 56, 218-19, 220
Scenarios for nuclear war, 213
Schlesinger, James R., 334
Schmidt, Helmut, 182, 187; Schmidt-Brezhnev communiqué, 169, 170; Schmidt-Giscard communiqué, 185
Selassie, Haile, 283
Shah of Iran, 283, 309
Shishko, Robert, 235
Shock-power, 146, 147
Siberia, 291
Sino-American alliance, 257
Smith, Adam, 238
Socialism/socialist, 128, 131, 135, 171, 176, 183, 187, 189, 239, 247, 248; in Eastern Europe, 165, 203; and revolution, 143; scientific, 244; World socialist system, 174
Somalia, 313
South Africa, 16
South Asia, 242
South Korea, 139-40
South Yemen, 173, 280, 299-300, 314
Southeast Asia, 62, 200, 289
Southwest Asia, 182, 289, 310, 311, 319, 320; defense of, 321-23; and Europe, 321-22; and Japan, 321-22; and the United States, 320-21
Soviet Union: aid to North Korea, 140; aid to other countries, 142-43; air force, 147; air offensive strategy,

223; and arms control, 8, 22, 91, 106, 162, 166, 177, 183, 185, 196, 291–92, 294, 313; and the arms race, 24, 285; arms sales to China, 169; and Atlantic alliance, 21, 174, 317, 331; Central Committee, 245, 250, 261, 296; and Central Europe, 145, 164–65; Central Group of Forces, 37, 39; and change in Europe, 170–83; and China, 169, 278–79, 285–86, 310, 315; civil defense programs, 309; combat role, 296; Communist party, 185, 241, 245, 249–50, 295–96; conventional variant strategy, 223; conventional war options, 147, 325–26; and CSCE, 166–70; and Czechoslovakia, 37–38, 42; decisionmaking apparatus, 207, 252–55, 296; defense capabilities, 245; Defense Council, 252–53, 254, 282; defense policy/strategy, 244–45, 293, 324–25; defense spending. *See* Defense spending, Soviet. and détente, 163, 166, 170–72, 178, 184–85, 187, 189, 199, 203, 246–47, 260, 264, 279, 289, 293–94, 313, 315–16, 340; deterrence policy, 106, 243, 327; diplomacy, 204; domestic policy, 248; economy, 107, 173, 203, 233–34, 239, 241, 246, 253, 255–56, 258–59, 261, 262–64, 283, 314; and Eastern Europe, 1, 20, 133, 146, 162, 164, 188, 197–98, 202, 279, 283, 314; energy policy, 181–82; and Europe, 162–64; and European political change, 21–23, 170–83; first-strike capability, 10, 143–44; five-year plan, 248, 254; and flexible response, 3, 210; force modernization, 39–40, 146, 202, 246, 263; force structure/design, 80–84; Foreign Ministry, 296–97; foreign policy, 124, 127, 137, 141–50, 167, 170–71, 172–73, 185, 187, 189–90, 198–99, 204, 244, 245, 246, 248, 264, 279–81, 296–97, 313, 317; General Staff, 253; global role, 287–88; GNP, 235; ground forces in Central Europe, 37–38, 83–83, 147, 165, 291; and high technology, 262–63; ideology,

172–73; imperialism, 313–15; industry, 285; and international politics, 130, 172; interpretation of Western policies, 19; interventions/ invasions. *See separate listings for specific countries.* and Japan, 183; leadership change in, 257–58, 261–64, 277, 340; and MBFR talks, 165–70; and Middle East, 21; military alliances, 249; and military balance, 166; military buildup, 10, 20–21, 80, 233, 235, 240–42, 246–47, 252–53, 258, 259, 308, 310–11, 319, 327; Military Industrial Commission, 252–53; military policy, 140, 202; military power, 3, 4, 6, 8, 11, 12–13, 18–19, 21, 24, 101, 123–27, 129–36; 141–50, 173, 178–79, 196, 200, 203–05, 243, 245–46, 249–50, 263, 290, 298–99, 307–13, 319, 332, 334; military strategy, 143–47, 211, 223–24, 254, 264–65; military technology, 311; Ministry of Defense, 252–53, 297; and NATO, 124, 145–46, 163, 176–77, 284, 286, 317, 331; naval superiority, 311; and Near East, 21; nuclear preemption doctrine, 106; and nuclear war, 128; nuclear weapons of, 2, 13, 176, 178, 184; offensive strategy, 223, 289–90; peace policy, 178; and Persian Gulf, 11, 315, 325, 340; and Poland, 244, 257, 279, 283, 287, 320; policymaking apparatus, 261, 281–82; political alliances, 249; political-economic system, 18; political objectives, 19; political strategy, 20–21, 143–45, 329; as political threat, 195; and the Rimland, 148–50; security agreements, 169–70, 300; security policy, 6, 162–70, 177, 183–84, 243, 255, 256, 264, 290–92, 330; Soviet-Cuban relations, 282, 299, 300; Soviet-East German relations, 331; Soviet-European relations, 2, 291; Soviet-French relations, 197; Soviet-German relations, 180; Soviet-Sino relations, 278–79, 285–86, 291, 294–95, 310, 315; Soviet-U.S. relations, 3–4, 8, 10, 132, 139, 278, 280–81, 288, 289, 297–98, 331; Soviet-U.S. security

partnership, 196; Soviet–West
German relations, 161–62, 177–78;
Soviet–West European relations, 10,
124, 125, 145, 162, 164–65, 168,
174, 179, 183, 186, 200, 202, 279,
291, 332; Soviet–Western relations,
6, 8–9, 10–11, 12–13, 19–20, 23,
25, 173, 176–77, 204, 331, 338.
See also East–West relations. State
Planning Committee, 252; strategic
policy, 135, strategic superiority,
324, 327, 329; as superpower,
90–91, 179–81, 188; systematic
social engineering policy, 171–72;
and the Third World, 124, 142,
143–44, 149, 169, 172, 173, 179,
185, 247, 257, 279, 286, 288,
293–300, 311–12; as target, 208;
and TNF decision, 180; TNF
posture, 89, 91, 185, 186, 210–11;
Trade Union Central Committee,
261; and U.S. foreign policy, 257;
and U.S. policy, 277–78, 295; and
U.S. strategic doctrine, 133–36,
288–89; and war, 147, 184,
292–93; weapons. *See specific
weapons.* weapons acquisition, 254,
and Western security interests, 18;
Westpolitik, 11, 21. *See also* Warsaw
Pact
Spaak, Paul–Henri, 198
Stabilization, 185
Stalin, Joseph, 1, 146, 242, 247–48,
249, 260; anti-Stalinism, 251; neo-
Stalinism, 260
Stiftung Wissenschaft und Politik, 23
Strategic analysis, 10–11
Strategic defense capabilities, 327
Strategic nuclear superiority, 135–36
Strategic parity, 150, 177, 178,
179–80, 183, 197, 228, 255, 290,
309, 334, 336. *See also* Balance of
power
Strategic restoration, 318–29
Submarine-launched ballistic missiles
(SLBMs), 96, 98, 102, 285
Submarine-launched cruise missiles
(SLCMs), 97
Supreme Soviet, 250, 253
Surface-to-air missiles (SAMs),
40–42, 65, 72, 92, 220; British,
73–74, 87; interceptor defense, 62;

NATO, 73–75, 77, 78, 87; Soviet/
Warsaw Pact, 73–75, 78, 81, 85–86,
87; U.S., 73, 74, 85–87; West
German, 87
Surface-to-surface missiles (SSMs),
211–12, 224; NATO, 97; Soviet/
Warsaw Pact, 96
Suslov, Mikhail, 172
Sweden, 198
Syria, 299

Tactical sensors, 218
Talensky, N.A., 128
Tanks, 40, 42–46, 211, 219; British,
44; East German, 44; French, 30,
44, 87; NATO, 42, 44, 45; Soviet/
Warsaw Pact, 42–45, 81–83, 87,
147, 285, 291; survivability of, 219;
U.S., 44–46, 87; vulnerability of,
220; West German, 44–46, 87
Target acquisition, 54, 57, 65, 218
Targeting, 103, 328
Technological automatism, 253
Technology: antitank, 50; armament,
220–22; conventional, 226; high,
221–23, 262–63; intelligence-
gathering, 221; military, 239, 308;
missile, 65, 67; transfer, 246, 247,
286
Terminal guidance, 50
Theater nuclear force (TNF) negotiations, 31
TNF systems, 180; delivery vehicles
for, 92; French, 93; long-range, 98,
102–04, 109–12, 202, 210; mid-
range, 98, 102–04, 109–12, 202;
offensive, 92; short-range, 93, 98,
104, 109–12, 202; Soviet/Warsaw
Pact, 96–97; U.S., 108, 328;
warheads, 93–96
Third World, 179, 280; defense
spending, 238; security in, 319;
and the Soviet Union, 124, 142,
143–44, 149, 169, 172, 173, 179,
185, 247, 257, 279, 286, 288,
293–300, 311–12; and the United
States, 175, 284, 288, 294
Thirty Years War, 34
Threat perception, 203
Throw-weight, 148, 282
Treaty of Washington, 204
Trofimenko, Henry, 134, 136–38

Tucker, Robert, 126
Turkey, 320, 322–23

Unacceptable damage, 326, 327
Unilateralism, 9, 333
United Nations, 183
United States: and arms control, 6–7, 186; brigades, 84; CIA, 235, 258; civil defense programs, 309; and containment, 318, 326; conventional forces, 136; crisis diplomacy, 138, 140; and defense of Europe, 105; defense options, 145; defense policy, 138, 336; defense priorities, 7; defense research and development, 328; defense spending. *See* Defense spending, U.S. Department of Defense, 92, 93; détente policy, 197, 277, 339; deterrence policy, 15, 23, 25, 125, 132, 243; and disarmament, 186; economy, 3, 264, 283–85, 336; energy policy, 181–82; and Europe, 181–82, 284; force modernization, 264–65; foreign policy, 18, 137–39, 257, 264, 295; global role, 287–88, 293; GNP, 238; ground forces in Central Europe, 37, 38, 83–84, 87; and Guatemala, 138; imperialism, 176, 182; industry, 285; leadership of, 277; and Middle East, 182; military buildup, 256–57, 264; military policy, 130, 150, 264–65, 286; military power, 139, 175–76, 179, 180, 182, 200, 210, 307, 309, 312; military technology, 308, 311; and NATO, 87, 178, 333; navy, 311; nuclear superiority, 308; nuclear weapons, 13, 92–93, 136, 228–29; position of strength posture, 178, 180; and SALT, 6; security, 7, 292, 324; Seventh Corps, 38; and Southwest Asia, 182; and Soviet manpower, 308–12; Soviet policy 277–78, 288–89, 316, 328; strategic doctrine, 132–36, 138–40, 243, 323–29; strategic inferiority, 324; strategic superiority, 326–27, 329; as superpower, 179–80, 188; Third Corps, 38–39; and Third World, 175, 284, 288, 294; U.S.-European relations, 180; U.S.-German relations, 6–8, 196, 336; U.S.-Sino

relations, 257, 283, 294–95, 298, 310; U.S.-Soviet relations, 3–4, 8, 10, 132, 139, 278, 289, 294–95, 297–98, 331; U.S.-Soviet security partnership, 196; U.S.-West European relations, 18, 19–20, 22, 182, 187, 197, 333, 336; and Vietnam, 8, 37, 138, 139, 200–201, 237, 257, 282–83, 286; war capabilities, 106, 328
Ustinov, Dimitri, 253

Vienna agreements, 197
Vienna negotiations, 7
Vietnam, 140, 257, 282–83, 289–90, 300, 310, 314
Vietnam syndrome, 130
Vietnam War, 8, 37, 138, 139, 200–201, 237, 286
von Stein, Lorenz, 3
Voznesenskii, N.A., 248

War/warfare, 146, 247, 324; antiship, 92; antisubmarine, 92, 101; causes of, 13; chemical, 99; combined arms, 220; conventional, 100, 223, 225, 324–25; conventional-chemical-nuclear, 89, 99, 100, 105; defensive, 217; economic, 256; and foreign policy, 133, 138; general, 325, 327–29; in Europe, 13, 16, 21, 89, 99, 100, 101, 324; intercontinental, 100, 106, 324–25; lightning, 107; maneuver, 217–18; Marxist–Leninist concept of, 249; NATO/Warsaw Pact, 91, 100, 105; nature of, 243; nuclear, 90–91, 100, 102, 105, 125, 128, 132, 190, 202, 210–12, 223, 225, 240, 324–25; offensive, 217; political utility of, 128–29; probability of, 316, 318; and revolution, 129; sanctuary, 183–85; strategic nuclear, 100; and society, 249; tank, 45; theater nuclear, 100; thermonuclear, 128. *See also Attack; and specific wars*
Warsaw Pact (Warsaw Treaty Organization): air offensive advantage, 224, 226; and arms race, 207; combat capabilities, 35, 37–38, 128; conventional variant strategy, 229; defense budget, 237; defensive

advantage, 222–23; and détente, 188; dissolution of, 163; divisional units in Central Europe, 34–36; escalation dominance, 105–06; and first use of nuclear weapons, 167; force expansion, 37; force modernization, 35, 39, 105, 309–10; ground force offensive, 225–26; ground forces in Central Europe, 34–37, 40, 104; military buildup, 32, 209; military strategy, 225–26; mobilization potential, 216–17; and NATO, 31, 89, 91, 100, 184, 208; nonnuclear aggression, 106, nonnuclear force capabilities, 101; nuclear strategy, 104–05; and nuclear war, 90–91, 105; offensive superiority, 64, 91, 106, 212; proposal for dissolution of blocs, 162; strategic weakness, 107; technical capability, 209; TNF data sources, 108–16; TNF inventory, 91–99; TNF modernization, 93–99; TNF posture, 89, 90–91; TNF superiority, 228–29; theater nuclear operational concepts, 99–105; theater targeting, 103, 104; war strategy, 101; weapon inventory, 40–42, 46

Watergate, 332

Weapon/weapons: aerial, 40–42; conventional, 40, 79–84; 100, 202, 212, 214, 328; conventional NATO, 40–42, 80–84, 209, 214; conventional, Soviet/Warsaw Pact, 40–42, 80–85, 209, 214–16, 223, 229; conventional, U.S., 85; enhanced radiation, 335; fire power, 217–18; nuclear NATO, 85, 319; nuclear Soviet/Warsaw Pact, 85, 229, 319; nuclear West German, 175; offensive, 78, 104; systems, 34; technology, 77–80, 217, 220; unmanned, 34

West/Western: and arms control, 185, 210; confrontational policy, 24; and containment, 330; defense options, 145–46; détente policy, 24, 130–31, 210; deterrence strategy 11, 12, 15; East–West relations, 15–16, 20, 22, 125, 167, 168, 170, 185, 196, 199, 247, 308, 315, 331, 333, 340–41; foreign policy, 5;

military policy, 144, 149, 333, 336; military power, 18; military vulnerability, 216–17; negotiating options, 89; nuclear options, 89; peace policy, 14–16; policy of management, 8, 12; political changes in, 4–5, 13, 22, 24; political strategy, 20; rearmament policy, 167; security policy, 4–6, 9–10, 12, 14, 18, 21, 23, 317, 336, 338; security threats to, 16–17; use of force, 140; West–Soviet relations, 6, 8–9, 12–13, 19–20, 23, 25, 173, 176–77, 204, 331, 338. See also Atlantic alliance; NATO; United States

Western alliance, 7–8, 24, 149, 196, 298; and arms control, 31; and balance of power in Europe, 3; military response options, 17; military strategy, 17, 326; Soviet policy, 5; war strategy, 329

Western Europe, 308; and arms control, 22, 185; defense policy, 7–8, 197, 198, 203; and détente, 339; economy, 205; energy policy, 205; and Europe, 326; and France, 197; military policy, 2, 204; military power, 18; and NATO, 125, 204; nuclear deployments in, 9; and Persian Gulf, 334; political integration in, 2–3, 205; security of, 148, 185, 196, 205; social system, 176; and the Soviet Union, 10, 124, 125, 145, 162, 164–65, 169, 174, 179, 183, 186, 200, 202, 256, 279, 291, 332; as target, 203; and TNF decision, 186; West European–U.S. relations, 18, 19–20, 22, 182, 187, 197, 333, 336

West Germany, 38–39, 189, 335, 336; ground forces in Central Europe, 83; military power, 165, 213; rearmament policy, 195; and the Soviet Union, 169, 177–78

Westpolitik, 11, 21

Wiatr, J. J., 248

Window of opportunity, 265

Wolfe, Thomas, 147

World summit, 167

World War I, 217

World War II, 1–2, 249, 255, 258

Yepishev, Aleksei, 143
Yom Kippur war, 332

Zagladin, Vadim, 168–69
Zhukov, Marshal, 146, 248
Zhurkin, Vitaly, 138–39
Zimbabwe, 280

ABOUT THE EDITOR

Uwe **Nerlich** is Director of Research at the Research Institute of Stiftung Wissenschaft und Politik in Ebenhausen, West Germany. Educated in philosophy and mathematics at Frankfurt and Cambridge Universities, Nerlich is Vice President of the European–American Institute for Security Research in Los Angeles and a Council Member of the International Institute for Strategic Studies in London. In 1974–75 he was a Fellow at the Center for Advanced Study in the Behavioral Sciences at Stanford University; and in 1981–82, a Visiting Distinguished Professor at the Naval Postgraduate School in Monterey. Nerlich has published widely on international relations, strategy, and arms control, and coedited *Beyond Nuclear Deterrence: New Aims, New Arms.*

ABOUT THE CONTRIBUTORS

Abraham S. Becker joined the RAND Corporation in 1957, where he is now a Senior Economist. Educated at Columbia and Harvard, Becker has been a lecturer at the University of California, Los Angeles, and Visiting Professor of Economics and Russian Studies at the Hebrew University of Jerusalem. He was the U.S. member of the United Nations Expert Groups on Reduction of Military Budgets in 1974 and 1976, and is the author of numerous monographs and papers on various issues of the Soviet economy and foreign policy.

Fritz Ermarth is an analyst of Soviet and strategic affairs. His areas of research include Soviet military policy and strategy as well as the comparative analysis of Soviet and American strategic thinking. Ermarth has worked for the RAND Corporation, the CIA, the National Security Council, and the Northrop Corporation. He is the author of the monograph *Internationalism, Security and Legitimacy: The Challenge to Soviet Interests in East Europe, 1964–1968.*

Harry Gelman is a Senior Staff Member in the Social Science Department of the RAND Corporation. He joined RAND in 1980 after retiring from the U.S. Government, where for many years he served as a specialist on Soviet political and strategic affairs. In 1962–63 he was a Senior Fellow at the Research Institute on International Change, Columbia University; and in 1973–74, a Fellow of the

Hoover Institution, Stanford University. Gelman has published many articles on Soviet and Sino–Soviet affairs.

Phillip A. Karber is currently Director of the Strategic Concepts Development Center at the National Defense University in Washington, D.C. and adjunct Professor in the Georgetown University Graduate School. Karber was a member of the U.S. Army Science Board and served in the Pentagon between 1974 and 1978 as Director of National Security Study Memorandum 186—A Comparative Assessment of U.S./Soviet and NATO/Warsaw Pact General Purpose Forces. Karber has been a contributor to several books and the author of numerous articles on European Security.

Robert Legvold is a Senior Fellow and Director of the Soviet Project at the Council on Foreign Relations in New York and Adjunct Professor of Political Science at Columbia University. His areas of research include Soviet policy in Europe and Africa, Soviet security policy, and the Soviet role in the world economy. As part of the Council's Soviet Project, he is currently writing a study of Soviet policy toward the United States from 1969 to the present. He is the author of *Soviet Policy in West Africa* and has published articles and contributions in a variety of journals and books.

James J. Martin is a Senior Vice President at Science Applications Inc. in La Jolla, California and manager of SAI's National Security Studies and Systems Group. During 1968–76, he was a systems analyst in the Office of the Secretary of Defense, where he led or participated in many of the administration's studies on SALT, nuclear weapons employment policy, and the theater nuclear force posture in Europe. Dr. Martin has published several articles on nuclear weapons issues.

John Van Oudenaren is a member of RAND and was educated at M.I.T. in Political Science. In 1982 he was a Research Associate at the International Institute for Strategic Studies in London. Van Oudenaren has specialized in the area of Soviet policy toward Western Europe. His publications include *The 'Leninist Peace Policy' and Western Europe* and *U.S. Leadership Perceptions of the Soviet Problem Since 1945.*

Lothar Rühl is currently State Secretary in the German Defense Department. Previously, he was Deputy Spokesman of the federal government in Bonn. Educated at Bonn and Paris Universities, Rühl worked from 1954 to 1969 as a Paris correspondent for German newspapers and between 1973 and 1980 he was a correspondent for German television. Rühl has published numerous books and articles on security policy.